The Feeling Intellect

William Blake, Plates 9 ("I want! I want!") and 10 ("Help! Help!") from the series *Gates of Paradise*.

The
Feeling Intellect

Selected Writings

Philip Rieff

Edited and with an Introduction by
Jonathan B. Imber

The University of Chicago Press
Chicago and London

Philip Rieff is Benjamin Franklin Professor of Sociology and University Professor at the University of Pennsylvania. He is the author of *Freud: The Mind of the Moralist, The Triumph of the Therapeutic*, and *Fellow Teachers: Of Culture and Its Second Death*, all available in paperback from the University of Chicago Press. **Jonathan B. Imber,** Whitehead associate professor and chair of sociology at Wellesley College, is the author of *Abortion and the Private Practice of Medicine.*

The University of Chicago Press, Chicago 60637
The University of Chicago Press, Ltd., London
© 1990 by The University of Chicago
All rights reserved. Published 1990
Printed in the United States of America

99 98 97 96 95 94 93 92 91 90   5 4 3 2 1

Library of Congress Cataloging-in-Publication Data

Rieff, Philip, 1922–
    The feeling intellect: Selected Writings / Philip Rieff.
        p.   cm.
    "Bibliographia Rieffiana": p. 375.
    ISBN 0–226–71641–4 (alk. paper). — ISBN 0–226–71642–2 (pbk.:
alk. paper)
    1. Philosophical anthropology—History.   2. Psychoanalysis and
culture—History.   3. Personality and culture—History.   4. Religion
and politics—History.   5. Education—Philosophy—History.
6. Freud, Sigmund, 1856–1939.   I. Imber, Jonathan B., 1952–
II. Title.
BD450.R479   1990
081—dc20   89–28360
                                                                    CIP

To Our Students
and to the
Students of Our Students

**Earl of
Gloucester:** Here, take this purse, thou whom the heavens' plagues
Have humbled to all strokes: that I am wretched
Makes thee the happier:—heavens, deal so still!
Let the superfluous and lust-dieted man,
That slaves your ordinance, that will not see
Because he doth not feel, feel your power quickly;
So distribution should undo excess,
And each man have enough.

King Lear, IV, i, 65–72

Contents

Political Faiths and Their Futures

Intellectuals and Education

Character and Culture

Preface

I began my formal study with Philip Rieff fifteen years ago. In the remarkable transition that leads from fate to faith, I had, a year earlier, found *Fellow Teachers* on the review copy shelf of my college newspaper. That is one book I have been reviewing ever since. I had been encouraged by an undergraduate teacher to study with Rieff because, she thought, my intuitions about sociology were similar to his.

With intuitions in mind and a copy of *Fellow Teachers* in hand, I arrived at his first seminar prepared to take course notes and to study social theory in earnest. I had no idea that we were to begin reading Friedrich Nietzsche's *Beyond Good and Evil* or that I and others were to "unpack" its first question: "Supposing truth is a woman—what then?" Within weeks I discovered a small group of fellow students who were able to feel and see where and how such words and sentences took us into the present shapes of our social order. We unpacked for hours on end, ignoring the clock. Doing theory in this way, we read realities suddenly there before us.

Those seminars were preparations for brief encounters with the truth. Ours was the only exegesis that mattered, and this pedagogic design forced each of us to become the only living Nietzsche, Plato, Paul, Weber, Kafka, and Freud. These great theorists became our masters, and for the purpose of the exercise, our mastery of them required that we speak and feel in their voices in order to bring alive what would otherwise remain dead for all time. As a matter of course we were not permitted to use writing instruments during class; we were also prohibited from eating and drinking. In those days Rieff's two Dandie Dinmont terriers often accompanied him to seminar, and we were regularly advised of their superior workings through of passages that refused to yield anything to us. At least they knew their master's voice.

Philip Rieff's devotion to teaching confirmed my own. Social theory, for those students who studied with him and who repeated the same seminar with different texts, had only partly to do with what now passes for theory in the social science journals. The aims of theory, as Rieff describes them in *The Triumph of the Therapeutic*, are of two distinct and often fused/confused kinds, conformative and transformative. Conformative theories are present in the original and originative works of what can be called generally the traditions out of Jerusalem and Athens, tested and so again trusted in every generation. Transformative theories are those that brilliantly test all that is felt and known: Nietzsche, Kafka, and Freud are great transformative theorists. This second kind of theory dominates what there is of the current and enduring social theory.

In teaching the transformative theories or their opposite, conformative, numbers (Paul's *Romans*, for example), the teacher must encompass and measure both of these stipulated kinds of theory, which, when unpacked, reveal what is otherwise concealed from the mind's eye. The task is to keep these opposing schools separate. Unpacking can lead to surprising moments when what is highest in the vertical of authority and what is lower, even lowest, are felt and seen as personal knowledge, transferable from person to person, never impersonal.

In the social sciences today, transformative theory is largely in the hands of self-obsessed activists and impersonal quantifiers, neither of whom can stake claim in measuring their transformations against the conformative theories whose sights are raised above reality precisely to reveal what is most true about it. "In the absence of news about a stable and governing order anywhere," the transformative theories direct us nowhere and to no higher purpose. There is Nothing authorizing. The seminar I attended for three brief years aimed at teaching how we can and why we must catch "glimpses of an order that is eternally right and good." These glimpses raise our sights to what is most true about ourselves against the endless possibilities of lesser choices and lowered hopes.

Ours is a time in which higher motives and authority in its higher ranges are suspect, specially among the re-educated, and both are so treated as a mirror of power. Teachers of transformative theory see right through it but also see nothing but the struggle for power. In this teaching book, Philip Rieff examines the sources and directions of these suspicions as they wind their way through Freud and the twentieth century. Freud is one central figure of address in the papers, essays, introductions, and reviews gathered here. But as central as the life of that figure is, it is the minds of moralists that Rieff has sought to understand. In Freud's mind, the twentieth century was his century. Respectfully, Rieff has taken this transformative mind to task. I would announce along with him that this century is ending in displays of such unfeeling and therefore blind intellect that the vertical of authority, the world constantly recreated in truth, appears upside down. With transgressions above and interdicts below, a passionate intensity now triumphs while conviction awaits its instruction.

In the next century, to which this book is dedicated, the vertical of authority will reappear right side up for those taught the original and commanding truths that are as present as their negational/transformative opposites. This teaching book will serve as a guide to that feeling intellect in its reappearance, which is my hope for my fellow teachers and their students.

Introduction

Early in *Fellow Teachers*, Philip Rieff observes: "There is no Method for achieving the proper distances of feeling intellect; there is an institution within which we can keep trying. Only in our schools can our students hope to achieve a humane and perceptive inner distance from the social struggles in which they may be—need be—otherwise engaged. School can be drawn too close to society. To make distances may help save this society from its cruel infatuations with one damnable simplification after another" (73:1, p. 5). Feeling intellect is first and foremost a conviction about the spiritual organization of our schools. That organization has never successfully closed out social and cultural struggles, but the distances made are the special responsibilities of teachers whose authority, insofar as it is recognized as humane and perceptive, conveys always what is higher in higher education.

In older ladder languages of faith, the feeling intellect was continually represented as that mindfulness of higher truths within which all life finds its decisive meaning. The language games of our higher education, since Nietzsche, forbid mention of an invisible, yet presiding, intellect, otherwise called our "creation myth." Philip Rieff's sociology, above all else, has been constructive in its intentions and various demonstrations. Contemporary sociology is characteristically deconstructive: it sees in "social control" only power and no authority; it struggles after an ever receding "equality" in the belief that all persons are infinitely separable from their "roles"; yet it denies this and that unalterable and unique identity of every living thing—the invisible "I" behind each visible "me"—without which we can be nothing but our roles. Feeling intellect recognizes what it cannot see directly: the authority that directs each self in its own will to be someone; it is the body ego revealed in our dressings up and our dressings down; it is the affirmation of our modesty as we survey the vast terrains of false guilt over which the modern mind presides.

The teaching of false guilt is a profitable enterprise and occupies a confident and secure place in our colleges and universities. There are countless sociologies of false guilt, the class struggle being the most imaginative and most popular. To teach otherwise, no doubt one must learn otherwise. Resistance movements within sociology have their polemicists on the left and the right. The refutation of error, the principal aim of polemical discourse, rarely permits the rereadings and supersessive interpretations that distinguish schools from vanguards. Therapeutics and polemicists together stand against those teaching traditions in which the true distance between oneself and the world is never completely bridged by the endless changes of either. That true distance is what feeling intellect achieves. I modestly submit that careful and patient reading and rereading of the writings gathered here will instruct in that feeling intellect which is Philip Rieff.

Absent in this instruction are oral teachings (now called seminars) without which the written word lacks its completion in the most special meaning of community, an oral tradition. There is no such thing as a "defense" of tradition by writing alone. The search for core curricula and general education requirements cannot be conducted without teachers who teach with personal authority, the only defense we teachers have. The writings contained here reveal a life of teaching. They address the authority of feeling intellect in the shape and substance of particular persons and ideas. By reading backwards and forwards in the order of selection as I have established it here, something of that teaching authority can be found by all who aspire to teach.

On Freud and Psychoanalysis

In part one, I have selected pieces that chronicle Rieff's working through of what I will call Freud's imperial intellect and its vicissitudes in the West. The emergence of psychological men and women remains the latest stage of self-assertions that seek to resolve, for the sake of health, who we are. Freud's contribution has yet to run its course insofar as it offers recognizable names for those self-assertions. Whereas symptoms, a highly recognizable name for one type of self-assertion, were once sins in religious terms, they are now the basis for a self-assessment that strives primarily to assure peace of mind in the name of personal well-being. "In the culture to which psychological man is heir, there has been an acute sense of the weakness of human character but a diminished capacity to feel compassion for it" (p. 13). Our diminished capacity to feel compassion has opened the way to a remarkable lowering of what is expected of character. This turning of the screw is a loosening, not a tightening, of expectations about the right conduct of living. Freud's gloss on character was to dress it down, thus making what is higher pretentious and what is lower a matter of endless fascination.

No single case in Freud's case histories exemplifies both respectful interest and endless fascination with what is lower than that of Dora's. If contemporary feminism iconizes Dora as a victim of the power and control of psychoanalysis over women's lives, it has succeeded only half-way to the truth. Half-truth in this case conveys something of Freud's power over Dora but conceals Freud's denial of the authority which inspired both his relentless analysis and her resistance to it. In the final analysis, Dora resisted the bisexual adulteries, real and imagined, of her parental circle: "Thus Freud bypassed the patient's insight into the rot of her human environment . . . he suspected her insight as an instrument of her neurosis instead of as the promise of her cure" (p. 26). Here imperial intellect, cruel in its effort at mastery, triumphs over feeling intellect, which Freud also deeply possessed. Dora's understanding of her own life had not given her the power to change it. The "power to change life was Freud's test of truth" (p. 22). But Freud's is the half-truth, the same shared by many who oppose him. Dora's "tenacious and most promising of all forms of resistance" (p. 26) may be read as her blind address to the authority of one interdict deeply installed in the consciousness of the West as one of its Ten Commandments.

The struggles apparent in Dora's case lead to a more direct assessment of psychoanalysis after Freud. What is distinctive about Freud's intellect in its imperiousness is also what is most transformative about psychoanalysis and psychology more generally. Therapy succeeds salvation and imitates it. Psychoanalysis sells salvation by the shilling and uses reason which "is no longer divinely ordered or natural, but, rather, a therapeutic fiction" (p. 35). Freud was not unaware of the implications of this fiction. In its name the assault on guilt knowledge has been enormously successful: Freud's "ambition to exhaust the sense of guilt by clinical exposures of it in its every detail may be dangerous, as he himself realized, to the life of a culture that is always necessarily (by his own definition of it) on the defensive" (p. 40). One's health may finally not depend on being made morally better. As the culture disavows all recognitions of what is and what is not morally better, the fiction grows.

Freud's sense of his own Jewishness serves as a key to the unlocking of our present therapeutic culture. Compare Rieff's unpacking of Kairos in Freud's thought, published in 1951, and his decoding of Appendix G in *Moses and Monotheism*, published in 1981. The unmusicality of Freud's response to his Jewishness should first be read as a symptom of his imperial intellect. A further reading suggests that in the absence of a feeling intellect for his Jewishness, Freud chose Moses as that figure in authority against whom to mount his "final assault upon repetition, the form of faith" (p. 62). Repetition, the form of faith, cannot be an orthopraxy. The obediences of feeling intellect are not constituted, anywhere at any time, by compulsives of cleverities who eat kosher and think unkosher so as to live lives liberated from the commanding truths of revelation. Truth and therapy, eternal and historical truth are merged, and obediences to Moses' divine commandments are reduced to the familiar deconversionist symptoms of compulsively therapeutic characters. How the Jews acquired their character and what they have to lose by losing it are questions in the blind spot of Freud's vision. (See Sentence IV.)

On Religion and Politics

One principal aim of Philip Rieff's work has been to explore the inner and outer meanings of cultural stability and change. In part two, I have selected three groups of essays and reviews that confirm the intimate connections between religion and politics and their mutual importance for understanding the dynamics of culture. The forms of faith and their vicissitudes are not confined to churches. They penetrate the organization of persons and polities and are, to this extent, inseparable from them. In *Freud: The Mind of the Moralist*, Rieff writes: "Politics and religion, understood by Freud as originally ways of reuniting the many under a single authority, came into existence together, as the profoundest expressions of the ambivalence of human will" (59:1a, p. 194). The selections in part two chart the course of this ambivalence from its Jewish and Christian expressions to its attenuation in the present therapeutic culture.

Disraeli, who chose not to forget he was a Jew and who claimed the Jews for the sake of his political uniqueness, found in his romantic fiction of himself a way to address and experience the nostalgia for his Jewishness. In making the "return to the past the guiding principle of his politics" (p. 76), Disraeli hoped for the creation of a presiding elite that would serve equally well in aristocratic and democratic times. And by conferring a literateness and respectability upon English conservatism, he infused the political culture of England with a high sense of itself. The symbol of this high sense was his choseness as a Jew. As a symbol it *was* what it represented. In this way, "Power is not the predicate of choseness, but choseness of power" (p. 80).

Freud's thrusts against this choseness reappear as attacks against the eternity of the Jewish symbolic of choseness. Disraeli insisted that "the dynamic of English culture was its Hebraism" (p. 85). Freud's view of religion as delusion when read back upon Disraeli's nostalgia for his choseness thus reveals a relation between two very different fictions. Disraeli's fiction was ennobling just as his dressing up to the point of dandyism was the outer representation of his inner choseness. The Freudian symbolic introduces the negational fiction of this choseness. Freud went so far as to claim Moses chose the Jews instead of the Jews choosing Moses (59:1a, p. 284). If the proto-Zionist Disraeli had a hand in shaping Zionist rhetoric since then, as Rieff proposes, the unmusically Jewish Freud had a hand in lowering the boom on the eternal covenant from which Disraeli took his sustenance, leaving us clearer on the competing fictions of our time.

Taking up these competing fictions or cultural struggles in another way, the reader will find references to the idea of "psychological Jewishness" as it pertains to Hannah Arendt's study of totalitarianism. Like Freud, Disraeli was certainly a psychological Jew, insofar as neither one was a religious nor ghetto Jew (see also "On Leon Trotsky"). Arendt's view of modern anti-Semitism as the Jews' punishment for trying to assimilate has been met with powerful denunciations precisely because this degree of intellectualizing, as Rieff argues, has "rationalized the rule of the guilty" (p. 89; see Sentence V). Yet Rieff offers an equally powerful affirmation of Arendt's attempt to come to terms with what she called totalitarianism's "consistent elimination of conviction as a motive for action" (quoted in 73:1, p. 210). In *Fellow Teachers*, Rieff concludes that "Terror and therapy, East and West, converge in something genuinely new—neither politics nor religion in any sense earlier received within the orders of Western societies" (73:1, p. 210). Arendt recognized this convergence in ways that continue to command attention.

In the second section of part two, I have brought together several sustained pieces on Christianity and Protestantism in particular. I begin with Rieff's observation in his evaluation of Harnack's *History of Dogma* that "Theory, in any case, criticizes belief. One cannot have a thoretical belief" (p. 123). (Compare: "Theory admits no blind obediences," 73:1, p. 103 n.) The cultural theorist embarks upon a dangerous enterprise, dangerous in the sense that the driving force of belief is never too difficult to criticize, but the driving force of criticism may overtake belief and diminish the capacity of belief to instruct. For teachers, the balancing act of belief and criticism is often clumsily handled. The extreme tilts, whether fundamentalist belief or radical criticism, have absorbed much of the attention of re-educated minds deprived of instructive examples other than their own experiences or what they read in newspapers. (See Sentence XXXII.)

One sign of our therapeutic culture is evident in the inability to recognize when criticism functions to revitalize the energy of belief and when it pretends to replace belief. Harnack's criticism of dogma was intended to invigorate the Gospel faith. He sought to release that faith from the "dead generations of believers." In the ambivalence of his own intellect, he called for a dogma that would express faith clearly without the trappings or intellectualizings of metaphysics. Augustine was his hero because "he penetrated beyond doctrine to a moral psychology of faith" (p. 121). What Harnack hoped would replace dogmatics was an apologetic literature of personal confession. In the struggles to be heard, "a strict dogmatics of proclamation cannot be expected to excite attention—let alone opposition" (p. 122). But the cultural logic of apologetics, that is, the attraction between personal confession and the willingness to listen or be heard takes on a special importance in a therapeutic culture. The effect of an apologetic may dissipate until "nothing remains except the smile on the face of culture" (p. 122).

Ferments of real religion have posed another danger, as Rieff argues in

"The Evangelist Strategy": "In the history of evangelism there are inevitably more agitators of genius than comforters" (p. 127). The anxieties raised by the genius of Jonathan Edwards were eventually met with the "liberal institutional answer" of Horace Bushnell. This answer establishes the priority of an institution over the faith it excites and promulgates. Yet the dynamic tensions between faith and institution remain, inviting fresh responses that neither depend upon the incantation of authoritative texts nor accept a Sunday religion that denies any link to the conduct of life during the rest of the week. (See Sentence XXII.)

An apologetic for unbelievers, a necessary address to teachers who find little use for faith, must be part of the evengelical strategy of feeling intellects. As the organized and evangelical churches of our culture assume evermore the character of recognizably political forms—left and right—the university in its feeling distances from these forms must maintain a faith in its own distinctiveness apart from politics and religion (see Rieff's remarks on Marsilius of Padua, p. 166ff). Value-neutrality is a poor name for these feeling distances, because everything to teach and everything to learn turns on what is meant by value. The testing of convictions cannot become an end in itself for teachers anymore than it can for religious evangelicals. The resonances between the personal confessions of the evangelicals and the secular therapists who dominate the anxieties markets of our culture offer evidence enough that teachers have a sacred responsibility to impress students with the difference between learning and being saved (or saving the world). Perhaps an apologetic for unbelievers in our schooling institutions can offer hope that we have no final answers but that we will give the necessary training and the disciplining of mind to find and keep them.

In his brief assessments of works by Paul Tillich and Teilhard de Chardin, Rieff considers two sides of the same coin. On Tillich's side, "the question of being and the meaning of God" are central to the great tasks of theology, however his particular treatment may now be judged and however ignored those tasks are by minds secure in fundamentalism and secularism. On Teilhard's side, "A book that imagines the total development of life, from origins to end, cannot be so essentially peaceful and yet true." The struggle over who will define origins remains a source of warfare between theology and science. Here is one war that no one wishes to see waged in universities again. This nineteenth-century fray has not disappeared; it has shifted its attention to other fronts in the same war. If the evolution/creation dispute has been transformed into a fight for the hearts and minds of fifth-graders, abortion and euthanasia remain powerful inciters of holy and secular wraths among grown-ups in the educated classes. Does any theology now stand against a scientific rationalism that sets no limits for itself? A piety seeking to reconcile itself with science may become only a pious science. But the sanitary terrors of our time, at the origins and ends of life, point to life lived between these two poles and therefore to the "question of being and the meaning of God."

In "Eros Cross-Examined," Rieff examines the fate of Agape, the form of Christian love that stands over and against Eros. The triumph of Eros has emphasized the "right and power of the individual" over "the purity of obligation" (p. 139). The revolutionary character of Christian Agape was expressed in the rebellion of the spirit. Its opposition has always been a rebellion of the flesh. The revolutionary character of Eros has sought to break the link between imperfection and the flesh. Only human mortality, I suppose, has kept that link from finally being broken. Beyond good and evil, there is a powerful freedom to do unto others as one desires, whether in the name of self or science. Nietzsche completed the intellectual work required to permit the entry of Eros into the educated classes. In so doing, he stands behind Freud who took up the clinical responsibilities of seeing to it, however inadvertently, that love would never be spoken of again in the twentieth century without first looking down.[1]

In the third and final section of part two, "Political Faiths and Their Futures," the reader will discover more specific evidence of the transitions to a therapeutic culture. In probing the three stages of the liberal imagination, exemplified in the literary mind of George Orwell, Rieff writes: "The first stage is being Christian without being liberal—action with belief. The second stage is being liberal without being Christian—action without belief. The third stage is the post-liberal—neither action nor belief" (p. 148). In this third stage, the quest for certainty has "revealed itself in its specifically modern form, the quest for security" (p. 149).

Orwell saw the new society emerging out of the decay and exhaustion of the old one. His pessimism about the meaninglessness of the old Christian and capitalist world and the "total shabbiness of the inevitable future" (p. 150) are signs of that liberalism going beyond itself: "As liberals who

---

1. Wordsworth's use of feeling intellect in the *Prelude* (Book XIV, line 226) owes its formulation and direction to an androgenous sweetness and a "higher love" whose pedigree is best traced back to the tradition of Eros and Plato rather than to that of Agape and Jesus, though both traditions are co-present in Wordsworth's work, in pantheist and romantic displays. The first tradition of feeling intellect, the Deuteronomic, had Moses as its chief spokesman. I place Philip Rieff's feeling intellect in the first tradition, repeating, as Moses does for a second time in Deuteronomy, the Law before which each of us stands whether or not we acknowledge this sacred order within which social order establishes its directions upwards and downwards along the vertical of authority. The epigraph of this volume from Lear and the illustrations by Blake are evidences of a sacred order that can never be raised within social order by some impersonally transferable science of intellect, whether positivist or deconstructionist. Personal knowledge, following Polanyi, must be a feeling resistance to the identifications downward that lead to the present therapeutic culture. That culture intends to help us destroy the historically known predicates of feeling intellect. If it succeeds, then identifications upwards and downwards in the vertical of authority will disappear, and so, too, feeling intellect. (See further, sections xv and xvi, in "The Cultural Economy of Higher Education.")

have not yet accepted and no longer know how to reject the meaningless world around them, they are full of the last fine activity of the liberal: imagining the utter destruction of this commercial world" (p. 150). Such energetic imaginations persist, with or without the false hopes of some more organized future. With those hopes, talk of "alternative futures" *for everyone* abound. Without them, that is, without the "escape back into the old whale" (p. 151) a new acceptance appears embracing the worst in an eternal present that has never looked toward an "alternative future" for its improvement.

Orwell embodied the tension between intelligence and morality distinctive of the liberal mind. He could neither accept everything nor reject "the world." His literary fiction invents transitional characters who have experienced the loss of belief in exchange for intelligence. Beyond the transition, in the vast forgetfulness of our present discontent, even the sense of losing anything is lost. Orwell could only imagine characters beyond the transition. Their laughter, as if heard ahead in time, is directed back toward us in the present. As we hear it more clearly, and join in it on occasions, hope and despair will be evermore peculiar to contemplate. In preparation we may strip down the ethic of responsibility until it is only a self-referential meeting of the demands of the day, what Rieff calls an ethic of action. For the exhausted liberal, small hopes are still better than none at all.

The temperament of intellects caught between not believing and not knowing fully why is nevertheless easily disturbed, producing outbursts of enthusiasm and resignation about whether the world is worth saving. Sexual desire and apocalyptic moods fuel these outbursts and have been repeatedly expressed in a post-liberal literature that laughs at itself and its readers as they give to it and take from it nothing of themselves. Entertainment has replaced instruction just as biblical criticism once displaced and then replaced faith. Henry Miller is Rieff's and, to a large extent, Orwell's instructive example of graceless entertainment. We know this because it is not laughter as such that feeling intellect resists but rather laughter at nothing.

The analysis, critique, and aesthetics of power are taken up in the remaining pieces of section three. The conflict between religion and politics, organized institutionally between church and state, has given criticism its sacred edge. As that edge wears off, criticism assumes its modern character, exemplified very well in Proudhon and Mills. The modern critic, following Proudhon, makes fun of everything, or, following Mills, is content with being on the side of dissatisfaction. (T. G. Masaryk taught his students "that it was the old God who created, while we new gods do not know how to create: we can only 'criticize the work of the old God,'" p. 174.) To feel in the minority when you are in the majority is one of the crucial experiences of being an intellectual. Proudhon's criticism has fed all manner of political belief while Mills's has become another name for integrity in sociology. This integrity is part of the new honesty to hold the hand that feeds you while promising to bite carefully and not too often. Mills would neither be deluded by "his socialism nor his respect for the liberal civilization of an earlier America" (p. 170), but he was also not prepared to move beyond his deconstructive sociology. Like Orwell, he possessed all the symptoms of the transition to a therapeutic culture that treats criticism as "another bright and shiny thing, to be admired and consumed" (p. 171).

"Aesthetic Functions in Modern Politics" has earned the status of precursor of the sociologies of mass communications, popular culture, and sport. The essential difference between it and these quite successful fields is its unwillingness to deny what is at stake in all performances. Ceremony emptied of its teaching content serves the cynical interests of those with power, whether for the purpose of naming the enemy or selling a product. At stake in all performances is the authority that they artfully acknowledge. Disraeli knew how to reach his public but also knew that both he and they were beholden to an authority that was not themselves. A sociology that forgets this last link, which is faith, will hash out millions of observations about the coercive powers of staged politics and sports (and, for that matter, everyday life) and never ascend the higher road of faithful criticism. (For more on what is implicit in the sociological faith, see "The Culture of Unbelief.")

On Intellectuals and Education

Part three gathers together various readings on the fate of teaching and learning in a culture that has grown inherently distrustful of both. The roots of this distrust are exposed in one way by comparing Max Weber and J. Robert Oppenheimer. Weber, like Freud, led those with conviction about their vocations to the great divide between reason and faith. By burning all the conscious bridges between the two, modern science in both its abstract and clinical manifestations has created a nonmoral culture described by Rieff in *The Triumph of the Therapeutic:* "With a commitment that is strictly vocational, the scientist personifies the latest phase in the Western psycho-historical process, one that refrains from laying down guidelines of moral intervention for the society as a whole. Whatever his professed intention, the scientist acts, therefore, as a spiritual preceptor to modern man. The therapeutic has everything—and nothing—to learn from the scientist, for in the established sense of the word, the scientist, as such, has no culture" (66:1, pp. 256–57).

One choice remaining to scientists who would profess guidelines of moral intervention is politics. Rieff describes Oppenheimer as "the priest-scientist of the Comtean vision, transforming history as well as nature" (p. 206). This vision also accounts for features of the modern revolutionary and bureaucrat. After the explosions of atomic bombs over Hiroshima and Nagasaki, scientists expressed a high moral conviction about their responsibilities for a creation that was the most creatively destructive use of nature yet invented. In the persona of scientist, creator and moral advisor over one's creation merged for a moment. But something intrinsic to the scientific mind would not permit moral conviction to constrain its imagination. The scientific imagination and the infinite universe it seeks to understand and control cannot be bound by politics anymore than by morality. Scientific genius, which can show fear in a handful of dust, has long since lost its connection to traditions of faith out of which the quest for certainty first emerged. (See Sentence XXIV.)

Oppenheimer's excommunication by the bureaucratic powers of the state signaled the permanent order of subordination of science to politics. And in an illustrative case of therapeutic gamesmanship, the state attacked his character and personal associations as a means of discrediting the counterpolicy he proposed. If this was unfair, even tragic, it was nevertheless a matching of wits between a state "without any dogma it cannot abandon overnight to catch the shifts of power" (p. 221) and a science without any dogma it cannot abandon overnight to catch the shifts of an imperial and, thus, unfeeling truth. Unfeeling truth, then, serves those in power and those in search of greater power. More recent mass movements opposed to the state production and administration of nuclear weapons appear unable to move beyond the will to power in politics and science insofar as their alleged transcendence of the interests of nation-states is viewed suspiciously as a skillfully played politics but played always for the wrong side.

Kelly Miller, far less known today than his contemporaries W. E. B. Dubois and Booker T. Washington, is, in Rieff's estimation of him, an exemplary figure in the pantheon of feeling intellect. Miller's defense of culture was steadfastly antiracist: "Race is the most terrible cultural simplification of all; in his wisdom and learning, Miller rejected the fatal simplicity that the provenance of a value determined membership in it" (p. 227). The fatal acceptance of this simplicity has deeply rocked our colleges and universities, to the point that race, class, gender, and "sexual orientation" are the new bottom lines for value determinations that typically originate in personal experiences and are then transformed into political convictions (see Sentence VIII). But Rieff teaches: "There are no values for whites only and none are black, whatever their origins. Our moral demands stand or fall on the proposition that they belong to those who enact those demands in their own lives" (p. 227).

The advocacy, however hidden, of a compensatory racism is now taught under the name of the sociology of race. (The older title "race relations" signified an acknowledgment of values that belonged to those, black and white, who were willing to enact moral demands in their own lives.) Students are cynically led to believe that nothing matters or that only the most violent tactics can pay back to Western culture what it has coming to it. Affirmative action in the external reorganization of work and school may achieve what the leaders of the Western cultural deconstruction and their falsely guilty followers intend. But after the deconstructionists may come a more powerfully organized thought police who already patrol college campuses in the adjunct offices specially created for their brand of intimidation called sensitivity sessions. In this struggle to determine what will be taught and how it will be taught, the defense of feeling intellect must be made fully and often.

"The function of the teacher is to help students to know the truth, even if they cannot love it" (p. 232). Here Rieff states the special responsibilities of teachers—as distinct from scientists, politicians, and publicists—who must regard education as "precisely the freedom and capacity to speculate that aristocracy or monarchy or totalitarianism may possibly be better than democracy. Otherwise, neither democratic values nor any others can ever be clarified" (p. 233). If education is "essentially a matter of authority" (p. 234), the teaching office cannot afford the terrible costs of its unclarified indifference to that authority. Our contemptuous indifference contains a strain of negation that regularly imagines itself as sophistication. (See Sentence VII.)

The final two pieces of part three are examples of teaching praxis and teaching theory. Since all data rise to meet theories—not the reverse—a corollary is that all praxes rise likewise. Notice in Rieff's recommendations for the organization of a science curriculum that he is "not above wishing to see a certain piety, a certain sentiment, developed for our masterworks and leading ideas" (p. 240). We teachers are reluctant to admit pieties that praise rather than condemn, preferring instead to avoid shared intellectual experiences that are the true core of all higher educations. The vacuum formed by a historic withdrawal from naming, scrutinizing, and defending our masterworks and leading ideas has pulled numerous politicized agendas, mostly from the left, into the vacant center. Plato will not save the academy or America from its closed mind; neither will his forced removal (see Sentence XXV). Despite the present climate of tirades against all parties culpable for destroying the life of the mind, a vast reservoir of teaching integrity remains to be tapped for the sake of enabling students to see why "Preaching is not teaching, except in a church" (73:1, p. 2).

Fellow teachers of my generation, those born after the Second World War and before the presidency of John F. Kennedy, are members of the multiversity, now more than ever. The quiet life of teaching, the life necessary for feeling intellect, is a foreign, forgotten thing. That life has been replaced by the pursuits of soft money and hard science, each transforming itself into the other. The most ambitious and occasionally most talented flee teaching first in search of promotions awarded for anything but teaching. Beneficient foundations and government confer awards that degrade teaching further. So many pies need slicing that entire careers are made for those who slice and consume them. In this tropical climate, no greed is too embarrassing to contemplate. The insider trading in our colleges and universities must be exposed for what it is: the abandonment of the teaching life and its feeling intellect. In "The Cultural Economy of Higher Education," Rieff gives forty instructions against the abandonment of No feelings, truthfulness, modesty, and an order of authority that cannot be abolished. (See Sentence XXX.)

On Character and Culture

Part four consists of studies in character and culture, though, by this point, the reader will recognize that all Rieff's writings aim toward constructing the necessary links between the two. Instruction in character begins with a child's feeling recognition that there are remissive spaces between an authority that demands a certain behavior (i.e., morality) and the behavior enacted. Saintliness is the closing of those remissive spaces. For the rest of us, it is enough to acknowledge the difference and accept our punishment (the most elemental of which is guilt). Reynard the Fox is a creature of radical remissiveness. In his world, "there are no saints, only litigants" (p. 268).

A culture of radical remissiveness makes a game of punishment, allowing no recognitions of what is not to be done, yet done. But the remissive children's tales are not without acknowledgments of judgment. While the stories entertain, they also instruct in the "violence inherent in winning" (p. 268). If this is learned in childhood, then adults will understand why playing by the rules is an achievable enactment that winning cannot guarantee. Not that losing is a virtue, unless one is a saint. Losing invites violence wherever charity is overorganized and bureaucratically mandated.

Rieff's description of the Organization Man over and against "his ruthless Protestant predecessor" (see also, p. 272) is not without ironic hopefulness: "He mixes more pleasure with business, and takes his pleasures in a less furtive way. He has regard for his health. He is kind to his children. He is reasonably happy. He is a far more civil creature" (p. 272). As for the cultural implications of the new sociability, the view is less sanguine: "The free man must learn how to cheat power masquerading as knowledge. He must cultivate that double consciousness which permits the Organization to mount a plausible version of himself in the bureaucratic showcase without for a moment believing that the mounted creature is really he" (p. 273).

More than thirty years later that "double consciousness" is central to the public/private debate among intellectuals uncomfortable with the defense of a characterless individuality, now called privacy, and opposite to what was once meant by hypocrisy. Of course, in Rieff's priorities, the "he" behind the "mounted creature" is directive of, not in flight from, the public fronts of sociability, politics, and work. Our civil indifference masks a more open hostility about being told what to do and how to live. The moralizing functions of culture have been largely assumed by state bureaucracies of foster care. Such care is a sign of the larger indifference once fought with the modest strengths of individuals, families, schools, and churches. A vanity that would save the entire world in the name of politics or that would attend to one's self-improvement exclusively is nothing more than a therapeutic smokescreen behind which all commitments can be construed as private choices. Doing good by oneself first, no matter how long that may take, is less a strategy for changing the world than a pious indecisiveness about the difference one can make in it. One can stay too long in school as easily as in politics. The early retirements of the overprivileged nowadays include endless stints in graduate study where criticism is confused with learnedness and entertaining is mistaken for teaching. (See Sentence XXIX.)

The essays on Oscar Wilde and Charles Horton Cooley are studies in contrast. Wilde's intellect was supremely remissive in its aesthetic justification: "Whatever is realized is right." The greatness of his artistic achievement reminds us that "There are no neutral powers in the permanent war of culture" (p. 277). In one sense, Wilde's imprisonment was a reminder of last resort insofar as the culture he challenged was already deeply confused about the attractiveness of his art. In another sense, his imperfect artistry forced him into direct confrontation with official inhibitions. A more perfect artist, Rieff argues, might have escaped the last resort of a culture to define itself over and against those who challenge it. His failure became his martyrdom, and time has transformed that personal failure into a social movement of much greater seriousness than Wilde ever intended.

The cheap, mass-produced imitations of Wilde's art have made the sophistication of his masterful assaults into trivialities, as trivial as bumper stickers that announce "Question Authority." The questioning and question of authority have preoccupied all revolutionaries in politics and art. The would-be artist who seeks to put into practice what he fails to achieve in his art is the most recently dangerous type of all (see Sentence XXXIII). Wilde's example, on the other hand, is instructive for what it may teach about the functions of culture. Figures in authority, so as to be in authority, cannot express everything and are rarely entertaining. Wilde's vision of a new culture, beyond the sheerly expressive entertainment it could afford, raised the ante on the questioning of authority to whether authority itself was necessary. He attacked an image of authority external in its appearance, believing, as did many others who were far less talented, that nothing so high-minded as authority was worth achieving inwardly. The art of abandonment practiced cleverly, cowardly, or brutally gives authority its external appearance. Wilde understood that character was dangerous to an art that guided last of all within. The transformative power of his art was released upon a world whose figures in authority were no longer clearly present. This remains so in our present.

Yet Rieff concludes: "Wilde's attack on all authority is too easy. When authority becomes so external, then it has ceased to be authoritative. The heaviest crosses are internal, and men make them so, that, thus skeletally supported, they can bear the burden of themselves. Under the sign of this inner cross, a certain inner distance is achieved from the infantile desire to be and have everything. Identification is a far more compelling concept of authority and includes imitation. True individuality must involve the capacity to say no, and this capacity is inseparable from the genesis of no in authority. A man can only resist the polytheism of experience if his character is anchored deeply enough by certain God-terms to resist shuttling endlessly among all" (p. 286). I have quoted at length because it is at this point that the full implications of the anticredal or therapeutic character become apparent. Whether achieved by totalitarianism or therapy, or by some combination of the two, the anticredal character emerges as that new type of private/public artist heralded in the writings of Freud, Marx, Nietzsche, and Wilde. The short pieces on Foucault and Ariès enable Rieff to theorize further on the end of the civilization of authoritarian rationalism and the death of meaning in the death of human beings, both examples of the anticredal desire to abolish all that is certain.

Cooley, like Kelly Miller, lives on in the pantheon of feeling intellect. His case against individualism, the moral imperative in his sociology, was a prescription for sociology itself. Rieff concurs: "The function of the sociologist is both scientific and pedagogic; dealing with moral problems, he must teach moral lessons—otherwise, his sociology fails to be social enough" (p. 296). In its teaching capacity, sociology was for Cooley and is for Rieff a counter to doctrine and ideology; in its permanent tentativeness about its analytic perspectives, sociology achieves an "intellectual-aesthetic capacity" that enables it to deal "as Cooley put it, 'with life in its fullness'" (p. 297).

As the full measure of its capacities, the plurality of theories and methods stands in constant tension with the pedagogic motive to achieve some stability over what is known. For Cooley, the primary group served as both an analytical perspective on American life and an answer to what was most important about it. Rieff calls this mixture of vision and motive a God-term. What is superior in all God-terms is the motive to give order to what is seen. This motive was once embodied in doctrine, and as Rieff describes with devastating precision, all methodologies in the social sciences are "styles of analytic address in which the doctrinal motive has been repressed" (p. 298). All data are interesting, regardless of the method used to obtain them, only by virtue of the fact that the doctrinal motive both reveals and conceals what it addresses. I see no way to save this fact from its own impoverishment in the hands of an army of lesser minds who turn texts into textbooks for students unable to distinguish between directive symbols and identification tags. The primary group refers to more than what is meant by family and the close network of relations around it. In Cooley's symbolic, it stands for hope and serves as the moral ground of his ethic of responsibility.

The more authentic sociology in an age of symbolic impoverishment is foreboding rather than hopeful. The critic is chief spokesman, as we have already seen in Proudhon and Mills, for what does not work. Cooley's constructive sociology contained elements of a naïve optimism, especially about the promises of industry and technology. His belief in an ethical culture in which all will be improved by an instructive and edifying mass communications is less a hope than a symptom of a directionless doctrine that is all form and no content. But this is also the greatest difficulty for sociology as a discipline: in its "critical" theories it may assume that all the old answers are permanently dead, if not completely forgotten; its constructive theories must raise the dead, but how can they in a world in permanent transition from its saving doctrines? Harnack, Orwell, and Cooley all shared in this dilemma from each one's special precinct of feeling intellect. Each knew that the release from the past was not complete without some new commitment in the present. Cooley's hope that human nature would find its fullest expression in the social order was a commitment to two fictions that may balance at short distances but may not in the long run. Unlike Weber, Cooley did not use his liberalism to define the limits of meaning. And unlike Freud, he did not measure the conserving quality of his sociology against a backdrop of unreason and mass unruliness. He instead promoted a form of togetherness that can only be preserved in a living content of stable re-enactments. With the content all but spent, the sociology of the family now replaces the family as a less stable re-enactment of what family means. Looking for meaning in this way, no invented criticism is too unbelievable to mount. Sociology is thus a shadow game that could just as easily build up what it tears down. This would require a fundamental shift in its mode of criticism.[2]

2. To my fellow teachers in sociology: if you were to teach a sociology that is constructive rather than deconstructive, then your deviance courses would consist entirely of examples of saintliness rather than sinfulness; if you were to teach social problems, then the cover term "problems" would point you back to the character of individuals not ahead to the illusion of some perfect social order in which "problems" disappear because professors or states say so; if you were to teach theory, then you would ask questions that are not the stock-in-trade of ideologists. If you were to teach about the law; then you would acknowledge what it upholds rather than what it holds down. The dread of looking up is nothing compared to the mindlessness of a discipline that stakes its integrity in the fascination with the endless releases from and denials of authority. Our social planners, who herald Comte or Marx, have ample empirical evidence for their strategic contributions to the world mess, and our deconstructionists, who defy the gravity of moral and civil existence for the sake of the experience of

Rieff's elaborations of a theory of culture, begun systematically in the introductory chapter of *The Triumph of the Therapeutic*, are taken up successively in the next three pieces. Once again Cooley's sociology serves as the inspiring occasion to formulate a theory in terms of minimal and maximal culture. "Toward a Theory of Culture" introduces the language of interdict, remission, and transgression. "By What Authority?" establishes the inescapable order of authority in its full range of expression as interdict, remission, and transgression. Treating these three pieces as finger exercises in a grander composition, I will quote from each one in order to sound the leitmotifs destined to be repeated in work beyond the appearance of this volume:

> "Sociological theory can become constructive if, and only if, it uses its critical powers to plan a cultural reconquest of the therapeutic thought-world" (p. 319).

> "Finally, Freud leaves us with that most revolutionary attitude of all, the analytic attitude, which closes off in the resolution of the transference the ancient possibility of creating, by its successes, yet another ideology of the superego—yet another moral demand system" (p. 330).

> "This essay proposes, without hope, a counterenlightenment" (p. 331).

The reader who has come this far will recognize the irony so profoundly a part of all the writings collected here.

"For the Last Time Psychology" ends what was begun in "Reflections on Psychological Man in America," the first chapter in this volume. With the emergence of psychological man confirmed, Rieff explores in this final piece the "unholy trinity of character types sovereign over the modern anticulture, of which therapy is the modal experience" (p. 356). That anticulture does not so much dominate what is taught as it makes impossible the recognitions of "the eternally given *Nots* of our historically received faiths" (p. 357) (see Sentence XXXVIII). Concealed within Rieff's ironic and irenic unpackings of these historically received faiths is the truth of our age as it pushes uncontrollably toward the abolition of sacred fear and its guilt knowledge and places upon the world stage "what endless balancing acts, what multiple perspectives, what rich shows of lifestyles, what a riot of selves" (p. 363). Nothing could be further from the Truth.

The aesthetic of Philip Rieff's irony, the artfulness of his feeling intellect,

---

release itself, flirt with nihilism as if it were the only game left to play in a relentlessly antitheoretical discipline. Between planning and unplanning, a scholasticism now abounds in sociology, offering rehashes so polished that no further interpretations of the classics will ever be necessary. Theory, as a vision of the highest, acknowledges authority in its living character here and now. Our classics are of antiquarian interest to the extent that their acknowledgments are no longer ours.

cannot completely protect him or us from the accusation that we are unfeeling defenders of abandoned faiths or that the interdicts are merely taboos. Theory, in its ironic habits, can neither revive faith nor invent taboos. The endless series of unprecedented repetitions and ungodly refinements that give genius its *repressive/expressive* character and morality its concealing enactments will have to be made to each succeeding generation of students personally instructed in what is at stake in living the high life of feeling intellect. This is Philip Rieff's sociology in all of its ennobling possibility. To advance this ennobling possibility is what a sacred sociology would be, as the governing phrase now runs, "all about."

Sentences

In order to complete the aesthetic design of this teaching book, I have compiled forty Sentences in the tradition of Summas and Sentences. In this tradition it was customary to write succinctly and in highly concentrated and focused ways, addressing always the sacred order from which thought in the social order derived. This same tradition reappeared in the composition of aphorisms. I might add that several of the Sentences here aspire to the canons of maxims and adages. It is for others to judge which canonical status is most appropriate.

Freud and Psychoanalysis

1

Reflections on Psychological Man in America

Before Freud and after

Three character ideals have successively dominated Western civilization: first is the ideal of *political* man, formed and handed down to us from classical antiquity. Plato was the greatest psychologist of political man and his most persuasive teacher. From Plato we first learned systematically to divide human nature into higher and lower energies. As it turns out, in Plato, the health and stability of a person is analogous to—and, moreover, dependent upon—the health and stability of the political order: that is, a proper subordination of passions to intellect will follow from the subordination of the uneducated classes to the educated. Elaborated as a doctrine of human nature, Greek political philosophy was also, at the same time, Greek psychology.

The second dominant character ideal of Western civilization borrowed the Platonic dichotomy between higher and lower energies and adapted it for different cultural purposes, chiefly religious. Although originally a naive and straightforward, even ecstatic, faith, Christianity could not resist going to the Greek philosophical schools. As a result, the *religious* man that Christianity formed and handed down to us shows certain recognizably Greek traits. The Christian doctrine of human nature grafted faith onto the place once occupied by the idea of life as a continuing intellectual and moral reeducation. Both therapeutic functions merged, and the church became at once a saving and a pedagogic institution. Certainly "The Republic" is one vast school, complete with intellectual and vocational programs, for the better training of more and less capable citizens. And the Gospels are the ideological basis for one vast church, for the better training of the capacity for faith. Adapting Greek intellectualism to its own pur-

Reprinted with permission of Abbott Laboratories (Abbott Park, IL 60064) from *What's New*, no. 220 (1960), Abbott Laboratories What's New Anniversary Issue, Contemporary Comment no. 13: 17–23.

3

poses, the main Christian institution developed a Western personality type that organized itself around the expectation of achieving faith, asserting it as superior to reason, which could, at best, merely support and confirm the religious gift.

In the slow accretion of self-images that is the mortar between periods in the history of our civilization, a third character ideal emerged, in part from the failure of the previous two: *economic* man, one who would cultivate rationally his very own garden, meanwhile solacing himself with the assumption that by thus attending to his own lower needs a general satisfaction of the higher needs would occur. A moral revolution was the result: what had been lower in the established hierarchy of human interests was asserted to be higher.

But economic man, as I have suggested in *Freud: The Mind of the Moralist*, turned out to be a transitional type, with the shortest life-expectancy of all; when this typical character of the enlightenment showed a faltering belief in his own superiority to his predecessors, a successor began to emerge—the *psychological* man of the twentieth century.

However intellectually sophisticated that psychological man is, he is anti-intellectual. However church-going still, he has reason to be dubious about the therapeutic efficacy of faith—which he believes to be the main purpose and function of his religion. However much involved in getting and having things, psychological man knows that the satisfactions he wishes to own, as his property, carry no certain price tag. For these reasons he is profoundly skeptical of the received hierarchy of values to which even his immediate predecessors assented. Yet psychological man cannot completely shake off his past. He has in fact the nervous habits of his father, economic man: he is anti-heroic, shrewd, studying unprofitable commitments as the sins most to be avoided, carefully keeping a balance of his satisfactions and dissatisfactions, but without the genial confidence of his immediate ancestor that the sum will mount to something meaningful and justify his entire life. He lives by the ideal of insight—practical, experimental, and leading to the mastery of his own personality.

It was at the tag end of the period during which economic man was the dominant character ideal that Freud first began to see his patients. Because they were unprepared for an ideal of insight as a way of accommodating to life—as a substitute for the earlier ideals of might or right, faith or productivity—Freud's patients of the turn of the century were incredulous and naive. But the Freudian pedagogy has had its effect. Now, half a century after Freud first began to teach the new ideal to patients anxious to unlearn the old ones embedded painfully in their personalities, the patient more often comes armed with Freud's own jargon, and may even bring along his own diagnosis—so ready is he to adopt the new character ideal.

He Is Ill, but Differently

Contemporary patients are not only educated in a different way from those of the periods when political, religious and economic pedagogies were successively dominant, but they are ill in a different way from the patients Freud first saw. A successful attack on the ancient dichotomizing of human nature into categories of higher and lower has taken place. But every cure creates the risk of encouraging a new disease. New forms of anxiety have been produced, peculiar to the healthy new character type. What is new—indeed revolutionary—about this latest image that Western men have of themselves is that it repudiates the hierarchical master-idea of "higher" and "lower" to which all the predecessors of psychological man have been addicted. Yet, perhaps in part because of this repudiation, the new character ideal generates its own peculiar nervous tensions. His anxieties may be less the consequence of inner repression, built into, as Freud believed, his native psychological endowment; instead, the new anxiety may reflect the ambiguity that surrounds his new-found freedom.

Freud understood this fresh turn in the history of human anxiety. Against the clear implication of his analysis of life as devoid of anything more than an endless network of trivial meanings, Freud offered no large new cosset of an idea. His is a severe and chill anti-doctrine, in which the final dichotomy to which Western man is prey—that between an ultimately meaningful and meaningless life—must also be abandoned. Freud's genius was analytic, not creative. To him creativity seemed to belong to the childhood of the race, not to its maturity. At its best, psychoanalytic therapy is devoted to the long and difficult task of rubbing a touch of that analytic genius into less powerful minds. For this reason, Freud rightly understood therapy as a form of reeducation; he specifically called it that.

Therapeutic reeducation is therefore at once a very difficult and yet very modest procedure. It teaches the patient-student how to live with the contradictions that bind him (or constrict him) into a unique personality; this is in contrast to the older moral pedagogies, which tried to reorder the contradictions into a structure of superior and inferior, good and evil, capabilities. To become a psychological man is thus to become kinder to the whole self, the private parts as well as the public, the formerly inferior as well as the formerly superior. While older character types were concentrated on the life task of trying to order the warring parts of personality into a hierarchy, the Freudian pedagogy, reflecting the changing self-conception of the times, is far more egalitarian: it is the task of psychological man to develop an informed (*i.e.*, healthy) respect for the sovereign and unresolvable basic contradictions that galvanize him into the singularly complicated human being that he is.

Freud's most important ideas finally may have less to do with the "repression" of sexual impulses, which explains neither the past discontents of our civilization nor the present ones, than with "ambivalence." Being a strange new kind of prophet—one who asserted that, after the most complete self-searching, men must learn to accept themselves as they are—Freud placed his hope precisely in that human capacity which is also the mainspring of the human problem: the human capacity to reverse feelings. This hope is grounded in Freud's assumption that human nature is not so much a hierarchy of high-low, good-bad, as his predecessors in the business of prophecy believed, but more a democracy of opposing predispositions, deposited in every nature in roughly equal intensities. Where there is love, there is the lurking eventuality of hatred. Where there is ambition, there is the ironic desire for failure. Although he wishes not to know it, a sore loser may be sore mainly because he almost won and is reacting against his wish to lose. Psychoanalysis is full of such mad logic; it is convincing only if the student of his own life accepts Freud's egalitarian revision of the inherited idea of a hierarchical human nature.

Yet, although he announced this major revision in the Western self-image, Freud was himself sentimentally attached (as a consequence of his own traditional education) to the old hierarchical assumption. The great healer of the tear in human nature was himself a torn man. (A genuinely analytical biography of Freud has yet to be written.) On the one hand, he analyzed the damage done by this hierarchical structuring of human nature into pejoratively toned "higher" and "lower" categories—indeed, it was precisely this damage that he made it his business to mend. On the other hand, he hoped that somehow, despite the near equality of our warring capacities, reason, the old Greek tyrant over the roiling democracy of emotions, would cleverly manage to reassert itself—not in the authoritarian way suggested by Plato and his Christian successors but in a modest and fresh manipulative way. This way actually demands, I think, the kind of character ideal I have called "psychological," in order to contrast it with the preceding ethically fixed types.

We can now better understand why Freud was an inveterate finder of double meanings, even of some that may not be there. For the latent makes sense only as it contradicts the manifest; the aggressive movement behind the friendly gesture needs the complement of the friendly gesture behind the aggressive movement. Thus Freud succeeded in challenging every simplicity, including moral simplicity. He encouraged a tolerance of what used to be called, in general, the "low," just as he encourages a new and profound respect for the young, for the deviant, for the shocking. There was about Freud a calm awaiting of the unexpected that subverts the expectations of a life based on older schemes of an authoritative, set, hierarchical order of living—including the structure of the family, and, moreover, of the "head" of the family. The Freudian pedagogy carries special implications for the position of the father as the main maker of the rules of the moral game as Western children must learn to play it. For the father is the very personification of all those heights of repressive command that Freud leveled.

The Freudian Flock and "Better" Living

To Freud, a tolerance of ambiguities is the key to a genuinely stable character. Yet it is possible, I think, that just such a capacity may lead finally to an attitude of knowing acquiescence as somehow superior to ignorant rejection. Being able to recognize the equivocations of which behavior is composed need not, of course, mean their encouragement. Yet there is a sound basis for what are otherwise hypocritical objections to the immorality of interpretation with which Freudians can rip away the facades of moral action. Hypocrisy is a precious thing in any culture. Like reticence, it may help build those habits of avoidance that swerve us from honest but head-on collisions against one another. Nothing about psychoanalytic therapy encourages immoral behavior. The immorality of interpretation aims merely to reveal the false morality of some behavior. But this means that psychoanalysis discourages moral behavior on the old, simple ground—out of what is now called a *sense* of guilt rather than guilt.

To help us distinguish between guilt and a sense of guilt, between responsibility for an offense committed and fantasy about offenses only intended or merely imagined, seems a moral enough as well as therapeutic aim. To suffer from scrupulosity is, after all, a well-known perversion of moral ambition, even according to the most elaborate of our established casuistries. But psychoanalysis is more than a mere surgery of handwashing. Freud cuts more deeply than that. His ambition to exhaust the sense of guilt by clinical exposures in its every detail may be dangerous, as he himself realized, to the life of a culture that is always necessarily (by his own definition of it) on the defensive. If a self-trained casuist gets along better by resolving his guilt into a sense of guilt, then he is the healthier for that resolution. This is a vulgar and popular misinterpretation of Freud; but there is something about the presuppositions of psychoanalytic therapy that encourages just such misinterpretations. A man can be made healthier without being made better—rather, morally worse. Not the good life but better living is the Freudian standard. It is a standard to which Americans find it specially easy to flock.

Vienna . . . Everywhere Vienna

Our lives are no longer modeled after the Christian or the Greek. Nor is it modeled after that of the humanist. The political man of the Greeks, the religious man of the Hebrews and Christians, the enlightened economic man of the eighteenth-century European (the original of that mythical present-day character, the "good European"), has been superseded by a new model for the conduct of life: the psychological man of the Americans. He is untraditionally European, or uniquely American, in a very clear sense; for both Socrates and Christ taught economic man to be at least slightly ashamed when he failed to sacrifice lower to higher ideals.

Freud is America's great teacher, despite his ardent wish to avoid that fate. For it was precisely the official and parental shams of high ideals that Freud questioned. In their stead, Freud taught lessons which Americans, prepared by their own national experience, have found peculiarly easy to learn: survive, resign yourself to living within your moral means, suffer no gratuitous failures in a futile search for ethical heights that no longer exist—if ever they did. Freud proclaims the superior wisdom of choosing the second best. He is our Crito, become intellectually more supple than a sick and old Socrates, who might be foolish enough still to justify his own death sentence rather than escape from the prison of his own crippling inhibitions about the sanctity of the state, which he mistakes for his father. Freud appeals so because his wisdom is so tired. But surely he is not to be blamed for living in a time when the inherited aspirations of the Greek, Christian and humanist past had gone stale, when both Athens and Jerusalem, along with their later European outposts, no longer could compel the spirit of Western man to embark upon life as a sacrificial pilgrimage. Instead, Freud teaches, every man must learn to make himself at home in his own grim and gay little Vienna.

There is a darkness about Freud's vision of the existing external conditions, toward which it is the ego's function to adjust, that makes his an "ego psychology" more profound and yet more modest than it has become among those of his successors who have appropriated "ego psychology" as their own. Clever disciples first narrow their master's doctrine in order later to broaden it. Such effrontery is inevitable, if disciples themselves aspire, after the death of the master, to acquire the title of master. The ambition to theorize flares especially strong in the orthodox, who must compensate for the restraints of orthodoxy by claiming at some point to enlarge upon it. In order to satisfy their own egos, the most able of Freud's followers have accented his as an "id psychology." Of course psychoanalysis was from the beginning an ego psychology. Understandably, however, the disciples have been unable to tolerate the ambiguity of the master's vision, his understanding of the pathetic weakness of reason and its neutrality before the chaos of conflict with which it must cope.

To a surprising extent, Freud leaves the task of ordering this chaos to the unneutral and rather unintelligent superego. The moral agent of the inner man inherits from the parental culture a certain common imagination of meaning which it imposes arbitrarily upon the meaningless whole of life. But with the decline of the superego, in a parental culture without enough moral earnestness to hand to its children, Freud's shard of traditional moralism, which he put over the emptiness he found in the very center and bottom of our lives, cannot appeal to his successors—in particular to his American successors. Their recourse has been to the strange fiction that the ego is really a very powerful and independent person, who can by conforming to reality master it. Correspondingly, the external conditions to which the ego adapts (and in adapting, masters) are painted by Freud's successors in colors far less dark than those grays and blacks favored by Freud. Ego—this delicate European intellectual ectomorph of the psychic trinity—has been padded out by Freud's American disciples until he appears now, in the psychoanalytic literature, as a muscular American sort of fellow, a regular mesomorph, willing and able to fight as well as connive for what he wants.

The "I" in the Middle of Every Head

What can the ego want? The selfish self of the ego-psychologists may be stronger than Freud made him out to be, but he is no better equipped to aspire to much more than his own survival—now by claiming less for himself, now by claiming more. The "I" in the middle of every head is an expandable and contractable thing, identifiable with the "me" and with the "mine" that once may have been "thine." Precisely here is the irreconcilability of the received Western hierarchical value system with any ego psychology, however keenly analytic about the pretensions of that value system the ego psychology may be. The psychological man of our therapeutic doctrine is not reconcilable with the moral man of preceding doctrines. If we choose the image of the trained egotist for our idea, we ought to be clear at least that such a choice runs exactly counter to the choice that once animated the West.

All three earlier answers to the standard question 'what is Man?' have been given in terms that could not be more opposed to the answer given by modern depth psychology. It is "because of his I, Mine, Me, and the like" that, according to the Greek and Christian traditions—and even, ironically, in our rationalist economistic tradition—men habitually fall into their sick condition. Man's first disobedience—or, put otherwise, his fatal cleverness—was to discover his commitment to himself. The old structured value system never preached "Man for himself"; not even the original doctrinal statements of economic man carried such a subversive message: "payola" was not a condition of the Wealth of Nations as originally conceived. In sum, all three major systems of hierarchical value rejected the moral implications of an ego psychology, which is the doctrinal basis for the emergence of psychological man. Even when the involvement of the ego is religious, as it is when the ego expands to include what Paul Tillich calls "ultimate concerns," no merging of images occurs: having acquired religion, psychological man nevertheless fails to resemble religious man.

Perhaps the image of man as a trained egotist is the one most appropriate and safe for use in this age. It is the self-image of a traveling man rather than a missionary. Unfortunately for culture and good taste, the salesman always cruelly parodies the preacher—without being able to help doing so, for his cultural history has dictated to the salesman the rhetorical style of the missionary. Freud distrusted that style, even for medical missionaries—or, more precisely, for missionaries of a saving medicine; he never "sold" his doctrine himself, as now many of his successors have done, to their profit. Freud's own personal style is more suited to the American temper, with its characteristic lack of piety toward "higher" things and a respectful interest in the "lower." How, finally, the American will solve his value problem, I do not know. It is certain, I think, that Freud has already contributed something significant toward that problem and its solution. (60: 1)

2

The American Transference: From Calvin to Freud

It was Freud who insisted that the analyst must be a veiled figure. In that way, Freud made himself available for therapeutic purposes; the patient saw in him that character, or tangle of characters, with which he was too deeply involved. The first analyst thus became, in a guarded way, whatever the patient needed to find in him—father, mother, brother, boss, competitor, latent lover, manifest object of hatred.

Into this intimate relation between doctor and patient are marched the unemployed emotions of the patient's life, in order that they may be sorted out and put in working order. Thus, the analyst gets to know the patient. In contrast, the patient learns to know himself through his therapeutic association with the analyst. Of the analyst he knows nothing except what he can imagine. From this imagining, and through the informed deference of his attention, the analyst learns much of what he wants to know about the patient. Yet Freud refused to realize that, in the doctor-patient relation, the therapist himself is an incalculable element, involved no less than his patient. If the two mysteries manage somehow to communicate, they accomplish that joint and greater mystery, a cure.

What the analyst can be to a patient, a doctrine may be, at times, to a

Reprinted from *The Atlantic Monthly*, Special Supplement, 208, no. 1 (July 1961): 105–7. © 1961, Philip Rieff, as originally published.

culture. In both cases, the main therapeutic factor is the transference. Like patients, cultures may purge themselves of an inner conflict, caused by lingering attachments to some old doctrine, by attaching themselves to a doctrine that is new and yet closely related to the old. Thus, the Russians have not ceased to be a religious people; their Marxism makes history redemptive, instead of Christ. But the motif of redemption—for which Americans have never found a place—remains. Quite without intention, Freudianism opened up a dead end in the American inner life, encouraging the replication of an old moral attitude and at the same time supplying an answer of denial. In psychoanalysis, the Puritan temper found a way to disapprove of itself.

Because it is so personal and humane a procedure, Freudian psychiatry has exhibited all the classic stigmas of a movement—splinter groups, rivalries within the leadership, secret councils, front men and Organization Men, passionate friendships turning into equally passionate hatreds. Freudian psychiatrists have had good reason to reject the notion that they are a movement. Any rending of the public veil can lead to a rending of private veils, which might endanger, or at least further complicate, the therapeutic effort. For therapeutic reasons, psychoanalysis is an esoteric discipline. As a movement, psychoanalysis necessarily sought to cover up the intense warfare of personality which, as a therapy, it sought to expose.

Unlike scientists free of the prophetic urge, Freud was not satisfied to work modestly along the lines laid down by scientific discipline: in a small company of researchers, chasing after collections of data with interpretations—and after interpretations with data. Psychoanalysis was valuable in theory, according to Freud, so far as it was successful in practice. It changed men's minds as it cured them. Freud felt compelled by the nature of his discoveries, which men had to resist, to be the leader not merely of a movement but of an embattled one; he planned for the future of that movement in terms that can fairly be called moral—even if not in defense of established moralities. "Some larger group" was needed, he decided, than the local societies of Freudians that had sprung up to spread his theory with its practice; he wanted such a large group "working for a practical ideal."

The size of Freud's pedagogic ambition comes through clearly in his motives for founding the movement as an international body. This was no simple strategy to develop some licensing procedure, in order to screen entrants into the profession. Indeed, the movement was not yet so professional, and when it became so, in the famous controversy about the function of the psychoanalyst without a medical degree, Freud found himself on the losing, less professionally oriented side.

Psychoanalysis is not libertarian. As Freud conceived it, his was a genuinely neutralist movement; more precisely, a movement offering a doctrine of maturity which might free the proper student of it from the compulsion to identify with any and all movements. Despite invitations to declare himself philosophically and otherwise, Freud remained a neutralist all his life. Psychoanalysis perfectly represents the neutralism of his character.

As psychoanalysis became more adaptable, the hidden force of Freud's character operated through the discipline, detached from his person and yet revealed in the neutral appearance that every analyst must present to his patients and, indeed, to the world. Despite periods of weakness, in which he toyed with ideas of linking his movement with others, Freud saw the dangers inherent in any such alliances. "We must in any event keep our independence. . . . In the end we can come together with all the parallel sciences." But that end appeared then, as now, far off; nor is it more clear now than it was at the time he gave this advice to one of his followers just which sciences are parallel to psychoanalysis.

As a movement, psychoanalysis was fortunate enough to achieve a counter-transference to America, that richest and yet, symbolically, most needy of all patients. To this symbolically impoverished culture, psychoanalysis brought not a new or compelling symbolism, but the next best thing: a way of analyzing symbols that is itself of symbolic (and, therefore, therapeutic) value. From being a movement, psychoanalysis became a profession, practical and immensely necessary. In America, the clinician found himself in a culture that considered itself a little crippled and broken. Freud's was the perfect doctrine to help a culture that no longer respected itself and yet had already rejected all the earlier, established alternatives. Moreover, there was something about Protestantism itself that made it ready, upon decline, for psychoanalysis.

For Protestant culture, it was Calvin, with his doctrine of predestination, who first turned all action into symptom. Only the most careful scrutiny of the outer actions could give even a hint of the inner condition, whether that be of grace or damnation. When Freud analyzed all actions symptomatically, he appealed chiefly to persons, trained and yet troubled, in just those cultures that had once been Calvinist, or otherwise rigorously ascetic. The therapeutic of the psychological age is successor to the ascetic of the religious age, with the economic man of the age of enlightenment (and capitalism) as a merely transitional type.

Continuously, in both ascetic and therapeutic cultures, there is an inclination to see symptoms everywhere—except, of course, that the symptoms point to different sources. In the age of psychological man, God's design and the hope of penetrating it may have vanished utterly, as, in fact, the Calvinist also discovered, often to his relief, that it had; nevertheless, there remains the passion, innominate from the decline of Calvinism to the rise of Freudianism, for acquiring some knowledge of one's personal destiny.

To the therapeutic of the mid-twentieth century, as to the ascetic of the

Reformation movements, all destinies had become intensely personal and not at all communal. The way to this self-knowledge, which may be in itself saving, is to trace back a person's conduct from symptom to the inner conditions responsible for that symptom. In the religious period, the symptom was called sin, and the neurotic, a sinner, self-convicted. The task of the clergy was to make the sinner hopefully aware of his sin; the task of the analyst is to make the neurotic therapeutically aware of his neurosis.

Residues of the old attribution of sin cling to the modern and popular usage of the term "neurotic." Like his predecessor, the sinner, the neurotic is most reluctant to admit his weakness. In fact, this failure to admit a fundamental weakness is the most obvious characteristic of the inner wrong which the sinner-neurotic commits against himself. Such failure was once called pride. The thankless task of old ministers and new psychoanalysts consists first in educating for that state of awareness from which a person can cope with his weakness.

A detailed admission of weakness is the beginning of emotional (or spiritual) strength, in both the ascetic and therapeutic traditions. It is not a condition easily admitted, for the weak one may consider himself strong, and only others, near him, may have to bear the burden of his weakness. In this sense, a family may be dominated by its weakest member, who, to the unanalytic eye, may appear strongest merely because he is the most aggressive or has succeeded otherwise in building his neurosis into his character.

In the culture to which psychological man is heir, there has been an acute sense of the weakness of human character but a diminished capacity to feel compassion for it. As the religious mitigations of weakness, built into the ascetic tradition, withered away, all that remained was a test of strength—successful action in the conduct of life. These mitigations, or devices of release from the tension of trying to be good or successful, remained operative in Catholic cultures. In consequence, psychoanalytic therapy never found as ready and receptive a public in those areas of Western culture that remained Catholic, or nonascetic.

Meanwhile, in those parts of the ascetic West that had lost their religious impetus, the contempt for weakness, inherent anyway in Calvinist doctrine, grew steadily more powerful. The individual, caught in this hard, dying culture, tried to hide his sense of weakness, for he no longer felt a compelling explanation for it; nor could he use something in his system of worship to escape this now intensely personal fault (no longer attributable to divine decision). The culture, always guilt-ridden, was no longer guilt-releasing. Without the remedy of grace or good works, conscience became the seat of emotional weakness rather than the sign of moral strength.

For Freud, strength was the rare bonus, weakness the common return on experience. By indicating again the universality of weakness—and, moreover, by suggesting new remedies for it—Freud challenged the tough indifference of the old ascetic attitude, while, at the same time, strengthening individuals to continue living in what remains a culture dominated by goals set in the ascetic period. In his determination to help an individual function more adequately in a situation essentially competitive from the cradle to the grave, Freud tempered the rivalrous mood of contemporary social life without challenging its validity. He thought thus to teach man how to snatch some personal success in living out of the general failure.

As a way of transforming the ascetic temper, now crabbed and mainly negative, psychoanalysis is no empty cipher, no shadow of religious doctrine. On the contrary, it is a doctrine suitable to this postreligious age. Even the goals of ascetic effort are disappearing in an economy based on leisure. If the former ascetic is to continue to work hard and live well, he must do so without any aim in mind other than the therapy of action which is living itself. The work of the ascetic must become the play of the therapeutic; that is the moral economy about which spokesmen of the new type, such as David Riesman, are theorizing.

As Freud saw him, psychological man had to learn how to accept life as if it were a game, earnestly played, with each player aware that in the beginning he is so unpracticed that the game must remain a series of errors and penalties. Yet, learning finally to be a strategist on his own behalf, psychological man could meet demands upon his energy and character quite as rigorous as those made during a time when he had a God on his side and the comfort of natural law instead of mere laws of nature.

There is something old-fashioned about the psychoanalytic movement; it is, in fact, although more subtly than ever before, a movement of self-help. For all the analyst can do is teach another how to become his own therapist, strong in the knowledge of his particular weakness. Freud insisted on this modesty of purpose, which many critics have viewed as an unwarranted pessimism. But the alternative to Freud's modesty is the optimism of a fresh religious sense of personal service to some object other than the self. Such therapies seemed to Freud to exploit the very weaknesses from which men suffered and for which they sought therapy in the first place. Doctrines of salvation are always therapeutic. In a culture no longer capable of inventing such doctrines, Freud proposed a therapy that did not try to charm the suffering out of humanity but only restored the capacity to endure living. For those no longer childlike enough to be charmed, a restoration of capacity is the one gift necessary and prior to any small giving of themselves.

I must emphasize that Freud condemned the religious repressions for instrumental reasons, because they were failing. Because religion could no longer compel character but only distract it, Freud dared suggest, in the name of science, a new ethical straightforwardness. Faith had become another form of anxiety. Despite his occasional protests about its neutrality and limited purposes, Freud hoped his own science would contribute in a major way to the working out of a more controllable and rational alternative to those imaginative systems of increasing anxiety that we call "religion." (61:2)

3
Ernest Jones's Biography of Freud

Great masters need great disciples; it is a prerequisite of greatness among those who found movements. Calvin had his Beza, Luther his Melancthon, Marx his Engels. Each disciple himself was great, not in his own right, but in relation to his master whom he interpreted to the world. Paul is the greatest example of discipleship in the history of our culture, for it is his Jesus that lives, not the historical one.

That master is fortunate who does not see, among his disciples, the closest fall away, jealous at being so near to greatness and yet not the greatest. Inevitably, Luther had his Carlstadt. Freud had not merely his Jung but also his Rank and Ferenczi. Fortunately for him, Freud retained his Jones. Of the original "Committee"—founded by Jones in 1912 to create a "bodyguard around Freud" and at the same time to carry his message out into the world—some died and others departed; Ernest Jones remained. Now at last, with this third and final volume of the memorial *Life and Work* of the master, Jones has taken his rightful place, as the greatest of Freud's disciples.[1] For with this work he has fulfilled, better than in any of his scientific writing and practical therapy, the historic function of great disciples: he has dispelled the loneliness and isolation of the master and has compelled the reader to venerate the man as well as to respect the idea. At the very end of his life, Freud saw that the world was coming to him. Jones has completed the task of reconciliation; he has brought Freud to the world.

Because this is a massive biography of a hero in our culture, we are likely to forget how much it has added to the stature of the biographer, Jones himself. A great part of the life of Ernest Jones is in this *Life* of Freud. Clearly, these two characters resemble each other more than any two others in the story. Perhaps a certain common temper allowed this calm and shrewd Englishman to accomplish what Freud never thought possible, a biography that is at once admiring and yet honest. Personal loyalty—of disciple for master—appears frequently in this volume, as in the previous two. But this is not the personal loyalty of a mere follower but of a true disciple. In the

Reprinted from *American Sociological Review* 23, no. 2 (April 1958): 211–12.
1. Ernest Jones, *The Life and Work of Sigmund Freud, vol. III: The Last Phase, 1919–1939.*

process of writing, the portrait of the master may be transformed into an uncanny likeness of the disciple; but we shall never know that. For who now can possibly know Freud better than Jones? No greater compend of information about the master will ever be published. More important, perhaps, no finer example of the free allegiance of one man to another can possibly be offered. Authentically pious works, calm and certain of the greatness of their subject, are rare in our literary culture. Jones's *Life* of Freud is such a work. It lends greatness as well to the biographer. Not that this is a Boswell, who will threaten one day to overshadow his Johnson. Nothing is less likely. Biographies of Jones—and Ph.D. theses—must already be underway. But he will always remain at Freud's side where he has quietly demonstrated that he belongs.

Being honest and pious at the same time, Jones has not merely imposed his own interpretation upon the reader but upon all future honest biographers of Freud. There is enough raw material in these parent volumes for a dozen healthy offspring. Any man with talent and daring enough can now begin to write about the life of Freud with nothing more at his elbow than Jones. But he cannot be so daring as to contradict the *Life* Jones has created. Anything written hereafter can only tip the interpretation slightly, one way or the other. For Jones has created the *Life* of a man in perfect balance. To destroy the balance would be to destroy the entire interpretation, and this would be a task more difficult than is at first apparent. Add something to Freud's pessimism and an equivalent optimism can be cited. Subtract something from Freud's kindliness, and utter kindness can be cited. No doubt Jones's interpretation is the true one. Freud must have been a giant of common sense and a character in perfect equilibrium to have led amicably and for so long such erratic and scheming followers in a highly moral intellectual movement to scrape clean the encrusted moral intelligence of western culture.

On the other hand, it cannot be pure accident that this model *Life* is written by the most sensible and well-balanced of the disciples, the steadiest and longest lived, the one who has outlasted all the others and brings the master to the attention of a posterity that is moved as much by great lives as by great ideas. There is something very English about the Freud that lives and dies so equably, under the most distressing circumstances, in these volumes. All that antinomian imagination is hedged off neatly by an unimpeachable private life; all that passion countered by stoic calm; all that friendship muted by reserve; all that desire to lead tempered by encouragements to epigones striking out on their own. The Freud that emerges from this volume, as from the two that have gone before, is a man of balance. He is in fact the ideal product of psychoanalytic therapy, the long-sought physician who has cured himself, to whom his own privately won self-knowledge has brought "harmony, peace of mind, full efficiency." Freud is a new kind of genius, a healthy one. Psychoanalysis cannot be expected to produce such geniuses. It can be expected to produce healthier men. Yet a significant number among Freud's closest disciples did not become healthier, but ill in a new self-conscious way. Despite their constant life as analyst and analysand, major disciples did not escape being the "unhappy, neurotic" wretches, "torn by conflict and inhibited in [their] social life" that Freud set out to cure.

In Freud himself, Jones portrays for us a harmonious and efficient genius, living until almost his last hour to the maximum of his emotional and intellectual capacity, tolerant and yet capable of judging even the meanly immoral men in the hypocritically moral little society that was his own "Committee" of disciples. It is the portrait of a modern man achieving peace with himself. Such a condition is so rare in modern culture that the Jones image of Freud is bound to achieve a kind of secular sainthood. His condition is desired by every thoughtful person nowadays, not as an end in itself but to assure each modern at least that he is himself and not merely acting out various roles in the unending large farce of the world. Other Freuds may emerge, now that the model one is fixed in our biographical literature. Jones has left shadows and depths around the edges of his clear portrait, and more may be added, by less English and less loyal interpreters. But the dark-souled one, the sinister Freud, is buried forever by the effort of his main disciple. The light-souled one will remain for posterity to admire, however they may color him in where Jones permits. Later shading will never again imply the exotic Viennese Jew of legend, plotting the overthrow of the moral order. The energetic, superabundantly intelligent and utterly fair human being that Jones remembers will, on the strength of his conviction, pass beyond refutation and influence into the collective memory of heroes of our culture, from which the educated classes now draw their pieties. It is a good omen that Freud is being thus incorporated into the culture. The days of a culture are numbered, its true life over, when it can incorporate no new and hostile insight. The celebration of Freud, in these popular volumes of biography, indicates further that our culture has some capacity still to absorb its critics. And Freud is a very ambiguous critic, at that. The monsters and grotesques that he slew, in the deepest and darkest interior of our culture, have many lives, as he knew. Some of these lives he himself declared to be immortal. This critic of the very foundations of culture has done as much as any apologist to generate new respect for it. He may be remembered by posterity as a saving critic rather than a damning one. The issue is far from settled.

That Freud did not care for posterity means only that posterity will care the more for him. Smashing up the past, denying any meaningful future, Freud concentrated entirely on the present. Posterity will revere him as the first prophet of no other time except each man's own, the first visionary to look neither forward nor backward except to stare down projections and penetrate fixations.

If Jones's biography guides it, posterity will revere Freud for his dying, as for his living. Jones is wise to give his readers the details of Freud's terrible illness. For here, against the longest odds, Freud's lifelong achievement of self-mastery paid off. Without complaint or moment of weakness, Freud met the demands of the day until almost the final hour, at which time he requested the drug that brought to him the release of death.

The word "fate" occurs in Freud's talk, as Jones records it, perhaps as significantly as the word "sexuality." Because he considered that fate had done so much to shape his life, there is something of the tragic hero about Freud's own self-image. He is neither guilty nor innocent; upon him the terms can no longer enforce their old meanings. Fate has shaped his life and he has placed himself at the service of fate. The most he could do, in order to raise himself a little above fate to choice, is to become a student of both guilt and innocence. (58:2)

4

Dora: An Analysis of a Case of Hysteria

On 14, October 1900, Freud announced to his epistolary confessor, the Berlin physician and biologist Wilhelm Fliess, that he was onto a case worth recording as history. "It has been a lively time, and I have a new patient, a girl of eighteen; the case has opened smoothly to my collection of pick-locks." On 25, January 1901, another letter went off to Fliess, reporting that the case was closed, the history written; "the consequence is that today I feel short of a drug." The intoxicating effort was his history of the case of an hysterical girl, called here "Dora."

The day after he had finished the writing, Freud felt certain that this case history was "the subtlest thing I have written so far." The subtlety of it would be enough to put people off, "even more than usual," he concluded, thus showing even more than his normal suspicion of the reading public. His ambivalence toward that public rarely subsided. In this case, he had composed a specially valuable hostage to posterity, and yet, bound by ties of ego to the present, Freud worried about the way in which this case history would be received. He therefore postponed publication for years. The young lady had broken off treatment on the last day of the year 1900 (Freud sometimes had a

Reprinted from *Dora: An Analysis of a Case of Hysteria, Collected Papers of Sigmund Freud*, edited and introduced by Philip Rieff (New York: Collier Books, 1963), 7–20. Introduction copyright © by Macmillan Publishing Company, a division of Macmillan, Inc. Reprinted with permission of Collier Books, an imprint of Macmillan Publishing Company.

poor memory for dates, and as late as 1933, in a footnote added to the main essay of this volume, insisted that the case had ended exactly a year earlier than in fact it did). Freud wrote the case in the month immediately following. He sent the manuscript in for publication and then quickly retrieved it, holding back until 1905. Such reluctance on the part of an ambitious author may reflect uncertainty about the quality of the work or about the adequacy of its potential audience—or both. Patently, Freud was confident about the work; it was the audience that he suspected.

If it is admitted that art and science have the power to do good, then it must also be admitted that they have the power to do harm. Moreover, the audience for a given work of art or science may receive it in a corrupt way, thus corrupting it. As there are corrupt works of art, so are there also corrupt audiences. Freud was aware of the dangers to which his work was specially vulnerable, once he let go. A case history, for example, has a cast of real characters. To reveal the ambiguous inner dynamics of outwardly blameless or pathetic lives was to risk cruel misunderstanding. Freud spends much of his preface arguing, not the merits of the case, but the merits of publishing the case. Much of the prefatory matter is thus now obsolete. In the name of truth and art, we publish everything nowadays, no matter how prurient the reader's interest or how unprepared his taste. Think how few readers there would be for, say, the most famous publications of Henry Miller if only those with serious literary interest and training constituted their readership. Nowadays, authors have markets rather than readers. In a preface to paperback editions of any of Freud's writings, it may be worth saying that there is nothing in any of them for the market, but only for readers.

Dora suffered from a confusion of inclination toward men and women. Her unconscious lesbian tendencies were allied to a painful tangle of motives that only a master of detection like Freud could have picked apart—and yet held together in their true pattern, so that the reader can see the whole of Dora's predicament in all its irremediable complexity. The complexity is there in the subject, the life history of a human being. It was Freud's genius not to simplify and yet make clear. On the surface, the organization of this essay can be easily followed: there is an introductory résumé of the girl's life and of her symptoms—nervous coughing, chronic fatigue and other more painful, if not uncommon, miseries. Then follow two chapters concentrating on two of her dreams; and then a concluding section. Yet, just beneath this apparently simple scheme there is a labyrinth into which the narrative thread soon disappears, replaced by a mode of presentation calculated to help us see events, remote and near, simultaneously—all having their effect upon Dora. This is literary as well as analytic talent of a high order; indeed, the fusing of these two talents was necessary to the case history as Freud developed that genre. A narrative account would have distorted the psychological reality that Freud wanted to portray; no linear style, however precise, could catch the eerie convergences of cause and effect sought by Freud. The general point was made by Freud in the course of his next major case history of a woman,[1] written nearly twenty years after that of Dora: "Consecutive presentation," he writes, "is not a very adequate means of describing complicated mental processes going on in different layers of the mind." Thus the case history is, indeed, a history—but not historical in the sense familiar to readers of either the novel or any of the classic forms of written history. Precisely at this point Freud may yet alter the way in which both the novel and history will be written. We see in the "anti-*roman*," as well as in older experiments with the expression of interior consciousness (e.g., Joyce, Woolf), efforts to break beyond the narrative art form. The historians have been slower to learn from Freud; more precisely, they have learned the wrong lessons. So far as it has been influenced by Freud, the writing of history has merely added a checklist of symptoms and their social expressions to the personal factor, as a category of historical causation, instead of using Freud to open up the possibility of reorganizing the structure of historical writing on other than a linear basis.

Organized as it is, along multiple analytic perspectives, all converging upon Dora's repressed desires, the case, read as preparatory exercise in a new mode of historical writing, has a sheer brilliance which is still breathtaking. Freud pushes the protesting girl back through her inner history—of which she is largely unaware—descending ever deeper, cutting across levels of the same event, beyond the outer shell of her protective self-interpretations, to her relations with her mother, father, brother, governess, other girls, and that famous couple: Herr K. and his wife. When the dazzled reader finally arrives at Frau K., he will be ready to admit, I think, that few greater pieces of detection have been written.

And yet there is no leading to a single culprit as the cause of Dora's misery: not Dora herself, nor her father, nor the man she loved, Herr K., nor the woman she loved, Frau K. Characteristically, Freud's case histories have no villains, only victims; Freud's world is populated by equally culpable innocents and sophisticates. It is the complicity of the innocents in their own unhappiness that Freud seeks to eliminate—at worst, by making that complicity sophisticated, and at best, by eliminating the complicity altogether.

What follows is the story of how Freud, the spiritual detective hired by Dora's worried father, catches up with her fugitive inner life—and, moreover, with that of her father and the others mainly involved in this group illness. The sick daughter has a sick father, who has a sick mistress, who has a sick husband, who proposes himself to the sick daughter as her lover.

1. Cf. "The Psychogenesis of a Case of Homosexuality in a Woman," *Sexuality and the Psychology of Love*, Collier Books edition BS 192V.

Dora does not want to hold hands in this charmless circle—although Freud does, at one point, indicate that she should. Her reluctance is a problem to which I shall have to return later in this essay. My point here is that all the others are also cases, so to speak, the very predicates of Dora's; and yet they are, except in minor ways, inaccessible to Freud. Moreover, Freud accepts this inaccessibility without serious theoretical question. His entire interpretation of the case—and also his efforts to reindoctrinate Dora in more tolerable attitudes toward her own sex life—depends upon his limiting the case to Dora when, in fact, from the evidence he himself presents, it is the milieu in which she is constrained to live that is ill. Here is a limit on the psychoanalytic therapy that neither Freud nor his orthodox followers have examined with the ruthless honesty appropriate to their ethic. "Milieu" therapy would involve a revolution in our culture.

Freud's own unexamined acceptance of the limits of his therapeutic effort to that of the doctor-patient relationship affected the way in which he indoctrinated his patients. That he was engaged in a work of indoctrination, which is the equivalent of interpretation, there can be no doubt. Elsewhere he speaks of having "expounded . . . a specially important part of the theory," a part touching very near the patient's own problems.[2] Interpretation involves indoctrination; the two cannot be separated in the psychoanalytic combat between therapist and patient. For the therapist is engaged in the effort to change his patient's mind by an exemplary deepening of it. In this case, Dora refused to change her mind and suddenly quit as a final act of denial against the truth of Freud's insights.[3] This is not to say that Dora's own insights were incorrect; they were at once correct and yet untherapeutic. Freud is not interested in all truths, and certainly not in Dora's, except insofar as they block the operation of his own. Because Dora's insights are part of her illness, Freud had to hammer away at them as functions of her resistance to his insight. Her truths were not therapeutically useful ones, even in the limited sense proposed by William James, when James understands the "higher happiness" of religious believers as a check and mitigation on their "lower unhappiness."[4] Even in Jamesian terms, Dora's habits of thought had brought her no "higher happiness." Indeed, she suffered from both higher and lower unhappiness. Her intelligence and imagination had rendered her the chief victim in a cast of characters made up exclusively of victims, in one degree or another. Finally, for so destroying the moral truths with which she protected her illness, and which were components of that

2. Cf. ibid.

3. Dora did return once more for treatment, and again, years later, sought help from a psychoanalyst. In each situation, her symptoms abated during treatment, but she remained, to the sad end of her days, a severely handicapped woman.

4. William James's *The Varieties of Religious Experience*, chapter 2 (published in Collier Books edition AS 39).

illness, Dora took her revenge on Freud: by ending the treatment before Freud had completed the expounding of his general theory into her particular case.

By any practical test, Freud's insight was superior to Dora's. Hers had not helped her win more than pyrrhic victories over life, while Freud's, engaged as he was in the therapeutic re-creation of her life, demonstrated its capacity to make Dora superior to some of the symptomatic expressions of her rejection of life. Her own understanding of life had in no way given her any power to change it; precisely that power to change life was Freud's test of truth. His truth was, therefore, superior to Dora's.

But the mystery of character never submits entirely, even to the greatest masters. There are fresh reserves of motive which, unexamined, will not yield to reason, however therapeutic might be the experience of yielding. Moreover, reason itself depends upon motives that are not themselves rational, thus limiting its strength severely at the very point of origin. Freud counted on something more than reason to achieve something more than a remission of symptoms. The *experience* of psychoanalysis was not a merely rational exercise upon fact but also a transformation of attitude. At this second level, the psychoanalytic case history crosses the barrier artificially erected between a literature of description and a literature of imagination. It matters little whether Freud's case histories are called science or art. Freud's interpretative science was itself, in practice, an art, aiming at a transformation of the life thus interpreted. All such strategies of moral interpretation—whether called art or science or religion—are characterized by their transformative function. Moreover, the decline of any science, or art, can be measured by a weakening of transformative effect. Thus do religions become neuroses; and thus, too, do psychotherapies become religions characterized by a desperate faith in themselves. We have yet to write the history of modern psychotherapy in a way that approximates the complication of motives from which it suffers.

The case history, in Freud's usage, records precisely such a complication of motive, beyond the emotional or intellectual capacity of a patient. Indeed, what distinguishes the patient from the therapist is just that capacity to handle the complexity of motive. There is, therefore, a hint of intellectual combat in this case history. When the modern detective of the soul meets his client, he must, like Sherlock Holmes, immediately exercise his mind. "Now," says Freud to the girl, almost in the words Holmes often used in first reconnoitering a case, "I should like you to pay close attention to the exact words you used." The battle of wits then begins: Freud matched against every unconscious device that this intelligent young girl can muster to protect her hard-won present level of misery from the danger of disturbance—for, under prodding, misery can grow more acute.

The tessellated quality of Freud's mind cannot be better viewed than from the vantage point of this case history. That tessellation is inseparable, of course, from the fusion of his own mind, as it confronts the experience of Dora, with his own inner experience. Freud's scientific knowledge is highly personal, an achievement first won with himself as patient. Dora ached with anger at everyone near her—including herself. Freud's task was to dismantle Dora's anger and to substitute for it that informed instinct for life to which he had himself, in his own self-analysis, won through.

The emotional combat between the therapist, experienced in the control of his suffering, and the patient, inexperienced and without the means of control, had to take an intellectual form, for Dora's was a failure to understand her true emotions. Her failure was a *willful* failure, as in all neurotic cases. But it was also a failure of intelligence, and in this "intelligent and engaging" eighteen-year-old girl both failures had to be corrected at the same time, at first by the agency of the transference, in which the girl would alter the current of her affection in such a way that Freud could gain the needed therapeutic authority; secondly, by the agency of the interpretation, in which the girl would see, in the locking of her mind with Freud's, how cruelly her own understanding had deceived her. In order to wage this private war, Freud's own intelligence had to become rather cruel at times. Dora would propose explanations of her wretchedness which Freud criticized, countering with his own; or Freud would spin out his arguments, ending with a fair challenge to his patient—"And now, what have your recollections to say to this?"

Everybody becomes indurate in the requirements of his own life. The neurotic girl hardened in her stand against Freud's interpretations; the intellectual therapist probed all the more deeply, in this case and in others where the quality of the patient was not quite so admirably suited to intellectual sparring. It was not just Dora's fine intelligence, remarked by Freud, that made disputation possible. The discursive web of treatment was spun to suit not merely this precocious girl. It characterized the method long after Freud's own stated preference for bright patients dropped out of the canon. The psychoanalyst must have something of Freud's intellectual virtuosity or he is not truly an analyst.

Virtuosity of intelligence, however, can lead to crude errors as well as refined truths. In the case of Dora, various clues indicating the nature of her neurosis implicated a certain event recorded in this case history: the girl's unresponsiveness to the sexual advances of Herr K. With irresistible brilliance, Freud followed the strings of complex motivation back to one of the painful knots in Dora's psyche, finding that, despite her refusal, Dora *wanted* to accept Herr K.'s proposition, which she understood and rejected, violently, even before he had finished making it. Dora was in love with the

man she thought she detested. "We never discover a 'No' in the unconscious." Sexual distaste, like other forms of rejection, may be dishonest
emotion, a defensive tactic of conscience against desire. Negation is for
Freud (Bergson held a similar view) a purely "psychological" fact. A denial
expresses that revision which follows the disappointment of some expectation. Dora had been disappointed by Herr K. The very words with which he
began his erotic proposition had been, she knew, used before—and recently; she was not his only love. Nevertheless, because a "negative judgment" is simply the "intellectual substitute for repression," each denial
makes an affirmation. A "No" from the patient confirms what the analyst has
proposed. Thus, when an explanation of his "was met by Dora with a most
emphatic negative," Freud could consider, rightly, that this "No"

> does no more than register the existence of a repression and [also] its sever-
> ity. . . . If this "No," instead of being regarded as the expression of an impar-
> tial judgment (of which, indeed, the patient is incapable), is ignored, and if
> [the analytic] work is continued, the first evidence soon begins to appear that
> in such a case "No" signifies the desired "Yes."

By presuming the patient incapable of an impartial judgment, the therapist
is empowered to disregard the patient's denials, substituting a positive feeling for the subject matter of the association. A patient says: "You may think
I meant to say something insulting but I've no such intention"; or, "The
woman in my dream was not my mother." From this the analyst may conclude, "So, she does mean to say something insulting; so it was his mother."
    This suspicion of dislikes can sweep dislike away. We are urged to attend
to all cases of vehement reproof, what people despise and what they loathe.
As Georg Groddeck writes: "You will never go wrong in concluding that a
man has once loved deeply whatever he hates, and loves it yet; that he once
admired and still admires what he scorns, that he once greedily desired
what now disgusts him." But to charge that all aversions breed from their
opposites is as misleading, put thus in unexpected principle, as to accept all
aversions without questioning their ancestry. Rejection is a proper activity
of the superego. And the superego is not a superficial, weak thing, without
its own instinctual ancestry. To uncover an acceptance beneath every rejection is to be incredulous of human goodness.
    It encourages too easy a wisdom, this principled suspicion of our dislike.
The ancient "Yes" to everything reigns, in the unconscious, near the sovereignty of an almost equally ancient "No," installed there by the social experience of the species. And that "No" keeps expanding its territory, at the
expense of the primitive "Yes." Moral reasons may themselves have an
erotic color. Dora could have turned down Herr K. for several good reasons.
Perhaps, at fourteen, and with a beau nearer her own age standing in the

wings, so to speak, she had not yet either the aplomb or the coarseness to relish an affair with the man who was, after all, the husband of her father's mistress. Moreover, this would have been to identify with the object of her profoundest affections, Frau K., and thus, understood even on Freud's own terms, surely an act more pathological than her refusal. Possibly, too, she did not find him quite as attractive as Freud believed. Herr K. was another counter in a most complicated quarrel between Dora and her parental generation. Freud takes Herr K. too much at face value. All he saw, conveniently, as his own interpretative powers flagged in this labyrinth of connections, was that this young female did not respond to the sexual advances of an attractive male: he had seen Herr K. and noted that he was still "prepossessing." Even supposing Herr K. quite as attractive as Freud thought, nevertheless he belonged to the older generation with which Dora was (with good reason) at war. She had become a pawn in her elders' pathetic little end-games, her cooperation necessary in order for them to salvage something erotic for themselves in a loveless world. The game had gone too far; Dora refused to play. Nor, had she played, would she have been spared her difficulties, for eroticism too is a form of neuroticism. There was no love in Dora's parental circle; her rejection of Herr K. was an effort, however confused and ambivalent, to break out of the circle. Yet Freud's interpretation makes of her neurosis a sort of *hubris* of distaste; the neurotic makes too many rejections. In rare moments of libertarian sentiment Freud arrives at such conclusions; mainly, however, he never confuses the sovereignty of personal taste, in love or work, with the slavery of neurotic rejection. There are no psychoanalytic formulae to discriminate this difference. Every analyst must find the line where it is drawn, finely or heavily, in the complex patterns of acceptance and rejection which define each individual case.

As a therapist, Freud had to suspect Dora's resentful objections to erotic games; they had offended her too deeply. She was not yet old enough, or defeated enough, to take what she could get, just because it was offered. Freud ignores her youth, and the fire of youth, however painfully it may burn inside. Dora was caught in a charade of half-lives and half-loves: those of her father and Frau K. She objected to being pulled into the game entirely, at the same time that she was fascinated by it and wanted to play. Thus, at one time, "the sharp-sighted Dora" was overcome by the idea that she had been virtually handed over to Herr K., her middle-aged admirer, as the price of tolerating the relations between her father and Frau K.

Of course, Freud knew that the girl was right. He had to admire Dora's insight into this intricate and sad affair-within-an-affair. Yet he fought back with his own intricate insights into the tangle of her own motives; that was his error; there is the point at which the complexity of Freudian analysis must reach out, beyond the individual patient, to the entire tangle of motives of all the bad actors involved in this affair—father, mistress, would-be lover, stupid mother. Only then would the analysis have been complete, and true, and adequately pedagogic.

Freud went far—far as time and the fatal limit of the doctor to his one patient, instead of to the complex of patients, permitted. His mind moved with breathtaking speed and accuracy. The evidence led him to know swiftly that, unknown to herself, Dora had got her libido engaged on all the possible levels: that she was at once in love with (of course) her father, the would-be seducer Herr K., and, at the deepest level, with Frau K., her father's mistress; this last Freud called "the strongest unconscious current in her mental life" because it was not in any way overt, and yet dominant. Dora expressed disbelief; she detested Frau K. Freud persists. He speaks of using facts against the patient and reports, with some show of triumph (this is no mean adversary), how he overwhelmed Dora with interpretations, pounding away at her argument, until Dora (who had already secretly made up her mind to quit) "disputed the facts no longer." Yet these facts were none of them visible; they were all of them of the highest order, taking their life from the precise truth of Freud's multiple analytic thrusts into her unconscious.

But, despite this victory, Freud still had to face the difficulty that if the patient has spun her own "sound and incontestable train of argument . . . the physician is liable to feel a moment's embarrassment." Dora was a brilliant detective, too, parrying Freud's practiced brilliance with a strength of mind that at once delighted and dismayed him. Her own interpretation of her situation was sometimes so acute that Freud could not help asking himself why his was superior.

In this earnest debate, Freud's tactic was not to dispute Dora's logic but to suspect her motives. "The patient is using thoughts of this kind, which the analysis cannot attack, for the purposes of cloaking others which are anxious to escape from criticism and from consciousness." Dora reproaches her father and Herr K. because she wishes to conceal self-reproaches. Her logic covers a deeper passion. Thus Freud bypassed the patient's insight into the rot of her human environment as part of the misleading obvious, when it was, I think, the most important single fact of the matter; he suspected her insight as an instrument of her neurosis instead of as the promise of her cure. Years later, still unable to brook disagreement, Freud was to call this tenacious and most promising of all forms of resistance—"intellectual opposition."

To relax Dora's intellectual tenacity, Freud's tactic was to insinuate a set of self-suspicions until he managed to convince her that she was too logical and reasoned too closely for her own good. Here his skepticism toward intellectual self-understanding is most apparent: let there be insight, yes; but too much too soon inhibits the creation of that therapeutic replica of the troubling situation for which the analysis strives. Prematurity of insight endangers the credulity basic to a successful resolution of the case; it is the most intractable form of resistance, because the patient cannot use such insight to relieve or control his anxieties or other symptoms as they arise. Freud made allowances for Dora's protective insights, for, as it turned out, her intellectual verve was just a mode of defense. Dora's acumen was obsessive. She could not let go of her painful interpretation of others in the net and look at herself; she persisted in her thoughts as a mode of revenge, while "a normal train of thought, however intense it may be, can be disposed of." Her exaggeration of rationality was no longer rational. This lively minded person was using her thoughts like symptoms, as articles of accusation against those she loved and hated.

For the patient, Freud advocated a balanced, flexible standard of reason; persisting too long in any train of thought resigns "omnipotence" to it. In a curiously exact way, Freud's own therapeutic habits—spinning out beautiful and complicated lines of argument—meet all the requirements of neurotic brilliance; he had, therefore, to exempt himself at least, as an analyst, from the critique of excessive ratiocination.[5] Freud saw little contradiction in his double standard of reason. He derogated conventional insight for tending to suppress unauthorized trains of thought—in sum, for harboring all sorts of discriminatory refinements that increased the burdens of conscience beyond the limits of consciousness. Reason aspired to no final solutions, and Freud is far from recommending insight in every case. Indeed, sometimes the psychotherapeutic effort is downright inadvisable. Freud made no brief for universal psychoanalysis and certainly not for any doctrine of rationalism. He was too much aware of the profound and irremediable irrationality of life to become a fanatic of reason. To expand the jurisdiction of consciousness did not mean that the unconscious could be conquered, or that fate and luck would abdicate their powers over our lives. No more moderate rationalist has ever challenged unreason to permanent warfare. (63:4)

5. The relentless beat of their "Freudian labors" upon themselves is often reported by Freud's early disciples. See, for example, A. A. Brill, *Basic Principles of Psychoanalysis* (New York, Doubleday and Co., 1949, p. 48). In one of his interpolations in his English translation of *The Psychopathology of Everyday Life*, Brill gives us some of the flavor of "the pioneer days of Freud among psychiatrists. . . . We made no scruples, for instance, of asking a man at the table why he did not use his spoon in the proper way, or why he did such and such a thing in such and such a manner. It was impossible for one to show any degree of hesitation or make some abrupt pause in speaking without being at once called to account. We had to keep ourselves well in hand, ever ready and alert, for there was no telling when and where there would be an attack." Brill does not comment on the military simile. The warfare of the Freudians among themselves was not entirely for the sake of truth, I suspect. Aggression appears even among professional students of aggression.

5

On the Sexual Enlightenment of Children

A happy childhood? The idealization of childhood originated in the old literature of the privileged and in the universal wish of all men, facing the inevitable disappointments of adulthood, to find something in their past that was supremely satisfactory. I remember the time when I happily spun out, for myself, family romances quite like those Freud discusses in the essay just preceding the case of "Little Hans" in this volume. Freud has had the major share in smashing the sentimental cult of the child—sentimental because it is insincere, refusing to take in the depth of suffering and complexity of thought of which children are capable. This breaking of the cult of the child has been to the benefit of children. Sentimentality went with brutality. For the new sentimentality, in which the child is given too little sense of the authority of his elders, Freud is not responsible. On the contrary, the very nucleus of child training, according to Freud, is the proper accommodation of the child to authority figures. Having made this accommodation, with Freud's help, "Little Hans" may be said to have had a reasonably happy childhood.

Hans was a perfectly ordinary little boy; he loved his mother and had rather more mixed feelings toward his father. Brighter than most, but otherwise, in Freud's own term, "normal," Hans exhibited, in his own small and attractive person, the contradiction that complicates all human character and renders suspect even our most moral anxieties. For, according to Freud, the moral sense grows out of a painful effort to divert our aggressive impulses from their original objects, by substituting an object that we imagine is hostile to us. In Hans, this effort at diversion took the form of a phobia. He feared that horses—any horse—would bite him; more precisely, that a horse would bite off his genitals. If that happened, he could no longer compete with his father for his mother; nor could he be like his father, who was the chief authority of his inner world. Hans's phobia thus had a positive function: it helped him shift his animus from his father to a father-substitute—horses; permitting him to hide his anger and express it, at the same time, and with equally sinister innocence.

Freud did not personally conduct the analysis of this five-year-old boy. Rather, this was, in one sense, the rarest case Freud ever had, one in which the fusion of father and physician became literally true. The analysis was

Reprinted from *The Sexual Enlightenment of Children, Collected Papers of Sigmund Freud,* edited and introduced by Philip Rieff (New York: Collier Books, 1963), 7–13. Introduction copyright © by Macmillan Publishing Company, a division of Macmillan, Inc. Reprinted with permission of Collier Books, an imprint of Macmillan Publishing Company.

conducted by Hans's father. Thus, in 1909, Freud wrote up a case in which the ideal elements were combined: on the one hand, a pliable, intelligent and dependent patient, on the other, a therapist who showed both the "affectionate care" of a father and the "scientific interest" of an analyst. The case was a complete success.

It was a case that interested Freud specially, not only for its inherent complexity but also because it provided him with his first chance to test inferences about childhood sexuality that were derived, until Hans came along, from the analysis of adults. Since the motives of later neurotic disturbances were rooted in childhood, the case took on a formal importance beyond the immediate exigencies of Hans's personal problems. In fact, the analysis had the effect, according to Freud, of a prophylactic. When Hans came to see him, years later, he was a strapping lad, "normal" in a second and more important sense: he had, with the help of his analyst-father, so outgrown the Oedipal situation that not even the memory of it remained. As the first analysis of a child, the case history of little Hans is precursive of what is now a vast and popular literature. Child analysis carries with it the implicit promise of remission from later miseries that would not otherwise be avoided; it does not carry the promise of remission from those disorders of character which do not appear specifically as symptoms, but rather as an impoverished quality of life. And yet, the case of Hans remains important, for although the way in which Hans exhibited the contradiction in his nature was his own, the contradiction itself is "the common property of all men, a part of the human constitution." To see the contradictions operate so transparently in Hans reveals, in a memorable way, that point of confluence between the particular and the general at which Freud penetrated, more deeply than ever before in our intellectual history, the mystery of the human character.

The ambivalent structure of human nature cannot be altered; but it can be better managed, and the harm we do ourselves can be diminished. Hans learned, during the course of the analysis, really to trust his father, who was the object of his distrust, by the therapeutic process of learning to trust himself, to the point where he no longer feared his own destructive impulses. At that point, his phobia disappeared, for it no longer was needed to protect him from knowing something of the dark side of his own nature.

However, before this success was achieved there was a long game of hide-and-seek, the father seeking the real Hans and Hans avoiding the confrontation with his own instinctual conflict. The game was involved and highly intellectual. Success was assured when it finally engrossed Hans's attention and his enthusiasm. Thus, this first case study of infantile sexuality was as much a study in infantile intellectuality. Hans's total person had to be engrossed in the effort. The contract in exemplary trust by which the psychoanalytic exploration proceeds needed to be complemented by a contract in exemplary distrust, with the patient trying to take over, for his own defensive purposes, the conduct of the analysis. Hans was a clever little boy, and he fell into the pattern of the game quite willingly. The game consisted in asking all sorts of questions of his parents and other adult authorities, thus opening himself up to counter-questioning. Hans's father and mother, determined disciples of Freud, had a solid respect for the traumatic sequence. They did not discourage him from first believing and then doubting the usual lies: about stork, God and all. Apparently the parents (whom Freud reports as among his "closest adherents") felt duty bound to give Hans the benefit of normal traumas, lest their special know-how untie too quickly the standard knots in the line of libidinal development. This pedant's respect for the inevitability of the traumatic sequence Freud himself shared—if one may surmise from a comment which he made on an incident reported by Hans's father. (Note that the analysis was conducted, with one exception, by correspondence, Freud meeting this youngest among all his patients only once.) When Hans's mother found the child fondling his penis she dutifully threatened: "If you do that, I shall send for Dr. A. to cut off your widdler. And then what'll you widdle with?" Hans's unregenerate reply, so psychoanalytically revealing was, "With my bottom." Upon this Freud comments heavily: "He made this reply without having any sense of guilt as yet. But this was the occasion of his acquiring the 'castration complex,' the presence of which we are so often obliged to infer in analyzing neurotics, though they one and all struggle violently against recognizing it."

The boy did what he could to help, not yet being old enough to hinder, like an adult neurotic. Near the end of the analysis, he was strongly enough identified with (and residually hostile to) his father-physician to try to take on the chore of communicating, through the mails, with the ultimate father-physician, of whose omniscient presence, just outside the scene, he was aware. "We'll write to the Professor," he announces happily. Dictating some excremental fantasy, he interrupts himself to exclaim, with evident delight at being like his father, "I say, I *am* glad. I'm always so glad when I can write to the Professor." Having grasped the principle that the Professor collects stories relevant to his own sexual interests, Hans took to analysis as a convenient way to further express that interest, within rules acceptable to both sides. When his father gave him a cue with some moralizing reproof ("A good boy doesn't wish that sort of thing"), Hans retorts with theoretic exactitude, "But he may *think* it." To his father's mechanical counterthrust, "But that isn't good," Hans offered, more ingenuously, a new rule, which indicated how fully he was engrossed in the analytic situation: "If he thinks it, it *is* good all the same, because you can write it to the Professor." It was fine sport, this: "Let's write something down for the Professor." The case history shows, here and there, a droll effect, partly because Freud himself seems unaware of the drollery.

Little Hans's cure followed the rationalist Freudian pattern. Remission of his phobic fear of horses followed upon "enlightenment," as Freud calls it. All Hans's anxieties and questions—except the one about the female genitals—were evaded, his fears allowed to ripen (although, of course, Freud understood from the beginning what, in the formulae of the unconscious, "horse" equaled) until the case reached its peripety: the brief single consultation in which son and father sat before Freud and "the Professor," at last in the flesh, revealed to the long-prepared Hans that *Horse* stood in his mind for *Father*. Directly after the visit with Freud, Hans's father noted the first real improvement: the child played in front of the house for an hour, even though horses were passing by. Henceforth, Hans's anxiety abated, although it did not disappear. When, in their trained unwillingness to teach Hans what he must learn at an appropriate time for himself, Hans's parents still hesitated to supply the long-overdue information about the mechanics of birth, Hans took "the analysis into his own hands" by means of "the brilliant symptomatic act" of ripping open a doll. Thereupon his parents knew that this was the propitious time to enlighten him.

As the case ended, after two years in which the game of confronting Hans's contradictory emotions with irenic explanations was played out, the father wrote to Freud that there was just one "unsolved residue." Hans kept "cudgelling his brains to discover what a father has to do with his child, since it is the mother who brings it into the world." On this Freud comments with expected good sense that, had he full and direct charge, he would have explained the father's sexual task to the child, thus completing the resolution.

Hans had characteristics that are always charming in children, less so in adults. In fact, he was already a probationary adult, trying to make choices on the basis of inadequate information. Thus he had a love life—"which showed a very striking degree of inconstancy and a disposition to polygamy." What adult male, in his right mind, has not felt the same disposition, in very striking degree? He was interested in little girls, and he also showed a "trace of homosexuality." In fact, like all children, little Hans was a "positive paragon of all the vices." Yet, of course, Hans was "not by any means a bad character; he was not even one of those children who at his age still give free play to the propensity towards cruelty and violence which is a constituent of human nature." This was an "unusually kind-hearted and affectionate" boy. For this very reason, because he loved his father at the same time that he would have liked to see him dead—he needed a phobic protection against his own impulses. The fear he felt was not generated by horses, or by his father, but by part of himself. Like everyone else in creation, Hans was made up of "pairs of contraries." He could only be relieved of his phobia by excavating to its instinctual source: his death wish toward his father and his sadistic feelings of love toward his mother.

A phobia opposes and restricts both intelligence and sexuality. But this does not mean that in resolving a phobia either intelligence or sexuality are released in some absolute sense. Freud emphasized the contrary. "Analysis does not undo the *effects* of repression." Rather, it "replaces repression by condemnation." Thus the moralizing effect is preserved, while the pathogenic process is replaced by one within the range of personal and conscious control. What is automatic becomes purposeful, what is excessive can be made temperate—but the controls remain; only their side effects are withdrawn. Once having been analyzed, Hans did not then carry out his death wishes against his father or his erotic fantasies of sleeping with his mother. Rather, in Freud's terms, he became both more stable and more civilized, by lowering for himself the cost of acting like a civilized young man.

Unless both the destructive and erotic impulses are brought under the control of consciousness, the moral systems erected upon the unconscious will continue, according to Freud, to work in curious ways, inducing outbursts of immoral action in the name of morality itself. There is, indeed, a streak of nihilism in contemporary radical moralizing precisely because our new moralizers defend the autonomy of the very instincts over which Freud advocated more conscious control. While Freud merely proposed to maintain effective moral control in ways less damaging to our vital energies, some post-Freudians seek to eliminate the moral effect with the repressive cause. In so doing, they are seeking a freedom from both repression and control that is, in the psychoanalytic view, merely another premonitory dream of destruction. If Freud was not a moralizer, in the old sense of supporting repressive symbolic forms, he was also not a nihilist of the new wave, advocating the liberty of the instincts. Sometimes this new instinctualism parades in the uniform of authority, at other times in the literary loincloth of rebellion. In response, Freud tried to create a new authority figure, in the image of the father-physician, helpful, but unwilling to abdicate the moral controls which he both criticizes and yet also represents. (63:5)

6

On Studies in Parapsychology

There are no easy triumphs in the world of the intellect. Freud's essay on "The Uncanny" is an outstanding example of the fact that, though he be-

Reprinted from *Studies in Parapsychology, Collected Papers of Sigmund Freud*, edited and introduced by Philip Rieff (New York: Collier Books, 1963), 7–13. Introduction copyright © by Macmillan Publishing Company, a division of Macmillan, Inc. Reprinted with permission of Collier Books, an imprint of Macmillan Publishing Company.

came the intellectual master of our age, his was not an effortless mastery. Freud worked hard—on himself and at his writing. Thus, a minor triumph, "The Uncanny," lay in his drawer from the unknown date of its first drafting until the month of May, 1919, when he dug it out for rewriting. The essay lay waiting an interpretative category that would give it life and coherence.

It appears likely that, while working on *Beyond the Pleasure Principle*, Freud turned back to "The Uncanny" and transferred to that essay, earlier conceived, a vital idea from the later work. In the famous "compulsion to repeat," Freud found the concept that was to give unity and truth to an essay which, without such a transfusion of theory, would have remained a relatively pale piece of erudition about problems that had long embarrassed both science and art—eerie feelings, premonitions, telepathic communications, terrifying fantasies, and the like.

Freud's explanation of the whole range of the uncanny has never been bettered. In default of serious competing theories, we will have to be satisfied with the idea that the uncanny is "something which is secretly familiar, which has undergone repression and then returned from it. . . . Everything that is uncanny fulfills this condition . . . [although] not everything that fulfills this condition . . . is on that account uncanny."

All of Freud's best writing has a certain tension, a reaching out for that which is just beyond reach—more precisely, an effort to say something not yet said, by fusing data all too familiar (and therefore a little contemptible) with an unfamiliar theory. The effect is rather uncanny. And not a few readers have this feeling of something uncanny in reading the work of a powerful mind capable of "laying bare . . . hidden forces," as Freud himself noticed. The reader comes to a work with ambivalent motives, learning what he does not wish to know, or, what amounts to the same thing, believing he already knows and can accept as his own intellectual property what the author merely "articulates" or "expresses" for him. Of course, in this sense, everybody knows everything—or nobody could learn anything. The effect of every first-rate piece of writing is to combine the familiar with the unfamiliar. Freud's genius was not really in the discovery of new facts but rather in the supplying of new perspectives on old and often disused facts, such as those upon which shamans, quacks, mediums, and mystics have based modes of knowing outside the respectable precincts of our rationalist culture. It is, thus, as a *theoretician* rather than an *empirical* research worker that his genius persists.

Freud was a rare rationalist, one who respected the irrational. In his intuition of the unity of truth, he leaped upon all manner of experience, even those dismissed as false and fraudulent by minds with lesser capacities to entertain the conceptual unities that are the constituent truths of the worlds of both science and art. It is at this point, indeed, that intellectual certainty, the only substitute for anti-intellectual faith, is achieved, through the fusion of analytic and aesthetic capacities. Freud was able to fuse these capacities. He was gifted with a sense of intellectual certainty, of the sort every scientist and artist needs. But for this sense of certainty he often has been blamed, as if this sense is not the cost of every creative act.

Having found his own mode of certainty, Freud had the courage to let it lead him into jurisdictions where he would not otherwise have entered. These essays are far from the main lines of psychoanalytic investigation. Yet, given the intellectual weapons with which he was gifted, Freud made incursions into the field of parapsychology, which is even more remote from the settled credulities of science and common sense than infantile sexuality is from that of theology and moral sentiment.

In these essays Freud is intent on breaking the hold of the "omnipotence of thought" over those areas of experience that are the investigative jurisdictions, nowadays, of the parapsychologist. Being a psychoanalytic rationalist, he knows the limits of the power of consciousness. It is a limit that rationalism itself has been reluctant to accept; what, then, can be expected of irrationalist doctrines? All doctrines of the irrational are essentially in praise of the unconscious, asserting the power of that level of mind even over matter. Freud belonged to the skeptical majority, of which I, too, am a member. Those of us who have directed our wills, with only random success, upon the required number in a game of cards, or with equal futility, diffused more mental than physical english over a pool table, know how powerless mind remains over matter. We await a theory that, by freeing the will, pockets the ball. Until that millennial time, the "omnipotence of thought" remains for most of us moderns a merely psychical reality, the stuff of neurotic fantasy, eerie fiction, and occult rackets. The mind cannot, upon Freudian or other rationalist hypotheses, act volitionally upon, say, falling dice. Such volitional possibilities, still devoutly wished by some and patiently investigated by others, would revolutionize our pleasures. But, then, I remember: nowadays no revolution can be good. Caught between an inadequately trained consciousness and an untrainable unconscious, our pleasures have a poor prognosis—dying things—like flesh.

Among its more extreme proponents, parapsychology is a kind of religion, and, indeed, raises the same ultimate promise as our historic Western religions: that, after all, we never quite die. Yet, from the evidence adduced, survival after death promises a boring time. Even the great late psychical researcher, F. W. H. Myers, in that part of his personality which (he thought) might retain the capacity to enter the minds of others, could, according to the most devoted witnesses of his re-entry, only express his old academic passion for classical literature; surely it would have been preferable that he remain forever silent. Myers had his say, at Cambridge and in books, when his personality was incarnate. Nobody has a supernatural right to go on talking shop from the Beyond, as if he were eternally at a faculty

party. There is too much talk in the world as it is; a science that would allow
the dead merely to repeat themselves can hold out no hope for the living.
More seriously, I should say that science has no business being either hopeful or hopeless. A science of personality disincarnate cannot be concerned
with the question of whether that personality is transformed in fading away;
such transformations are the waking dreams with which religions have com-
forted the living, by imagining something better than life itself. On the evidence thus far, death has no meaning, except as it is a projective symbolism
expressing the fears and hopes of the living.

As a psychoanalyst, in these essays Freud reviews some of the problems
of parapsychology. Sociologists must fear even to look in the direction Freud
thus took occasionally. The departmental gods will be offended. But it is not
taboo to be reminded by other worlds of one's own. In reading psychical
research reports, I am often reminded of an area over which sociology now
rules: religious behavior. (Sociology picks up subjects by default, the psychologists having abandoned this one as less amenable than pigeon behavior
to their rigorous testing devices.) There appears a remarkable uniformity in
the way extrasensory knowledge is acquired, and, moreover, a remarkable
similarity in the attitude of percipients. These extraordinary ways of knowing would appear, to a sociologist, as secular modes of what used to be
called "mystical understanding."

Although it will not please theologians to think so, religion has been one
major way in which people have saved themselves from the strain of excessive intellectualism. Reason cannot do everything. Since the eighteenth
century, the long supremacy of intellect has been undercut not least by the
rationalists themselves. Finally, with Freud, at least in the first two stages of
his intellectual development, reason was made a constitutional monarch,
charged with the function of appointing ruling parties to office from the par-
liament of emotions, and occasionally reading out a message on future policy from which that parliament could take its cues for action. But the
majesty of reason now needs all kinds of clever supporting publicity; it is no
longer divinely ordered or natural, but, rather, a therapeutic fiction.

Mystics, not only of western but even more emphatically of oriental traditions, were never much impressed with either the majesty or power of reason. On the contrary, of the two types of religion, that generally called
mystical is constantly at war with the other, which is intellectual and doctrinal; the second often feeds upon the first, transforming mystical experience into rationalist dogma. Science is the inheritor of the second tradition,
specially powerful in the West, almost to the exclusion of mysticism. What
was once heresy is now abnormality. Science, equipped with Freudian instruments, is almost ready to pick apart the dynamics of mysticism. But, in
this culture, mysticism has never mattered, except as a release from rationally ordered routine. Now, rationalist science, in the shape of depth psy-

chology, pursues the harried, tired old thing to its last hiding place, out beyond the respectable precincts of church and laboratory, into the back rooms where consolations are sold cheaply, mixed with petty shrewdness by mediums with some small gift.

I say "gift" advisedly; the telepath, the clairvoyant, the medium, the automatist have what Gardner Murphy calls a "special gift for the paranormal." That gift consists in relaxing the intellect, almost as in a trance. It is the gift of the religious—or those who, without being aware of their yearning, would be religious if being so did not carry along unbearable institutional restraints.

Parapsychological theory will develop further, I think, when the percipients themselves are more carefully studied from perspectives other than parapsychological. With what questions will they be studied? That Rhine's first and greatest ESP subject, at Duke, was a student in the divinity school, religiously disposed, and from a family apparently so disposed, leads to a sociological question about the transmission of "sick" and "healthy-minded" attitudes. Again, incidents of telepathy are, with significant frequency, as Freud noted, of disasters; this leads to another sociological question. For personalities with mystical inclinations, social life is a sequence of disasters; through their telepathic experience, they perform a therapy of transformation upon their disgust at existence. One of the last of the great American mediums, an old Yankee whom William James used to visit, would put it to James that "the experience of mediumship was a transforming experience in which everything looked different. He looked out, for example, at 'this rusty hayrick,' to which he pointed, and it would become beautiful. It was transformed, took on meaning." Gardner Murphy quotes another person mystically inclined, a Pole who had the "ability . . . to read hidden messages. . . . 'I concentrate, and then in those moments'—here his face was bright with animation—'I become a Christian.'" [1] The dynamics of personality transformation—whatever the social value attached to such transformations—are better understood than ever before, in part due to the work of Freud. It is difficult to say, however, whether the next advances in understanding can take place strictly within psychology. Perhaps, at the stage to which Freud has helped bring us, historical and sociological analysis will help carry the investigation of parapsychological phenomena further than the psychologists can go on their own. Take, for example, the problem of the decline in the number of first-rate mediums in our culture. The era of great mediums lasted from about 1880 to 1925; this terminal date coincides fairly with the end of the Protestant era. Perhaps survivalist expe-

1. See, for a useful introduction to the problems of parapsychology and psychical research, Gardner Murphy, *Challenge of Psychical Research, A Primer of Parapsychology* (New York, 1961). For a more popular account, see G. H. Estabrooks and N. E. Gross, *The Future of the Human Mind* (New York, 1961).

rience was the genteel form of revivalist experience, fit for those rare creatures who could not otherwise express their sense of the overall meaning of life in a culture that, in both its waning religious and waxing scientific phase, denied the legitimacy of mystical modes of understanding.

A telepath "learns" in the same way that a mystic "knows," with intense emotion and vivid imagery. Both cherish their private knowledge as an untransferrable possession—more precisely, as a knowing that has possessed them, relaxed them, and in a historically familiar way, released them from the rational superficies of everyday life. It may have been this sense of release, so incredible that it had to be believed in, that the residually religious brought, for examination, to the few investigators who, like Freud, were interested in so exotic a subject as feelings of release and possession in a culture that denied the possibility (and efficacy) of either. In Freudian terms, the mystic is a vehicle for the expression of feelings that otherwise must remain repressed, at least in this culture. But the modern mystic, the telepath, is of a very special, historical kind: he reports knowledge of evil, terrifying and out of balance with good. Finally, the events of modern history have emptied out the category of the uncanny. The repressed has returned, in full vengeance, and therefore repression may no longer be the unit of analysis upon which to build a psychology of real horror, as contrasted with the fictional chills that Freud used for illustrative purposes. (63:10)

7

Further Reflections on Freud and Psychoanalysis

On Morality

In Freud's dramatistic structure of personality, the seat of criticism always tries to preempt the function of the ego. The superego is also the ego ideal; and this is, of course, a pejorative imputation.

The traditional description disagrees with Freud's: conscience is not an outer check before it can become inner. Morality is not always negative, the frightful original aspect of power; the thou-shalt-nots do not annul the circumcision of the heart. The cannibal spirit of the Freudian view of morality,

This chapter is made up of excerpts from the following previously published works by Philip Rieff: "Freudian Ethics and the Idea of Reason," *Ethics* 67, no. 3, part 1 (April): 169–83, © 1957 by The University of Chicago, all rights reserved; Introduction to Sigmund Freud's *Collected Papers of Sigmund Freud*, 10 vols., edited and introduced by Philip Rieff (New York: Collier Books, 1963), specifically *Character and Culture*, 9–13; *Three Case Histories*, 7–11; *Therapy and Technique*, 7–24; *General Psychological Theory*, 7–20; *Delusion and Dream and Other Essays* (Boston: Beacon Press, 1956), 1–21.

its hostile absorption of the images of parents and teachers and other authoritative personalities, does not allow enough to the equally original compassionate spirit. Freud represented compassion to be the tender depression
that comes when passions are spent—or, in his other view, the clever way in
which the weak imitate the strong. (57:3, p. 174)

On Reason

Freud's reason is the "sense of reality," and he thought the demands of conscience invariably "unrealistic"; since the id is unavailable to change,
reason's essential task is to revise the superego, the critical is moral. It
would seem that psychoanalysis, since it inevitably must criticize the origin
of criticism—society—is, therefore, compelled by the terms of its genetic
analysis, to be a reformist doctrine. But Freud as social critic of Victorian
morality cannot be identified with the Freud of individual pedagogy. Because of a sound pessimism about cultural capacities, the Freudian reason,
for the weight it throws on adjustment to the given, to this extent agrees with
the established ethics of a liberalism that has lost its nerve of protest. Freud
as a rationalist of a sort does not protest what is; instead he suggests we
reconcile ourselves to it. Any treatment of Freud as a descendant of the Enlightenment must take account of the fact that he largely discounted the
Enlightenment possibility of the given as irrational. The given was simply
given. The problem was to adjust to the world, for the world will not readily
adjust to you. (57:3, pp. 181–82)

Reason is a bourgeois gentleman, with proper desires; security and success,
not insight as such, is the aim of reason. It is an admonition to childish
minds: "But, my dear child, be reasonable." Reason is chiefly prudent, the
cautionary voice of experience, a method of mastery. The "why" questions
are transformed into "how" questions; for, to ask where we are going and
what we are to do is eliminated as unscientific, as archaic teleologians of a
religious past, when reason was still somehow compatible with revelation.
Psychoanalysis, like politics, is an empiric art of successfully grasping those
opportunities that nature, out of its richness, has to present. (57:3, p. 182)

On Idealism . . .

To build a theory that is at the same time a therapy goes far beyond the
canons of nineteenth-century rationalism and of science; indignation against
Freud among the scientists was therefore understandable. Without really
comprehending the drift of his genius, the scientifically educated at first saw
Freud as a traitor to their class. They feared in him—and some still fear—
the return of dark old superstitions in clever new disguises.

In merging a therapeutic concern for what ought to be with a theoretic concern for what is, Freud offered to our culture the first audible word of an idealism that was fairly new and disquieting. It is an idealism concerned primarily with the hardening of the self rather than the softening of the world, an idealism that sets for each poor individual creature of a world he never made the task of saving that remnant of time he may still make his own.

In his idealism, Freud is never sentimental. He spares us all the latest insincere designs in "values" or the other awkward tumbrels of modern ethics. He does not force our suspended beliefs to dance, as if they were alive. Though he escapes being a designer of ideals or, like Carl Jung, being a master in the puppetry of traditions, Freud goes to another extreme. He is dangerously unsentimental. His systematic candor about the inherent aggressiveness of mankind has become a formula for aggression among the educated against themselves. (63:9, p. 10)

. . . and Realism

Freud never indulged in the religion of science. On the other hand, he did not delude himself with any form of the older tradition of wishing: for some meaningful end toward which we are all, in our otherwise separate histories, tending. Therefore he was caught in the middle, between scientism and religion, a thorn in both sides. Probably the middle is the most interesting place to be; it is the one position of strength remaining, once the weakness of all positions, including its own, has been exposed by it.

Freud's is really a psychology of weakness, founded as it is upon the condition of man at the time of formative beginnings. Neuroses are a form of denial of certain weaknesses, in a misdirected effort to stabilize them; to these weaknesses some men return, by way of symptoms or more subtle protests, when they must for reasons neither Freud nor anyone after him has made sufficiently clear. More precisely, we do not really return; rather, our weaknesses, specified in our infancy and childhood, are always with us. Why some men succumb, sometimes in bizarre ways, while others, no less latently weak, are spared, remains a mystery, involving not only ourselves but possibly also our forefathers and certainly the cultures to which we are subject. What is a disease entity in one culture may be a glorious capacity in another. Freud has made a start toward getting away altogether from doctrines of disease entities toward a truer psychology of processes by which men become what they are. (63:7, p. 8)

Neither the ascetic nor the therapeutic bothers his head about "ultimate concerns." Such a level of concern is for mystics who cannot otherwise enjoy their own leisure. In the workaday world, there are rarely "ultimate concerns," only immediate ones. Therapy is that respite in everyday life during which the supremacy of the immediate is learned and the importance of what some religious intellectuals call "ultimate concern" is unlearned. Such remote areas of experience are brought up as examples of the neurotic displacement of emotional attention, thus the better to understand them and put them in their properly subordinate place as dead events and motives rather than as the models for events and motives of the present life. Nietzsche's announcement that the gods were dead seems a little premature, in view of all the difficulty Freud had in rooting the ordinary household god out of every unconscious, where it is deposited by our common childhood experience. Psychoanalysis is thus a form of reeducation toward making Nietzsche's poetic announcement a prosy fact of life. (63:3, pp. 16–17)

The alternatives with which Freud leaves us are grim only if we view them from the perspective of some possibility passed, either as political or religious men. Assuming that these character types are, in his terms, regressive, the grimness is relieved by the gaiety of being free from the historic Western compulsion of seeking large and general meanings for small and highly particular lives. Indeed, the therapy of all therapies, the secret of all secrets, the interpretation of all interpretations, in Freud, is not to attach oneself exclusively or too passionately to any one particular meaning or object . . . With Freud, individualism took a great and perhaps final step: the mature and calm feeling that must keep the individual a safe distance from the mass of his fellows can now, in therapy, be so trained that the individual can withdraw an even safer distance from his family and friends. With Freud, Western man has learned truly the technical possibility of living his inward life alone, at last rid of that crowd of shadows eternally pressing him to pay the price for a past, in his childhood, when he could not have been for himself. This isolation, however, is no longer confining, as Tocqueville, with his classical prejudices favoring political man, thought it must be; rather, in Freud's opinion, it is liberating. At last, in the assurance and control of his consciousness, the Western individual can live alone because he likes it. (63:3, pp. 21–22)

On Death

Despite Freud's attempt . . . to construct a genuine parity between [Eros and the death-instinct], a fundamental disparity remained. The difference between life and death is that death has no character; life has three. The Freudian characterology is entirely of the development of the libido into three stages: the oral, the anal, and the genital. It is an important sign of Freud's failure to equalize the life and death instincts that, in a doctrine free with name-givings, there is no name for the energy of the death instinct equivalent to "libido" ("aggression" is not an energy), and no characterology for aggression, the microcosmic expression of the death instinct to parallel the libidinal. The Freudians excuse this lapse by remarking that since Freud discovered death thirty years after libido, "research" has yet to catch up. But the utopia of research will never end, and a characterology of aggression distinct from the libidinal will never be found. The structure of the theory itself admits of no academic excuses. (63:6, pp. 14–15)

On Analogies

There is great ease in the Freudian method. The husk of events is removed and only kernels of meaning remain. Actions become transparent and at last one can look inside at what is really interesting, the agents; and inside the agents, there are the emotions making everything move. Freud provided gossip with a theory and made history nothing more than the quintessence of gossip. His method would halt the perverse quoting of state papers, as if they were significant data, and return social research to its original concern with the oddities of personality and the regularities of events, as if this movement or that did not differ from those of the "heavenly forces." Historians, who aspire to something more impersonal and respect more obvious facts like the impotence of a revolution as well as the impotence of a revolutionary, accuse Freud of encouraging the barbarism of the historyless. The historians, though they are too hostile, may be correct. Freud's analogies permit uncontrolled shifts in the presentation of evidence and arbitrary devaluation of the larger contexts within which given psychological processes operate. The results survive him in a remarkable narrowing of historical interest among those he influenced. Contemporaneity, the failure of memory, is the characteristic mark of modern barbarism.

But the new barbarism induces an ease greater than the mere condensation of history in psychology. By a strange chemistry it dissolves worlds of moral difference into the absurd sameness of psychological roles. Hitler and Christ are both father-images, and fathers must be moral. One does not choose one's father. Psychology makes it all accidental which morality one acquires, discerning a natural morality that precedes Bibles and swords and makes of them only the narrowest family prejudice. Psychoanalysis can too easily arraign substantive issues of justice, morality, and freedom as evocations of psychic functions. Freud's social theory is dependent on the reduction of substantive to functional, public to private. The psychological was primary and causative, while the historical event was the secondary, or resultant. (63:6, pp. 18–19)

Freud's analogies reveal the sharpness of his polemic. Philosophers are not simply ingenious moralists; there are gods who are not fathers, or before that, mothers; a nun counting beads is not an obsessional counting buttons. They are not; but Freud's analogies imply guilt by association. He explained the connection between the private motive and the public action genetically;

but genesis does not tell right from wrong, good from bad. Indeed, saintliness may be a development of the oral character, but certain emotional
states, certain developments of character are, if not inherently then by in-
spection of consequences, known to be good; a satisfactory explanation can
not discount them as pathological. The good need not be pathological because it is rare or because it is no progression beyond a certain stage of
development. (63:6, p. 20)

On the Aesthetic Imagination

Nothing more clearly overrides the autonomy of the aesthetic imagination
than Freud's attempt to rationalize it. As an intellectual equivalent of the
industrial process, rationalist science finds a uniform production of symbol
and myths and works of the imagination so that all these can be classified
and identified with each other. As the early Deist and rationalist students of
comparative religions simplified Christian dogma until they discovered in it
the same ultimate truths as, say, in Zoroastrianism, so the modern psychological rationalist simplifies the variety of emotive expression to find the
same meanings beneath. The separate and often irreconcilable details of
myths, religions, dreams, and art are made, under psychoanalytic heat, to
melt and merge. The Freudian method is thus entirely reductionist as to
genre. It tends to reduce art, myth, dream, fairy tale alike to the same basic
stock of plots and symbols. For psychology is the science of motivation and,
motive-wise, different works of art may look very similar. An interest in
motives shared by the generality of men offers little basis upon which to
distinguish among works of the imagination. Further, this exclusively moti-
vational analysis retains no way of dealing with what aestheticians call the
sensuous surface of a work of art. The qualitative experience of the senses is
dismissed by Freud as mere "forepleasure"; his aesthetic criticism is purely
intellectual.

What Freud has to say about art applies to all art, good and bad. It is
somewhat accidental to the psychoanalytically minded critic what is being
scrutinized. In various writings, when he turns, for illustrations of psychological dilemmas, to *Oedipus* and *Hamlet*, to *Macbeth*, to *Richard III*, to
plays of Ibsen, Freud develops some brilliant insights. Yet it all seems very
arbitrary. Works of lesser stature could as well have exemplified his theme.
It is revealing that Freud's one full-scale examination of a novel [Wilhelm
Jensen's *Gradiva: A Pompeiian Fantasy*, in *Delusion and Dream* (56:6)]
fixes on a work of fragile aesthetic merit. But aesthetic merit, or the limit of
a particular genre, is not Freud's concern. His interest caught on *Gradiva*
not for any reason of literary excellence, but ostensibly because the novel
could be read as an ingenious prevision of the psychoanalytic love cure. We
may agree, I think, that *Gradiva* would not be very memorable in itself,

lacking Freud's gloss, and this perhaps is an ideal state of affairs, from the view of psychoanalytical interpretive technique.

I should not like to imply that *Gradiva* supplied the raw material of Freud's reductive technique and no more. However slight a work, *Gradiva* is to some extent true to the center of the novelistic tradition. It relates a quest for the recovery of the personal self; it is a story that praises the liquidation of the burden of the past and ends happily, with the opposite sexes walking into an open future. Just these are the themes most central to the novel since the inception of the romantic period of our culture. And since depth psychology, too—as well as the novel—lives off the presuppositions and questions of the romantic period, it seems apt that Freud acknowledged what happens in the novel as an analogue to the healing mission of his own science.

This raises a larger question, which can only be touched on here: the question of the relation between psychology and the novel. Certainly at the present time it would seem to be a congenial relation. Like the novel, Freudian psychology still accepts the individual as the unit of analysis. Yet, in historical context, the general habits of introspection and solicitude toward the self which Freud's method sponsors raise at best a defensive enclave into which the individual may retreat. The literature and science of the individual—the novel and depth psychology—take on an added import of consolation in an age in which the individual counts for less and less. For in our society the individual has been severely challenged. Change has been built into the ordinary rhythms of social life. Caught up in the frightening acceleration of historical events, personal decision has lost the moral import it had in slower times. As if in compensation, just when he is becoming a cipher, the modern individual has learned to play with utter earnestness at the ancient problem of "discovering himself." Psychotherapy cannot be for most more than a luxury experience, a bracketed area in which the individual can face the problem of making decisions as if they are his to make.

Nevertheless, it is fair to say also that depth psychology repudiates the conception of the moral life which is implied in the novel. Against the novelistic tradition, which is Protestant and individual, our psychology has emphasized that the self is a fiction—a composite of instinctual and social mandates. In his psychological theory, Freud allows only the smallest margin for the self-determining individual. And this self-determination (located in the *ego*) amounts merely to a skill at playing off against one another the massive sub-individual (*id*) and supra-individual (*superego*) forces by which the self is shaped. Idiosyncrasy, decision, habits of moral stocktaking can be referred back to the generic motives which they merely exemplify. And not only in theory but in the presumptive rules of interpretation which are set down in therapy, there is a rebuke to our inherited sense of self. To be always plucking universal motifs from behind the ear of the prone subject, to seize exemplifications of sexual symbols out of a hat—surely this magic is impressive but more impressive is its ethical import.

In his essay on Jensen's *Gradiva*, Freud wears the face of an emancipator, physician to sick individuality in search of its abrogation in the instinctual life. Norbert Hanold, as Freud tells us, suffers alienation from love. His illness is essentially "the rejection of eroticism." But sick as his erotic nature is, much as it has disordered his reason, he is still driven, by the very agency of his delusion, within reach of a lover. And love, incarnate in the long lost Zoë, cures him. According to the erotic ethic of Freudianism, he has been saved; his body has been reconciled with his mind. The lesson of Norbert Hanold's life, that one cannot starve the emotions, that one has to obey the imperatives of nature, Freud takes as the model of psychoanalytic remedy.

Yet Freud had another face—turned always against "the lie of salvation" (see his letter to Wilhelm Fliess in *The Origins of Psychoanalysis* [New York, 1954], p. 366) in any form, including salvation through sexuality. The erotic ethic of *Delusion and Dream* is only part of the Freudian ethics, perhaps the lesser part. Freud is not only the approving commentator on Zoë's maneuvers toward the act of love. So far as he encouraged the passions, he did so in a complex and self-canceling way. *Delusion and Dream* gives little idea of the reflective discipline of self-consciousness which he made a prerequisite for divesting oneself of one's symptoms, if not one's deeper illness. If, in *Delusion and Dream*, Freud is the champion of the erotic life, he is also, in other places, the master of an ironic view of life. It is a fairly chilly permissiveness that psychoanalysis fosters—more a matter of prudence than passion, more science than sex. While psychoanalysis is engaged in permitting us to experience our emotions without hindrance from images of the past, it also engages its adherents in a more dispassionate task: that of testing the logic of the emotions themselves. (56:6, pp. 17–21)

8
Fourteen Points on "Wilson"

Only when the doctor has been deeply touched by the illness, infected by it, excited, frightened, shaken, only when it has been transferred to him, continues in him and is referred to himself by his own consciousness—only then and to that extent can he deal with it successfully.

Viktor von Weizsäcker

Reprinted from *Encounter* 28, no. 4 (April 1967), 84–89.

1

What makes this book important? [1] Diagnostic revelations about the twenty-eighth President of the United States? Nothing new here. Woodrow Wilson is almost too obviously an Oedipal case. Indeed, so obvious a case that the authors, in their zeal to denigrate him, distort the sense in which the unresolved remnants of Wilson's early ambivalence to his father facilitate, as well as limit, his achievement. In the Preacher, the Reverend Professor Joseph Ruggles Wilson, his son possessed from the beginning a figure of what he might become. Freud would have it otherwise. It is not at all clear that he had much knowledge of Wilson's American-Presbyterian (Scotch-Irish) culture. The perfunctory and insensitive treatment of Wilson's Presbyterian origins reminds me rather of Ernest Jones's treatment of Freud's Jewish origins.

Probably this book will acquire an importance beyond its merit: as yet another symptom of the decline of idealization—bad, good, but never indifferent—in modernizing societies. Freud, not Marx, may be considered the presiding genius of modernity; and it is Freud, not Wilson, who is the significant presence in this book. We cannot be certain what is Freud's and what is Bullitt's; there are crudities here that are most unlike Freud. But he gave his name to the book; more important, he shaped its diagnostic intention. In this "Psychological Study," the doctor performs a deep operation: he divests of his authority that rare but native American type, the preacher as politician. In effect, at least upon the educated classes, Wilson is likely to be further imprisoned within a reductive psychological portrait. This portrait is all warts, sharp nose, too often out of joint, and asses' ears. The diagnosis of Wilson's unresolved Oedipal relation to the figure of authority in his life, his preacher-father, is at once a posthumous arraignment and punishment. It is also an arraignment of a Presbyterian style in American politics: the style of "moral crusades." (How can one help, nowadays, but put such styles inside quotation marks?) Under the impact of the drumfire of which this book is only one shot, there is developing, in advanced societies, a new cultural type: the anti-leader. Without Freud, the type (as it is developing in the United States) is inconceivable.

2

The book is ablaze with contempt for Wilson, not merely in the "Digest of Data" on Wilson's life (for which Bullitt is explicitly responsible) but

---

1. Sigmund Freud and William C. Bullitt, *Thomas Woodrow Wilson: Twenty-eighth President of the United States: A Psychological Study* (London: Weidenfeld & Nicolson, 1967).

throughout the long diagnosis of Wilson's career, which reads like a parody of an analysis. Wilson becomes a standard case of an unconscious ambivalent transference: his acts and illnesses are the precipitate of hostile feelings to his father, unknown to him and inadmissible into consciousness.

But there are two sides to every analytic situation, the patient's and the analyst's. Bullitt and Freud tell their readers that they have overcome their negative countertransference to their subject. The evidence, as I read it throughout this book, is to the contrary. So far as it is hostile, even contemptuous, the mood of the book abrogates Freud's own methodological canon. In his own view, such contempt would ruin the therapeutic relation between analyst and patient and distort the analyst's insight. Of course, Wilson is not a patient. Yet the essential devices of this psychological study are psychoanalytic. Freudian knowledge is never so impersonal that the mood of the knower becomes irrelevant.

What happens when it is not the patient who achieves the negative phase of the transference but the analyst? The result here is polemical psychologizing.

3

How shall we account for the appeal of psychologizing, in both the post-Wilsonian and post-Marxist period? Psychologizing organizes the modern convulsion of belief. The doctor supplies a basis for treating those who dare to preach to us. Viewed in the psychoanalytic style, the Communist, too, as revolutionary, is neurotic.

> Theoretical Marxism [Freud wrote, in his *New Introductory Lectures*] as realized in Russian Bolshevism, has acquired the energy and the self-contained and exclusive character of a *Weltanschauung*, but at the same time an uncanny likeness to what it is fighting against. Though originally a portion of science and built up, in its implementation, upon science and technology, it has created a prohibition of thought which is just as ruthless as was that of the religion of the past. . . . And although practical Marxism has mercilessly cleared away all idealistic systems and illusions, it has itself developed illusions which are no less questionable and unprovable than the earlier ones.

As a new political idealism, Marxism earned Freud's grudging respect: at least it did succeed in shifting away from the property system the instinctual restrictions which Freud considered essential and necessary for the working of any social order. Wilsonian idealism, in his view, accomplished nothing—worse than nothing. For a brief while this miserable neurotic, who could not enjoy his victories (did Calvin enjoy his victories?), became another false Messiah, a focus for popular illusions of a radically new order of social life—peace on earth. For his self-idealization, in which Wilson finally identified himself with God and the Son of God, Wilson earned Freud's contempt.

4

The book reinforces the already widespread credibility of discounting "idealistic" and "oratorical" politics. The word "neurotic" might have excused Wilson as a private man; as a public man, and the subject of a book about his character and action, Wilson is denigrated by the relentless display of his neurosis. The study of Wilson may be read as an assault upon all our inherited political styles, including the Communist. Lenin would have done as well as Wilson, though Gladstone makes a more familiar candidate. Between the Presbyterian gentleman and the psychological doctor there is implicit one of those struggles of credibility by which entire societies are empowered to change their sense of what they are really about. Wilson loses: not surprisingly because the terms of the struggle are entirely psychoanalytic. Can anyone imagine a religious analysis of Freud, not to mention a persuasive Calvinist attack on his therapy as a precipitate of his lack of faith?

5

Bullitt and Freud may have overplayed their hand. Wilson is too obviously the enemy; not simply those twin enemies of psychological man, id drives and superego demands, but Wilson's ego is the enemy as well. The whole man, in the integrity of his neurosis, is too consistently reconstructed. The analysis is too tidy, the quotes out of Wilson's own mouth too neat. The young academic Wilson is even denied his real interest in sport. Moreover, their zeal outstrips their purpose. In one characteristic passage, Wilson's "excessive uncertainty" about bringing America into war is laid mainly to his "identification of himself with Christ." That Wilson wept openly, on the Cabinet table, when he reflected what his message of war to the Congress meant ("Think what they are applauding. My message today was a message of death for our young men. How strange it seems to applaud that. . . ."), becomes an expression of his immaturity, of his dependence upon his father. They must nail Wilson to his neurosis in his best as well as his worst moments. Did Harry S. Truman act "like a man" rather than as a child when he lost not a single moment of sleep over Hiroshima?

The crudity of such an assault may be Bullitt's, but the intellectual responsibility is Freud's; it is Freud's *doctrine* that can so easily be translated into a form of contempt and personal rejection. How Freud must have had to struggle against his own excesses: after all, contempt is the readiest emotion of one intellectual confronting another.

That contempt, that unresolved and only grudgingly admitted hostility against Wilson, is what interests me, as a sociologist, about this book. Wilson's unresolved and unadmitted hostility to his father is more obvious. It is also less interesting, less vital to an understanding of conditions inside those readers who are the true objects of this final fragment of Freud's grand assault on the conscientious moralizing of social order. Freud, not Lodge, is Wilson's final antagonist, no petty role in a world to which "Meester Veelson" once appeared as an earthly Messiah. Dos Passos once summed up the Freudian thesis in a sentence: "Woodrow Wilson believed in his father's God. . . ." This is very different from saying, however, that the properties of Wilson's life and conduct were ordered by instinctual determinants. "Father" is not a usable middle term between instincts and gods, except as one or the other polar term is collapsed into the middle one. It is not at all clear why the term "instinct" should not be equally subject to such collapses toward the sociological middle. When "instincts" are seen as gods now are, the analysis of Wilson's life (or any other) will involve us in answers that take us beyond Freud.

6

The therapeutic relation demands a worthy patient. Wilson remains forever unworthy, for he can never admit the sources that at once flawed and facilitated his idealism. The historical patient emerges as an enemy, as the actual patient is always in danger of becoming. Both as a branch of medicine and as an intellectual discipline, psychoanalysis must struggle constantly, and sometimes unsuccessfully, against contempt. As part of the medical subculture, doctors of psychoanalysis, too, grow callous about their patients. More important: as closely related antagonists in the postreligious culture of modernity, analyst and patient are engaged in a struggle of competing interpretations. The patient's interpretative system must be utterly routed. That is the cure: a conversion to the point of view implicit in the analysis. Wilson can never be converted; he can never be cured. His self-interpretation can only be exhibited to a third party, the reader. It is the reader who is the real object of the therapeutic thrust hidden inside this book.

7

Freud wrote other studies of historical figures: Moses, Dostoevsky. In both cases, he admired the man who was his subject. Moses is to him a creedal personality: a moral hero, enforcing, by the destiny of his character, a new symbolic of renunciation upon recalcitrant and distraught individuals, successfully forging them into a cultural, if not political, identity. Dostoevsky was creative in a narrower sense, a supreme figure of the modern artist, representing in the power of his art the true individuality of men who have to live on the verge of madness. In Freud's version, Woodrow Wilson was not a great man, but merely a neurotic who may have just managed to avoid slipping away into psychosis. His temporary greatness, the adulation he received upon reaching Europe, as the "Saviour" of mankind, exemplified that larger enemy against which Freud set himself: the established process of idealization. In attacking Wilson, Bullitt and Freud are continuing an intellectually elaborate assault on a culture that depends, for its motivating energies, not simply upon the renunciation of drives but upon an idealization of those renunciations. Can renunciation work without idealization? Or does Freud misunderstand what it is that must be renounced? For in the great systems of conduct preceding that of modernity, it is precisely ego that had to be renounced. Such a renunciation is so difficult that our gods have killed themselves in the effort.

8

Moses too idealized his necessary renunciations. But in *Moses and Monotheism*, the polemical thrust, or countertransference, is positive, in Wilson negative. Compare Erikson's superior book *Young Man Luther* (1958). Here again the polemical thrust is positive, mainly because

> Luther accepted for his life work the unconquered frontier of tragic conscience, defined as it was by his personal needs and his superlative gifts: *"Locus noster,"* he said in the lectures on the Psalms, *"in quo nos cum Deo, sponsas cum sponsa, habitare debet . . . est conscientia."* Conscience is that inner ground where we and God have to learn to live with each other as man and wife. Psychologically speaking, it is where the ego meets the superego; that is, where our self can either live in wedded harmony with a positive conscience or is estranged from a negative one. Luther comes nowhere closer to formulating the auditory threat, the voice of wrath, which is internalized in a negative conscience than when he speaks of the "false Christ" as one whom we hear expostulate *"Hoc non fecisti,"* "Again, you have not done what I told you"—a statement of the kind which identifies negatively, and burns itself into the soul as a black and hopeless mark: *conscientia cauterisata.*
>
> [Luther] was made for a job on this frontier. But he did not create the job; it originated in the hypertrophy of the negative conscience inherent in our whole Judaeo-Christian heritage in which, as Luther put it: "Christ becomes more formidable a tyrant and a judge than was Moses."

Freud is a great man, too, in the sense that he again moved the frontier of the tragic conscience and appeared for a time to have supplied a new hope of conquering that frontier.

9

In attacking the mandate under which Wilson lived, Freud's explanations must themselves try to take the place of the defeated mandate; that is the lawlike nature of the confrontation between explanatory modes, "neurotic" and "realistic." But the Freudian mandate carries us back to the Father-Mother polarity from which it is the task of men, if they would be "normal," to emancipate themselves. Elaborating the analysis of this polarity, Freud's achievement constitutes a rebellion against that very polarity. We are now so impressed by the Father-Mother polarity that it has become one negative principle around which the present internal world is organized, giving its own cast to social and personal reality. Wilson's culture is not quite dead; it lives on as the Devil-term in the present antitheology of Freud and his epigones.

10

The demands of the superego (culture) have a structure far more complex than the instinctual demands of the id. In Bullitt and Freud, this historical complexity is reduced to Father-Mother, in Joseph Ruggles Wilson and Jessie Woodrow. In a period of history in which other institutions of Wilson's culture were undergoing rapid disintegration, Freud assimilated all other historical contents to a particular image of the family as a Father-Mother polarity. But the Father-Mother polarity is itself part of a complex structure in which the meanings cannot be held as stable as Freud held them, for reasons that have to do, in part, with the generalization of Freud's own assault on a particular Father-Mother image. Freud takes that image for an ordained, suprahistorical reality, when in fact his own analysis signals a change in its cultural potential as authority. At a distance, Freud's rebellion appears ambivalent: an effort to teach a new respect for the power of the dominant imagery and yet lay the ground for a true rejection.

11

Freud has it both ways: he appeals to external reality as if it were something more than family, yet in his own time he understands that reality is dominated by the internal world of the family. The playing-off of the less definable external world against the defined internal world constitutes Freud's therapeutic effort against the dominance of a particular internal world. Both the drives of the id and the demands of the superego are enemies. The only acceptable ally of the therapist in the structure of the internal world is the ego, that is, the representative and agent of Reality. But what reality could Wilson's ego represent that would not have been mediated through yet another internal world, objective and external to the will of this particular actor-patient? *"Nichts ist drinnen, nichts ist draussen / Denn was ist innen, das ist aussen."* In the light Freud casts on his inner life, Wilson was not a free man. Suppose we could grant him his freedom from the authority that constituted his deepest being. In what would Wilson's freedom consist, except the freedom from this inmost authority? To say that Wilson could have lived this nearer reality is to say he would have lived nearer the surfaces of life. There is a sense in which freedom is superficiality. On Freudian terms, the structure of character is built up out of depths and surfaces. It is in this sense that rational freedom, when and if it can be achieved, carries an implication of superficiality. The very assertion of such freedom, less in the arts than in the social sciences, signals a most important movement in and against our inherited culture: a lost emotional content, taking the form of an effort to destroy the creative sense of guilt (and the "inexorable psychological law of ambivalence") from which culture—as religion, art, and moral judgment—has always taken its energies. In the arts there is a movement no less calculated to destroy the creative sense of guilt. But here the assertion is of irrational depth, as instinct against superego, with ego in the service of instinct.

12

Bullitt and Freud do not even try to put Wilson in his time and place, except in the most perfunctory, camera-eye, way. Wilson breaks with the tradition of his fathers, and goes into politics. This means more, in the America of Wilson's time, than Bullitt and Freud make of it. There is no real history in this book. Instead, the conflict between the instinctual demands of the Woodrow id and the conscientious demands of the Wilson superego becomes the timeless Freudian family romance turned inside out, the romance rendered as analysis.

But Wilson's passive-aggressive reactions are animated by the special moralizing demands of his paternal Presbyterian culture. The intensities are specific to his internal-external world, and very realistic. Freud himself put the point (for Wilson and every other child born into any culture) in his essay "On Female Sexuality":

> It is easy to observe how, in every field of psychical experience . . . an impression passively received evokes in children a tendency to an active response. They try to do themselves what has just been done to them. This is part of their task of mastering the outside world and may even lead to their endeavouring to repeat impressions which they have good reason to avoid because of their disagreeable content.

The "impressions" of the Presbyterian culture that Bullitt and Freud find so disagreeable are precisely what facilitated the Wilsonian activity. The psychological study of Wilson constitutes another example of a new myth attacking an old one. One ministry of the word displaces another. It remains to be seen whether such a ministry, become therapeutic, can abolish itself.

13

In Wilson, Bullitt and Freud argue, idealizations have become mere words. Wilson is a rhetorician, in the pejorative sense of the term; and he is the son of an even more pious rhetorician. Wilson's idealizations become mere words for reasons of which Bullitt and Freud seem unaware. It is true that Wilson meant, and did not really mean, what he said. Idealizations can lead to self-idealizations. But the neurotic style is not his own. It is a powerful remnant of Protestant evangelical culture that Bullitt and Freud attack in Wilson. In attacking him as an orator, they assault his strongest point. But they do not know, I think, why it is also his weakest. Wilson was a lover of words, but words are not "mere words," or so much hot air. Such a prejudice against words is itself a product of our commercial culture, where only money really talks, and of a materialist-positivist ideology in which facts are like things, with an apparent authority beyond the words attached to them.

14

Bullitt and Freud explain Wilson's "intensity" along the usual line. Prohibition (of thought and activity against the Father) involves frustration, which leads to a particular kind of submissive facility: in this case, oratory and inclinations to "moral" crusades. The Presbyterian intensity is still to be found among some Americans: in the search, for example, for a cause serious enough to merit the investment of moral aggression. (The civil rights movement was the most recent focus for Protestant self-justification.)

But after Wilson came Harding. Immediately after Wilson's time, I think, American Protestant intensity, the tenacity and ambition with which a man could consider himself the chosen instrument of a higher and sovereign authority, ceased to be a portent of the working of that higher authority. Rather, with a vengeance that betrays its origin, intensity was reserved for precisely the unportentous: for trivia, hobbies, leisure-time "activities," gardening, edifying lectures, cheap entertainments, crossword puzzles, whatever passes the time without having to be taken as a sign of surpassing importance. In short, intensity passed to what is now called "Culture," which is without authority. The American whirligig of art, fashion (in dress and in doctrine), and hobbyism—the entire "Culture Boom"—is a post-Protestant phenomenon. Intensity no longer represents an ego mobilizing energies for the service of authority, some deeply installed will, but the new freedom of man, disabused of such sovereignties, to be himself rather than an agent of God. Americans continue to demonstrate abundant tenacity and ambition, but as men of power rather than as delegates of authority. I wonder if Freud would have liked the thirty-sixth President of the United States better than he liked the twenty-eighth? (67:3)

9
Kairos in Freud's Thought

Freud was prepared to illustrate his idea of history by the metapsychological history of the Judeo-Christian tradition. Kairos, for Freud, was, of course, the "primeval experience in the human family,"[1] the killing of the primal father. Moses is the "tremendous father imago" of the Jews.[2] The forgotten kairotic event in Jewish history is the killing of Moses. Had not Freud picked up this "suggestion concerning Moses' end, the whole treatise [*Moses and Monotheism*] would have to remain unwritten."[3] Fortunately for Freud's treatise, the Jews, "who even according to the Bible were stubborn and unruly toward their lawgiver and leader, rebelled at last, killed him,"[4] suffered remorse, and so became religious and Jews. The history and religion of Jewry is an outwork of the Jewish Kairos, the teaching-struggle and death[5] of the man Moses.

Originally entitled "The Meaning of History and Religion in Freud's Thought." Reprinted and abridged from *Journal of Religion* 31, no. 2 (April 1951): 114–31. © 1951 by The University Chicago. All rights reserved. [Parts of this essay were later revised and incorporated into *Freud: The Mind of the Moralist*. See 59:1a, pp. 194–96—ED.]

1. Sigmund Freud, *Moses and Monotheism*, translated by Katherine Jones (London: Hogarth Press, 1949), 204.

2. Ibid., 174. The Jewish masses are "his dear children."

3. Ibid., 95.

4. Ibid., 98.

5. The teacher is, for Freud, the universal martyr image—characterized by his charisma and wisdom, suffering the resentment of his students and public, who are his children. There is no doubt that Freud, as a great teacher, identified himself with Moses. Although he considers himself no art connoisseur, Michelangelo's "Moses," in the Church of San Pietro in Vincoli in Rome attracts him irresistibly. "It always delights [me] to read an appreciatory sentence about this statue. . . . For no piece of statuary has ever made a stronger impression on me than this. How often have I mounted the steep steps of the unlovely Corso Cavour to the lonely place where the deserted church stands, and have essayed to support the angry scorn of the hero's glance! Sometimes I have crept cautiously out of the half-gloom of the interior as though I myself belonged to the mob upon whom his eye is turned—the mob which can hold fast no conviction, which has neither faith nor patience, and which rejoices when it has regained its illusory idols" (*Collected Papers*, IV, 259–60). Perhaps this is the most intimate self-image the new Moses ever wrote, to the unconvinced, faithless, impatient, illusion-ridden, idolatrous, mob that is the public.

Freud at first concealed his authorship of *Moses*, and his "inner misgivings" during the composition of the essays involved not simply the consequences of his outer situation, a refugee in London at eighty-two. The "inner difficulties" were not to be eased by the freedom of England. Freud was still "uneasy." He was wrestling with the problem with which he had closed grips a quarter of a century before, in *Totem and Taboo*: religion. Now, with *Moses*, as he wrote, he felt like a bad dancer, balancing on one toe. But he found the problem, to the end, "irresistible" (see *Moses and Monotheism*, 164). [A shorter version of this note appears in 59:1a, pp. 282–83n—ED.]

The Jewish historical Kairos created the Jews, as Jews. It gave to them their permanent national character. Freud does not doubt that the Jews have a national character and that it is now what it was in antiquity. It is expressed by their "unexampled power of resistance"[6] (cf. Nietzsche, on how the Jews, "the little people of the great prophets," have been able to maintain themselves). The national character of the Jews is a consequence of the "special character" of their Kairos. The Jewish Kairos is the advent of the Mosaic idea of chosenness.

Freud insisted that it was the Egyptian, Moses, who chose the Jews, rather than the Jews who chose Moses. Moses stamped the Jewish people with its special character: "It was one man, the man Moses, who created the Jews." At Sinai the chosenness of the Jews was "through Moses anchored in religion; it became a part of their religious belief."[7] As God had chosen his people, so Moses "had stooped to the Jews"; they were his "chosen people."[8] To Moses, then, the Jews owe their character, their "tenacity," their moralism, and the hostility that their tenaciousness and moralism had met, if not wholly created. Moses first and thereafter "definitely fixed . . . the Jewish type."[9]

Freud had first to emphasize the historicity of the Kairos and its dynamic of repression. The Mosaic religion "exercised influence on the Jewish people *only* when it had become a tradition."[10] The point is the necessity of the event, and the establishment of a historical tradition—the creation of the Jews by the giving of the Law and the occasion of the primal murder—as a psychic constant in the Jewish generations. Kairos created the Jews. It gave them their history. The inner meaning of kairotic history remains true and operative to this day, according to Freud. It is in this sense that the Jews may be said to have kept a tradition, and tradition may be said to have kept the Jews. Freud thinks it did not matter that the Jews once renounced their religion, the teaching of Moses. Renunciation confirmed the religion, "the tradition remained."[11]

Freud understood the historicity of the idea, however, in a very specific way. Meaning is polarized as inner and outer. All meaning is historical. But inner meaning is the psychological pole; outer meaning is contextual, eventual. Outer meaning "reproduces" inner in an infinite variety of events. The eventual reproduces the psychological. The outer process, deprived of its autonomy, documents the inner.

If for the great historians of the nineteenth century, it is ideas that work themselves out as events, for Freud it is psychic states that work themselves out as events. A comparison of the systems of social causation of Freud, Marx, and Weber may be useful at this point. If we may list the levels of

6. *Moses and Monotheism*, 166–67.
7. Ibid., 168–69.
8. Ibid., 73.

9. Ibid., 69.
10. Ibid., 201. (My italics.)
11. Ibid., 81.

causation as (1) *idea*, (2) *psychic state*, (3) *event*, Freud may be said to locate the genesis of both ideas and events in psychic states. A famous example of this location might be taken from the Freudian literature on culture history and religion, from one of the most brilliant and perhaps the most relevant of Freud's epigoni, Erich Fromm. For Fromm, prior to Protestantism as both idea and event is Anxiety. The former is finally reducible to a symptom of the latter, as for Freud prior to Christianity as both idea and event was the psychic state of guilt.

It would be unfair to say that Marx locates the genesis of both ideas and psychic states in concrete events. The early Marx, at least, reconciled all three levels of historical causation in the dialectical unity of consciousness and existence. Nevertheless, Weber alone clearly rejects an ontological emphasis. He is a causal pluralist, asserting the autonomy of the three levels. Ideas may be said to be autonomous, for Weber, as they may originate as the spontaneous insight of a charismatic man. In turn, once having located the autonomy of ideas in the existence of a genius, Weber notes that ideas may become premium systems for the selection of useful psychic states, out of the multiple psychic states available in a culture. The event, in turn, has a logic of its own, turning ideas and psychic states to unforeseen uses. Thus Weber arrives at his most delicate evasion, in a lifetime of delicate evasions, in the problem of social causation: the irony of history, the surprising thrust of the unintended consequence, so much ignored and despised by other sociologists but nevertheless crucial to Weber.

For Freud, there is nothing that is eventual except as it is the outer meaning of the psychological. Outer meanings are to be subsumed under inner. This is to say, history operates, in the first instant, in terms of its inner, psychological articulation. It is only in this sense that Freud could write of "historical truth." The eventuality of the suffering Redeemer, for example, is, as event, quite secondary to the inner meaning of the redemptory role. Psychologically, the Redeemer is always the same tragic hero, "the chief rebel and leader" against the Primal Father. "If there was no such leader [historically], then [e.g.] Christ was the heir of an unfulfilled wish-phantasy." If, on the other hand, the hero was an event, the (e.g., Christ) was one of a number to take the role, the "successor" to it, the "reincarnation" of it.[12] Thus, social action is ambiguous. It expresses itself as an action-myth. To understand an action, one must understand its "inner source," the "secret motives"[13] that are the psychological meaning informing it.

There are other evidences of the elaboration of historical meaningfulness into primary inner-psychological, and secondary, outer-eventual, a distor-

12. Ibid., 140. Here is Freud's basic insight into the structure of myth. A myth may be defined as an action narrative, containing, in interrelation, both the elements of meaning, the inner-psychological and the outer-historical. *Moses and Monotheism* is in this sense a study in the structure and meaning of myth.

13. Ibid., 18.

tion and disguise of the inner. Whole structures of institutions are projections of psychic states. Freud called institutions such as the "institution of remembrance festivals," and totem feasts, collective "screen-memories." [14]

The history of religions gives Freud further evidence of the dynamic interplay of inner and outer meaning. Christianity, for Freud, is a "Son religion." Judaism is a "Father religion." Christianity, in terms of its inner meaning, is the institutionally organized remembrance and recurrence of the deposing of the father by the son. In Freud's construct, Judaism stands for the true Father, against the spurious assumption by the Christians of his Son. The Christian tradition is the recurrent filial revolt, "just as in those dark times every son had longed to do." [15] But the fate of Christianity is that it cannot escape Judaism, any more than the son can escape the father.

In the inner beginning, then, was the primal crime, reproducing itself historically in the persons of Moses and Jesus. Why not then a Moses or Jesus every generation if Christ is the "resurrected Moses and the returned primeval father"? [16] We must turn, therefore, to the doctrine of the psychic trinity—Father, Son, and People—according to Freud.

Both Moses and Christ are vessels of ambivalence in the mythos of history. Thus Christ is constructed, in one sense, as the Incarnate God, Father of the rebellious sons (the People—who must kill him), thus recapitulating the primal crime. In another sense, equally true, Christ is the Son of Man, facing and suffering the Father God. Here the Father of the people becomes as well the Son, dying by the wish of the Father. This is the double role of all tragic heroes, Oedipus and Hamlet as well as Moses and Christ: to die the representative deaths of both sons and fathers. This is, for Freud, the most profound meaning of the scapegoat mechanism, and thus, for example, of anti-Semitism.

The question of a continuous reproduction of the Kairos remains. Freud, indeed, believed the Mosaic Kairos to have a special inner meaning for Western culture. It reproduced the model crime (the killing of the primal father), for the historical consciousness of Western culture. It is safe to conclude, then, that there can be but one Kairos. Each subsequent Kairos is epigonal (e.g., Moses, Christ), and thus more and more spurious, inauthentic, at least unrevealing of any new psychic states. (Here the idea of epigonal Kairos may be assimilated to the Marxist understanding of history as repetition, first as tragedy, then as farce. See the great opening passages of *The Eighteenth Brumaire*.)

On the other hand, each Kairos is new and unique in its contextual mask. Calvary is not Sinai, even if the inner meaning is the same and Christ is simply a resurrected Moses. It is more important to emphasize, however, that every Kairos is a recurrence, the return of the repressed, the latest return of the ever-same. Returning "from the forgotten past," the primal crime

14. Ibid., 133.   15. Ibid., 141.   16. Ibid., 145.

"produces an incomparably strong influence on the mass of mankind, and puts forward an irresistible claim to be believed."[17] Freud is not interested in the truth of the claim. Rather, the truth of the claim is the power of the claim itself.

Religion itself, for Freud, is something quite different from Kairos. It is a neurotic elaboration of the power of Kairos, much like the impact of a charismatic leader among the masses. Within its liturgy and dogma, religion, like mass politics, seeks to routinize Kairos by reproducing it ritualistically. Freud seemed to believe that religions and significant political movements cannot originate except in Kairos, nor live except off its kairotic capital in terms of ritualist manipulation of interest in the Kairos. (Thus, Henry Wallace attempted to manipulate what he thought to be a Rooseveltian Kairos.) The capital of the Kairos must serve the investment of the epigone in it. If, in Marxian terms, one wishes to translate Freudianism into a bourgeois thought form, capital may be said to be fetishized in a psychological form. Kairos is funded capital, in bourgeois categories, or, in feudal terms, an entailed estate. It is in this sense that Weber thought of the grace manufactured by the Catholic saints as the church's investment for the future. The problem of salvation may well be discussed in terms of the economics of grace.

Kairos, coming up out of the past, breaks with revolutionary power against the present. Freud recognized the past as true, as Marx recognized it as only ideologically true, and only true for the revolutions before the proletarian. Freud recognized the conservative character of all revolutions, as Marx recognized their progressive character. In Freud's "shortest formula," the dialectically conservative character of revolutionary movements, like the traditionalism of the prophets, illustrates again "the well-known *duality* of . . . history."[18] Freud is far from astonished that in revolutions, particularly the most recent, for him the Russian and the Nazi, "progress has concluded an alliance with barbarism." It is only the resurgence of the past that preempts the present for the spurious future.[19] The starting points of progress are always at the return, in shifting contexts, of the repressed.

17. Ibid., 136.
18. Ibid., 84. Freud's image of history as almost a Manichaean ambivalance is clearest in this passage: there are always "*two peoples* who fuse together to form one nation, *two kingdoms* into which this nation divides, two names for the Deity in the source of the Bible." And to this he must add two new dualities, discovered by himself: "the founding of *two* new religions, the first one ousted by the second and yet reappearing victorious, *two* founders of religions, who are both called by the same name Moses and whose personalities we have to separate from each other. And all these dualities are necessary consequences of the first": the presence or absence of Kairos. "One section of the [Jewish] people passed through what may properly be termed a traumatic experience which the other was spared." (Freud's italics.)
19. Ibid., 89. Here Freud provides the sociology of revolution with its most penetrating insight: that revolution is precisely that event which allows the most archaic to bisect the most recent accumulations in the psychic state of man. Freud thought the Bolshevik and Fascist

Then, the Christian revolution, for example, is reactionary, if the term is understood correctly, at the same time and for the same reason that it is progressive. Christianity advanced beyond Judaism precisely so far as Christ was the surrogate, not alone of the resurrected Moses, but also of the returned Father. Paul, when he developed the doctrine of original sin as the "murder of the Father who later was deified,"[20] and the doctrine of guilt and salvation in the Son who was also scapegoat, advanced Christianity beyond Judaism to the extent that he executed a greater regression. Here Freud has made the role of the regressor-prophet Paul the most crucial to the dynamization of Christianity into a socially significant tradition. The Christian doctrine of salvation is fundamentally Paul's own ideological screen of regression. To the extent that Freud believed there was in Judaism no idea of salvation by the admission of guilt, to that extent Freud seemed to show more sympathy for that neurosis than for its inherently hostile child.[21] Like the dominant schools of modernist sociologists of religion, including Weber and Klausner, Freud identified Christ as a Jewish revival. The break, he believed, is located in Paul, as the figure who pushed the regression beyond the revival.

It is a further illustration of his location of inner meaning in history that Freud concludes that the Christian tradition must be anti-Semitic. Freud de-

---

revolutions examples of this dialectical unity between progress and retrogression, though perhaps he was too naïvely impressed with notions that Mussolini had "educated," however regressively, the Italians to run their trains on time and that the Bolsheviks had truly deprived their subjects of "the anodyne religion" and had been "wise enough to grant them a reasonable measure of sexual freedom" (see ibid., 90), however primitively cruel had been the coercion to freedom.

20. Ibid., 139.

21. Ibid., 141–41. Freud's debt to the modernists is plain. What early theological training he had in the Jewish community was not very useful. "My youth was spent in a period when our freeminded teachers of religion placed no value on their pupils' acquisition of knowledge in the Hebrew languages and literature" (quoted by A. A. Brill, *Freud's Contribution to Psychiatry* [New York: W. W. Norton & Co., 1944], 195–96). Freud considered himself as "little an adherent of the Jewish religion as of any other." Like Weber, he considered himself religiously unmusical. "I consider them all most important as objects of scientific interest, but I do not share the emotional feeling that goes with them." Freud's religious unmusicality, however, did not contradict his community with Jewry. A famous passage in the literature of consolation of secular Jewry reads: "I have always had a strong feeling of kinship with my race and have always nurtured the same in my children" (quoted from a letter to the editor of the *Judische Presszentrale* [Zurich], 26 February 1925). Nevertheless, his "scientific" passion for religion was great. As early as 1911, in a letter quoted by Brill (op. cit., p. 192), Freud declared he "was extraordinarily absorbed in the study of the psychology of religion." The absorption lasted a lifetime. His last book was *Moses and Monotheism*. In another school of analysis, older than Freud's, Freud's concentration on the meaning of Fatherhood and the Father-God-Son triad would have been interpreted as a well-known expression of a religious type, the "God-intoxicated man," the famous phrase used by Novalis to describe the excommunicate Jew Spinoza.

velops a specific analysis, in *Moses and Monotheism,* of the necessary anti-Semitism of the Christian tradition. It will be summarized here as further illustration of the constructs described above.

The irresistible claim of the Christian Kairos to be believed is to be understood rightly as the claim of the original killing of the primal father, of which all Kairoi are outworks. Anti-Semitism is the process of resentment by those personalities influenced by the Christian Kairos. It is a resentment against those who will not admit their guilt and thus seem somehow outside of and dangerous to a community held together in some significant measure by guilt. The Jews, Freud observed, refuse to admit their guilt. "The poor Jewish people, who with its usual stiff-necked obduracy continued to deny the murder of their 'father' [i.e., the inner meaning being equivalent to the primal father, the outer meaning to Christ], has dearly expiated this in the course of centuries. Over and over again they heard the reproach: You killed our God." Freud concludes: "And this reproach is true, if rightly interpreted. It says in reference to the history of religion: 'You won't *admit* that you murdered God' (i.e., the archetype of God, the primaeval Father and his reincarnations)."[22]

Thus, he concluded, Christianity, in its inner meaning, is anti-Semitic. A major cause of anti-Semitism is not, as some would have it, the resistance of Christians to Christianity. Rather it is the acceptance of the inner meaning of Christianity, of its essence, that works anti-Semitism.

However, Freud's construction of psychoanalytic truth allows him to assert that the reverse is equally true. He conceives of the rebellion against both Father and Son, Judaism and Christianity, to be a dynamic of anti-Semitism. The pagan character, never thoroughly restructured by a religion that was missionized politically, has always sought to unburden itself of Christianity by the displacement of anti-Semitism. Thus one can understand in Freudian terms that the spearhead of anti-Semitism in Germany developed as a cultus of Teutonic paganism. If the Christians did not powerfully resist anti-Semitism, the most active anti-Semites were those seeking a regression to pagan culture, or at least a compromise of Christianity as a Son religion by rechristening Christ a Nordic.

There are important weaknesses in the Freudian reconstruction of the genesis of political society. The chief critical point to be made is at the problem of the concept of Kairos as meaning the primal-father murder. Freud has picked and chosen without regard to all the data. The father-murder myth is but one theme in myth literature. In the myth material available—and myth was for Freud the link between social and life-history, social and individual psychology—the fratricide image stands beside the parricide image. It is difficult to choose the one to the exclusion of the

22. *Moses and Monotheism,* 145.

other. If the images of the parricide theme—Oedipus and the other regicide characters of the drama—stride so movingly across the universal stage, the images of the fratricide theme—the sons of Oedipus, Joseph and his brothers, Cain and Abel, Arthur and his Knights, the Trojan peers, the *Niebelungen*, indeed, all the brothers and sisters who have been so fatal to one another—stride across the same stage, equally moving in the myth mind.

A third myth rises to complicate the Freudian selection: the Abraham myth (cf. Kierkegaard, *Fear and Trembling*). In it, it is the father who kills the son, not the son who kills the father. And, as we have noted before, the propitiatory sacrifice of the Son of God (Moses, Christ), on behalf of his sinful people, must be viewed as much a Son-killing as a Father-killing. That the killing of the Son of Man by his own brothers, the masses, may be viewed as commanded by a more primary Father, God, appears only as a sublimated solution of the scapegoat mechanism as a fratricide.

The great murder myth of the Old Testament is the killing of the primal brother by the primal brother. The first moral question of Western politics, as expressed in the story of Cain and Abel, seems to have been not, as Freud insists, "Am I my father's son?" Rather, the primal question was: "Am I my brother's keeper?"

In terms of the primal-murder myth, it is the war of brothers, not the revolt against the tyranny of fathers, that is the psychological origin-condition of man's social existence.[23] *Hamlet* can perhaps be read, psychoanalytically, in a way neither Freud nor Ernest Jones considered. After all, it is the killing of the brother that is the demiurge of the plot. Claudius himself instructs Hamlet, in their first scene, that nature's most "common theme is death of fathers . . . from the first corpse till he that died today." But the first corpse was a brother. The primal curse is the usurpation of the throne by fratricide. Hamlet sees the horror of brother against brother. The ghost— the dead father who is, more important, the brother—bids Hamlet: "Remember me." What the ghost reveals is the fratricide, and fratricide is what is rotten in the state of Denmark. Freud seems to have been deaf to the meaning of fratricide, although it fairly shouted at him in his brilliant analysis of *Lear* and of the ninth of Grimm's Fairy Tales, *The Twelve Brothers*. Instead he writes as he rarely wrote, belaboring the obvious: the symbolism of death as dumbness in myth literature.

But the primal war of brothers is accounted for in Freud's basic myth of the origin of the polity. He was led to assert, finally, a "sort of . . . social

23. However, for a presumption of the equivalence of the father and the brother murder myth and totem supporting the Freudian presumption cf. Freud's mentor in these matters, Sir J. G. Frazer, *Creation and Evolution in Primitive Cosmogonies* (London: Macmillan, 1935), 17–18. According to Frazer, in primitive cosmogonies the subject of the myth and the totem animal may be, evidently indifferently, either father or brother.

contract" theory.[24] The contract, he thought, came out of a Malthusian calculation of the value of scarce resources and the necessity of restraint, in this case the value of the female commodity in a scarcity situation. But even the hard light of the economic-sex calculus cannot spoil the grandeur of Freud's myth of the origins of society. In the social contract of brothers there came into being the first true society—that based on the renunication of instinctual gratification. The establishment of man came through an act of renunciation.

The act of renunciation is at once the establishment of man in society and of the Father as God. The war of the generations ends in the deification of the dead Father and in the socializing guilt of the brothers. Men, as a band of brothers, stand at the genesis of society when they renounce their aspirations to become, each above all, the supreme Father. Renouncing the promise of being the godlike Father on earth, they worship the Father they have murdered (e.g., the primal father, then, Moses, Christ, et al.) as God in heaven. God, according to Freud, is the positive projection of the act of renunciation. Then man is by nature, at his origins, a killer, and religion is the history of his guilt. Freud aimed to cure man of his guilt and thus to abolish the history of it. (51:1)

24. *Moses and Monotheism*, 132.
Reprinted from *Humanities and Society* 4, nos. 2 & 3 (Spring & Summer 1981): 197–201.

10

Intimations of Therapeutic Truth:
Decoding Appendix G in *Moses and Monotheism*

The essence of the decoding procedure . . . lies in the fact that the work of interpretation is not brought to bear on the dream as a whole but on each portion of the dream's content independently, as though the dream were a geological conglomerate in which each fragment of rock required a separate assessment.

Sigmund Freud

An endlessly critical culture game is the play characteristic of modern intellectuals so far as they no longer claim to arrive at a commanding truth, but only at a therapeutic interpretation. Bound as it is to be replayed here and elsewhere, the game calls for me to take as my text for decoding the curious passages on "*historical* truth" and "eternal *truth*": Appendix G of *Moses and Monotheism*. Note that the italics are Freud's, not mine. Here we see our greatest player arriving so near the commanding truth that it appeared to him therapeutic. Freud suffered from a myopia in this matter that amounted to his genius. Misreading the object of the game, he tried to play it, on our behalf, to an unrepeatable end: one in which truth and therapy merge, like God and man in an older mythology.

Appendix G is Freud's final assault upon repetition, the form of faith. *Moses and Monotheism* in its entirety constitutes an effort to decode eternal truth in such a way that there is at least the ghost of a chance that it will become merely historical—and therefore resolvable. Playing for a fantastic stake, eternal truth, I shall try to decode Freud's decoding. Really, there is nothing to lose in this kind of game. All the players, if they play at all, must come out winners. What else is critical intellect about, if not these endless recensions of such texts as supply the players with the source of their criticism? Unless otherwise noted, page references, the sources of my criticism following, are to the *Standard Edition*, volume 13, pages 127–32, Appendix G, titled "Historical Truth."

"*Historical* truth" directs human conduct when it is transferred by indirection into "tradition"—that is, when *historical* truth becomes repressive, through the shaming, forgetful affect of the retreat from popular consciousness of a thoroughly defeated and consequently unrecognized interdictory figure (pp. 127–28): in this case, the figure of Moses. "Meaning" in history is implicit in "tradition," as the working through of defeated interdicts— what is not to be believed, yet in time believed. Tradition is to society as repression is to character; an unrepressive history would be a meaningless one; an unrepressed mind would do, instantly, whatever came into it. Historical memory repeats interdictory truth, elaborated by cadres recognizing their interdictory figure, made internal as character. The defeat of tradition is tantamount to puerility of character.

How does a tradition live through time? The history of a high culture is the thrust downward of its highest excuse for existence by an interdictory elite. Tradition is conveyed by generations of interdictory cadres directing meanings as if they were dreams from above. These dreams derive from their store of experienced obediences to commands of the defeated interdictory figure. In this manner of transmission, historical truth may be understood as the slow return of a repressive teaching administered by patient generations representing their defeated teacher.

There must be "some other factor" present in the return of what has been repressed as *historical* truth (p. 128). What "other factor" can there possibly be, except that metamorphosis of guilt into knowledge, *guilt/knowledge*, consequent upon the primal crime and its repetitions? That repetitive "other factor" pointed to the limit of *historical* truth: but it was a limit Freud would find it most difficult to accept. To his way of thinking, only "pious believers" have no difficulty in divining a "portion of the eternal *truth* which, long concealed, came to light at last and was then bound to carry everyone along with it" (p. 129). Note that Freud has remarked, immediately before, that what he calls "the idea of a single god" is only a *portion* of the "eternal *truth*" and, moreover, that that idea "produced such overwhelming effect on men *because* it is a portion of the eternal truth" (p. 129; my italics added). Here, "at last," is that mysterious other factor, "something that matches the magnitude both of the subject and of its effect" (p. 129).

Immediately, however, Freud withdrew from this advance by what is interdictory toward his own intellect; he faltered just at the moment when eternal *truth* is that to which *historical* truth points. That that latter truth, as symbol, is what it represents is precisely the truth of symbolism Freud denies, in this case, in order to admit it into his theory. So historical and eternal truth are separated at their crux.

At this crux, Freud did not admit into his theoretical effort his own metapsychology, where historical truths come to rest eternally in the "death instinct." He retreated to his own most cherished preference: to "assume the right to correct a certain distortion to which this [for him, both repeatedly metapsychological and entirely historical truth] has been subjected on its return." Eternal truth is reduced to a "certain distortion" of historicity by Freud's final effort, in his *Moses*, to deny its return into his own mind—to resolve it by therapeutic explanation—by (1) the indirective (that is, distorting) myth he has constructed for it; and by (2) the interdictory figure who bequeaths his will as historically ordained—worked-through—"meanings" that are equivalent to repressions, or what I have called the metamorphosis *guilt/knowledge*.

Freud reduced eternal *truth* to its repeated interdictory transfiguration, repressive historicity, and at the same time raised his interdictory figures to truths eternal in their repetitiveness. By this doubly negational strategy, Freud tried to resolve eternal truth into its historicity and release us, as his contemporaries, from the directedness of that historicity: its repeated interdictory development as character. So his essays on Moses might have been titled, had Freud been self-defeated enough to be more direct and conscious of his purpose, "How the Jews Acquired Their Character."

Why should "historical truth" repeatedly "return"—indeed, until our own time, never fail to "return"? Freudian theory would make its users complicit in a historicity become therapeutic; those returns of what is interdictory, in its figures, are created by the dynamics of our own *guilt/knowledge*; advances in intellectuality ordain further renunciations of instinct; pieties of obedience to what is interdictory are identifiable as belief; critical intellect is self-defeated as "pious argument" (p. 129). In Freud's therapeutic reworking, historical truth became impious argument, a repetition of what is interdictory for the sake of its resolution.

Freud's theory of our unconscious historicity raises hope for a qualitatively different advance in intellectuality, the opposite in affect of all earlier advances. To see eternal *truth* as a "pious" version of *historical* truth depends upon a conceptualization of historical repetition as neurotic contemporaneity. The theoretical steps may be as follows: make over repeated returns of what is interdictory into a repressive mechanism; make primal repression metapsychologically equivalent to historic *guilt/knowledge*; make what was great in the past small in the present. We are left with a storied, generation-burdened sentence which transforms the towering presence of the past into the small neurotic of the present: "We do not believe that there is a single great god today, but that in primaeval times there was a single person who was found to appear huge at that time and who afterwards returned in men's memory elevated to divinity" (p. 129).

In such a way, *historical* truth may be made resolutive instead of reproductive. Psychoanalytically toned, historical unconsciousness joined the modernist movement to abolish itself. You may see this movement take its abolitionist direction no less well, and certainly with at least equal bemusement, in Joyce's *Ulysses* as in Freud's *Moses*. Joyce took the cultures of the European past as one vast rubbish heap and recycled its dead artifacts into movements of his own mind that amount, in their incredible detail, to a vast emptiness. Freud's *Moses* amounts to an equally gigantic nullity. The "idea of a single great god—an idea which must be recognized as a completely justified memory" (p. 130), emerges as the first of many murders of figures of authority. That memory of a murder, both true and distorted, has had a "compulsive character" (p. 130). But even as it extended its command over the Jewish character, forming it, the idea was "distorted [and] may be described as a *delusion*" (p. 130). What happens when this ancient delusion is worked over yet again, as material for an analytic essay or two? Nothing remains, in those essays, of the huge apparatus of Mosaic tradition. The commanded acts, the illuminative relations of daily life to the "idea of a single great god," are treated in that dismissive phrase: "effects of a compulsive character." Both the psychical and external realities of living inside the Mosaic, or any other, dispensation are put into different perspective when *historical* truth is so deeply understood that even its distortions are "recognized" and "completely justified" as a socially functioning "delusion." What was once there and, in its thereness, "*must* be believed," must now lose its "compulsive character," except in new truth, so compulsive in its own way that Freud declared, at the beginning of his *Moses*, nothing could induce him to put it aside.

In the compulsive character of this new truth, it is Freud, not Moses, who commands a return of the authoritative, character-forming past, but this time resolutive rather than reproductive. Freud's new truth, offered in the form of a book, commands us to nothing except belief in its critical argument. Freud's new truth embraces, in a pitiless and suffocating Yes, not unlike the Yes in the last and punishing forty pages of Joyce's *Ulysses*, both *historical* truth and eternal *truth*. It is in their own works, as art or science, that truth now resides. "Insofar as it brings a return of the past, it must be called the *truth*" (p. 130). This is exact, more exact than Freud himself knew, I reckon. Here, in a terminal truth, is the end of "pious argument," of "pious solution," of "optimistic and idealistic premise" (p. 129). Superior to *historical* truth, as repetitions of eternal *truth*, is yet another: *therapeutic truth*. Appendix G, decoded, is an exercise in *therapeutic truth*. That truth, long concealed in its antecedent forms, eternal and historical, comes to light at last in the critically modern culture game which has carried everyone along with it. True moderns do not believe even in their criticism; that criticism is too ephemeral for belief and is mounted only to lead to criticism of the criticism. Of course, there is piety in this practice of endless criticism— this "we do not believe." *Moses and Monotheism* is one of the most pious works in the canon of modernist art, I reckon. At Appendix G, negational theology turns fully into historical psychology. That full turn makes the critical climax of the work, the point with which the veil of eternity is finally drawn (cf. another work of modernity, Picasso's "Les Demoiselles d'Avignon"). Then, and only then, what is repetitive need no longer be taken seriously, except as the oldest version of the greatest game. (81:2)

11

Freud Will Fade Only from Faddists' Minds

A short acquaintance approached my dinner table at a local restaurant the other night, planted one fist to steady himself, and, waving his free hand in a gesture of exorcism, said: "You know, Freud is just a passing fancy. He is like Zen Buddhism, a fad. He'll fade." Of course, my acquaintance was slightly drunk, and therefore in a very generous mood, ready to spend his saved-up aggressions. It was one of those specimen crises, a thin slice from the psychopathology of everyday life, that Freud has taught us to expect. With a few more technical words about the differences between theory and practice, the exorcist departed, satisfied that I knew that he knew that he was being provocative. Freud had been dismissed, along with the author of a book on Freud. It is an unfortunate sophistication to which psychoanalysis sometimes tempts its patients, as in this case. In fact, too often nowadays Freud provides the formula behind which the civilized can continue to be uncivilized toward one another.

If Freud should fade, it will be only from the minds of faddists. This is entirely possible, for one way the fashionable remain fashionable is by trying to stay a little ahead of the game; counterfashions are the ultimate weap-

Reprinted from *San Francisco Sunday Chronicle* (21 June 1959): 23.

ons of the miseducated who like their ideas brand new and yet of a quality that does not change their minds. Whether in popular favor or disfavor, Freud remains important, for he thought profoundly about matters that must always concern not merely scholars and scientists but even drunks and diners-out. The psychoanalysts have plenty of customers; what is perhaps more significant, an even greater number of potential patients can think of nowhere else to go. But the permanent influence of Freud depends on a fact of an entirely different order: that Freud embodies the rarest event in our history—a great mind. Those countersnobs who suspect that what is influential cannot have merit are, in this case, as mistaken as the snobs who are capable of finding merit only in what has been declared influential. (59:4)

Religion and Politics
Judaism

12

Disraeli: The Chosen of History
Uniting the Old Jerusalem and the New

George Saintsbury thought not only that Disraeli "founded a remarkable school of fiction," but that his politics were as romantic as his fiction. The most romantic thing in Disraeli was the motivation of both his fiction and his politics, a motivation to be found in his Jewishness—his quite particular kind of Jewishness. For it was not the Jews that claimed Disraeli—Disraeli claimed the Jews. Baptized into the Church of England in what would have been the year of his Bar Mitzvah, Disraeli *chose* not to forget he was a Jew. And it was not simply a reaction to the "hostile consciousness of others," as Sartre would interpret the sense of Jewishness. Rather the hostile consciousness of others was a reaction to his perverse claim to Jewishness.

The hostile consciousness of others can best be read in three unsigned articles, probably written by Goldwin Smith, the Liberal historian and polemicist, printed in consecutive numbers of the *Fortnightly Review* from April through June 1878. "The secret of Lord Beaconsfield's life," Smith wrote, "lies in his Jewish blood. . . . Lord Beaconsfield is the most remarkable illustration of his own doctrine of the ascendancy of Hebrew genius in modern Europe. . . . Certainly a century and a quarter of residence in England on the part of his ancestors and himself has left little trace on the mind and character of Lord Beaconsfield. He is in almost every essential . . . a Jew."

One of the missing essentials was that Disraeli was a member of the Established Church. And yet he played at being a Jew far more seriously than Heine played at not being a Jew. (To play at being a Jew is usually more serious.) Disraeli, who hated the universalist rationalism of his country, refused to be accepted as simply a "man," and yet he was certainly not simply

Reprinted by permission from *Commentary* 13, no. 1 (January 1952): 22–33. All rights reserved.

a Jew. Sartre has developed no category for him, neither "authentic" nor "inauthentic." Disraeli neither fled from nor stayed with his Jewishness: he was pushed out too early to make either choice. But he remained a Jew in a peculiar way that deserves its own study—in his nostalgia.

The critic D. H. Harding has said that the word "nostalgia" ought not to be used "unless the quality of feeling to be described is recognizably similar to the common experience of homesickness, the feeling of distress for no localized, isolated cause, together with a feeling that one's environment is . . . vaguely wrong and unacceptable." Then the word is used quite properly to describe Disraeli. His writing is an expression of an experience recognizably similar to homesickness, and Disraeli certainly felt from the very beginning of his life to the end that his environment was vaguely wrong and unacceptable. His feeling of discomfort in his environment began at home, with his family.

Disraeli's grandfather—Benjamin D'Israeli, merchant, for whom the grandchild was named—came to England from Italy around 1748, when he was eighteen. He joined the Jewish community in London, became a member of the Sephardic synagogue of Bevis Marks, and married a Jewish girl who never pardoned him his name. Her nagging self-hatred in time drove him into retirement, but not before he had made a small fortune. Her only child, Isaac, suffered the burden of never being forgiven for being a little Jew. His existence, writes the second Benjamin in the *Memoir* of his father, "only served to swell the aggregate of many humiliating particulars. [He] was not to be to her a source of joy, or sympathy, or solace. She foresaw for her child only a future of degradation. . . ."

Isaac D'Israeli became a "timid, susceptible" boy, in his youth and early manhood suffering from what his son later decided must be called something other than a physical illness. He put it down, in his famous *Memoir,* as a "failing of nervous energy." Disraeli was amazed that the best medical men for a long while diagnosed his father's illness as "consumption." "The symptoms," he writes, "are physical and moral . . . lassitude and despondency." He knew the case could not have been consumption, for he had had the same symptoms in his own early manhood. The disease was really self-hatred. "One of his few infirmities," Benjamin concludes of his father, "was . . . a deficiency of self-esteem."

Disraeli remembered his grandmother, even in his later life, as "a demon," and the journeys to her home were the horrors of his boyhood. But he came to understand her very well. "My grandmother, the beautiful daughter of a family who had suffered much from persecution, had imbibed that dislike of her race which the vain are too apt to adopt when they find that they are born to public contempt. The indignant feeling that should be reserved for the persecutor, in the mortification of their disturbed sensibility, is too often visited on the victim and the cause of annoyance is recognized not in the ignorant malevolence of the powerful but in the conscientious conviction of the innocent sufferer."

His grandmother, he concluded, was "so mortified by her [Jewishness] that she lived till eighty without indulging in a tender expression." His father became an intellectual, the son of a rich Jew searching for mankind in libraries. He read Bayle and Voltaire, and especially Rousseau. When he had been a young boy he imagined his name was Emile, not Isaac. He was too mild to break with the synagogue, or to marry other than a Jewess. His wife, Maria Basevi, took over the practical affairs of the family and bore him four sons, Benjamin, Raphael, Jacob, and Naphtali, and a daughter, Sarah. Benjamin was born 21 December 1804, "or according to the Jewish reckoning the nineteenth of Tebet, 5565," as his chief biographer, Monypenny, puts it. "On the eighth day the boy was duly initiated into the covenant of Abraham, the rite of circumcision being performed by a relative of his mother's. . . ."

In 1817, when the grandfather died, Isaac agreed to have all his children baptized, and Benjamin was received into the Anglican communion at St. Andrew's Church, Holborn, 31 July 1817. Isaac had grasped at a petty reason to break with the synagogue. He gave it in an essay on "The Genius of Judaism": the "lone and sullen genius of rabbinical Judaism" cut him off "from the great family of mankind." Isaac D'Israeli spent the remainder of his life taking flight into the universal in his library, where he read and puttered all day and most evenings, and wrote such books as *Calamities of Authors*, which sold well to "the middling classes." But he himself did not become a Christian—that was no more "reasonable" than to remain a Jew. And the family name remained the same, D'Israeli. Indeed, D'Israeli had allowed the baptizing of his children only after considerable urging by a gentile friend, the historian Sharon Turner, who convinced him that baptism would help their careers if not their souls. Civil office and much land and business were closed to Jews, not to be opened until Benjamin Disraeli himself helped do so.

There is no evidence that the twelve-year-old boy resisted baptism. Neither is there any sign that he welcomed it. Boys do not usually have opinions on such matters. What had happened was quite simple, and sudden—and, most of all, expedient. But the young Disraeli was certainly aware of his Jewishness. Until the year he was baptized, a man came every Saturday to the Christian school he attended and gave him Jewish religious instruction. When the rest of the boys made their daily prayer, Benjamin had to go to a corner and turn his back, as was the custom developed at that time to take care of this sort of situation.

And there was always his name. Even after he had been received into the Church of England he had to fight his schoolmates to defend his name. The D'Israelis sent him to a Unitarian school, but even there he had to fight and they soon took him home. Benjamin stayed at home, alone, and read hard. The lonely boy decided he would be a famous man, and quickly. After all, Pitt had become prime minister at twenty-one, and Byron a star in Europe's culture at twenty-five. Young Benjamin made himself sick wondering what role to choose in order to be great.

Disraeli's father thought he ought to go into law; at seventeen he was articled to a firm of solicitors in Old Jewry. (A year later he dropped the apostrophe from the spelling of his name.) But he had already discovered another role, which he loved and which was to make him at least famous. He was writing a novel, *Vivian Grey*. And when it appeared it made him the literary lion of London, at twenty-one. *Vivian Grey*—and a period of deep depression—saved him from the law. Still, he could not decide what he was, or even *who* he was.

Troubled, he took his *Wanderjahre*, and returned home, irresolute. His depression drained him until he could not "write a line without effort." He wandered aimlessly about his father's house in "solitude and silence," unable to work enough to break the depression, but doing some reading and thinking. He worried about his appearance. "I grieve to say my hair grows very badly." Now his interest in dress became quite intense. He took to green velvet trousers, a canary-colored waistcoat, low shoes, silver buckles, lace at his wrists, and his hair in ringlets. He made himself into a complete dandy.

He lived "in perfect solitude for eighteen months." And he was "still suffering." It was the malaise his father had once suffered from, but Benjamin understood it better. In his letters, the word "ill" appears often in quotation marks. And his consequent reaction was quite different from his father's. What reading he did was in the history of the Jews. What thinking he did was of the Jews. Though every line was an effort, he began a second novel, to be called *Alroy*, whose hero was a Jew. But he dropped this. He could not be heroic. He began another, *The Young Duke*. The young duke is young Disraeli, and both are quite despairing, even if their despair seems unfashionably Byronic now. "The drooping pen falls from my powerless hand, and I feel—keenly, I feel myself what indeed I am—far the most prostrate of a fallen race."

Finally, the son announced to his father what had been on his mind during the despair of all his solitudes and silences: he proposed to visit Jerusalem. This would be his cure. (Disraeli sent his heroes to Jerusalem to end their malaise.) His announcement was vetoed with all the cold calm his father could muster. Almost twenty years later, in his novel *Tancred, or The New Crusade*, Disraeli imagined how his father must have reacted to his announcement. "Why should Benjamin go to Jerusalem?" the father must have insisted to himself. "Unreasonable boy!" And if he reaches there what does he think he will find? Religious truth? Political justice? Let him read of Jerusalem in travel books for restless young gentlemen. "They tell us what it is, a third-rate city in a strange wilderness." Isaac thought it was a folly, and his wife, who was a practical woman, agreed.

But Benjamin found a way to go. Some wealthy friends, the Austens, financed the trip. And he got as his traveling companion the wealthy fiancé of his sister Sarah, William Meredith. They set out for Jerusalem in June 1830. His trip was an effort to get at himself by traveling back through his past to what he considered to be his beginning. The first important stop after England was Spain, land of the Sephardim. The next, Jaffa. He passed through Ramleh, and rode into Jerusalem in February 1831.

The impact of Jerusalem upon him is recorded in his letters from that place to his sister Sarah; and, at a twenty years' remove, in *Tancred*.

Tancred, troubled young Lord Montacute, having always been fascinated by theology and troubled by the past, goes to find the mystery of that trouble in Palestine; it is his private crusade. If he is to go to the very beginning of his past, a learned Sephardi advises him, he must retrace his steps "from Calvary to Sinai." When the pilgrim comes finally "within sight of Sinai" he is "brooding in dejection, his eyes . . . suffused with tears." Tancred is in a "reverie," the style, at least, if not the condition, in which Disraeli often expressed his own Jewishness—rather, his nostalgia for it. The pilgrim Tancred stands at Sinai. "It was one of those moments of amiable weakness which make us all akin, when sublime ambition, the mystical predispositions of genius, the solemn sense of duty . . . and the dogmas of . . . [religion and] philosophy alike . . . sink into nothingness. The voice of his mother sounded in his ear, and he was haunted by his father's anxious glance. Why was he there? Why was he, the child of a northern isle, in the heart of stony Arabia, far from the scene of his birth and of his duties?"

Disraeli calls it "an awful question." But he thinks he knows the answer he ought to assign to Tancred. The answer is in one of Disraeli's favorite parliamentary devices: the rhetorical question. Was he, then, a stranger there? Uncalled, unexpected, intrusive, unwelcome? Was it a morbid curiosity, or the proverbial restlessness of a sated aristocrat, that had drawn him to these wilds? What wilds? Had he no connection with them? Had he not from his infancy repeated in the congregation of his people the laws which, from the awful summit of these surrounding mountains, the Father of all had himself delivered for the government of mankind? And were not the wanderings of the Jews in the wilderness "the first and guiding history that had been entrusted to his young intelligence, from which it had drawn its first . . . conceptions?" Disraeli decides that Tancred is neither morbid tourist nor jaded young aristocrat. Tancred is here because he was here before he went to other lands. "Why, then, he had a right to be here! He had a connection with these regions; they had a hold upon him." He was not visiting a foreign land, like an educated and refined Hindu curious about Europe. He was visiting his own land, foreign as it was, "his fathers' land." Tancred's most passionate desire was "to penetrate the . . . elder world, and share its . . . divine prerogative. Tancred sighed."

Disraeli, who had written to John Murray that he might never return home, sighed and turned home. On their return trip, Meredith died of small-pox. Sarah never married. Instead, she became her brother's devoted sister. Her brother needed all her devotion. Having failed to find himself in jour-nalism (at twenty-one, he had been important in pushing John Murray to publish a rival to the *Times*) or in novels, Disraeli finally decided on poli-tics—this, while he was still in Jerusalem. He returned to England "in fa-mous condition—better indeed than I ever was in my life and full of hope and courage."

Disraeli was twenty-eight when he returned to England. He was a famous novelist and a bad poet. Most of all, he was a young man of letters with a public, and this had given him a precarious professional income and an an-noying habit of picking up large debts. But his sense of failure was still with him. A sense of failure, and something else, had driven Disraeli to Jerusa-lem. But Jerusalem, at this point, was a dream, and he knew he could have waking greatness only in action—on another blessed plot, that New Israel, this England.

Disraeli's position in English society in 1832, when he first stood for Par-liament, was that of an intellectual, a dandy, an exotic. His novels had made him important to a society that, after all, did read novels. And his dandyism had made him even more ingratiating to a world that was, after all, a world of fashion. But the relation of the dandy to high society was that of a pacesetter of fashion who was also an outsider. The dandy might well be an aristocrat born, but if, like Disraeli, he was not one, he was never quite accepted—nor quite rejected.

"To enter high society, a man must have either blood, millions, or a ge-nius." Disraeli thought he had at least genius. And he was in a hurry. He sought out the great with a purpose: to be great with them. They represented action and power. There was only one aristocracy above the English—the Jews', the universal, eternal aristocracy.

Disraeli used dandyism to legitimate his exoticism, which was his Jew-ishness. His dandyism merged with his Jewishness. This was the image the public had of him all his life, or at least until he became Lord Beaconsfield. The combination, Jew-dandy, gave him a name as a *farceur*, and he remains forever the Jew at play, overdressed and tongue in cheek, piping a cynical tune. Nothing about him was assumed to be true—except his Jewishness.

The diarist Wilfred Blunt decided Disraeli's Jewishness was the only real thing about him: "Aesthetically our good Jew was a terrible Philistine; and politically . . . a very complete *farceur*. I don't like to call him anything worse than that. . . . Only you cannot persuade me that he even for an instant took himself seriously as a British statesman, or expected any . . . to accept him so. His *Semitic* principles of course were genuine enough. For his fearlessness in avowing these I hold him in esteem—for a Jew ought to be a Jew. . . . [But] the wonder is that anyone should have been found to take him seriously . . . after such beginnings as his had been."

Disraeli's exaggerated Jewishness was a pleasure, a revenge, a resource. It was the center of his strength. Disraeli, wrote Emma Lazarus, had inherited and cultivated the pose of the Jew, "the simulated patience to submit to [humiliation, defeat, and brutality] without flinching, while straining every nerve and directing every energy to the aim of retaliation and revenge." Emma Lazarus thought Disraeli shared with Shylock, as a representative Jew of the Diaspora, "the rebellion of a proud heart embittered and perverted by brutal humiliations, and the consequent thirst for revenge, the astuteness, the sarcasm, the pathos, the egotism, and the cunning of the Hebrew usurer." As in Shylock, she found in Disraeli "the poetic, Oriental imagination dealing in tropes and symbols, the energy, or rather now the obstinacy, of will, the intellectual superiority, the peculiarly Jewish strength . . . not only to perceive and make the most of every advantage of their situation and temperament, but also, with marvelous adroitness, to transform their very disabilities into new instruments of power."

Disraeli's pose gave him his perfect grip on himself. But the price of a perfect pose is to be unknown, alone, and this was the rock-bottom price he had to pay for power. An outsider—an intellectual of sorts, a Jew of sorts—cannot let the insiders get too close to him. It would only deepen their suspicion or, at least, their confusion about him. And confusion is the same thing as suspicion in politics.

Disraeli was an opportunist. This did not strike him as being unethical, only political. He made no bones about his opportunism. After silence, it was the highest law of politics. If he was unfair to Peel in the famous debates in which he destroyed his party leader and opened the way to make over the Tories under his own leadership, he was unfair with a clear eye that this was his main, perhaps his only, chance. Politics is a game of time. And times change. Peel knew that, too. But Disraeli knew it better. When Peel attempted to change the Tory protectionist policy, Disraeli rose to defend it. It was his chance to separate the Tories from their leader, and he made the most of it. He became the leader the protectionists had to accept, finally. No one else could speak so well for them.

But this was later, after Disraeli had been elected to the House. His first stand, in 1832, failed. He was too suspect. Neither party took him seriously. Opinion had it that he was a Radical. Disraeli failed as well in his second stand, and in his third, and in his fourth. By this time he had decided to be a Tory. Failure makes conservatives out of near-radicals.

The Conservative party was in a quandary when Disraeli entered it;

"having rejected all respect for antiquity, it offers no redress for the present, and makes no preparation for the future." Disraeli gave English Conservatism in the nineteenth century its program and its purpose. To prepare for the future, a political movement must return to its past. So Disraeli believed all his life; he was a dynamic conservative. And the conception of a return to the past organized his own energies, if it did not supply them.

Disraeli's "active and real ambition" was to be a great man, even prime minister of Victoria's England. As his fiction was in some measure a nostalgia for his Jewishness, so his political ideology was founded on nostalgia for a past that Britain, like himself, perhaps, had never had.

Disraeli made the return to the past the guiding principle of his politics. The program of "Young England"—the label of his ideas before they acquired the later label "Imperialism"—was avowedly old: "To change back the oligarchy into a generous aristocracy round a real throne; to infuse life and vigor into the Church, as the trainer of the nation . . . to establish a commercial code [this is the age of child-labor capitalism] . . . to elevate the physical as well as the moral condition of the people, by establishing that labor required regulation [that is, protection] as much as property; and all this by the use of ancient forms and the restoration of the past rather than by political revolutions founded on abstract ideas."

This is how Disraeli viewed his political religion, from the perspective of the general preface to the 1870 edition of his novels. The return to the past—the program of Young England—was at once the expression and the distortion of his nostalgia for his lost Jewishness. Disraeli wanted to unite the aristocracy and the masses against the Whig oligarchy and the upper middle classes. He viewed the crown and the aristocracy as the protectors of the people, with the Established Church as the propaganda department—the praying section—of the state. In turn, legislation had to be careful not to cut the basis of power out from under the aristocracy. Disraeli well understood that property was power in his time: he became a corn protectionist to keep it so. What was needed was a hierarchy with sensibility, and with a sense of *noblesse oblige;* "an aristocracy that leads . . . since Aristocracy is a fact." But that Democracy—the mass age—was coming was equally a fact. Then let it be led by that older, and higher, fact—Aristocracy. In any case, this was good politics for aristocratic parties.

The industrialists and the commerical oligarchy must be rapacious in business, and so must be irresponsible in government. The Whigs cannot care for the people. Rather, they have divided England into two nations, the rich and the poor. By the *coup* of 1832, the Whigs had finally set up the dictatorship of the bourgeoisie. "To acquire, to accumulate, to plunder . . . to propose a Utopia to consist of *Wealth* and *Toil*, this has been the breathless business of enfranchised England for the last twelve years [since 1832] until we are startled from our voracious strife by the wail of intolerable serf-age." The Whigs, according to Disraeli, had made modern history the ugly history of class struggle. But it need not be that way. A dedicated elite could change modern history. Capitalism, which is Whiggery to Disraeli, has divorced the idea of property and power from the idea of duty, and thus has divorced power from responsibility. But in the English past, responsibility was joined with power. The connecting link was a dedicated elite. Dedication is, after all, the price an elite ought to pay for its power and for its property.

Chartism was the first answer of the English masses to industrial capitalism. Among the politicians of the time, Disraeli alone was not afraid to hear it. He almost welcomed it. He thought the alliance of the true gentlemen and the good people was perhaps just around the corner. Let the sheep and the shepherds together stand off the wolves. This was Disraeli's program, and he tried to educate the Tory party to it. He was a first-rate teacher, but somehow the lessons failed to get across. His pupils were inclined to another tactic: to domesticate the wolves, who seemed to them much more manly than Disraeli. The Whigs, after all, were of the gentry. So the Tories refused to become Disraeli's gentlemen: they suspected that Disraeli did not know, really, what a gentleman was. He never belonged at Brooks's. And if he belonged at the Carlton—in fact to become enshrined there—he had to mount a great deal of pressure to get in. Even his friend Bentinck did not think he was a sportsman. Certainly, Disraeli knew little about horses.

But he knew more and cared more about politics. It was almost all of his life. Politics made his life successful, he thought. And he played politics everywhere, even where there was no politics. Disraeli was a completely political man. After race, all was politics.

As a political man with the common touch, Disraeli knew, before most of his contemporaries, the value of public opinion. He called it the "cry," and he always knew how to "play with a cry," as he put it. The novelist turned politician was an early modern master of mass manipulation and the first modern politician to assert the supremacy of his art. He used the press, then the most powerful means of mass manipulation, as no other politician before him. And he was proud of his craft. "I am a Knight of the Press," he once said, "and have no other escutcheon." This was rare in an age when politics still demanded escutcheons of a more biological, or, at least, economic, sort.

Disraeli discovered how to manage that new political integer, the People. One got along with the People in the same way one must get along with women—say, Queen Victoria. The trick, of course, is to flatter them; in fact, "to lay it on with a trowel." They will know it is flattery, but will love it anyway. Disraeli's best advice to politicians was always: "Talk to women.

Talk to women as much as you can. This is the best school. This is the way to gain fluency, because you need not care what you say, and had better not be sensible."

If Disraeli gave Conservatism a grip on the public, he equally made Conservatism legitimate for the intellectuals, who are always anti-public. The point is clearer when American Toryism is compared with the British variety. As Crane Brinton has said, American Toryism is "dull and stuffy, singularly lacking in intellectual graces." Robert Taft is not quite bright enough to attract the bright young people, and Catholicism, in America, is still Irish. Disraeli gave English Toryism grace. He added books to good tobacco, drawings, and the University, even though he himself did not smoke and had not attended a university. Disraeli made politics respectable for young gentlemen, semi-skilled intellectuals, and old ladies who love literature. The image of the literate Conservative is Disraeli's work, after Burke.

The man who remade Conservative politics almost failed to become a politician. The cry "Shylock!" rose to meet him as he rose to speak. The public was put off by his "physiognomy," which seemed to them "strictly Jewish." If it was not "Shylock!" the alternative greeting was "old clothes!" And some of his opponents declared to their audiences, in asides, that they could not "pronounce his name aright."

Disraeli did not complain. He could not. In any case, he had already formulated the ruling motto of his life: "Never complain, never explain." Rather, he returned insult for insult. He gained a reputation for being a very insulting young man. Later, when he was older, his reputation was as a mysterious reservoir of cynical truculence. Aristocratic ladies, in their memoirs, list as one of their constant fears that they would come under Disraeli's wrath.

After four tries, Disraeli was elected to the House of Commons from Maidstone in 1837. He stayed forty years. But the first speech of perhaps the greatest parliamentary orator of the nineteenth century ended as a humiliating farce. The hostile members met him with hoots and catcalls. It was the laughter, however, that brought him down to his seat, his speech unfinished. But his final words were a taunt he was to make good: "I sit down, but the time will come when you will hear from me."

Much of what England heard from Disraeli is outside the limits of this essay. Its task is rather to follow the voice to its origins, that is, to Disraeli as Jew.

On the surface, Disraeli seemed never to be disturbed by anything. This—and his talent for dramatic silences—was the mask that so infuriated Gladstone while it charmed England's salons. It was also the mask that gave face to the myth of the Jew Satanas, the "superlative Hebrew conjuror" who led poor old England by its nose.

"Someone wrote to me yesterday," Lord Acton said in a letter to Gladstone's daughter Mary, "that no Jew for 1800 years has played so great a part
in the world. That would be no Jew since St. Paul; and it is very startling.
But, putting aside literature . . . I have not yet found an answer." And further: "Let us . . . call him the greatest Jewish minister since Joseph."

Consciousness of Disraeli as a Jew appears in all English writing of the
period and later. His biographers and the political writers of his day cannot
shake their awareness of "that Oriental tendency in his nature." And they
are made uncomfortable by his defiant outbursts of racial scorn for the "barbarians," who, of course, were the gentiles, the "flat-nosed Franks" who
worship a Jew, and "who toil and study, and invent theories to account for
their own incompetence." The only "barbarians" Disraeli excepted from his
scorn were the ancient Greeks. Nevertheless, his advice to students of civilization is: study the Jews. In the Jews, and in the Jews alone, can the
exhausted gentiles "discover new courses of emotion, new modes of expression, new trains of ideas, new principles of invention, and new bursts of
fancy."

It was the impressive, death's-head face, which *Punch* saw as the sphinx
or, at least, as the face of old Jewry, that exasperated Carlyle to ask how long
"this Jew would be allowed to dance on the belly of [England]." Disraeli's
face fascinated—and still fascinates—Englishmen. It seems to them to express the witty, ironic, dancing character of the Jew. It was not simply his
dandyism. The upper classes knew and included many dandies. Rather, it
was his thin face; the "lividly pale" skin; the large "black eyes"; the long
nose and heavy underlip; the jet black hair, curling near the big ears; and,
finally, the stoop of a thin body. It was the face and stoop of Irving's Shylock,
so popular that it has been the classic portrayal of the role from that time
to this.

But the disturbing question of his Jewishness can best be read in the
snatches of Disraeli's memoirs and in his novels. In his novels, particularly,
Disraeli lifted "the veil that hides his own personality," and opened up the
"hidden motives" to deep underneath his "public pretenses," as he says of
the partly autobiographical character Sidonia (who is also Lionel Rothschild) in his finest novel, *Coningsby.*

One of the more significant accounts of his secret life is in his *Memoir* of
his father, written as an introduction to a three-volume edition of Isaac D'Israeli's *Curiosities of Literature.* Most revealing is his fantasy about his name.
He simply decided that his name came to be Disraeli because his ancestors
"assumed the name . . . in order that their race might be forever recognized." Thus they would be forever D'Israeli—of Israel. Disraeli invented a
romance by which his name became a deliberate emblem of dignity, a badge
of pride, an irrevocable identity, a "we" to the world's "they." There are
elements of his "ideal ambition"—of his Jewish fantasy life—in each of his

novels. It is especially obtrusive in the rhapsodic *The Wondrous Tale of Alroy*. He writes in his *Diary:* "My works are the embodification of my feelings. In *Vivian Grey* I have portrayed my active and real ambition: in *Alroy* my ideal ambition . . . [it] is the secret history of my feelings." In another place, Disraeli further explains his purpose in *Alroy:* "It is meant to be the celebration of a gorgeous incident in the annals of that sacred and romantic people from whom I derive my blood and name."

Disraeli published *Alroy* soon after his return from Jerusalem. It was never one of his popular novels. The critical public judged it absurd where not unreadable. But it provoked a reaction reserved for creations less absurd than annoying. A number of parodies of Disraeli's rhapsodic attempt appeared. One opened: "O reader dear! do pray look here, and you will spy the curly hair and forehead-fair, and nose so high and gleaming eye of Benjamin Dis-ra-e-li, the wondrous boy who wrote *Alroy*, in rhyme and prose, only to show, how long ago victorious Judah's lion-banner rose. . . ." But the most furious critical baiting was done by "Thomas Ingoldsby," a famous pseudonym of the magazine world of the time. "Thomas Ingoldsby," the Reverend R. H. Barham, published a parody of *Alroy* in *Blackwood's* in 1832, calling it: *The Wondrous Tale of Ikey Solomons*—Ikey Solomons was a notorious receiver of stolen goods.

Alroy is a story of the Jews of the Diaspora. David Alroy is a "Prince of the Captivity," full of Byron and brooding on the degradation of the Jews. Alroy, of the princely people, is sick—to the Byronic verge of action—of the slavery of the chosen: "God of my fathers! For indeed I dare not style thee God of their wretched sons. . . . Thy servant Israel, Lord, is born a slave so infamous, so woebegone, and so contemned, that even when our fathers hung their harps by the sad waters . . . why it was paradise compared with that we suffer."

Alroy refuses to suffer. He prefers to lead the Jews back to power, to national identity. Disraeli sets Alroy in a number of characteristically revealing conversations. One of these is with an ex-Jew who has risen to power in the gentile world. Alroy argues the problem of commitment with the ex-Jew, now high in government service.

"After all," Alroy insists, "thou art a [gentile]."

"No," the ex-Jew, called Lord Honain, answers.

"What then?"

"I have told you, a man." Honain asserts he is neither Jew nor gentile, and that most of all it is foolish to belong to a frail minority. It is better to belong to the strong majority; there is power, there is chosenness. Alroy has only one answer. Power is not the predicate of chosenness, but chosenness of power.

"We are the chosen people."

"Chosen for scoffs, and scorns, and contumelies. Commend me such a choice," Honain answers.

Alroy stubbornly commends the choice to him. Further, he insists to the ex-Jew that he cannot now understand the Jews. Honain is too well off, too strong, and so he cannot understand why the Jews must fight for power. The fight for power is clearest to those who are powerless but superior: the Jews.

"The world goes well with thee, my Lord Honain. But if, instead of bows and blessings, thou like my brethren, wert greeted only with cuff and curse; if thou didst rise each morning only to feel existence a dishonour, and to find thyself marked out among men as something foul and fatal; if it were thy lot, like theirs, at best to drag on a mean and dull career, hopeless and aimless, or with no other hope or aim but that which is degrading, and all this too with a keen sense of thy intrinsic worth, and a deep conviction of superior race; why, then perchance, [you] might discover 'twere worth a struggle to be free and honoured."

Alroy's brooding discomfort, and the guilt he feels at his inaction, is ended when he kills a Moslem who has tried to violate his sister, Miriam. He flees into the hills, to the retreat of the militant rabbi Jabaster, who is his ideologue. The rabbi instructs him in his mission: to raise the Jews first to revolt and then to independence. But first, Alroy must make a pilgrimage to Jerusalem. The fantasy at the "Tomb of the Kings" in Jerusalem is the most remarkable in the pattern of fantasies in Disraelian fiction. Solomon incarnate appears and hands down to his descendant, David Alroy, the rod of leadership. David returns to raise the revolt. With Jabaster as his chaplain, he leads the Jews to triumph. Alroy is, indeed, a Prince. But power, of course, corrupts him. He wants to be Alexander instead of David.

"The world is mine: and shall I yield the prize, the universal and heroic prize to realize the dull tradition of some dreaming priest and consecrate a legend? . . . Is the Lord of Hosts so slight a God, that we must place a barrier to His sovereignty, and fix the boundaries of Omnipotence between the Jordan and the Lebanon? . . . Universal empire must not be founded on sectarian prejudices and exclusive rights."

Seeking power for his people, Alroy had become intoxicated with it for himself. The Prince of the Captivity was corrupted by the vision of power in a Gentile world. He marries a gentile, the daughter of the Caliph, and makes Baghdad his capital. When it becomes apparent that he has abandoned his Jewish ambitions for other pleasures, Jabaster leads the Jews in revolt against him. This gives Alroy's wife the opportunity she has wanted to eliminate Jabaster, who is beheaded at her insistence. Finally, the Moslems defeat Alroy, and he is sentenced to death by the restored Sultanate. However, he is offered his freedom if he will renounce his Jewishness. This last irony amuses him. His refusal to renounce religiously what he had already renounced politically is his near-final affirmation of Jewishness.

But his final affirmation is more positive. Failure has taught him more about his Jewishness than success. What had been fatal, for him, Alroy now understands, was his attempt to de-Judaize himself. He makes what he considers to be a historical analogy: "The policy of the son of Kanesh—'twas fatal. He preferred Egypt to Judah, and he suffered." Alroy is a convinced Jew now, even more than he was when he was an ambitious Jew. His ambition is now for the Jews. In the same speech, he continues: "Sires, the Lord has blessed Judah; it is His land. He would have it filled by His peculiar people. . . . For this He has by many curious rites and customs marked us out from all other nations, so that we cannot at the same time mingle with them and yet be to Him." Alroy comes to what proves to be the final conclusion of his life: "We must exist alone." The Jews are meant to "preserve this loneliness." Loneliness is "the great and holy essence of our law."

The other side of the Jews' historic loneliness is Zionism. Alroy comes to understand this in what is perhaps one of the earliest Zionist perorations given in Western literature. He is asked what he wishes for the Jews:

"You ask me what I wish? My answer is: a National existence, which we have not. You ask me what I wish? my answer is: the Land of Promise. You ask me what I wish? my answer is: Jerusalem—all we have forfeited, all we have yearned after, all for which we have fought—our beauteous country, our holy creed, our simple manners."

But Alroy is troubled by the thought again, that the Return may be the Jews' last illusion. "Is there no hope?" he asks himself. His answer is to quote the Prophets, that religious hope exists most of all in the hopeless situation: "The bricks are fallen, but we will rebuild with marble; the sycamores are cut down, but we will replace them with cedars. . . . Yet again I will build thee, and thou shalt be built, O . . . Israel!"

Alroy is a confession. It is an assertion that the Jew is the clue to history, and its demiurge. But the most passionate statement of Disraeli's fantasy of Jewish chosenness is made by his most romantic character, the Jew Sidonia in the novel *Coningsby*. Sidonia is Disraeli's affirmation of the myth of the super-Jew, superior because a Jew. Disraeli insists: "Race is everything; there is no other truth." Sidonia is proudest that he is "pure" Sephardic— for him, the Sephardim are the purest Jews. Sidonia is Disraeli, although he is made to look like Lionel Nathan Rothschild, who was to become the first man to enter the English Parliament as a Jew; that is, without having to take his seat "on the oath as a Christian." Guedalla calls Sidonia, in a try at a joke, "Disrothschild."

As Disraeli's proudest projection, Sidonia is the most powerful, the most learned, the most shadowy man in the world. He is also the loneliest. Sidonia is an alien, detached, without intimates or a permanent home. It is his homelessness that makes him intensely interested in the problem of political and cultural stability.

Disraeli offers in Sidonia a character who has the insight of an outsider. But his insight and his power are pathetic—for they must be the insight and the power given to an outsider who can never quite use his superiority to bring him into a community. His power and insight are the masks, the weap-

ons, of his detachment. Sidonia "was admired by women, idolized by artists, received in all circles . . . and appreciated for his intellect by the very
few to whom he at all opened himself; for though affable and generous, it
was impossible to penetrate him; though unreserved in his manners, his
frankness was limited to the surface. He observed everything, thought ever,
but avoided serious discussion. . . . He looked on life with a glance rather
of curiosity than contempt. His religion walled him out. . . . He perceived
himself a lone being. . . ."

This is the image Disraeli accepted for his own self: walled out, a lone
being. But Sidonia chooses to remain walled out and to turn his loneliness
and exclusion into a premise of insight. Disraeli turned his own loneliness
into both a pride and a political tactic. Yet the lonely, proud man titillated
himself with the fancy that English Jewry found a secret, private joy in him,
whispering among themselves that "he is one of us." The Jewish hero,
walled out from the Jews as well as from the gentiles, nevertheless is aware
of his irrevocable connection with the Jews.

Disraeli, in his fantasy, saw in the Jew the demiurge, as well as the measure, of history. Sidonia expresses this: "The fact is you cannot destroy [us].
It is a . . . fact, a simple law of nature, which has baffled Egyptian and
Assyrian kings, Roman emperors and Christian inquisitors. No penal laws,
no physical tortures can effect that a superior race should be absorbed in an
inferior, or be destroyed by it. . . ."

Sidonia insists that the Jews are not only the super-race, but now and
always responsible for whatever is great and good in history, despite the attempt of their inferiors to degrade and to destroy them. The Jews, according
to Sidonia, are superior by more than force of intellect. The Jews are favored
with genius by nature, as a divine gift. Try as the gentiles might to destroy
them, the Jews are indestructible. They are the intermediaries between man
and God, the divine "link" that gives to mankind its humanity, the priestly
people in a world that would be best organized as a theocracy.

Disraeli avowed Sidonia's manifesto for his own in the famous twenty-
fourth chapter of his political biography of his friend Lord George Bentinck,
which repeats many of the same things. This chapter, quite out of place in
the story of Bentinck's life, is a wholesale defense of the Jews, past, present,
and future, and an unqualified assertion of their superiority over other
"races." Disraeli's belief in the Jew as the indestructible hero of history led
him to claim for the Jews every historical glory of Western civilization.
Christianity, at its best, is a Jewish religion, and what is not best in it is not
Jewish. He could not allow many pages to pass before he must repeat one of
his favorite taunts: that, after all, the gentiles worship a Jew and a Jewess.
This is also the taunt of his beloved heroine, the Jewess Eva in *Tancred*. The
taunt was meant as a challenge delivered by Disraeli in his own name to the
Gentile world.

The Jew is chosen for eternity, Disraeli proclaims in the same chapter of his *Life* of Bentinck. He does not know too much of Jewish theology or history—or of Christian theology or history, for that matter. For Disraeli, these are all lumped together as the "great Asian mystery." But knowledge, he thinks, is not so necessary to insight as faith. Neither as prime minister nor as a proto-Zionist did Disraeli allow lack of information to inhibit his certainty. He is sure that the Jews, "sustained by a sublime religion," are the chosen of the earth. Each Jew proves his chosenness. Opportunity makes him the Tory prime minister of Great Britain. Persecution makes him a revolutionary leader in Europe. It does not matter what the world does to Jewry, Jewry always gives proof of its chosenness.

But Disraeli has still to answer a taunt returned to his own taunts: that he, D'Israeli of Israel, was a convert to Christianity. Disraeli gave a Jewish answer to an impossible question. *He* the convert? A *converted* Jew? It is the gentiles who are the converts, he answers. And that is something that in their confusion about the real nature of Christianity they quite forget. The answer is, admittedly, not equal to the question; but it has its cogency.

To Jews who thought themselves "better" converted, Disraeli showed an icy humor. He saved some of his sharpest irony for those "young ladies" who are "ashamed of their race, and not fanatically devoted to their religion, which might be true, but certainly was not fashionable." And he directed what he hoped were his most telling thrusts at the most sophisticated, and so the most vicious, type of assimilationist. This was the "animated" creature who "was always combatting prejudice" and who "felt persuaded that the Jews would not be so much disliked if they were better known." All they had to do, Disraeli minced, "was to imitate as closely as possible the habits and customs of the nation among whom they chanced to live. . . ."

Like many more modern Jewish intellectuals, Disraeli wrote partly to protect himself against the completest assimilation: the loss of his own consciousness as a Jew. Assimilated before he could choose another way, he hated assimilation. A master of practiced nonchalance all his life, he could barely tolerate the "practiced nonchalance" of the assimilationist ladies of his time. He expected a good woman to be "enthusiastic for her race" and unashamed, at least, of her religion. The first requirement for the role of heroine in his novels is that the lady be loyal to her "old faith," whatever that "old faith" be. This accounts for the affection he displays in his novels for noble old Catholic families, and for loyal young Catholic ladies.

But the Catholic heroine is simply a variation of the Jewish; of Eva, in *Tancred,* and of Miriam, the sister of Alroy. Catholicism, as a loyalty, appeals to him because it is a loyalty in the midst of disloyalties. The Jews are alone in the world as the Catholics are alone in Protestant England. Loyalty is the one characteristic a Jew cannot give up and still remain a Jew. The test of loyalty is to continue to live separately, no matter what the temptations of victory or defeat. "The Hebrews have never blended with their conquerors," says Eva to Trancred, proudly. In his novels, the heroine is the vessel of loyalty—a quality that makes his good women altogether flat, always superior and virtuous. Miriam is a better Jew than her brother, the great David Alroy; Disraeli dedicated *Alroy* to his sister, Sarah.

Finally, Disraeli made the Jew the image of what he thought to be his own politics. The Jews, he decided, "represent the Semitic principle; all that is spiritual in our nature. They are the trustees of tradition, and the conservators of the religious element. They are a living and most striking evidence of the falsity of that pernicious doctrine of modern times, the natural equality of man." The Jews are the "natural aristocrats" of man. Disraeli's entire "education" of the Tories was to recall them to the responsibility of their aristocracy, as trustees of the English political tradition. And his image of the English aristocrat was struck off from the image of the Jew. Disraeli insisted that the dynamic of English culture was its Hebraism. "Vast as the obligations of the whole human family are to the Hebrew race, there is no portion . . . so much indebted to them as the British people. It was the sword of the Lord and of Gideon that won the boasted liberties of England; chanting the same canticles that cheered the heart of Judah and their glens, the Scotch, upon their hillsides, achieved their religious freedom. [And] who is the most popular poet in this country? Is he to be found among the Mr. Wordsworths and the Lord Byrons . . . ? No; the most popular poet in England is the sweet singer of Israel. . . . There never was a race who sang so often the odes of David as the people of Great Britain."

Disraeli's sense of the past made him a consistent advocate of aristocracy as the decisive basis of English politics, and of the Jews as the aristocracy of history. In *Tancred,* he calls the gentile world sordid, and he makes Sidonia dismiss gentile Christianity as an immature imitiation of the peoples with a master past. The past and the present, as Sidonia says, "explain each other." The Christian clergy knows "nothing about these things. How can they? A few centuries back they were tattooed savages. . . ." Politics and theology, Sidonia concludes, are not yet within the mastery of Christian civilization. They require "an apprenticeship of some thousand years at least; to say nothing of clime and race."

Disraeli was often sentimental and could move himself to tears by his own words. But his sentimentalism was the hardest thing inside him. Sentimentalism, in the form of nostalgia, defines his politics and his fiction. It represents his sense of the past, and of his chosenness in it. It gives him his ideology, and has had a hand in shaping British political rhetoric, and Zionist rhetoric since then. (Churchill's epigrammatic, nationalist sentimentalism is straight from Disraeli, not from Gibbon, as some students of Churchill's rhetoric think. Gibbon was neither a sentimentalist nor a nationalist.) Disraeli felt himself twice chosen, as a Jew and as an Englishman, a representative of the Old Jerusalem and the New, the past and the present united.

Disraeli was pleased to make his sense of chosenness the basis of his

politics throughout his life. His belief in the mystery of Israel's chosenness
gave him a basis for his belief in his own chosenness in English politics. It
gave him the necessary aggressive mystique he needed to survive in English
politics, a unique achievement for a man in his position, unrepeated in England since. Disraeli did not simply hint at the doctrine of election, he asserted it. And his prophecy to England was a romantic conservative vision,
like Cromwell's, of England, that blessed plot, as a New Israel. It was Disraeli's nostalgia for his Jewishness that enabled him to present this vision in
English political history. (52:1)

13

The Theology of Politics: Reflections on
Totalitarianism as the Burden of Our Time

Burckhardt's reflection on Machiavelli's *History of Florence* applies equally
to Hannah Arendt's *The Origins of Totalitarianism:*[1] "Even if every line
were demonstrated to be false, the whole would still present an indispensable truth." Even if Miss Arendt's book should, in some important parts, be
an error, it is, by its sweep and passion, a creative error. And better a creative error than the uncreative truth that passes for some types of contemporary social science. It will become the kind of creative error that provides a
myth useful to the very time it analyzes. Her vocabulary—the "mob" and
the "masses," "psychological Jewishness," etc.—provides new pegs for the
ongoing conversation that is the intelligentsia. It will make public opinion,
as much as it tries to understand it. Miss Arendt, who studied philosophy
under Jaspers at Heidelberg and theology at Marburg (her first book was on
The Concept of Love in St. Augustine), has, with this book, become a guiding
mind in contemporary social thought. It is well for theologians to notice her
closely.

Reviewers in the popular journals (see, e.g., David Riesman's review in
Commentary, October, 1951, where Miss Arendt is placed with Comte and
Freud, among others; or Dwight Macdonald's in the *New Leader*, 15 August
1951, where the contents of the book are hailed as the greatest advance in
social thought since Marx) have adored it. It remains to be seen how the
reviewers in the scientific journals will treat it. *The Origins of Totalitarianism* is, like *The Decline of the West* (which Spengler wrote in 1911, before

Reprinted from *Journal of Religion* 32, no. 2 (April): 119–26. © 1952 by The University of
Chicago. All rights reserved.
    1. Hannah Arendt, *The Origins of Totalitarianism* (New York: Harcourt, Brace & Co.,
1951).

prophecy could become hindsight), a vast spiritualization of history—that is, her data are organized to reveal the spirit that informs history. Miss Arendt's book is a massive prophecy of hindsight, reaffirming the hopelessness of the modern situation to another even more despairing postwar intelligentsia.

The original title—*The Burden of Our Time*—better expresses Miss Arendt's prophetic intention than the title given to the American edition. More precisely, the two titles ought to be read together. In Hannah Arendt's theology of politics, totalitarianism is the burden (punishment) of our time, visited inevitably upon Western man for *hybris;* for a politics whose dynamic is expansion for expansion's sake; for a morality that believes everything is possible and everything is permitted. Evil, however, must be locatable. Men are never satisfied to know evil merely exists. They must know where to find it, whether in a man, in a race, in a nation, in a class. For Miss Arendt it is the bourgeoisie, as a class, fascinated by crime as a style of life and as a political weapon, that has become radically evil. Evil was, by the time of the nineteenth century, bourgeois. Miss Arendt's negative theology has created a counterimage to Weber's middle-class Puritan. The ethical Puritan has been transformed, some two centuries later, into a criminal bourgeois.

Miss Arendt has learned a great deal from Marxism. But where Marx would be interested only in the politics of theology, Miss Arendt is more interested in the theology of politics. As the bourgeoisie inevitably turned to crime, it has been destroyed along with what it has destroyed (p. 124). This is not to say Marx did not recognize the nature of evil. But for Marx evil was the restriction of man to something below his full humanity. For Miss Arendt evil is the expansion of man to something beyond his limited humanity. The leap into freedom has freed man only from his humanity. The peripety denotes the changed temper of Western culture.

Mr. Riesman and other reviewers have been disturbed by the tone of inevitability in Miss Arendt's constructions. But her tone is not simply, as Mr. Riesman would have it, the fanaticism of great and systematic minds. This is not a systematic history (which is neither praise nor blame). Rather, Miss Arendt has written a set of essays into special phases of modern history. Its cohesion comes from the passionate subjectivity of the author, its astuteness from the unity of her analytical direction, its power from her vocabulary of forces—for example, the mob and capital, the Jews and the nation-state—pointing everywhere toward a vista of doom. Miss Arendt's total construction is grounded in her belief that the demonic principle has triumphed in modern history. Man's demonic will to freedom has led him beyond the limits of his reason and humanity, beyond the limits of old political orders, beyond the limits of old social and religious communities; it has led him away from the saving social graces of small functions and personal responsibility.

The demonic is the destruction of form. It rises as shapelessness and

rootlessness. Man becomes demonic when he considers his natural propor-
tions merely historical and feels free to break through them. Miss Arendt
has been rightly paired with Simone Weil. The one is the overt theological
expression of the other. What is implicit in *The Origins of Totalitarianism* is
explicit, for example, in *L'Enracinement:* Evil is rootlessness, Good is
particularity.

But it is precisely Miss Arendt's covert theology that has made her attractive to an antitheological intelligentsia. And this is what theologians must
notice in a great deal of the most important contemporary social thought.
Much of the best writing in contemporary social science is covertly religious-
ethical writing. It takes its peculiar charm from its refusal to admit it.

Miss Arendt has reversed the Marxist and humanist image of man. For
Marx, as for humanist thought generally, the vocational-religious-national
character mask that particularizes man cripples him, alienates him from his
humanity or his divine relation, and is therefore a denial of his humanity.
Miss Arendt's man is alienated from his humanity as he becomes without
vocation, without nation, without his religious community. Man emancipated from his particularity becomes not human but demonic. Where the
humanist Hölderlin saw cobblers, Jews, Germans, but no men, Miss Arendt
sees men only when they are cobblers or Jews or Germans. (The Nazis were
not really nationalists, and this is the measure of their demonry.) The ideal
of the humanist man, or of Christian universalism, has become the nightmare of the mob man. Totalitarianism is his polity of chaos.

In the absence of limits, evil becomes everyman's lot. Everyman is "coresponsible" (i.e., guilty). Indeed, the world cannot become much worse. Totalitarianism marks the last discovery of Western man in his search for the
limitless. It marks the end of our time. Miss Arendt offers as consolation the
prophecy that perhaps totalitarianism, too, "will one day simply disappear,
leaving no other trace in the history of mankind than exhausted peoples,
economic and social chaos, political vacuum, and a spiritual *tabula rasa*"
(p. 430).

A theological vocabulary is quite unnecessary to theological assumptions. Miss Arendt nowhere explicitly generalizes modern politics and social
relations as at the same time punishment and a revelation of man's pride.
But her assumptions will out, as in the concluding paragraphs of the
Preface:

> Without the imperialists' "expansion for expansion's sake," the world
> might never have become one; without the bourgeoisie's political device of
> "power for power's sake," the extent of human strength might never have been
> discovered; without the fictitious world of totalitarian movements . . . we
> might have been driven to our doom without ever becoming aware of what has
> been happening.
> And if it is true that in the final stages of totalitarianism an absolute evil

appears . . . it is also true that without it we might never have known the truly
radical nature of Evil.

The passage seems incomprehensibly cruel if not recognized as an expression of Miss Arendt's covert theological assumptions. The punishment
visited as totalitarianism, like the punishment visited by God through history, is at the same time a revelation of the abyss of possibility. The punishment is, therefore, an opportunity to repent and to live under a "new law."
For the punishment has revealed that "human dignity needs a new guarantee
. . . a new law on earth, whose . . . power must remain strictly limited."
Like men, even the new law must be limited, lest it become demonic. God,
after all, must not ask Abraham to sacrifice his son.

Hannah Arendt has written not simply as a historian. She has written as a
prophetess, claiming, of course, like all late prophets who have nothing to
prophesy, that she is against prophecy. But all prophecy is historical, and
all prophecy is history, even if all historians are not prophets. Miss Arendt
is a prophet-historian, moralizing history as the burden of our time. She is
neither cool, aloof, nor impartial. She is without the pseudo-objectivity
which masks itself as the moral achievement of modern social science.
Plainly, detachment is, for her, morally despicable. It is nothing but the
complacency of academics far from the shooting. (Acton's judgment seems
final: "The strong man with the dagger is followed by the weak man with the
sponge.") Miss Arendt will not wipe the blood off anybody's hands. Her
moral absolutism, in its context of select fact, has given her judgments a
wrath and credibility beyond the empty moralizing capacity of theology
alone.

But Miss Arendt's theology of politics has given her book the weakness of
its strength. No one is innocent. She smites right and left, high and low, Jew
and Gentile, with equal indignation. No one comes off well. Almost everyone is damned, either directly or with faint praise.

The difficulty is, as Miss Arendt has noticed elsewhere, that an indictment, like a self-accusation, is weakened when it includes everyone. And,
of course, the indictment is bound to be untrue. The innocent still exist. It is
the deadly fault of the modern intelligentsia that it refuses to assert even the
possibility of innocence. Thus, whether in their Freudian or pseudo-theo-
logical (for example, Kafka cultus) phases, the intellectuals have rationalized the rule of the guilty. That is their treason.

Miss Arendt cannot tolerate innocence. The Jews, for example, are
equally guilty, "coresponsible" for the crime against them. A victim, she
writes, "does not simply cease to be coresponsible because it becomes the
victim" (p. 6). The reason for the Jews' "coresponsibility" is not so much,
she thinks, the decline of their function in the nation-state (for which they
can hardly be judged even metaphysically responsible) but the manner of
their assimilation. Modern anti-Semitism is "interconnected with Jewish as-

similation, the secularization and withering away of the old religious and spiritual values of Judaism" (p. 7). Miss Arendt cherishes a special indignation, not so much against the Jewish rich, but against the Jewish intellectuals, who in "searching for a road into society . . . quickly discovered the force that would open all doors [into the corrupt gentile, bourgeois world], the 'radiant power of Fame'" (p. 52). A "great proportion of cultural institutions, like newspapers, publishing, music and theatre," became "Jewish enterprises" as a strategy of assimilation.

But Miss Arendt does not report what she must know: that the doors the Jewish intellectuals forced open were precisely the doors the Germans left open to them. The Jews became "reviewers, critics . . . and organizers of what was famous" because the Germans would not. When, even in "the century of free trade," was there "access of Jews to all professions" (p. 36) in Germany?

What drove the Jewish intellectuals into the culture occupations was neither their tradition of culture nor their corrupt spur toward fame (and notoriety) as a conscious or unconscious strategy of assimilation. Rather, those culture occupations attached to capitalism and the mass market were open to Jews precisely because Germans despised them. The German bourgeoisie, assimilated after 1848 to feudal and militarist society, did not have its own culture. As an appendage to the German ruling strata, the German middle classes despised both humanist culture and capitalist techniques for its diffusion, thus leaving these fields open. The German intelligentsia, on the other hand, remained trapped within the legacy of small-town life. Neither the Latin salon nor the English club was available to it. Thus the German intellectuals became domestic workers, cut off from the urban market situation. They developed, as a rationalization of their position, a moral hatred against those culture occupations that revolved around the cash-fame nexus.

Despised occupations (in this historical case: journalism, the arts, banking, etc.) are always left to despised groups. The status and value hierarchy of German society excluded the Jews from the officer caste, from the land, and from the civil service; just as, in American academic society, Jews tended to be excluded from history departments but found it easier to enter newer and less honored disciplines like sociology. What was left to the Jews was beneath respectable German aspiration.

It is only when socially despised occupations become respectable, because of (1) the closing of more respectable opportunities (for example, in a nation of demobilized and defeated officers with only a 100,000-man army), or (2) the new relevance of despised occupations in shifting income and power contexts (for example, when the movies become important economically and politically), or (3) when changes in the structure of despised institutions make them indistinguishable from respectable institutions (namely, when German banking became more and more a bureaucratic agency of the government), that the ruling upper-status groups resent the "crowding" of the Jews.

If, "whenever [the Jews] were admitted to . . . society, they became a well-defined, self-preserving group" (p. 13), then they were well-defined and self-preserving because of their occupational and status limitations, not because of their privileges. Miss Arendt misses an entire analysis of social structure. It is simply untrue to write: "Without the interests and practices of governments, the Jews could hardly have preserved their group identity" (p. 14). It was society, not the state, whose interests and practices identified the Jews: moreover, the internal dynamic of Jewry itself, through two thousand years, must be taken into account.

The distinction between "political anti-Semitism" and "social anti-Semitism" serves as Miss Arendt's substitute for an analysis of types of anti-Semitism in terms of social structure. "Political anti-Semitism developed because the Jews were a separate body, while social [anti-Semitism] arose because of the growing equality of Jews with all other groups" (p. 54). She concludes that "in Europe, [social anti-Semitism] had little influence on the rise of political anti-Semitism" (p. 55).

As Miss Arendt draws it, the distinction between political and social anti-Semitism seems quite spurious. First, political anti-Semitism rises as social anti-Semitism becomes a form of self-penalization of the anti-Semites themselves, closing off certain newly desirable opportunities. Thus, political anti-Semitism can grow out of a shift in the value of social anti-Semitism. Miss Arendt verges on the point: political anti-Semitism "in its most sinister aspect owed much of its success to [social anti-Semitism] which virtually constituted a consent [to political anti-Semitism] by public opinion" (p. 87). Plainly, if Miss Arendt is right on page 87, she is wrong on page 55.

Second, the best explanation of political anti-Semitism may still be the one Miss Arendt dismisses most vehemently because it vitiates her ethic of coresponsibility: the scapegoat theory. As Daniel Lerner has noticed in his study of the Nazi elite, the Nazi propagandists (as listed in the *Führer-Lexikon* [1934]) were of superior status, education, and travel experience. Political anti-Semitism among the Nazi propagandists, then, cannot be explained by shifts in the value of social anti-Semitism. Rather the political scapegoat theory—even the conspiracy theory—is still operable and adequate. Educated and sophisticated Nazi propagandists climbed to power partly by manipulating the fright-mask of *The Jew*. Miss Arendt has substituted her own subtle and ambivalent judgments of Jewish motives toward assimilation for a reading of the basic facts of German social structure.

She is equally hard on the German intellectuals. If the emancipated Jewish intellectuals came to the Germans, the Germans also came to the Jews. The weak bourgeois strata of German liberals welcomed support from any quarter. The intellectuals, Germans and Jews, met because they had no place else to go, except to each other. Miss Arendt notices the point in her discussion of a short-lived Jewish salon (pp. 59 *et passim*).

The rise of the doctrine of "innate personality" (p. 31) is treated as if it were a peculiarly German phenomenon, a sinister status weapon in the hands of the intellectuals. Thus, in Germany, "personality worship developed as the only means of gaining . . . social emancipation" and equal, even superior, status with the nobility (p. 168). But personality worship neither was a German invention nor did its peculiar development take place there. She does not mention Shaftesbury or Rousseau, the two great virtuosos of humanity. The omission is crucial in a book by one so erudite. It indicates that she is pleading a very special case. If the ideas of "innate personality and natural nobility prepared the way intellectually for race-thinking in Germany" (p. 170), Miss Arendt must explain why the same ideas, even more powerfully and originally expressed, prepared the way intellectually for democratic thinking in England and America. To relate the idea of "innate personality" and "natural nobility" to race-thinking is a distortion of its meaning and of the intention of its promulgators. All pedagogical thought in the eighteenth century aimed to liberate man from his conventional fetters. Equally, the ideological mission of all bourgeois liberalism of the time was to emancipate man by appealing to his innate capacities and natural sentiments. The doctrine of "personality worship" is Miss Arendt's sinister version of the humanist ideal of *l'uomo universale*, endowed with natural morality. It was the ideology of Goethe and Schiller, a perhaps naïve belief that one could transcend the limits of being Jew, German, even writer, and be Man. If Marx is correct, the doctrine carried the essential meaning of toleration: each according to his capacities. Miss Arendt has turned personality worship, the serene doctrine of the best minds of the eighteenth century, into a polemical weapon against the German intellectuals in their search for emancipation, as she has converted culture-worship into a polemic against the emancipated Jewish intellectuals.

Miss Arendt is herself a Jew and an intellectual, and she suffers from a fear common to both: "the prejudice of the masses" (p. 3). The traditional Jewish fear of the masses is "deeply rooted in and . . . unconsciously shared" not only by the "vast majority of Jews" but by Miss Arendt as well. The vast majority of Jews, as a minority group, react, like the Negroes in the United States, out of a calculation of majority-group pressures and out of the intuition that there is more distance and therefore less conflict between themselves and the higher classes than between themselves and the lower classes. (Thus the Jewish love of aristocracy, as Miss Arendt notices it, is not different from the American Negroes' love of the American upper classes.)

But the reaction and calculation that informs the intellectuals' fear of themselves is of a different quality. In *The Origins of Totalitarianism* Miss

Arendt's calculation of the role of the masses is at the heart of her analysis of imperialism; and her reaction to that role is the reaction of a conservative intellectual. Thus, her analysis of imperialism as the "union of superfluous men [the mob] and superfluous wealth [capital]" (pp. 150–51) is best summarized in a passage from Hegel's *Philosophy of Right:*

> When the masses decline into poverty . . . and when there is a consequent loss of the sense of right and wrong, of honesty and . . . self-respect . . . the result is the creation of a rabble of paupers. At the same time this brings with it, at the other end of the social scale, conditions which greatly facilitate the concentration of disproportionate wealth in a few hands.
>
> This inner dialectic of civil society . . . thus drives it . . . to push beyond its own limits . . . [pars. 244–46 of Knox's trans.].

Here is the conceptual basis, in brief, of Miss Arendt's theory of imperialism, for the coupling of the aristocracy and the mob, of the gentleman and the criminal. To write of the "mob, begotten by the monstrous accumulation of capital, accompanying its begetter on those voyages of discovery" into imperialism seems a perfectly Hegelian thesis (p. 151).

Miss Arendt's theoretical connection with Hegel places her in a great tradition of conservative social thought. Her reduction of the highly stratified masses of Western society into Hegel's rabble, or Marx's *Lumpenproletariat*, reminds one of Burckhardt's internal barbarians or Toynbee's internal and external proletariats. The reduction is in the air. To substitute the word "mob" for one of the older terms is no more valuable as an analytical device now—banalized by pocket editions of Ortega or rarified by Eliot's sociological lectures—than it was in the hands of the conservative critics of the nineteenth century. That is the reason a reviewer like Macdonald, who has been searching for something to replace her lost Marxism, can hail Miss Arendt as Marx's successor. Her massive spiritualization of history provides the most sumptuous refuge yet made available to an American intelligentsia in full retreat from Marxism and unable to accept an avowedly theological interpretation of history. A dispiritied audience hails Miss Arendt as Marx's successor because she belongs with Marx's predecessors.

In Hannah Arendt's theology of politics, modern anti-Semitism becomes the burden (punishment) of the Jews for their historic act of cowardice (assimilation). For the attempt to escape himself, the religious Jew has been burdened with an even more indelible mark: psychological Jewishness. The lesson must teach him that "from Jewishness there is no escape" (p. 87).

But perhaps the Jews' subtle and "tragic endeavor to conform [assimilate] through differentiation and distinction [exoticism and culture]" can be better understood in terms of the occupational sociology of despised peoples, as we have noted; and, in terms of the tendency of intellectuals, in certain epochs, to dandyism. Disraeli's dandyism was not, as Miss Arendt thinks, a daring

function of his "psychological Jewishness" but of his membership in an aristocratic smart set. Disraeli's education in the circle of Lady Blessington and
Count D'Orsay was probably more important than his "psychological Jewishness." Salon societies are always full of virtuosos. They are laboratories
for developing marginal types within the aristocracy. Salons are the elas-
ticity factor of the upper classes. Disraeli was no exception and certainly no
charlatan. Byron, and Fox, were dandies too.

What Miss Arendt fails to say about the Jew as intellectual is that all
intellectuals—Jewish or not—seem "mysteriously wicked or secretly vicious" to bourgeois society. Or, alternatively, they are treated as comic and
therefore harmless, for example, professors. Sweet, bumbling Mr. Honey
(*No Highway in the Sky*) is only one of the most recent in a lengthy line of
Hollywood reductions of the intellectual to the comic. Miss Arendt's assertion of a general "Jewish preference" (p. 67) for intellectuals is, of course,
correct. At their emancipation, the People of the Book only translated the
high prestige of religious learning into secular terms. The preference also
made Germany the land of "Jewish preference."

But the "Jewish preference" has shifted from the learned Germany of
the nineteenth century to the muscular, business America of the twentieth.
The transformation of the character of American Jewry is evidence against
the reality of Miss Arendt's image of the "psychological Jew." Many of the
People of the Book have become the People of the Bookies. Benny Friedman
and Sid Luckman are, of course, still quarterbacks and thus continue to express the "Jewish preference." But the Baer brothers were not very brainy
boxers, and there have been some very beefy-headed Jewish fullbacks from
Cornell to Southern California. (Perhaps, given the supremacy of sport in
our culture, the athlete has become the "exception Jew" of America.) If
there have been only a few Jewish generals (General Rose's father was a
rabbi), it is because West Point has not allowed enough Jews to prefer it.
The Jewish promoter in American does not promote culture. He promotes
junk. Thomas Mann's European impresario has become Garson Kanin's
American junk-dealer. Saul Fitelberg has been transformed into Harry
Brotz. The "intellectual" (he wears horn-rimmed glasses and cannot fight) of
Born Yesterday is a gentile drumming culture into the mistress of a barbarian
Jew. Surely, in America, the Jews have finally escaped their "preferences."

But for Miss Arendt the Jews are simply trapped. There is no way out.
She bypasses religious Jewishness. Psychological Jewishness is a perversion. And the world is implacably hostile. (Thus, in Europe, anti-Semitism
rose because the Jews had lost their social function, while in South Africa
anti-Semitism rose because the Jews had gained a social function [see
p. 205].) Heads the Jews lose, and tails they lose. However the Jew distorts
himself, there is only "universal hostility" (p. 120).

Miss Arendt's tragic view of Jewish destiny goes beyond Carl Schmitt's *freund-feind* relation. Both are suspect, friends and enemies, philo-Semites and anti-Semites. Indeed, friends are more suspect than enemies. Whether society was "strangely eager to associate with [Jews]" or hated them, "of course . . . relations with Jews never came to be taken for granted." Philo-Semitism "at best . . . remained a program, at worst a strange and exciting experience" (p. 65). And anti-Semitism? Evidently, at worst it was a program and at best a strange and exciting experience. Thus "philo-Semitism" (e.g., pp. 86–87) can only appear as a quotation of anti-Semitism. "Philo-Semitism" always ends by "adding to [political anti-Semitism] that mysterious fanaticism without which anti-Semitism could hardly have become the best slogan for organizing the masses . . . for wholesale extermination" of the Jews (p. 87). Without "philo-Semitism," "mere[?] political anti-Semitism . . . might have resulted in anti-Jewish legislation and even mass expulsion but hardly in wholesale extermination." Miss Arendt has overburdened the psychological aspects of anti-Semitism, as most writers now do. She ascribes too much importance to attitudes alone, at the cost of underestimating modern political anti-Semitism as a trained and manipulated mass hatred.

If the Jews must suspect their friends more than their enemies, they must withdraw. But to what? And where? Miss Arendt by-passes religion or the ghetto. Zionism is almost unmentioned. After two thousand years the re-establishment of Israel as a sovereign nation is not a sufficient hope. The direction of Miss Arendt's analysis is that the Jews, with the rest of humanity, must march resolutely backward to a reaffirmation of the eighteenth-century humanist ethic of a united humanity she has herself derided and to the ethic of formal legal equality. (Thus, the lesson of the Dreyfus affair ought to have been understood, according to Miss Arendt, as: justice for all.)

The ethic of a united humanity, supported by the legal tradition of the middle-class revolutions, is precisely the great failure documented in this tragic book. Both the ethic and the tradition Miss Arendt seems to recommend are so acceptable because they coincide with the sleight of hand of our everyday vocabulary. It is the phony language of the United Nations, trite and untrue for the men who mouth it and for those who listen. To recommend as a "new guarantee of human dignity" and as a "new law on earth" the tradition of the Enlightenment and of the French Revolution, to root the possibility of a renascence of what has proved to Miss Arendt to be an inadequate ethic and an empty legalism in vague "newly defined territorial entities," is a measure not only of the confusion of her book but of its abandonment of hope.

Finally, according to Miss Arendt, "at least we can cry out to each one of those who rightly is in despair" and listen to our own voices instruct us: "Do thyself no harm; for we are all here." Miss Arendt ends by quoting Paul. But for Paul the instruction is penultimate. There is salvation to come. For Miss Arendt the consolation is ultimate.

The old prophets lamented the past, or glorified it, and understood the present as a punishment and revelation. But they held out hope to the suffering. In this sense, Paul is in the prophetic tradition. And it is precisely the prophetic power of Marx that he grounded hope in a specific class, only vaguely outlined at that time. Indeed, in this way, he helped to create that very class. Plato, like the prophets, beheld a saving remnant, Calvin a holy community, Marx a new class.

Where is Miss Arendt's saving remnant? There is none. There is no hope and no prophecy. God is dead, and his saving remnant, like Progress, exists nowhere. All that remains to Miss Arendt is a belief in the equalitarian legal formalism of the French Revolution and the eighteenth century, so horribly inoperable in modern society. The "nineteenth century's greatest achievement, the complete impartiality of the law" (p. 91), is, perhaps rightly, dead. With differential educational and status opportunities for veterans (for example, the G.I. Bill), with special laws to protect Jews and other minority groups against economic discrimination (such as the New York State statute against job discrimination), and with special loyalty oaths for government employees, the "new concept of equality" that she calls the great challenge of the modern period (p. 54) has become a myth, now if not in De Tocqueville's time. The great movement of modern government has been toward substantive legal preferences and definitions. Modern Americans are more protected than ever by "differing circumstances and conditions." Legal formalism has created a civilization in which the rich and the poor alike were prohibited from sleeping under bridges. The reaction against this "equality before the law" was not only the arbitrary radicalism of despots but also the democratic demand for justice. There is lessening "equality" and lessening "impartiality before the law," not greater.

In yet another sense, equality is not the principle of modern society. Ascribed status is still more important than achieved status. Proust discovered men were only their representations. When he tried to find the real man behind the status mask, he found that what was most real about men was precisely their status masks. The discovery has made Proust the most insightful sociologist of our time.

Proust had to be a great sociologist to be a great novelist. The requirement says a great deal about the social structure of modern society. "Aristocracy" still rules the world, even where the slogans are democratic; indeed, especially where the slogans are democratic, as in the Soviet Union and the United States. The aristocracy that, according to Miss Arendt, once pervaded "the whole social body in the nineteenth century . . . by imposing 'the key and the grammar' of fashionable social life" (p. 86) has never been

overthrown. Rather, the ideal of democracy has degenerated one phase beyond Balzacian bourgeois egoism to the salon ideal of every man an aristocrat. Popular culture has made salon life available, as an aspiration, to
Everyman. The tension between the narrowly ascribed status of Everyman
and his self-image of aristocratic aspiration is one of the major contexts of
modern social life. The context has transformed modern literature into parody and modern art into caricature, wherever it has not escaped into privacy. The wheel has come full circle, from the tragedy of the revolt against
the aristocratic principle to the farce of its restoration. (52:3)

14

On Franz Rosenzweig

Professor Glatzer concludes his Introduction to *Understanding the Sick and
the Healthy* with a perfect and necessary remark.[1] The book, he says, "is
being printed and offered to the public not primarily as 'a contribution to
philosophical or religious thought,' but as a part of Franz Rosenzweig's very
life." Not that the philosophical or religious import of the book is in any way
slight. As a thrust at the immense airiness of German idealism from Kant to
Hegel—and therefore at professorial theology—it is quick and brilliant.
Rosenzweig was very clever; he averted getting hung out in the middle of the
same vacuum as the idealists by probing idealism from within himself and
for himself. This style may confuse unwary readers. A philosophical book,
yet it is a personal book, even a chatty book. It has no system. But then,
because German philosophical systems sealed off the life that ran inside
them, Rosenzweig's jab flickers out toward all system.

In approaching Franz Rosenzweig, Glatzer tries to resolve a destructive
impasse within modern Jewish thought. On the one hand, in this volume and
in an earlier one on Rosenzweig's *Life and Thought*, Glatzer has introduced
the American public to a saintly man. The Jew Franz Rosenzweig belongs in
the company of the sublimest characters his religion of character has produced. For modern and secular taste, Rosenzweig was almost embarrass-
ingly good. But then he was paralyzed and died young, and this will confirm
the secular prejudice that goodness is not for healthy dispositions. Dostoevsky tried to make the character of Alyosha good and his body healthy, but he
succeeded at the expense of Alyosha's mind; this brother, of all the Ka-

Reprinted from *Journal of Religion* 35, no. 4 (October): 262–63. © 1955 by The University
of Chicago. All rights reserved.
    1. Franz Rosenzweig, *Understanding the Sick and the Healthy: A View of the World, Man
and God*, with an introduction by Nahum H. Glatzer (New York: Noonday Press, 1954).

ramozovs, was the least intellectual. Franz Rosenzweig was a saint and an intellectual too, a combination that runs against the prepossessions of the intellectuals I know.

At the same time, Glatzer has struggled to bring the reader near the intimate mind and doctrine of Franz Rosenzweig. But in the generations of its submission to German learnedness Jewry has grown intellectualized. Receptivity to the person and personal message of Rosenzweig is very low. As author of *Hegel and the State*, he would probably get longer notices in more journals than as author of *The Star of Redemption* or *Understanding the Sick and the Healthy*. *Hegel and the State* is a theoretical work and therefore a safe excitement, for theory does not demand an intimate and practical response, as dialogue does. Theory does not address another person but another book. In the contemporary hospital atmosphere of culture, theory leads nowhere except to theorizing. Indeed, we are past the creative age of theory, and for this reason Rosenzweig attacked it. But this does not mean that Rosenzweig in any way accepted the present domination of empirical attitudes as an alternative. On the contrary, empiricism has become an even thicker disguise of established and rejectable fact. For empiricism pretends merely to observe fact, as if such observation were not the grossest idolatry of fact. At least idealism pretended to go beyond fact.

Rosenzweig expected thought to lead the thinker somewhere he had never been before, to new relations as well as to altered perspectives. *Understanding the Sick and the Healthy* is therefore not an academic book. In fact, it is an attack on the academic sickliness of modern thought. It is saddening to realize that probably the present fate of this book is to be absorbed into the glutinous world of the American academy, where all thinking people think they have to live. Yet, in its very format, *Understanding the Sick and the Healthy* exhibits the original hope of the author, his editor, and their publisher that it would be read in wider inclosures. It is a beautifully produced book, with the death mask of a beautiful man on its covers to give the reader a vision of what lies within. (55:3)

15
On Leon Trotsky

There has never been any easy way of accommodating the fact that so many great revolutionary leaders have been Jewish with the fact that they have been revolutionary leaders. Even such first-rate writers as Edmund Wilson have taken the line of least resistance and transformed Marx into a prophet;

Reprinted from *Chicago Jewish Forum* 13, no. 1 (Fall 1954): 66–67.

Lassalle, if never quite a prophet, has had his Jewishness treated as the wound that strung his bow. The connection, too generously developed from a psychology brilliantly proposed in the late nineteenth century and still in vogue today, establishes the drive for revolutionary power as a reaction of resentment to the frustration and injury of visionary and proud people.

It was Nietzsche who made the still persistent judgment of Christianity as an ingenuous revolution among the weak Jewish people against Roman power. And since Nietzsche the style of discussing Jewish revolutionaries has been set: the Jew, if he is revolutionary, must suffer from the ambiguity of being a Jew in the gentile world. Revolution is his revenge and at the same time his way out, as Christianity was the Jew's first revenge and also his way out of Jewishness. The Nietzschean theme has been played to project the most surprising characters; even Disraeli appears revolutionary when his psychological Jewishness is rediscovered by writers various as Hannah Arendt and Wilfred Blunt. Psychological Jewishness has had a special recommendation in the case of Freud, for Freud himself accepted the idea.

The first value of Isaac Deutscher's book [1] is that he quickly demolishes the established psychology of the revolutionary Jew, at least with respect to one of its most dependable cases—Trotsky. Trotsky was neither neurotic nor particularly Jewish. Mr. Deutscher makes his point in the first two chapters; it is a fair sample of an originality which, when the work is elaborated in a second volume, will certainly help make it the standard Life of Trotsky.

It is true the Bronsteins were Jews. But they were Jews in the same sense that many Americans are Jews, for although Trotsky's parents still carried their historical burden it was without renewal in that elective affinity by which the next generation can at least establish a nostalgia for its Jewishness. Unconnected with the Synagogue, the Bronsteins no longer lived within a Jewish community. What was left of their Jewishness was almost entirely negative: a capacity for hard and unfamiliar work and fierce, often oppressive, family pride.

Trotsky fits none of the images of the Jew-Communist, except (and this, I realize, has overwhelming importance) physiognomically; indeed, Trotsky may be said to have modeled the world image of the Jew-Communist leader, the militant urban intellectual leading the masses into the future. Yet this Jew was born on a farm and raised in a very rustic, unintellectual way. Trotsky did not know those frustrations of the lower middle class, intellectual, city sort of Jew upon whom the Communist parties are supposed to have drawn so heavily. His commitment to the revolutionary movement in his late teens does not admit of the Nietzschean explanation, or its more

1. Isaac Deutscher, *The Prophet Armed: Trotsky, 1879–1921* (New York: Oxford University Press, 1954).

recent psychoanalytic variants. His decision appears to have been as nearly and purely an act of moral intelligence as the human capacity for morality and intelligence allows. Trotsky, shorn of any special Jewish motivation, emerges a moral hero the more grand for his disinterestedness. Mr. Deutscher is to be congratulated for his restraint. The key of psychological Jewishness will not unlock the secret of revolutionary history, although it is a key that still seems to fit, not only for anti-Semitic and philo-Semitic but for less obsessive minds.

Yet Mr. Deutscher's restraint does no more than balance the issue, without resolving it. Trotsky's amazing faith in the future was certainly a psychological condition of his revolutionary activity. Yet it is as plausible to assign this to the tenuous influence of his Jewishness as to the even more tenuous influence of Marx when his faith was formed. Trotsky's god is history, but it is a history that takes sides in a way far more personal than Marx conceived. This history is like the primitive Jehovah, making a deeply personal promise of victory to his righteous. It is not surprising that Trotsky, despite his ignorance of either Hebraism or Calvinism, liked to compare the psychological effects on moral character of Calvinism and Marxism. At the least we cannot dismiss the eschatological character of Trotsky's mind. It is still stirring to read his declaration of faith, written during his first Siberian exile, under the title "On Optimism and Pessimism, on the Twentieth Century, and on Many Other Things":

> *Dum spiro spero!* . . . If I were one of the celestial bodies, I would look with complete detachment upon this miserable ball of dust and dirt. . . . I would shine upon the good and the evil alike. . . . But I am a *man.* "World history which to you, dispassionate gobbler of science, to you, book-keeper of eternity, seems only a negligible moment in the balance of time, is to me everything." As long as I breathe, I shall fight for the future, that radiant future in which man, strong and beautiful, will become master of the drifting stream of his history and will direct it towards the boundless horizon of beauty, joy and happiness! . . .
>
> The 19th century has in many ways satisfied and has in even more ways deceived the hopes of the optimist. . . . It has compelled him to transfer most of his hopes to the twentieth century. Whenever the optimist was confronted by an atrocious fact, he exclaimed: What, and this can happen on the threshold of the twentieth century! When he drew wonderful pictures of the harmonious future, he placed them in the twentieth century.
>
> And now that century has come! What has it brought with it at the outset? . . . Hatred and murder, famine and blood. . . .
>
> It seems as if the new century, this gigantic newcomer, were bent at the very moment of its appearance to drive the optimist into absolute pessimism and civic nirvana. Death to Utopia! Death to faith! Death to love! Death to hope! thunders the twentieth century in salvoes of fire and in the rumbling of guns.

Surrender, you pathetic dreamer. Here I am, your long awaited twentieth century, your "future."—No, replies the unhumbled optimist: You—you are only the *present*. (54:5)

16
Judaism and Democratic Action

I said unto Peter before them all, If thou, being a Jew, livest after the manner of the Gentiles, and not as do the Jews, why compellest thou the Gentiles to live as do the Jews?

Paul, in Galatians, 2:14

Christians have always wondered how Jewish they are. Some have wondered as an expression of their hostility to the Jews. Some have wondered as an expression of their resistance toward the significance of Jewry and Judaism. But western gentilehood has never been free of the question. At various times, each section of Christianity has either accused or stood accused of being crypto-Jews. It has been an integral aspect of the Christian sense of guilt.

Thus the Roman Church has always spoken of the Protestants as being crypto-Jews, accusing Wycliffe and the Lollards, Luther, Zwingli and Calvin, in turn of being too much influenced by Judaism. In turn, Calvin accused Servetus, who may be classified among the great forerunners of contemporary Unitarianism, and burned him; and Luther accused the revolutionary Munzerites. Too much Judaism: This was the favorite accusation of the Catholics against the English Puritans, and of the Puritans against the Catholics for their ecclesiastical legalism, as well as against the left-wing of the English revolution for their antilegalism, and anticlericalism. Zwingli had to deny he had studied the Bible with a Jew. The accusation frightened him so he implored the Jew in question to deny it. Only the Hussites, the revolutionary followers of the Protestant reformer Jan Huss, in Bohemia, and certain elements among English Puritanism may be said to have taken pride from the accusation of being crypto-Jews. For the rest, to be said to be too Jewish in their Christian faith was as crushing as being called a Red west of the Iron Curtain today, or a bourgeois-imperialist east of it.

Nevertheless; there have been gentiles, devout Christians, who have insisted upon their intimate connection with the Jews and with Judaism. This has been the case, not only for the Hussites and for the English Puritan of the Reformation periods in European history, and for some curious Scottish

Reprinted from *The Chicago Jewish Forum* 9, no. 3 (Spring 1951): 165–170.

and English sects cropping up here and there, now and then, but always persisting, from the sixteenth century through to the middle of the nineteenth. It is also the case among an interesting number of people in the United States today. But before one can understand the existence of "Jewish" oriented Christian sects in the United States today, one must understand the predicates of that orientation: *first;* the historical impact of the Jewish literature upon all parts of gentile culture, and *second,* the special social, political and economic situation of the members of such sects. Having elucidated the predicates of the "Jewish orientation" we will then examine the impact of Judaism on those elements of gentile society most receptive to it in contemporary society.

I

Rabbi Goldman's massive work on the Old Testament, of which two volumes, have been published thus far, has as a secondary task not so much the elucidation of the texts but the cataloguing of the supreme influence of the texts upon the mind and thought of Western civilization. Western prose style cannot be understood except by a student of the Bible; nor can one understand the temper behind that style. Rabbi Goldman makes the point in overwhelming detail. This is not the place to review the details of the history of the influence of the Jewish Book on the gentile mind. It is enough to say it has been the central influence. One example will suffice: the impact of the King James Version.

Hebrew, as Professor Crook, a great authority on the literary associations of the Bible has written, translates singularly well into English, better perhaps than into any other language. Any comparison of the Hebrew literary style of parallelism in its English and German versions, for example, clearly indicates the superiority of the English. This is not to say the English translators have been consistently more philologically precise than the German, or others. On the contrary. But the syntax of English seems to make for a more expressive translation of Hebrew poetry than any other.

Nevertheless, the Bible had as much impact, after the Reformation had made it available to every man, upon the Continent as on the British Isles. All politics, even the politics of the Humanists, felt the impact of the Old Testament imagery, of Jewish ethical valuations. All poetry felt the same impact. Neither Genevan government, nor Miltonic poetry is conceivable without the Jewish influence. Men politiked to build the New Jerusalem, and sang to the glory of the Jewish God. When Milton thought of the enemy of the English revolution, he called them "Gentiles" ("Why do the Gentiles tumult?"), when he wrote his magnificent *Sonnet on the Late Massacre in Piedmont* the voice, as Professor Marjorie Hope Nicolson, of Columbia University, has noted, is the voice of Milton, but the voice behind the voice is that of Jeremiah. Indeed, for Milton, as for the English in general, there is nothing in other cultures and literatures

> . . . to compare
> With Sion's[1] songs, to all true tasts excelling,
> Where God is prais'd aright, and Godlike men,
> The Holiest of Holies, and his Saints.

It was not only the educated Englishman, or German, or Scotsman who knew his Old Law, and his Hebrew. It was the pious man, the whole "Secret company of true believers." Class and formal education did not correlate at all with the Hebraism of the English Protestants, as Mathew Arnold and the best of modern scholarship know so well.

This is the final point to make about the impact of Jewish literature: it penetrated the entire social structure, and thus the entire culture. The world image of gentile hope is Jewish.

II

Plainly, the rich need not hope so much as the poor. Satisfaction is an adequate substitute for hope. Hope, however, is the bread of the lower classes. The world image of hope, coming out of classical Jewish literature has, therefore, broken with a consistently revolutionary impact on the lower classes. The lower classes, whenever they reacquire a dynamic, religious reorientation acquire it first of all in the frame of the Judaistic image of world hope. The first vital spark of each new religious breakthrough within Christianity has come as a return to the Bible. The vital spark of protest against the status quo, insofar as it has been framed in terms of the traditions of Western culture, has first come in terms of a prophetic protest.

Religion, not church-building, but creative movements of belief, is a lower-class phenomenon. Ernst Troeltsch, perhaps the greatest scholar of the sociology of religion, made the point, around which all sociologists of religion have to focus some measure, if they are to understand religious experience and movements:

> The really creative, church-forming, religious movements are the work of the lower strata. Here only can one find that union of unimpaired imagination, simplicity in emotional life, unreflective character of thought, spontaneity of energy and vehement force of need, out of which an unconditioned faith in a divine revelation, the naivete of complete surrender, and the intransigence of certitude can arise.

1. Milton's spelling.

A religious movement, first, as a sect, is born, then, out of psychological need and class situation. The rich do not have the problems of the poor, nor can they answer them. A bourgeois scholar-minister cannot talk to a poor Negro congregation. His philological musings, his temperate speech, cannot penetrate the craving for a new Jerusalem, or the resentment of complacency by the religious proletariat.

This is to say: all proletariats are religious. All religions arise out of proletariats. Christianity was itself at least a century in this world before it attracted any significant number of upper-class members. It was at that moment that Christianity became something other than it had been, in sociological terms.

It is, therefore, equally true to say: all religions die when the class that carries that religion is no longer lower. John Wesley, the charismatic founder of Methodism, clearly saw the paradox:

> I do not see how it is possible in the nature of things for any revival of religion to continue long. For religion must necessarily produce both industry and frugality, and these cannot but produce riches. But as riches increase so will pride, anger, and love of the world in all its branches.

He saw his own movement beginning to lose its religious integrity, out of the irony of religiously grounded success, much like western Jewry after the Emancipation.

> The Methodists in every place grow diligent and frugal; consequently they increase in goods. Hence they proportionately increase in pride, in anger, in the desire of the flesh, the desire of the eyes, and pride of life. So, although the form of religion remains, the spirit is swiftly vanishing away.

Wesley's answer indicates the insolubility of the paradox and the failure of an originally lower-class movement such as Methodism to preserve its religious dynamic. He cannot urge that the movement remain lower-class, although that is the logical alternative. Instead, he asks:

> What way can we take, that our money may not sink us into the nethermost hell? There is one way and there is no other way under Heaven. If those who gain all they can, and save all they can, will likewise give all they can, then the more they gain, the more they will grow in grace, and the more treasures they will lay up in Heaven.

Thus a dynamic religious movement inevitably becomes, with its success, a ladies-aid society, remembering its devout ancestors and forgetting the nature of the devotion. There are no historical examples available of the upper-classes giving up their status, or to use Wesley's terms, to "give all they can." Every upper class, to turn Winston Churchill's famous phrase, means to hold what it has. It only gives up what is taken away from it, or what it has learned, in its sophistication, is spurious and unnecessary to its status. Thus, only the lower classes can achieve the basic religious attitude, which is an ambivalence of hope and protest. Upper classes are incapable of genuine religious experience, although it is, of course, possible for individual members of those classes to be so alienated from them as to be capable of genuine religiosity. But this is true only of deviants, not of the typical or ordinary, who are far more important in characterizing the class basis of religion.

In summary: the world image of hope and protest is Jewish. The classes most receptive to that image, most capable of genuine religious experience are the lower. The connection between the Jewish world image and specific strata low in the social structure of gentile society may be illustrated at almost any period, from the Christological to the present. It may prove more interesting, in an article intended for a general readership rather than one for specialized students of the problem of Jewish-Christian ideological interrelations, to illustrate the connection in terms of contemporary religious movements.

III

The Negroes are the lowest class, indeed, a lower caste, in the United States. They are still, on the whole, the most genuinely religious group in the nation, granted the fact that as their status has improved their religion has declined. They fit Troeltsch's criteria for a creative religious movement more perfectly than any other group in the United States. Having a low level of education, the Negro imagination is comparatively unimpaired. The force of need out of despair, and all the other qualities Troeltsch lists, are also present in contemporary Negro life, particularly in the South, though not exclusively so, as witness the storefront churches in Northern urban centers. One other element is present, beyond Troeltsch's catalogue, that makes the Negro's religious experience both genuine and unique. This is his debt to Judaism, and more important his occasional attempt to assert that he is a true born child among the Chosen People, a blood Jew. A Negro sect such as the *Churches of the Living God* may prove significant and interesting example, less well known if no more significant than the better known Negro synagogues of New York City. A second perhaps even less known example of the use of Judaism among dynamic Christian movements will come out of our discussion of the community of Negro religious communists living in rural Virginia, *The Church of God and Saints of Christ.*

The Church of the Living God, Christian Workers for Fellowship is now two sects, the splinter calling itself, after the schism in 1902, the *Church of the Living God, the Pillar and Ground of Truth.* There have been other schisms, as in most sect histories, but they are so manifold and complicated that they cannot be traced in an article that is not devoted exclusively to the scholarly function of documenting religious movements. In any case the schisms are not relevant to our purposes. The relevant statistical statement to make is that the two major groups tally as follows: the first has about 100 churches and 4,500 members, the second 120 churches and 5,000 members. Thus the total membership of this unknown sect of poverty-stricken Negroes is probably greater than the card-carrying membership of the Communist Party in the city of Chicago.

The founder of the sect was the Rev. William Christian, at Wrightsville, Arkansas, in 1889. He founded it after a revelation gave him that divine mission. Indeed, the sect believes its leader can be "neither elected nor appointed, but holds his office by virtue of a divine calling. . . . No man has been given power to judge God's anointed." Christian died in 1928, to be succeeded by his wife, and she, in turn, by her son.

The rhetoric of the sect is plainly Old Testament. But the significance of the Judaic quality of the rhetoric is unclear until one examines the catechism of the sect, the basis for the instruction in church and to the young in Sunday school. The passage from the catechism of *C.W.F.F.* quoted below is a key to understand the religious hope and protest of this group of some ten thousand Negroes:

Q. Was Jesus a member of the black race?
A. Yes. Matt. 1.
Q. How do you know?
A. Because he was in the line of Abraham and David the King.
Q. Is this assertion sufficient proof that Christ came of the black generation?
A. Yes.
Q. Why?
A. Because David said he became like a bottle in the smoke. Pa. 119:83.
Q. What color was Job?
A. He was black. Job. 30:30.
Q. What color was Jeremiah?
A. He said he was black. Jer. 8:21.
Q. Who was Moses' wife?
A. An Ethiopian (or black) woman. Numbers 12:1.
Q. Should we make a difference in people because they are black?
A. No. Jer. 12:23.
Q. Why?
A. Because it is as natural to be black as the leopard to be spotted. Jer. 13:23.

The catechism speaks for itself. The amalgam of hope and protest that is the *fons et origo* of Negro lower-class religion is clearly expressed. But it is not simply that it is enjoined in Jer. 13:23, and is therefore the word of God, that one must not make a difference in people because they are black.

It is not simply that this Negro sect draws on its Judaistic source to protest its status and hope for something better. More curiously, it identifies itself with its source. Its own self-image is the image of Jewry, the line of Abraham and David the King.

What could be more curious than for one persecuted people to adopt the fiction that is another's. To be a Negro is tragic enough. To be a Negro Jew is a double tragedy. To be a Negro who asserts, falsely, of course, that he is equally, racially, a Jew seems an ultimate tragedy of irrational behavior.

But the irrationality expressed in the catechism has its own rationale. What is it to be a Jew, in the line of Abraham and David the King? It is to be a living expression of the highest ideals of human existence. It is to belong to the master race, in terms of the history of ethical valuations. The Negro sect, therefore, asserts the fiction of its Jewishness to assert its own dignity and equality, to express its hope and protest, in the myth of its racial history, by identifying themselves with the "racial" image of the dignity and equality of man.

The Church of God and Saints of Christ are an even more clear-cut illustration of the connection between racial protest and the impact of Jewish ethical valuations. Again the sect is colored, poor, southern (Virginia). Again there was a "prophet," who founded the sect after the experience of revelation. This time it was not a Rev. William Christian, but a cook on the Santa Fe Railroad named William S. Crowdy. Again the whole language is steeped in the King James Version of the Old Testament. However, this radical sect protest has been so thorough that it openly insists on two doctrinal points: first; that property be held in common, and that the thousand odd acres of land, the various small plants, the commissary, the school, and the homes for the orphans and aged be operated by and for the entire sect assembled. Indeed, *The Church of God and Saints of Christ* is a Negro Kibbutz, practicing what is believed to be the economic and social injunctions of the Lord God Jehovah.

The second doctrinal point is equally important for understanding the impact of the Jewish world image on lower class groups. The prophet's revelation disclosed to him that the Negro people are really Jews, simply children of the lost tribes of Israel. The pathetic reason that the Negroes have lost contact with contemporary Jewry, according to the doctrine, is that contemporary Jewry is no longer Jewish. The original Jews were black. Modern Jewry has changed color as a consequence of breaching the specific Deuteronomic injunction against intermarriage; that is, modern Jewry is guilty of miscegenation. However, the shoe is on the other foot. It is miscegenation in reverse in sociological terms. It is the Jews who, by becoming white, have degraded themselves. The *Saints of Christ* as Negroes, and true Jews, keep alive the mission and meaning of Jewry.

There is, therefore, great Jewish piety among the *Saints of Christ*. Cir-

cumcision is, of course, universal within the sect. The Holy Days are observed with minute pietistic scrupulousness. Thus members of the sect
gather from comparatively great distances to observe Passover for a week.
As in ancient Jewry, blood is smeared liberally on the houses at the appropriate liturgical points, and the saints, robed as they think the Jews must
have been robed, march solemnly in prayer to commemorate the historic
event of the emancipation from Egypt. The Jewish calendar, with its Hebrew
names, is used by the sect, without any feeling of strangeness or incongruity. E. T. Clark, perhaps the greatest student of sect life in the United
States, and my source for much material here, reports some of the names of
the saints: "St. Benjamin Watkins, St. Ethel Mai Tutwiler, St. Joshua Hurt,
St. Zebedee Daniels, St. Isaiah Williams." The chief of the sect is called
"Grand Father Abraham," the sect newsletter is entitled the *Weekly Prophet.*

Both illustrations might be multiplied by examples from seventeenth-
century Scotland, or England. In a few cases noted by sociologists, the
American Negro has turned to the Moslem religion for his image of hope and
protest. But, on the whole, not only the American Negro but the lower
classes generally, wherever the traditional, animating ethic of the western
democratic tradition is still operative, have turned the images created by
Jewry for its ideology and its model of action. Even Henry Wallace must
have thought at times he might, indeed, lead a Gideon's army.

Democratic action is, historically, always an upward thrust toward equal-
itarianism. Democratic action, whatever its purposes, however false its
base, has needed the Jewish world image to give it its dynamic. (51:3)

Religion and Politics
Christianity

17

Adolf Harnack's *History of Dogma*

Harnack's masterwork, the *History of Dogma*, first appeared between the years 1886 and 1890. In 1894, one of the leading Protestant book houses in England, Williams and Norgate, began to issue it in an English translation. The quantity of German learning translated for the English reader was already formidable in Harnack's time. It was made the more formidable, and the more important, through these seven volumes of narrative argument on how a living faith was laid away inside stiff ecclesiastical formulae.

The scholar Harnack was also a practical man of religious affairs, interested in reaching the educated laity. *Outlines of the History of Dogma*, here reprinted without change from the authorized English translation of 1893, represents his own subsequent effort to summarize the labor of his life in one volume.

It remains a great labor, even when seen in miniature. Few people nowadays, even those few studying church history in the seminaries, have read through the seven volumes; but many have been influenced by their general thesis. Thus the *History of Dogma* satisfies the criterion of a great work. It belongs in the select library of grand, sad case histories that argue decline and fall. The decline which Harnack narrates is of the Christian faith; the putative cause, that transformation of Gospel Christianity by Greek philosophy which hardened faith into dogma. Nevertheless, for all its sadness this history has a happy ending—at least one that promises a new beginning. For it ends with Luther, who, in the "beautiful years of the Reformation," from 1519 to 1523, waked the faith of Christendom from its dogmatic slumber.[1]

Harnack belonged to the unmitered hierarchy of Protestantism, the pro-

---

Reprinted from *Outlines of the History of Dogma*, by Adolf Harnack (Boston: Beacon Press, 1957): xiii–xxxv.

1. *Outlines*, 541.

fessoriat. He was a Protestant of the chair—a professor, and the son of a professor. Perhaps the most influential Christian historiographer of his time, Harnack was violently attacked and loyally defended. He progressed quickly through the academic hierarchies—from Leipzig, where he began as a *Privatdocent*, to Giessen; from Giessen to Marburg; from Marburg to Berlin. In Berlin he was not only a professor but also director of the Royal Library. It was a progress from province to capital, from local superiority to widespread influence. The attacks upon him, for unorthodoxy, made him even more famous. Harnack was honored and influential in the prime of his own lifetime. If he has been forgotten, enough time has passed now for a safe return of interest and respect.

Formidable scholars are not generally formidable persons. Harnack was not a formidable person. An immensely productive scholar, he simply did not have the reserves of passion and time necessary to engage himself fully in the controversies he stimulated. Yet he was not merely a great scholar. Out of his interest in reaching the laity came a widely read apologetic work, in the form of historical analysis, *What Is Christianity?* Harnack's scholarship had been organized, the immense learning marshaled, to remoralize Christian doctrine. Anything called doctrine which did not induce a believer to experience himself as a morally responsible agent was not authentically Christian.

For ten years, from 1902 to 1912, Harnack was president of the Evangelical Congress. In 1914 he was honored by the Kaiser, and became *von* Harnack. The social gospel disappeared in the smoke of national religion. Harnack died in the summer of 1930, too soon to see the renewed efforts—both the social gospel and Christian Socialism—by Protestant intellectuals to break out of the seminary into the world dissipated in the smoke of a national religion so profound and so popular that few Socialists and fewer Christians could have imagined it. Certainly the social gospel had never prepared anyone for what happened in 1933. That sin could be so original came as a shock even to the neo-orthodox.

When he died, at seventy-nine, Harnack had left a monumental corpus, much of it untranslated. His influence in England and America, as well as on the Continent, had been very great. This summary of the *History of Dogma* testified to his success. It came out in English almost at the same time as the original German edition. But neither the *Outlines* nor the seven-volume *History* has been reprinted since. The last generation of Harnack's students now approach old age. The generations between the Great Wars ignored him, and read inferior texts by up-to-date scholars. Nevertheless, despite inadequacies of translation, *Outlines of the History of Dogma* remains the most interesting single volume on the subject. If it is to be surpassed, someone of equal talent and energy will have to approach the subject from a different perspective. For Harnack has done all that can conceivably be done by a great historian hostile to his subject.

Harnack's Protestantism, shaped by scholarship and preached in seminars, is the Protestantism of the educated middle classes, at war on two fronts—against both the ecclesiasts above and the revivalists below. If on the upper front, it proclaims the un-Christian character of much of Christian learning, on the lower front it proclaims the unlearned character of much of Christian preaching. The main contest, however, was against the learned dogmatists.

Not that dogma had been useless or unnecessary throughout the historical developments of Christianity. Dogma was the instrument with which the early Catholic Fathers had kept the Gospel alive, in the face of competing— mainly gnostic—interpretations of the faith. Furthermore, lest he be misunderstood, Harnack made it very clear, in the Prolegomena of the *History*, that dogma was a very flexible instrument; it has been used to stifle religious life, but it could also be used to enhance such life. "Dogmatic Christianity stands between Christianity as the religion of the Gospel, presupposing a personal experience and dealing with disposition and conduct, and Christianity as a religion of cultus, sacraments, ceremonial and obedience, in short of superstition." And, Harnack added, dogmatic Christianity "can be united with either the one or the other"—with a religion of conduct or with a religion of superstition.

Harnack preferred dogma united with a religion of personal experience, shaping character and conduct. Even so, there was something dangerous to religious life in the presence of dogma. Dogma expresses "intellectual Christianity," Harnack tells us. "Therefore there is always the danger . . . that as knowledge it may supplant . . . faith, or connect it with a doctrine of religion, instead of with God and a living experience."[2] By the fourth century, the living Gospel had been masked in Greek philosophy. It was the historian's mission to pluck off the mask and thus reveal how different had been the original contours of the faith beneath. But Harnack knew that doctrinal masks, worn long enough, can reshape the face of religion; the mask acquires a life of its own. The historian knew that dogma—the Trinity, the two natures of Christ, infallibility and all the propositions seconding these dogmas—was the product of historical decisions and of situations that might have turned out quite differently. But a historical decision, once made, has power and logic; it can transform the very elements from which it emerged. If dogma was the product of the historical situation of early Christianity, it is also true that the historical situation of later Christianity was shaped by the

2. Adolf Harnack, *History of Dogma*, translated by Neil Buchanan (London: Williams and Norgate, 1894), I, 16.

presence of dogma. Nevertheless—early and late, product or shaping force—dogma remains what it has been from the beginning: a bad habit of intellectualizing which the Christian had picked up from the Greek when he fled from the Jew. The conversion of faith into dogma, the "work of the Greek [mind] on the soil of the Gospel,"[3] was responsible for what Harnack calls the secularizing of Christianity.

Theories of decline other than Harnack's are available to explain the tragic failure of Christianity to live up to its promise to the world. I shall mention only two other plausible explanations that have been frequently explored. One is the theory that identifies decline with the emergence of coercion as an instrument of Christian practice. The decline of Christianity is thus ascribed to the alliance of Church and State. A second theory of decline identifies the emergence of law, over against the spirit, as the fateful problem. No single theory holds the field. All, including Harnack's, continued to receive consideration from church historians and philosophers of history.

Harnack's theory, in brief, located decline at the point where philosophical creed had displaced religious life. The *History of Dogma* essentially narrates the history of this displacement. By this theory Harnack himself may be located historically, as one of the finest examples of post-Enlightenment Protestantism. Since the Enlightenment an evangelical army of erudites sought to alter the historic decision through which Christianity was made dogmatic. They founded a new Protestantism, more radically different from pre-Enlightenment Protestantism than the Reformation itself had been from Catholicism.

It was in the Enlightenment that the question of the historical nature of Christianity was first fully opened up. Voltaire, Lessing, and others had asked embarrassing questions about Christian institutions and doctrines. Was Christianity a corruption of the true religion, as Voltaire charged? Was it the perfected version of the religion of nature, which is accessible to all men in the light of reason, as Kant thought? Was the historical form of Christianity superior to natural religion, as Locke thought? Or was Christianity but one phase in the historical emergence of the final and true religion, as Lessing suspected? Long after these major interlocutors had departed, these questions, and others very similar, continued to disturb the piety of cultured Europeans. A new Protestantism, antidoctrinal in cast and social in justification, developed in response to these sorts of questions. The Enlightenment philosophers located the religious spirit in Reason, which is universal and thus cannot be contained within the specifically religious institution—the Church.[4] Harnack's post-Enlightenment institutionalism is

3. Ibid., I, 17. Cf. *Outlines*, 5.
4. Today the position of what one might call the Counter-Enlightenment—the defense of institutions by de Maistre, Bonald, finally, in its secular version, by Comte—lies hidden in

part of the nineteenth-century answer to the Enlightenment critique: for Harnack, the Spirit was nowhere if not in the life of the institution and could have no Christian existence except institutionally. Thus the antithesis between Gospel and dogma, to which Harnack ascribed the failures of Christian life, is by no means to be identified with the antithesis between the Spirit and the institutional shapes into which it is forced.

In his debate with the Church historian and jurist Rudolf Sohm, another great theorist of the decline of Christianity, Harnack's modified institutionalism was expressed most convincingly. The debate centered on the nature of primitive Christianity, where Sohm detected an immediate decline. For Sohm, according to Harnack's conscientious account of his view, "the Church is a purely religious and spiritual entity; she is the people of God, the body of Christ. In this sense she forms, it is true, a body but not a corporation, much less a Christian corporation, for it is only something spiritual (the spirit of God, faith) which makes her a body. Nor can she be at the same time a spiritual and a legal (corporate) unity, for that would be a self-contradiction." But, to Harnack, "it is impossible to see, if we simply eliminate everything earthly from the nature of the Church, how the Church can then be anything but *a mere idea, in which each individual Christian in his isolation believes*. Even so, this idea may be efficacious and powerful, but there is no Church here, only a number of . . . believers, who cannot be anything to one another, and who resemble a number of parallel lines which meet in infinity and not before."[5] Harnack thus poked some gentle fun at the notion of the invisible Church, against which his own institutionalist presuppositions were firmly set. And he goes on to a first-rate piece of sociological analysis which effectively challenges Sohm's position.

After all, Sohm does talk about a *Church*. And a Church, Harnack hurries on, is a social formation, a nuclear society. To say that wherever two or three people gather, in the name of Christ, is a Church may well prick Catholic pretensions of a mass Church. But Sohm's conception of the Church, according to Harnack, is not the correct alternative to the Catholic conception. The Church is "no mere idea of faith"; it is also a regulative institution. If there is an antinomy between the Church as a religious entity and as a social institution, Harnack answers that after all "it is the antinomy which runs through all human history." Wherever absolute values are objec-

---

the shadow of the Enlightenment critique of institutions. If the Enlightenment stimulated the private religions of liberal Protestantism, the Counter-Enlightenment subtly rehabilitated Catholicism as a social religion. It gave to Catholic institutionalism a renewed intellectual sinuosity, with which Newman and his successors built up an intelligentsia in the service of the church rather than of Christ directly.

5. Adolf Harnack, *The Constitution and Law of the Church in the First Two Centuries* (London: Williams and Norgate, 1910), 210–11. (Harnack's italics.) Cf. *What Is Christianity?*, translated by T. B. Saunders (New York: Harper, 1957), 107.

tified, the antinomy must exist.[6] Sohm, Harnack concludes, was correct in protesting, as a jurist and historian, against Catholic ecclesiastical pretensions; but Sohm's protest had gone too far and involved a rejection of the Church as an earthly institution. Yet Sohm's theory of decline—of the charismatic fellowship hardened into a legal organization—appeals to a very powerful and useful sentiment. From faith to institution, from charismatic founder to bureaucracy, from idea to organization—whether in religious or secular form, this theory of decline has conditioned what remains, by and large, the most compelling critique of the growing power of institutions. Contemporary moral letters would be deprived of its acutest angle of critical vision if some version of the Sohmian theory were disallowed, on some such grounds as Harnack proposes.

To be viable, dogma must be capable not only of developing into the future but also of conserving the past. Cardinal Newman, with Mill perhaps the finest English mind of the nineteenth century, declared (in his great *Essay on the Development of Christian Doctrine*) that there are laws governing such a development. And the chief law is that of the conservation of institutions, symbolically represented in the dogma itself. In sum, dogma serves to preserve the Church. Harnack would have understood the movement of this most exquisite of modern Catholic minds, from institution to faith rather than from faith to institution. In such a reversal is described the entire law of development, as Harnack rightly understood it. For the development of dogma remains the grandest effort in all western history to guarantee the prevalence of an institution against the competition of time. Thus, in Harnack's judgment, the Roman Catholic Church has become "the most comprehensive and the vastest, the most complicated and yet at the same time the most uniform structure which . . . history has produced."[7] To Harnack it was not an astonishing development—this movement of western religious energy from faith to institution. He understood that the entire movement was inevitable; the power-hunger of the western psyche remains always at work. And so Harnack concluded: "The end toward which from the beginning [the history of dogma] was directed in the Occident . . . revealed itself with astounding clearness: Dogma is institution."[8]

Against the decisive identity of dogma and institution what can the historian offer? Harnack offered his monumental *History of Dogma*. For, as a post-Enlightenment Protestant, Harnack advanced the discipline of history as a counter to the disciplines of dogmatics. "The history of dogma, in that it sets forth the . . . origin and development of . . . dogma, offers the very best means . . . of freeing the Church from dogmatic Christianity, and of hastening the inevitable process of emancipation, which began with Augustine."[9] Thus the writing of history functions as a religious task for the

6. Ibid., 215.   8. *Outlines*, 503.
7. *What Is Christianity?*, 246.   9. Ibid., 7–8.

Protestant intellectual whose historical sensibilities have been trained in the Enlightenment tradition.

That Harnack the historian was at the same time Harnack the post-Enlightenment Protestant is clearly the import of his own reflections on his tasks as a historian. "We study history," he said, "in order to intervene in the course of history and we have a right to do so . . . To intervene in history—this means that we must reject the past when it reaches into the present only in order to block us."[10] With Ernst Troeltsch, it was Harnack's ethical intention "to overcome history by history . . . and transform it into something better."[11] His mission, as a historian, was to free man from the dead weight of the traditions that merely burden conscience. In Harnack's opinion, Cardinal Manning had stated the issue clearly, however frivolously: "One must overcome history by dogma." Harnack would say just the opposite: "Dogma must be purified by history, and as Protestants we are confident that in doing so we do not break down but build up."[12]

As a historical religion, Protestantism itself needs to undergo creative transformations, in order to build itself up under new historical demands. For this reason, Harnack did not hesitate to advocate the transformation of a major article of Christian belief: that Christ is manifest in the Old Testament. But Harnack did not shy away from the logic of his own post-Enlightenment historicism. What would have been fatal to the Christian faith in one age may well be vitally necessary in another. Thus now, if not earlier, the time had ripened for Christianity to divorce itself from Israel. "To reject the Old Testament in the second century was an error which the great Church rightly rejected; to cling to it in the sixteenth century was a destiny from which the Reformation could not yet withdraw; but still to preserve it after the nineteenth century as a canonical source in Protestantism is the result of religious and ecclesiastical paralysis . . . To make a clean sweep at this point and honor the truth [namely, that the Old Testament could not be retained as preamble to the New] in confession and instruction is the mighty act—already almost too late—required today of Protestantism."[13] In fact Harnack superadded the verdict of scientific history to the gnostic and Marcionite rejection of the Old Testament; history now supported the suspicion of the first heretics that "the essentially Christian element could not be

10. Quoted in Wilhelm Pauck, "The Significance of Adolf von Harnack's Interpretation of Church History," *Union Seminary Quarterly Review*, January 1954, 15. Professor Pauck's inaugural lecture at the Union Theological Seminary contains a penetrating account of Harnack's self-interpretation as an historian. I have to thank my friend and sometime colleague, James Luther Adams, for directing my attention to Pauck's lecture—and, moreover, for his reading of the present essay in an earlier draft.

11. Ibid., 16.

12. Ibid., 21.

13. Adolf Harnack, *Marcion, Das Evangelium vom Fremden Gott*, 2d ed. (Leipzig: Hinrichs, 1924), 217. Quoted in Karl Barth, *Church Dogmatics*, vol. I, part 2, translated by G. T. Thomson and Harold Knight (New York: Scribner's, 1956), 74.

found in it."[14] Thus the historical sensibility of the post-Enlightenment Protestant compelled him to alter this enormous detail of Christian belief.

Other details, too, would have to be cheerfully sacrificed. But what, then, is the "essentially Christian element"? The answer given by his master, the theologian Albrecht Ritschl, remains superior to any Harnack developed for himself. In the liberal mood, Ritschl's definition of what is essential in Christianity has not yet been bettered, either by Harnack or by any other legate. "Christianity," Ritschl tells us, "is the monotheistic, completely spiritual, and ethical religion, which, based on the life of its author as Redeemer and as founder of the kingdom of God, consists in the freedom of the children of God, involves the impulse to conduct from the motive of love, aims at the moral organization of mankind, and grounds blessedness on the relation of Sonship to God, as well as on the Kingdom of God."[15] The parts of Ritschl's definition are scattered and elaborated throughout Harnack's writings. Trained in the Ritschlian school, Harnack examined the vast range of philosophical theologies and rejected them all as varieties of a Gospel *about* Jesus instead of the Gospel *of* Jesus. Jesus himself "nowhere speaks like a man who had assimilated any theological culture of a technical kind,"[16] and the true believer in Jesus need not assimilate that sort of culture. No theology or philosophy is really necessary. The Gospel is "something so simple" that no one "who possesses a fresh eye for what is alive, and a . . . feeling for what is great, can fail to see it."[17] It was right emotion that the scholar advocated, throughout his unsurpassed survey of what in the history of the Church has passed for right opinion.

The hardening of right emotion into right opinion had taken place early in the history of Christianity. Jesus had combined religion and morality;[18] the early Catholic Fathers had recombined the religion of Jesus with metaphysics. To Harnack the realignment appeared inevitable, and perhaps desirable. Primitive Christianity had to disappear in order that Christianity might become a major contender in the field of Greek culture. The higher righteousness had to compete with the higher symbolism. What more inevitable compromise than that the higher righteousness should clothe itself in the higher symbolism? "The most important step that was ever taken in the domain of Christian doctrine," Harnack declares, "was when the Christian apologists at the beginning of the second century drew the equation: the Logos = Jesus Christ."[19] To render the personal experience of Christian

14. *Marcion*, 223; *Church Dogmatics*, 79.

15. Albrecht Ritschl, *The Christian Doctrine of Justification and Reconciliation*, edited by H. R. MacKintosh and A. B. Macaulay (Edinburgh: T. & T. Clark, 1900), III, 13.

16. *What Is Christianity?*, 31.

17. Ibid., 14.

18. Ibid., 73. "In this sense," Harnack writes, "religion may be called the soul of morality, and morality the body of religion."

19. Ibid., 202–3.

faith as the rationalism of Greek philosophy "thus marked out the task of 'dogmatic' and, so to speak, wrote the prolegomena for every future theological system in the Church."[20] Thus, to Harnack, metaphysics spelled at once the ruin of the original and authentic faith and the making of the syncretic Church. But the paradox is that so long as Christianity remains bound to one system of metaphysics or another it severely limits its own range of life. For every metaphysics, being an historical formulation, is trapped in its own history. But, in a very important sense, the Gospel is historyless. Unencumbered by outdated metaphysical presuppositions, a fresh response of faith is always possible.

Yet, however it may have later encumbered faith, the metaphysical equation of Logos with Christ resulted in two immense victories for the Church: it made the new faith intelligible to the non-Jewish world, where formerly it had been unintelligible; it laid down a major permitting condition for the development of western rationalism. The latter victory has been less frequently explained than the first; I shall at least sketch in an explanation of this still important connection between the sophistication of western religion and the energy of western rationality.

With the triumph of Logos theology, God became a God not of disorder but of order. Christianity thus maintained the image of an ordered as well as an ordained cosmos. Furthermore, the Logos theology prevented the identification of Christ with the absurd; Christian revelation could not be so easily described as irrational. Equally important perhaps, Logos theology preserved for western science the idea that the world was not dominated by demonic forces that were unintelligible or would destroy man if he investigated them. A victory of gnostic dualism would thus probably have changed the entire course of development in the history of occidental rationality. It is fair to say that to Logos theology modern reason owes a great deal of its early training. The Logos incarnate acted to preserve the power of Reason for its later advent and domination over a world no longer dominated by the Christian myth. Without dogmatic Christianity, the mystique of Reason, by which western culture now survives and once flourished, might never have had the environment in which to mature into its own different—and finally anti-Christian—form. It was the Logos Christology of the western Church that supplied the symbolic environment for the rise of the rational technology of the western State. For without a prior development of substantial rationality, it is scarcely possible that technical rationality would have developed. Nowhere except in cultures conditioned by orthodoxy have men struggled with such sanctified conviction to transform the world. If the faith of contemporary rationalists in the transformative power of Reason is justified, then they must at least acknowledge how directly the sources of their faith run to

20. *History of Dogma*, II, 224.

a religious intellectualism now traditionally derided by the rationalists themselves.

I have said that the Logos theology rendered the new faith intelligible to the non-Jewish world. But the motif of intelligibility in the history of Christian apologetics is a very ambiguous one; intelligibility can become a danger as well as a necessity to the Church. To Harnack the danger of the Logos doctrine—and of other apologetic instruments used for bridging the abyss between Christ and culture—was as significant as its necessity. The intellectualization of Christianity marked perhaps the supreme propaganda victory in the coldest of wars. As in all propaganda victories, however, when the defeated are won over they bring with them, as the price of defeat, their favorite ideas. Greek culture may have been brought to its knees; but it worshiped the old truths, even if they were incarnate in the Church. The failure of nerve in the Hellenistic world was revenged in the Christian world: by the transformation of faith into doctrine. Weak and old philosophies, when they tutor strong young faiths, become their masters.

Perhaps the major error of Harnack's analysis was his insistence on associating gnostic formulae with Greek philosophy. Harnack's thesis on the Greek ancestry of Christian dogmatics rests heavily on this assimilation of gnostic to Greek thought. The thesis has been severely damaged by the researches of later scholars into the Oriental background of gnosticism. Nevertheless, if he considered gnosticism too narrowly as an expression of the Greek mind, Harnack took care not to overemphasize the singular effect of gnosticism on the faith. The Greek mind was in any event "already concealed in the earliest Gentile Christianity itself: it was the atmosphere which one breathed." If the gnostics "hellenized" Christianity, so had Paul.[21]

The gnostic controversy encouraged the Church to become intellectual, in self-defense, rather than sentimental, in self-assertion—as did the controversy with science in the nineteenth century. To compete with the gnostics, the Church adopted the decisive part of the gnostic program: "the conversion of the Gospel into a doctrine, into an absolute philosophy of religion."[22] The victor adapted the program of the vanquished. On reading Harnack, one has ample occasion to reflect on the hollowness of victories. The personnel of gnosticism was defeated. But in the very struggle against gnosticism, the Church created a frame of dogma which the gnostics themselves had advocated. Harnack sees the historical value of the Catholic victory—or of the gnostic defeat. The question regarding the nature of the Church first arose between Catholics and gnostics: whether Christianity was to be organized around definite and definitely interpreted creeds, or disorganized around a hundred different philosophies. Both sides "hellenized." The gnostics were merely the first to transform faith into doctrine. "They

21. Ibid., I, 217.
22. Ibid., I, 252.

were the first to work up tradition systematically. They undertook to present Christianity as the absolute religion, and therefore placed it in definite opposition to the other religions, even to Judaism." Not that Christianity is anything other than the absolute religion, according to Harnack. But to the gnostics, the content of the absolute religion was identical with the conclusions of religious philosophy, allegedly certified by the Christian revelation. Gnostics, we may conclude, were somewhat premature Catholics. The gnostic systems, Harnack tells us, represent the "*acute* secularizing or hellenizing of Christianity, with the rejection of the Old Testament." The Catholic system, he continues, represents a "*gradual* process of the same kind," except that the Old Testament has been conserved.[23] We have here the classic instance in the pattern of victory by moderates over extremists— a pattern repeated countless times since in the history of religious and political movements.

The faith of the historian is best detected in his discussion of the faith of others. Of all Christian minds, perhaps, Augustine comes closest to satisfying Harnack's personal taste. Augustine is praised as the finest Christian sensibility before Luther and after Paul. Even in this outline version of the *History of Dogma*, the exposition of Augustine conveys to us how important Harnack considered him.

In the history of dogma, Augustine exemplifies that fresh departure which always has made the development of any doctrine something more exciting, and more relevant, than the discovery of its origins. Augustine is favored not simply for his expansion of the basis of dogma. More important, he penetrated beyond doctrine to a moral psychology of faith. The Augustinian theology was linked to personal experience, not merely to erudition and to intellectual ingenuity. Augustine thus becomes a figure of Protestantism, theologizing from what he really knows: his own experience. In the name of Augustine, Harnack tests the Church against spirit. "He who disregards the formulas, but looks to the spirit, will . . . find in Augustine's works a stream of Pauline faith."[24] Augustine unfettered the sense of freedom in religion; "he rescued religion from its communal and cult . . . form and restored it to the heart."[25] Thus Augustine added a ferment of real religion to the history of dogma.

To replace obsolete dogma with real religion, Harnack hoped for a new sort of dogmatics—a literature of personal confession. In 1925 he told Karl Barth, when these two men, so utterly opposed, last confronted each other directly, that if he were to write a dogmatics it would be of the variety we now understand as anti-dogmatic. Had he the gift, Harnack would have

23. Ibid., I, 226–27. (Harnack's italics.)
24. Ibid., V, 88.
25. *Outlines*, 336.

written a personal apologetic in the genre intimated by Paul, occasionally used by Luther, perfected by Augustine, and characteristic of the best writing of Pascal and Kierkegaard. In that final conversation with Barth, then already embarked on the composition of the greatest and most proclamatory dogmatics since Calvin's, Harnack proposed, as Barth reports it, "that dogmatics in the older sense ought now to be replaced by the personal confession of someone who has attained the maturity and serenity of final convictions and spiritual certainties, a confession determined at its very heart by the history of Christianity." Harnack, Barth concludes, "was obviously speaking for Neo-Protestantism, whose proper object of faith is not God in His revelation, but man himself believing in the divine."[26]

Harnack's "Neo-Protestantism" stands up surprisingly well beside Barth's Neo-Orthodoxy. To whom the future belongs may be more problematic than current estimates allow. In Switzerland, almost the last Protestant culture on earth, it is still possible for Barth to construct a dogmatics, not an apologetics. A Church dogmatics speaks to the world in the language of the Church, not in the language of the world. Yet, to be intellectually relevant, it is doubtful that any Christian writer can be strictly proclamatory. He must necessarily write an apologetics, if he is to reach beyond the hard core; to teach the already well-instructed is not a sufficient reason for composing a dogmatics. And the culture that the Church has generally confronted listens best to apology and personal confession. In a culture so richly endowed with a variety of intellectual, aesthetic, and emotional exercises, a strict dogmatics of proclamation cannot be expected to excite attention—let alone opposition. Barth may be rejected, but not because he has been read; such rejections do not prepare for acceptances in the future.

In this respect, at the least, the sort of apologetics Paul Tillich attempts offers a valuable alternative to Barth's uncompromising dogmatics. Tillich uses radically secular terms and insights, in order to reconstitute the Christian argument from within modern culture. There is a danger in modern apologetics, of course. Any arrival at a new point of consensus can mean the fading away of the apologetic body until nothing remains except the smile on the face of culture. A similar danger waits for the contemporary Jewish theologian. Martin Buber employs apologetics brilliantly, minting anti-biblical dross into biblical gold—this in order to revive a response to the faith of Israel from the secular culture of world Jewry.

Of all Harnack's works, a small volume of his meditations, published three years after his death, *A Scholar's Testament*, comes nearest to being a work of personal confession. In it Harnack most clearly revealed his own anti-intellectual attitude toward religion. Religion, we learn, is an "energy." Specifically, the Christian religion is a moral energy, training the character and will, and therefore ruling life. Thus Harnack asserts the practical sover-

---

26. *Church Dogmatics*, 367.

eignty of religion, however philosophy may defeat it on a theoretical level. With his revered "Christian pagan," Goethe, Harnack is willing to measure Christianity by its moral effect, not by its theoretical coherence. Theory, in any case, criticizes belief. One cannot have a theoretical belief. Christian theory is a contradiction in terms. "We ought to regard [Christianity] as an energy"[27]; and as an independent energy at that, not measurable by one or another of the many standards of theoretical coherence. As a human energy, religion was incomparably superior to philosophy. Philosophy was for philosophers; religion was for suffering humanity. Not even the Socratic religion of conscience was a substitute for Christian faith. Of course, there were exceptions. But most men wanted to know more than how to be knowing and virtuous both; they wanted to know what it felt like to be saved. If not for every single man, then for humanity at large, Harnack asserted it was the energy of Christian religion that could "meet misery and wretchedness of every kind"[28]—the misery and wretchedness not only of those who do not know, but also of those who know that God exists.

Here, in *A Scholar's Testament*, Harnack spoke in his personal voice. The voice of the historian encouraged quite another attitude. For Harnack is never dogmatic; he is not even dogmatically anti-dogmatic. Piety could not advance without accepted proclamation, nor sentiment without expression. Even a temper so fundamentally hostile to dogma as Harnack's found a Christianity without dogma "inconceivable." Of course in this passage he means by dogma merely "a clear expression"[29] of the ever-present content of faith, not of some past historical content. If there could be no Christianity without dogma, nevertheless Harnack concluded that dogma should not be fixed by the attitudes of dead generations of believers—however inspired. Harnack's exposure of the historical limitations of dogma equally well indicates its continuing historical possibilities. If the churches expect anyone to listen seriously to them, they will need to rehabilitate both dogma and the personal voice, both traditional intelligence and fresh emotion. (57:4)

18

The Evangelist Strategy

The modern evangelist must confront the unique fact that this is no longer a Christian society. Earlier evangelists and other sorts of religious agitators faced a very different problem. They confronted instead of a secular a

27. *A Scholar's Testament* (London: Nicholson and Watson, 1933), 220–22.
28. Ibid., 225.
29. *History of Dogma*, I, 22.

Reprinted from *Religion and the Face of America*, chapter 4, edited by Jane C. Zahn (Berkeley: University Extension, University of California, 1959), 17–24.

church civilization, one that was, in fact as well as lip service, Christian. Every element of the art, music, recreation, philosophy, education, politics, manners, and morals of the civilization referred, by definition, to the Christian standard. To be heretical meant to be a deviant Christian. To communicate with the heretic was a high Christian intellectual art, perhaps higher than the art of dogmatics which is directed to those who are communicants but need further instruction. *Dogmatics* was the teaching device of the church. It was intended to keep the religious community, which was in that civilization identical with political, tightly cosseted within the frame of ideological consensus. Quite another kind of literary genre reached beyond the heretics on the very edge of the religious community toward those who did not belong altogether. This we may call *apologetics*, the literary address aimed at those entirely outside the religious community.

Apologetics usually develops two high points, I think. One is at the beginning and the other at the end of a given religious culture. At the beginning, as the doctrine for which it argues in the ascendant, apologetics are aimed confidently at incorporating old competing doctrines, failing yet powerful. This describes the relation between Patristic writing and Greek philosophy. But there is also a late flowering of apologetics, as the doctrine for which it argues begins to decline. Such a flowering announced the last period of European Christian culture. The first great apologist of that period was Blaise Pascal.

The *Pensées*, addressing, as they do still, those completely outside the church, compose in their fragmentary and personal character the first great modern work of apologetics. As such, it is a masterpiece. For it asks the final question of those who cannot muster their courage for faith: how long can the misery and futility of life without faith be tolerated?

The next great figure in the modern apologetic tradition appeared centuries later. Søren Kierkegaard wove his apologetics into a deliberate and brilliant series of attacks both on the dogmatic, institutional Christianity of the time and on the secular philosophy with which it allied. Both Pascal and Kierkegaard made private Christianity superior to public Christendom, as the early Christian community was assumedly superior to the civil religions of the Roman Empire. Without institutional responsibility, Kierkegaard is the very type of modern religious intellectual—essentially a free lancer, a religious critic. Promising candidates for the ministry must, during their years of study in the seminaries of Protestant America, be trained so far as possible as critics—without developing in them that painful allergy to the life of their own clerical institutions which rightly afflicts young Protestant intellectuals nowadays. The problem is to make these brighter ministerial students religious intellectuals, on the one hand, and yet capable of persisting in the parish ministry on the other. The loss of the most promising minds and finer sensibilities from the ministry, under the characteristic pressure of congregational life in America, is a very serious problem and one among many with which the seminaries across the country must somehow cope. The ministerial sense of futility can be appreciated, for the minister occupies a residual place in a culture which no longer adheres to the symbolic representation of itself that is still publicly sanctioned and even invoked. Pascal was perhaps the first figure to face squarely the need for a new rhetoric of support for the old Christian symbolism. In this sense he belongs in the evangelical tradition, followed by Kierkegaard. The evangelical strategy of both can be duplicated by examples from the strategies of far less weighty, if more popular, figures in the development of modern evangelism. Essentially, the strategy of Pascal, of Friedrich Schleiermacher, of Kierkegaard, does not differ from that of Jonathan Edwards. And, still, the Edwards strategy does not differ from that of Billy Graham. For all, the weighty and the trivial, the aim is first to disturb self-complacent humanity and then to quiet that disturbance with the Gospel.

Self-complacent humanity may be complacent precisely in its feeling of superiority to the Gospel. The test of successful evangelical strategy is not how it can develop and then use the anxieties of residually religious lower class and uneducated auditors. Rather, the test of evangelical strategy always comes when it is used against the emancipated, educated classes. The first deliberately concentrated literary effort at an evangelical apologetic aimed at the educated classes was composed by the German theologian, Friedrich Schleiermacher, who in 1799 published a volume of pretended *Addresses on Religion, to Its Cultured Despisers.*

Schleiermacher deliberately did not address some variety of Christian or even anti-Christian, but a far greater opponent: the indifferent. For it is not the opposition of another doctrine that the modern evangelist must confront but that most elusive and powerful of all opponents—one without doctrine because he is really without interest in the controversy. Thus the modern evangelist must first act the apologist and bring the characteristic anxieties of his auditors into the Christian frame of reference, thereby actually increasing the pressures of anxiety by putting them into a radically moralizing context. Slipped in among the anxiety-producing references is a new interrogative motif—whether the feeling of superiority to the Gospel is not itself, paradoxically, a major cause of the anxieties indubitably felt. From Pascal to Graham, the evangelists ask: Can a modern man afford to pass up this possible resolution of his characteristic anxieties?

This is not a purely rhetorical question. The great evangelists themselves have been often anguished, tortured figures, in search of an answer for themselves. The question of whether in the Gospels there is relief from anxieties is the hair-shirt that the evangelist wears with more or less public effect. Often his own preaching is deeply personal, as we find it in both Pascal and Kierkegaard. The anxiety they discuss is, in the first place, their own; and the solution they find—conversion in the light of the Gospel—a comfort somehow made available to them. The evangelist is very modern precisely in his autobiographical style of address, whether it be the philosophical personalism of Kierkegaard, or the autobiographical vulgarity of Billy Sunday. In Billy Graham there is a notable reserve, an antiseptic refusal to get personal or exhibit the stages of his own religious development—while all the time being personal about the intimate life of his ideal auditor—that marks Graham as a middle-class parodist of the evangelical strategy, lowering the intensity of anxiety to be produced and demanding a far less dramatic recourse to the Gospel. But Graham is dealing with a public already somewhat aware, in this advertising age, of the techniques of anxiety production. Therefore, although certainly not more subtle than his vulgar predecessors, he must be more cautious about not overreaching himself. The evangelist cannot survive failure. Such anxiety as he can exploit must be carefully worked, in the idiom of his public, and to the thresholds of their toleration. Thus Graham, like certain evangelists, adapts himself to the idiom of whatever subpublic his advance agents and scouts tell him he is likely to be confronting. In this strategic consideration there is no necessary dishonesty. The evangelist accepts the self-image legitimated for him in *I Cor. ix:22:* "I am made all things to all men, that I might by all means save some." Throughout the history of Christian evangelism, anxiety has been exploited for apologetic purposes. The apologist must, however, adapt his rhetorical means to conform to the class and cultural expectations of his auditors or readers, even as his apologetic end remains ever the same. Where, under the guiding influence of secular thought since the Renaissance, western man considers himself an autonomous agent able to reach decisions for himself, the evangelical apologist must meet him precisely on his own ground. There the classical evangelist strategy unfolds: it is to exhibit to western men, first, the panic of isolation underlying the security of autonomy and second, his fear of facing—let alone deciding—what his life means and whether it can continue to be lived in the present way. By confronting his auditor with the capricious fact of death, the evangelist raises the question implicitly whether the present life is worth living. Thus, more or less implicitly, the evangelist confronts his listener with a choice between fatal meaninglessness and saving meaning, through the Gospel interpretation of life. It is a mark of Graham's desperate situation, coming as he does at so late a time in the evangelical effort, that he has to make very explicit the opposition between the meaningless contemporaneity of life and the meaningful archaism of the Gospel. To all appearances he is himself up-to-date in gesture, dress, and all the stage managements of his campaigns. But in essentials he must deny the validity of leading the contemporary life, or risk the defeat of having the Gospel made again a Sunday belief or a purely inward experience, to no outer effect on conduct. The opportunity of the evangelist is that he must, in terms of his role, speak critically to the condition of his time. The danger inherent in this opportunity is that the evangelist will not be apologetic enough but rather will resort to the archaic text as if in mechanical inspiration. A parallelism of effort occurs; genuine anxieties are probed, but no bridge is really built between the terms of these anxieties and the archaic forms of comfort in the Gospel. This is the weakness of the evangelical polemic: that, in the second part of the strategy, it is not apologetic enough and rests too heavily on the incantation of authoritative texts. In his own sublime way, Pascal fails here quite as much as does a Billy Graham. Both can more persuasively raise anxieties than allay them. In the history of evangelism there are inevitably more agitators of genius than comforters. In fact, historically the first talent seems to exclude the second. Evangelical revivalist agitation tends to be mainly repressive in character, without compensatory cathartic release. Governor Bradford of the Massachusetts Bay Colony saw the danger thus inherent in the evangelical strategy. He wisely noted in his *History* that evangelical repression comes at a high price. "It may be in this case as it is with waters when their streames are stopped or dammed up, when they gett passage they flow with more violence, and make more noys and disturbance, then when they are suffered to rune quietly in their owne chanels. So wikednes being here more stopped by strict laws, and the same more nerly looked unto, so as it cannot rune in a comone road of liberty as it would, and is inclined, it searches every wher, and at last breaks out wher it getts vente."

The evangelist with the greatest native genius for agitating anxiety without a compensating genius for transferring with anything like the same power the comfort of the Gospel was Jonathan Edwards.

The first great revival in America, that of 1734 in Northampton, Massachusetts, shows immediately the dynamics of anxiety behind evangelism. Though comfortable, and with eminence achieved early, nevertheless, out of the pressure of his own personal religious problems, Edwards stepped from his role as minister to a respectable congregation into the role of disturber. The world of Northampton appeared to be affirming itself with fair smoothness when Edwards made his shattering denial, and raised the capacity for Christian denial of the world as it always is first among the members of his own congregation.

Edwards understood that the society around him was still formally Christian. It was precisely this formality that disturbed him. He detected the rot within the formal and imposing edifice of the civilization of authority at the apex of which stood the church, teaching agency of that society, as the state is its executive managerial agency. There is a splendid variety of relations possible between religious and political institutions. The church may be superior to the state or it may develop, say, the doctrine of the two swords, or it may be Erastian in character. More important, at that time both church and state were agencies of a coherent culture. They belonged to the same civilization, informing one another even in their conflicts. Thus, on a local level, to be a member of Northampton township—the political community—in the Massachusetts of the 1730s was at the same time to be a member of the religious community. A citizen of the community was by definition a member of the church. His standing as a citizen was defined in terms of his relation to the church. Society as Christian; Christianity was social. Edwards's revolutionary decision consisted in recalling the essential individuality of faith in Christ. Membership in the secular community no longer implied for Edwards membership in the sacred community. Nor was church membership sufficient. The idea of the invisible church returned thus to haunt the visible churches, shaking the doctrine of the "half-way covenant" that had long since become the main criterion for entry into local religious communions. In place of these social—even genealogical—criteria, Edwards put the criterion thereafter dominant in the evangelical strategy—the personal experience. Unless there was a distinct evidence of an inner experience of transformation, on the psychological level as well as on the level of social conduct, the most explicitly observant Christian, with a fine education in dogma, could not be admitted into full membership of the church. Edwards's profound book on the religious affections, which he wrote in 1746, spells out the theoretical basis of his evangelical strategy. In that book he argued for what was to become the major American contribution to western religious history: the primacy of the personal experience over the institutional identification. More seriously for Edwards than even for his Puritan predecessors, saints can never be known by externals. Edwards maintained the Puritan tension between the tentative comfort of being in the church and the permanent discomfort of being nonetheless uncertain of God's actual will. Conversely, he permitted the possibility of being outside the church and considered a sinner in the eyes of the world and being in divine fact already admitted to the invisible church. This double elitism, the one balancing the other, produced a most powerful and creative tension in Puritan culture. It is the one elitist theory—significantly a theological one—that had a flowering on American soil. Edwards's religious elitism persists natively in the anti-institutional animus of most revivalist movements. Compared with the inner experience of the self-isolated American, identification with a salvational institution continues to run a very poor second as a resource of stabilization for the anxious American. For this reason, psychoanalytic therapy has a strangely religious resonance, and the social religion that is Roman Catholicism still appears somewhat alien to the American temper.

Time waited for Horace Bushnell to give the liberal institutional answer to the evangelism of Edwards. It was Bushnell who finally wrote the great refutation of Edwards's evangelism called *Christian Nurture*, characterizing the whole rationalist attack on Edwards throughout American unitarianism and congregationalism and all of the other liberalisms that conquered throughout American religion. As a result of the rationalist counterattack, irrationalist evangelism was pushed westward in space and downward in the social class structure. Personal experience was not necessary to the pursuit of the good religious life, according to Bushnell. Liberal and rationalist theology posed the stable ethic of responsibility against the unstable ethic of conscience. After Bushnell nothing significant happened in American theology until the time of Walter Rauschenbush, who, as a figure of the pre-World War I period, drove the Bushnellian ethic of responsibility to its logical conclusion: the "social gospel." After Rauschenbush came the "anti-social gospel," so to say, in defiant reaction against the superficiality of an ethic of responsibility that had actually smoothed out the angular pain of the ethics of Christian conscience. A fresh ethic of conscience arose. Its spokesman was Reinhold Niebuhr.

We may now summarize the evangelist strategy. First, it appeals most powerfully to those who are suffering the specially added anxiety of having lost emotional contact with the traditional Christian rhetoric. These we may call the "residual believers" whom the evangelists must bring back into the fold. Second, there is the apologetic for unbelievers, whose anxiety levels are so high that they risk symptom formations of a grave kind if there is no therapeutic conversion experience—whether secular or religious in character. The evangelists are, therefore, mass therapists, operating mainly with the dynamics of suggestion in terms of ego ideals. Thus they are inevitably in competition, however indirect, with secular therapists equally concentrated on transformations of the inner experience of the anxiety-torn individual. In both, significantly enough, the emphasis is on the personally transformed experience and control of anxiety. In effect, then, the evangelical strategy is still widely practical in America, sometimes in secular, even scientific, disguise.

The alternative to the evangelical strategy is not congenial to Americans, despite its recent growth. The Organization Man remains uneasy about his trust in a saving institution. Such institutional identification is not the American way, to which the evangelists have contributed significantly.

Yet the encasement of the religious dynamics in American life within thick institutional walls continues. The growth of churches has more institutional significance than religious, in the classical evangelical sense. In the suburban church boom of our times we witness the usefulness of such institutional forms to a political order that is itself free of any religious commitment. The state can always use churches, as Machiavelli well knew. In his supremely intellectual comedy, *Mandragola*, Machiavelli writes of how decisively churches contribute to the "grandeur and felicity" of states. Religion, he notes, "produces good order" and good order is generally necessary to the success of any political undertaking. "A strict observance of divine worship and religion" always tends to increase the power of a state. "So a neglect and contempt of them may be reckoned amongst the first causes of the ruin of a state. For where there is no fear of God it must either fall to destruction or be supported by the reverence shown to a good prince which may sustain it for awhile and supply some form of religion in his subjects; but as human life is short the government must of course sink into decay when the virtue that upheld and informed it is extinct." In the *Discorsi*, Machiavelli presents much the same view. It is the view of the politician—whether as president or high priest—that is opposed by the view of the evangelist. The tension between religious experience and church organization continues, with more and more people who should know better and feel more deeply dismissing too easily the evangelical strategy even while continuing to suspect that there is a rather naive version of the Machiavellian position at the empty heart of the American religious revival. This same confusion informs the American fusion of the *moral* and *morale*, of the common welfare with social conformity. (59:2)

19

John T. McNeill's *A History of the Cure of Souls*

Primitive Christianity had offered another age of anxiety a missionary doctor, who would by his exorcism and charisma cure strange diseases vainly treated by more physical doctors, trained in less spiritual doctrines. Karl Holl, in his essay on "Die Missionsmethode der alten und der mittelalterlichen Kirche," notices how important the competition over the cure of souls was from the earliest moments of church history. "Surprisingly," he writes, "the early church from the beginning had an office which we have established only in recent times: the mission doctor. Certainly the mission doctor of that time was no such sober figure as is the modern doctor. But the range of activities which Christian exorcists and charismatics . . . engaged in was quite large. They practiced not only among Christians, but also among the heathen and even the Jews. . . . The Christian exorcists knew how to heal even the most severe cases, cases which Jewish and pagan exorcists had tried in vain. The trend of the time, in which anxious care for one's body played such a large part, met this very activity of the church halfway and with special eagerness."

Now again, Jewish and pagan exorcists are competing with Christian in the cure of souls; and perhaps more successfully than ever before. Sigmund

Reprinted from *Church History* 22, no. 4 (December 1953): 337–40.

Freud is only the greatest name marking the challenge to the Christian ther-apeutic tradition. That tradition has suffered a certain oblivion among Chris-tians themselves. Professor McNeill has taken an exemplary Protestant measure, in order to help right the balance in contemporary competition over the cure of souls.[1] He has written *A History of the Cure of Souls*, "to introduce to a wider class of readers a province of history of which there exists no other general treatment."

The treatment, then, is history. In the Protestant tradition, the abuses of the present have been cured first by presenting the uses of the past. Pro-fessor McNeill has been driven by his knowledge of that sickness, espe-cially affecting modern Protestantism, which he calls the "obsession with the contemporary" to try the therapy of history on the problem of the cure of souls itself. He has written a much needed history of *religio psychiatri*, as a prophylactic against that "new and strange phenomenon . . . a scientific psychiatry indifferent to religion and philosophy." His history is offered as a medicament, to put scientific psychiatry back "in something like its true historical perspective," and to humble the secular healer with "an invigorat-ing awareness of his membership in a unique and sacred profession that spans the centuries."

But the past is precisely what the scientific doctor of souls must seek to abort. Modern psychotherapy, in all its significant expressions, is not indif-ferent to religion and philosophy as such; only to Christian religion and to a philosophy still concerned with proposing that there are ends of man beyond life itself. Indeed, Freud viewed his new science as the inheritor of the de-clining authority of the Christian churches. "Psychoanalysis is a re-educa-tion," Freud declared. The scientific psychotherapy is not less a moral therapy than the earlier forms Professor McNeill reviews in this book. Sci-entific psychiatry is certainly aware of its religious predecessors. Freud at least pays Christian moral pedagogy the compliment of noticing the effects of its decline. Neurosis waxes, Freud writes, as religion wanes. He cited the "extraordinary increase in the neuroses since the power of religion had waned" to give his physicians some indication of "the intensity of man's inner irresolution and craving for authority."

Freud thought he saw certain resemblances between certain methods of the old cure of souls and the new. Particularly, "the Confessional . . . which the Catholic church has employed for centuries to wield her influence over her communicants . . . may be considered as belonging in the realm of psy-choanalysis." The Confessional, as a method of spiritual guidance, seemed to Freud a "leading up to (psychoanalysis), as it were." In fact, religious guidance in general seemed to this central figure of scientific psychiatry now only of "historical value." The religious cure of souls had exhausted its au-

1. John T. McNeill, *A History of the Cure of Souls* (New York: Harper & Brothers, 1951).

thority. The spiritual advisor of the churches would be replaced by quite another kind of physician, a "secular spiritual guide." In a famous passage, Freud concluded: "Indeed, these words, 'a secular spiritual guide,' might well serve as a general formula for describing the function which the analyst, whether he is a doctor or a layman, [Freud did not expect his best moral physicians to be doctors of the body as well] has to perform in his relation to the public."

After he had laid down his general formula for the new moral physician, Freud went on to attack the old. Both the Protestant and Catholic moral physicians only offered their sick relief "by confirming their faith." The offer may indeed be successful for a time, but precisely because they must confirm the old faith Christian ministers can afford at best a very temporary relief. Christianity is, for scientific psychiatry, itself an expression of the sickness that plagues the world, not a cure. Any relief a pastor can bring is only the passing flush that comes over the soul on first being received back into any community after the sickness of alienation that characterizes the "social dilemma" of being neurotic. The scientific moral physician, on the other hand, cannot "seek to bring [man] relief by receiving him back into the Catholic, Protestant or socialist community." Scientific psychiatry (the phrase is Professor McNeill's, not the reviewer's), whatever the protestations of leaders like Karl Menninger and Erich Fromm, must aim to free men from their sick communities. It is precisely in a total critique of Christian belief that Freud located "spiritual guidance in the best sense of the words."

It may be argued that Freud's epigones were less intransigent against the religious cure of souls than Freud himself. Professor McNeill's favorite scientific psychiatrist seems to be Otto Rank. But it is no surprise to discover that Rank, too, considered that since "psychoanalytic knowledge . . . is knowledge of mankind" a new kind of pastor, far more powerful than the old, had come into the world. With the psychiatrist performing his new pastoral functions, Rank writes, "the old family physician, the friend and counselor of the family, would thus again play his former role with an even deeper meaning. He would watch with understanding and know intimately the whole personality and would be able to exert an intelligent influence upon the development of a human being from his birth onwards, on his education, to throw some light on the difficulties of puberty and the choice of a profession, and on marriage, all more or less trying mental conflicts, as well as to deal with organic illness and mental disorders." As scientific psychiatry conceives its inheritance of the "role of counselor," it would by no means "be restricted to bodily ailments" but to all the ailments of the soul and of the body politic. "This doctor of souls," Rank proclaims, "would naturally exert through the family a still unconceived amount of influence upon society, its morals and its customs and thus indirectly effect an improvement in education and in this way contribute to the prophylaxis of the neurosis."

The scientific moral physician would unite in his own person all the knowledge "which has up to now appeared to be so heterogeneous" and so "contribute towards the unification of the sciences in general, which up to now have been too sharply separated into the natural and the mental (for example, cultural) sciences." All that was needed for a great new effort at the cure of souls was a dedicated army of psychiatrically trained missionaries. Another of Freud's epigones, Ferenczi, considered the necessity of training a whole "army" of disciples in right doctrine: not only practicing analysts, but teachers of all sorts, criminologists, social workers—in fact, everyone "whose work, in one way or another, has any bearing on the human soul." Freud himself dreamed of psychoanalytic colleges, to train the new missionaries "an ideal scheme, no doubt. . . . But an ideal which can and must be realized." He anticipated the cynicism with which his missionary demand would be received. It is true, he admitted, he wanted "some sort of a new Salvation Army." And then he directly challenged the older armies of salvation: "why not?" Other missionary movements had thought they knew the right way to salvation. "After all," Freud concluded, "our fantasy always follows existing patterns."

Professor McNeill is certain that "the role of the religious physician of souls is not played out." But he does not consider that this role may be renewed under quite another doctrine and in another institutional form. It is the specific weakness of Protestant intellectuals concerned with the problem of the cure of souls that they still believe, with Professor McNeill, that the scientific psychiatrist can be "an ally of the pastoral advisor"; indeed, he can. But the psychiatrist can be as well an ally of any other kind of advisor, and this should limit the possibilities of any alliance to a Christian pastorate. Psychiatry can serve any master. It is peculiarly liable to serve the modern state. But, despite the program, doctrine and political alliances of the new science, (the psychiatrist has a connection with armies and with warfare to which the pastor can never aspire) Professor McNeill sees no reason why there should not be an "effective correlation of religious and scientific psychotherapy." He quotes with favor David E. Roberts' suggestion that "theologians incorporate the therapist's conception of conflict in the doctrine of sin and his conception of healing in the doctrine of grace." It would be strange to see such radical secularizations accepted into theology. Such hopes for incorporation show a terrible failure to understand either the doctrines or the program of scientific psychotherapy, as a challenge to the cure of souls. Professor McNeill's assumption that "the solution of the tension between them will come by mutual recognition and not by the extinction of either" ignores the threat of extinction to a declining therapy inherent in the process of "mutual recognition." The Christian cure of souls must be bankrupt if it needs to hope for so much from its competitor.

Professor McNeill's fine history is thus somewhat vitiated by his failure to see the historic character of the present struggle to define the health of man; nevertheless, it is fine history. His book shows some of the rarer virtues of the historian's art. Knowing that he can "merely glance . . . at the problems and mysteries that are attracting new attention in our century," Professor McNeill has compensated for the necessary quality of survey in the book by forcing the intellectual virtue of an adequate survey—perspective. He has put the wise men, the scribes, the rabbis of Israel, of his chapter one, in the same perspective with the curates of the modern Anglican communion, the Lutherans, the Quakers, the great religious movements of Asia, the philosophic medicine of the Greeks, with the whole range of the Christian divisions and the radical secularizations of the contemporary science of the soul. The cures have remained remarkably stable, through all the changes of culture and denomination, and Professor McNeill takes notice of this essential fact.

In a volume covering such a tremendous amount of data, the author might have exposed his readers to the German disease; but there are almost no footnotes in this book. Professor McNeill has simply listed the books and articles he has consulted and left the general reader free of an apparatus he does not want at the same time that the specialist is freed from the distraction of an over-documentation he does not need. The erudition never obtrudes; its massiveness surprises the reader when he becomes aware of it. Professor McNeill is particularly insightful in the chapter from which the book really germinated, on the Celtic penitential discipline. The seeds of the romantic movement, in both religion and literature, are laid out freshly, from a point of origin little known to students of romanticism. Professor McNeill has the final, moral virtue of the historian, without which church history becomes foolish and loses its didactic purpose: he is not neutral. His value judgments, positive and negative, fall regularly upon his subjects. These judgments are deeply Protestant. Professor McNeill's book emphasizes the danger, which has manifested itself in forms more Roman than Catholic, of that "perverse and overbearing spiritual direction in which one person's will and conscience are yielded to another's." (53:5)

20
Paul Tillich's *Systematic Theology*

From the Reformation to the late eighteenth century, Protestantism held two truths to be self-evident: that the Bible was the literal word of God and that faith was a private possibility, available to each man in his personal relation

Reprinted from *The Chicago Jewish Forum* 10, no. 4 (Summer 1952): 294.

to the Bible's sources. The great Confessions (such as Westminster, Dort, etc.) served simply as constitutional fences around Biblicism and Pietism.

In the Age of Reason, Protestant doctrine began to disintegrate. Biblicism was attacked first. Natural reason undercut scriptural revelation and proposed natural religion as an alternative to revealed religion. At the beginning of the nineteenth century, Pietism was attacked by sentimentalism. Schliermacher's religion of the heart subtly transformed the older religion of individual *innerlichkeit*. If the eighteenth century was the Age of Reason, the late nineteenth and early twentieth was the Age of History. Protestantism was engaged in a quest for the historical Jesus, which has ended in the discovery of the centrality of myth.

But the Age of Reconstruction in Protestant doctrine began even while the Age of History was in full dominance. When Schweitzer gave up the historical quest for a missionary's life in Africa, the reaffirmation of the Protestant tradition had begun. Karl Barth is certainly the leading figure of the Protestant Reconstruction, but his reaffirmation has been in great measure an ideology of Restoration, returning to the authority of Biblicism. Paul Tillich has been engaged in quite another kind of Reconstruction, for he believes the restoration of the authority of Biblicism is a somewhat irrelevant effort in the modern world. It remains to be seen whether Tillich or Barth will prove the more important figure in the reconstruction of Protestant doctrine.

With the publication of his *Systematic*,[1] Paul Tillich is established as the greatest philosophical mind in modern Protestantism. If Barth may be said to express the highest passion of Protestant reconstruction, Tillich may be said to express its rarest intellect. For his *Systematic* is the first volume of a modern Protestant *Summa*. (Although he has sought to avoid that label, his kind of *Summa* is the only kind possible in the modern world.) It is an attempt at a systematic presentation of a radically reconstructed Protestant doctrine.

The *Systematic* cannot be a popular book. Even Protestant theologians have long lost the habit of reading *Summas*. The Protestant layman, secure either in fundamentalism or secularism, will not read it. It remains for those of any religious identification who are neither fundamentalist nor secularist to read it. For Tillich's importance is not only that he is neither fundamentalist nor secularist, but that he is so Protestant as to be almost unChristian. Indeed, Tillich is the most Judaic of contemporary Protestant theologians. His Christology is the weakest part of his structure. What remains of his Christianity is quite compatible with Judaism.

As a theologian relevant to Jewish readers as well as Christian, Tillich has attempted, in his *Systematic*, to reassert the ultimate concerns of man,

1. Paul Tillich, *Systematic Theology*, vol. 1 (Chicago: University of Chicago Press, 1951).

the only subject matter of theology. Therefore, this book does not expound the Bible nor does it heal souls or minds. It asks that question relevant to Judaism and Christianity alike: the question of being and the meaning of God. Those—Christians or Jews—who deny the reality of the question will be especially interested in Tillich's answers, if only they will read diligently in one of the most important books of our time. (52:6)

21
Teilhard de Chardin's *The Phenomenon of Man*

It is too early to tell which will prove more interesting to Father Teilhard's American readers—his sad life or his happy mind. I suspect it is the combination which will intrigue us, for here was a Jesuit (and trained scientist) censored throughout his lifetime for his cosmic optimism.

That Father Teilhard was not allowed to publish this,[1] or any of his speculative essays, during his own time once again demonstrates the specially keen nose of the church for the heresy that arises out of excessive piety. For it is clear in this book that Father Teilhard managed to reconcile his science and his piety—and in a grand manner at that.

Is the reconciliation true? Will it be useful? The fact that it has created such a stir among readers with scientific training who are far outside the Roman Catholic jurisdiction indicates the usefulness of the softening to which Father Teilhard has treated the evolutionary hypothesis. Here is evolution with the struggle for existence discreetly left out of the picture. Like Boris Pasternak, Father Teilhard is another of those moderns who retain the imagination of faith: not merely history, as for Pasternak, but all of life, from the original germ plasm to the final divinity of it, represents the upward steps that eventuate finally in God. (What appeared heretical to his superiors was Father Teilhard's own ambiguity about whether God exists at the beginning as well as at the end of the evolutionary process.)

To secular readers who are less strongly influenced by the imagination of faith, even if not completely divorced from it, this very good Father will have appeared to ignore willfully the terror that lies between the germ plasm and God. A book that imagines the total development of life, from origins to end, cannot be so essentially peaceful and yet true. Somewhere, perhaps in his own struggle for faith, Father Teilhard must have turned away in horror from the struggle for existence. (60:2)

Reprinted from *The Unitarian Register* 139, no. 5 (May 1960): 15.
1. Pierre Teilhard de Chardin, *The Phenomenon of Man* (New York: Harper & Brothers, 1959).

22
Eros Cross-Examined

For several generations the Swedish Church (Lutheran) has had the genial custom of making its ablest intellectuals bishops after a period of service in the universities. The Church of England employed its intellectuals similarly from time to time, as when Mandell Creighton, the historian of the papacy, was appointed Bishop of London, and the leadership of the English Catholic Church during the nineteenth century was remarkably intellectual. In the American churches and denominations, the ambition is generally reversed; it is the despair and hope of almost every Protestant intellectual after his experience of congregational life to return to a university, if not as theologian at least as college chaplain. But in Sweden, religious intellectuals have received sturdy and generous institutional encouragement. From their professorships at the University of Uppsala at the beginning of the century came both Bishop Soderblom and Bishop Billing, and later from the University of Lund (the other seat of Protestant learning in Sweden) Professor Anders Nygren was raised to Bishop of Lund.

Inquiry into the leading idea of Christianity has been the trademark of the Lundensian school of theology to which Bishop Nygren belongs; substantially the same method—motif-research as the translator renders the Swedish *motivforskning*—has informed the *Dogmatics* and *Christus Victor* of his colleague, Professor (aferrwards Bishop) Gustav Aulen. This movement of thought has been deplorably neglected even within English-speaking theological circles. Indeed, despite its rich texture of documentation from Gospel times to Luther, *Agape and Eros*[1] did not entirely persuade Anglo-American scholars, and the book's reception when issued in English translation in 1938 was decidedly cold. Until this present edition, the American reader probably has been more aware of extensions and critiques, like Father D'Arcy's *The Mind and Heart of Love*, than of the original work itself. In recent years, however, the reputation of *Agape and Eros* has circulated beyond the learned clergy to the secular culture elites, and now, made available for the first time by an American house, it will no doubt be treated with that particularly gratuitous praise reserved for the representatives of good old causes.

Certainly to exemplify Christianity in a single motif, which is the aim of Bishop Nygren, invites scholarly cavil. The Bishop's contention that Christi-

First published in *The Kenyon Review* 16, no. 4 (Autumn): 645–52. © 1954 by Kenyon College. Reprinted with permission.

1. Anders Nygren, *Agape and Eros*, translated by Philip S. Watson (Philadelphia: Westminster Press, 1953).

anity was one sort of Love (Agape) not another (Eros) must appear exaggerated to the historian. Agape as the essence of Christianity has a very attenuated and broken line, and some may prefer to read Nygren as a reformer suggesting what Christianity ought to be rather than as a scholar reporting what it has been. Nevertheless it is apt that the Bishop should have concerned himself mainly with the fate of Agape, not merely out of piety but because the refined classes are more erotic than at any time since the declining periods of antiquity. The masses have always been erotic. But never has Eros, in the variety of his cults and in the splendor of his advertisement, received more educated worship. Christian love has not survived the importunities of Eros, and even while Christianity was more lively the effort to keep Agape inviolate from Eros failed. Bishop Nygren's history is filled with the grief of improper unions, the harsh orthodox tone of a man who remembers lost distinctions and writes to revive them. The very language of the revolutionary Christian Agape—"that love which pronounces judgment on all that is not love"—had fallen from confusion into such disuse that it needed first of all a scholarly rehabilitation among even Christian readers. Bishop Nygren's desire to give some authority to the Christian side produced an exemplary case of committed history, partial and yet thorough in the exhibition of the other side.

As a comparative study in the wars of love, *Agape and Eros* stops at, respectively, the Reformation and the Renaissance. To pick up the theme nearer our own time Bishop Nygren's book might be read together with Mario Praz's. The Eros motif is followed in *The Romantic Agony* through its strip-tease in the eighteenth-century novel (for example, *Clarissa*) and its unique expression as a systematic philosophical viciousness in the work of de Sade, into the nineteenth century where the literary triumph of pagan love was complete without yet becoming vulgar. But *The Romantic Agony*, although it rightly concentrated on exploring the shadow of the divine Marquis, missed the connection between politics and literature. Prof. Praz failed to bring out the identity in Sade's mind of the political and the erotic. Sade proposed the sexual revolution as the only permanent and complete one, that would break not one regime or another but the regime of civilization as such. This particular connection between Eros and a total and revolutionary politics has been brilliantly assessed by Max Horkheimer, in his book with T. W. Adorno *Dialektik der Aufklärung*.

Agape and Eros is only as far removed from illuminating the connection between sexuality and politics as beginnings are from ends. But it may be more useful to the secular mind to begin nearer the end—with the late eighteenth century and the early nineteenth. Then, sexuality became again the subject common to the best literature and the most revolutionary politics. The revolutionary conception of Agape, once institutionalized, had been transformed into the uncomfortably conservative paradox that precisely through differences of social hierarchy could spiritual identity be proved. Agape is fully as revolutionary a conception as Eros, but, within the history of the successful church and its rivals, Eros had come to imply the right and power of the individual and Agape his inherent duties. Eros referred to the sense of achievement, to the purest and most private desiring, while Agape was the feeling of devotion, the purity of obligation. Thus, from the early gnostic writings to the first critical philosophy of industrial civilization, revolutionary thought and action has drawn on a deliberate anti-Christian eroticism.

The Fourierists, the Saint-Simonians, and following them in literature the "young Germans," were among the first who tried to reconcile spirit and flesh in one religion as the basis of a fresh civilization. This earlier more explicit relation between socialist and sexual revolution, before the conservative Karl Marx broke the connection with the pejorative word "utopian," was closer to being a real revolutionary movement—that is, from below—than we now can grasp, accustomed as we are by Marxism and its counterfeits to revolutions run by reason—namely, from above. The universal *Menschtum* of the radical vision was never chiefly of a classless society—the Marxist was a special demand within the more general one for a reconciliation of the high and low, the material and the ideal—but of a humanity freed from a false reverence for the general advantage. The great sex writers from Sade to Freud were all antiliberal, pressing in various degrees through the doctrine of an originally free instinct for the freedom of the individual against the burdens of social morality.

In the immediate pre-Christian period, when the antique world was suffering its own exhaustion, the utopian hope had been toward something higher, for it was a period of satiety and the needs of the flesh were only too well attended. In the post-Christian period—as the most advanced minds of the nineteenth century considered it—rebellion could only be in the name of the flesh. A great part of the fatigue of the time (the melancholy is most common in nineteenth-century French novels) was felt precisely with the Christian demands for a love too sublime for any response except pretense or guilt. The rebellion proceeds unconnected with popular obscenity, which is more closely associated with the escape mechanism of a repressive Christian civilization than with a revolutionary sexual life. Sexuality in the revolutionary doctrine would no longer be associated with the leer, once its connection (fixed long ago in the Platonic and Christian mind) with the evil of matter was broken.

The theme of liberation from a repressiveness more serious than that of any merely political regime was everywhere in the haunted air of the nineteenth century—in an acutely sexed literature, in a value philosophy (Schopenhauer) that by its interest in "values" questioned their validity, in strange political and religious movements that in the name of the future claimed to go deeper than politics and religion. With *Beyond Good and Evil* the sustained attack on spiritual love and the glorification of a humanity free to live in a more sensual way was philosophically complete and passed over into a commonplace of the educated mind. Love was examined with steady and detailed ferocity by literary men and philosophers until with Freud it entered into the twentieth century under a more persuasive definition—as science.

But in the nineteenth century it was still in lyric poetry (including the lyric philosophy of Nietzsche) and in the novel that the attack on Christian love was most advanced; science had not yet taken up the attack and carried it through. It was indeed in literature that the revolutionary erotic intention emerged in the clearest and still usable terms: in the reassertion of Hellenism against Hebraism, of beauty as the real object of piety. The romantics, even before the school of romantic agonists, had made their poetic avowals of the new harmony—Schiller perhaps first in the name of the glory that was Greece. Heine (whom Freud revered) also had taken up the French indignation with a civilization too long under the shadow of a too spiritual Law of Love. In England Swinburne watched the decline of energy and took the accusative voice: "Thou has conquered, oh pale Galilean; the world has grown grey from thy breath." In France, around the same time, Gautier wrote against "the Christian contempt for what is shapely and incarnate." There are passages in his *Mademoiselle de Maupin* that could have come out of a letter by Heine or from Swinburne himself: "Christ has swathed the world in his winding-sheet," or "continence, mysticism, melancholia—three unknown words—three new infirmities introduced by Christ." The point with later writers, such as D. H. Lawrence, has remained the same: humanity has grown sick and tired, living in the trap between good and evil. "I count Christianity as . . . the great . . . has been," Lawrence announced. Even the gods were drawn into the literary struggle against Christian love, to expose it as a secondary and oppressive sentiment. Just as Heine's monks in *Gods in Exile* turn out to be the most sensual of Greek gods, so Lawrence in *The Man Who Died* has Christ resurrected in body and soul through intercourse with Isis.

In the liberal theology of the nineteenth century, the pale Jew dripping on the cross gave way to the image of a virile young emancipator from the Galilean hills, most tolerant of men, himself chafing under the restrictions of a pharisaical culture. *Matthew XXI, 31*, was interpreted to make a revolutionary point: "Verily I say unto you, that the publicans and the harlots go into the Kingdom of God before you." Christian love, as opposed to Eros, valued no person more than another; but in the development of erotic doctrine this revolutionary abstention from valuing was ultimately transferred back to the realm of instinct. To value the objects of love differently, according to their merit or beauty, is not a Christian sentiment, but one trained by culture (which the Christians originally and still in the orthodox sense reject) in order to regulate the promiscuity of the erotic instincts. Thus in its modern psychological version Eros parodies the spontaneous and unmotivated character of Agape.

Christ, loving sinners more than the righteous, was transformed into an erotic modern by the theologians of Eros, perhaps most notably after Nietzsche by Max Scheler. It was Paul, the first clergyman, who in the standard erotic version of the gospel transformed the death of Jesus into a triumph over the rich dissatisfactions of living. From the high tide of the German criticism (Gfrörer, Ghillany, et al.) down to the recent book by Robert Graves and Dr. Podro, *The Nazarene Gospel Restored*, the living historical Jesus had been regularly saved for the ongoing rehabilitation of the flesh, toward the time when the innocence and capacities of the old Adam would be revived in the new. It is the familiar discovery of Mr. Graves and his collaborator that Christ really did not die and that the whole Christian mistake turned on a chance meeting of the Pharisee Paul with Jesus under the hot sun on the road to Damascus. By the nineteenth century the most disparate figures were prepared to admit the devitalizing effect of the Christian ethic of love upon the energies of civilized man.

From belief in the exhaustion of Christian love many of the great movements of late nineteenth-century art were nourished—symbolism and impressionism, the naturalistic novel, even the peculiar and violent rationalism of Ibsen, Shaw, and other more fanatic champions of the liberating irrational—*Trieb*, Instinct, *Élan Vital*. The powers of criticism were trained in one way after another upon the repressiveness of what had become a bourgeois as well as Christian culture, adding the insult of hypocrisy to the injury of asceticism. In the novel, far more explicitly than in the cultural polemics of the nineteenth century attending the decline of Protestantism, the erotic interest was high. Indeed, the novel in the nineteenth century may be said to have taken the erotic problem as its main subject. It is not enough to call the novel a Protestant and bourgeois art form, as critics from Newman to Orwell have done, and in this way award it a general ethical importance not matched by any other form of art. Both the Protestant and bourgeois springs of the novel can run dry, as we have felt it in our own time, and yet the vitality of the form remains. It is as the most psychological of art forms that the novel is uniquely vital—and modern. It depends for its main subject on the post-Christian division of man into natural impulse and social conscience or, as Max Stirner put it, into an "inner populace and an inner police." The war of desire with the delicate and selective sentiments of civilization—which constitutes the working conception of modern depth psychology—has been long the working conception of the novel. The modern novel has as its object to show the natural impulses of man breaking against the retaining walls of civilization.

Bishop Nygren has tried to break through this liberal-theological and novelistic tearing apart of man between impulse and conscience, to show how they are one in Christian love. It is a difficult task, made manageable by carrying the history of his problem only so far as the Reformation, after which the theological side steadily loses at least rhetorical power. In literature as in philosophy since the late eighteenth century, the great names have been all on the side of Eros—and this Eros is no longer Platonic, for it has been tracked back to its instinctual origins. Freud is the greatest name nowadays on the side of Eros, in direct descent (as he himself realized) from the psychology of Plato, to whom Bishop Nygren credits the original science of erotic love. No name—no combination of names—stands out on the Christian side to put against Freud's. Yet the recovery of sexuality as the foundation of a radical criticism of the established morality may have almost run its course. The rehabilitation of the flesh in the face of a declining Christian asceticism is now being offered strictly as therapy and with serious reservations about its capacity to finally bring man to that pursuit of happiness from which he was deflected by Christian ideas. The renewal of interest in Bishop Nygren's history is not extravagant; it has come mostly from a small minority among the educated who are dissatisfied less with the dead and almost forgotten Christian morality, whose very language appeals as strange and fresh, than with the argument against it by which our literatures and psychologies still proceed. If the Westminster Press succeeds in distributing this already classic volume, from the Christian view properly as much polemic as history, outside the seminaries, perhaps the logic of modern psychology and the modern novel will begin to get the reexamination it desperately needs. A mind so perceptive as George Orwell's, filled with the nightmare of a totalitarian culture, considered Henry Miller as the novelist of the future, pointing with a half naive, half macabre enthusiasm to the logical joining of the sexual and political revolutions. It is worth something to literary criticism if *Agape and Eros* can be used as a manual, to relearn how to test the canons of argument so long established in our literature; once the canons of argument are corrected in a form so intellectual as the novel the needed correction of taste may follow more easily. (54:6)

Religion and Politics
Political Faiths and Their Futures

23

George Orwell and the Post-Liberal Imagination

If there were a competition for saints in which liberals could bid, George Orwell would be their man; he satisfies at once the liberal nostalgia for action and their resignation to despair. Simone Weil might be another choice. There is indeed a similarity between these two martyr figures, the frail intellectual Jewess sickening unto death in the Renault factory and the tired Etonian holding his own among the tramps; both made the futile gesture of going down among the "masses." But Orwell remained a self-conscious representative of the cultivated, and his early books are defensive reports of his spiritual encounters in the depths of society; Simone Weil had a different intention. Her reports are not on the practical level of the novel or the memoir, and they have an oversubtlety that does not quite elude the ancient religious heresy she represents which finally makes her unacceptable not only to rationalist liberals but also to the conservative religiosi. Orwell remains the most adequate ideal. And in a liberalism that feels itself trapped by the Jewish question, he has the added advantage of not being Jewish. Moreover, Simone Weil, so far as she is relevant to secular questions, is no liberal. *The Need for Roots* serves, not altogether in agreement with her intention, the conservative polemic for a return to a traditionalist world, while the liberal mind prefers to live in more possible worlds. Simone Weil really looks beyond all present orders; one of Orwell's attractions for liberals is his immersion in the here and now. He wrote to the question of how to live in the possible world, not how to die in an impossible one.

Honest living has always interested liberals more than holy dying: Orwell's problem is how to live honestly in a world that is no longer liberal, and his unique perspective on the politics and poverty of the world was gained from being very honestly involved in both. Cyril Connolly had made the

First published in *The Kenyon Review* 16, no. 1 (Winter): 49–70. © 1954 by Kenyon College. Reprinted with permission.

basic point about Orwell's painful honesty in a biographical note on his old
Eton friend in *Enemies of Promise,* and in this character Orwell has descended to us. "He was a virtuous man," writes Lionel Trilling, in his introduction to the American edition of *Homage to Catalonia;* and this was, as
Mr. Trilling calls it, his "moral triumph," for Orwell's personal virtue was
practiced on the basis of a decisive confusion of principle. Orwell rose
above his principles and this confers upon him his peculiarly modern
saintliness. He is indeed worthy of our admiration, but the aura around his
nobility and courage has left the darker side—his mind—relatively unexamined. For liberals, Orwell's virtue as a man has obscured his significance
as a writer. Thus Wyndham Lewis, of course not at all reverent, becomes in
his recent *The Writer and the Absolute* the only critic who has treated Orwell
at any length as a writer. His critical judgment, however unfair and perverse, nevertheless recognizes that Orwell is, of all "the English war and
post-war writers, not alone the one most worthy of attention, but he is the
only one."

The flaw in Orwell's art, Mr. Lewis thinks, lies in what he takes to be
Orwell's socialist creed; only the last two popular books, *Animal Farm* and
1984, are passable by Mr. Lewis. Liberals praise Orwell on paradoxically
similar grounds: because Orwell was a socialist and because he recapitu-
lated the liberal disillusionment with socialism. Painfully teaching themselves to accept this uncongenial world, the liberals are still troubled by a
certain nostalgia for their earlier temper which finally, as socialism, sought
to reject this world. But both the conservative criticism and the liberal
praise of Orwell are, in his own terms, quite misplaced. The liberals had
never reached socialism, and Orwell calls the earlier temper by its right
name, "liberal-Christian."

"Verily," that strange accepter of all possible worlds (including Hitler's),
Wyndham Lewis writes, "this man was determined to identify himself with
the 'lowest of the low.'" Mr. Lewis is thinking specifically of *The Road to
Wigan Pier,* Orwell's book on the coal miners. As an anti-Christian himself,
Mr. Lewis thinks this is socialism. Rather, Orwell was that most liberal of
liberals, the Christian who has lost his Christianity, but keeps up the essential Christian action of brotherliness and compassion. *Homage to Catalonia*
opens with an expression of brotherliness and compassion and also with the
notion of its pathetic transience. George Orwell's active and compassionate
rejection of this world that describes the old liberal imagination, coupled
with his sympathetic analysis of the new temper of acceptance that describes the post-liberal imagination, make him the writer most worthy of attention at least for those imaginations still in process of transition. He
marked the transition more clearly than any other writer of his generation.

The first thing Orwell, as a liberal-Christian, could not accept about this world was the omnipresence of money. Rather, in his own liberal parody of religious indignation, he could not accept the omni-absence of it. Like his predecessors in the English novel of poverty from George Gissing to H. G. Wells, Orwell discovered that money was the root of all good. Money was the shield of faith that made the liberal-Christian life livable, "silky-smooth as the inside of a shell," a hard skin protecting those who had it, from the ultimate misfortune of being without it. The phrase is from Orwell's second novel, *Keep the Aspidistra Flying* (1936), and reports the suffering and resentment of the poor hero, Gordon Comstock. All of Orwell's leading characters (with the exception of Flory in *Burmese Days*) are consciously poor. It is their consciousness of their poverty that puts them in touch with reality. Poverty, the definitive experience of his heroes and one heroine, teaches them the poverty of the new world.

Orwell was stricken until death with the problem of poverty, and he made it the certain and rich theme of his writing. Poverty is as much the problem of his political tracts as of his literary criticism and fiction. Poverty connected both politics and literature. This does not contradict the fact that poverty is always treated in individual terms. The social reference, the programmatic perspective, is invariably superficial. The suggestions for reforms in hotel management and for the disposition of tramps appended to *Down and Out in London and Paris* (1931)—Orwell's first book, a memoir of a few months of his personal experience of poverty—are put forward with a curious dreamy self-consciousness, an artful childishness of statement. Poverty does not first appear in Orwell's writings as either a political or an intellectual problem. Poverty is material want. There are no myths in Orwell, and his literary manner is the English plain style. He goes directly to the point: rooming houses, vermin, sleeping under bridges, subways, cold, back alleys, orange peels, wet newspapers, hunger—all. Orwell's major aesthetic achievement is the communication of the infinite evil of not having the shield of money. There are passages in the early novels on vagrancy, on the niceties of picking through garbage, on begging and sniping, on torn clothing and compulsory camping out that are better than any others of their kind in English literature. But it is not easy to interest the educated book-buying class in such matter, and Orwell's pre-war novels were not popular. Only when he collapsed poverty into politics in *1984*, did Orwell locate that vast audience with money that could not be troubled by his original version of the politics of poverty—the simple absence of money.

The experience of poverty remained the common theme of Orwell's fiction. It is not an experience to breathe, since one does that every minute of one's life. Orwell is not interested in the poverty of the always poor, the authentic proles. The Orwellian heroine and heroes have to fall into poverty.

Their fall brings them what the original fall brought, knowledge of good-and-evil. Only those whose souls have been quickened by poverty really experience the world as it is. The experience of poverty is the loss of innocence. Falling into poverty burdens one with a problem neither the never poor nor the always poor suffer: quite literally, how one ought to live.

The experience of poverty is also the loss of faith, no less than the loss of innocence. In his first novel, *The Clergyman's Daughter* (1933), Orwell uses the absence of money to parody the liberal-Christian loss of faith. In a reverse conversion, Dorothy Hare loses her faith in the Christian mystery as she learns of "the mysterious power of money." This is her liberalizing experience. There are, indeed, three stages of the liberal imagination. The first stage is being Christian without being liberal—action with belief. The second stage is being liberal without being Christian—action without belief. The third stage is the post-liberal—neither action nor belief. Dorothy moves from the first stage to the second, but rejects the invitation to move on to the third. She can no longer take her Christianity seriously. Indeed, the religious element in her liberalism becomes for her a private joke, one she can't tell even her best friend. Nevertheless, Christianity remains the incommunicable but absolute base of her liberalism, of her wish to do good in this world.

Dorothy is reminded of a favorite joke of Mr. Warburton, the innocent, always rich man who is her would-be lover. "If you took I Corinthians, chapter thirteen, and in every verse wrote 'money' instead of 'charity,' the chapter has ten times as much meaning as before." Orwell thought so much of the parody of money as the *caritas* of capitalist civilization that he used it as the motto of his next novel, *Keep the Aspidistra Flying:*

> Though I speak with the tongues of men and of angels, and have not money, I am become as a sounding brass, or a tinkling cymbal. And though I have the gift of prophecy, and understand all mysteries, and all knowledge; and though I have all faith, so that I could move mountains, and have not money, I am nothing. . . . Money suffereth long, and is kind; money envieth not; money vaunteth not itself, is not puffed up, doth not behave unseemly, seeketh not her own, is not easily provoked, thinketh no evil; rejoiceth not in iniquity, but rejoiceth in the truth; beareth all things, believeth all things, hopeth all things, endureth all things. . . . And now abideth faith, hope, and money, these three; but the greatest of these is money.

Orwell hammered away in all his early novels at the shield of money. "Money, once again; all is money." Money did truly exclude but one evil, poverty, as Dr. Johnson said. But this described all evil. Poverty first opened up the problem of evil as such for Dorothy Hare. Before she falls into utter poverty, she refuses to believe evil exists. By the agency of Mr. Warburton, she loses her limited Christianity and acquires a new imagination, more suited to her condition. Poverty "had driven into her a far deeper understanding than she had before of the great modern commandment—the eleventh commandment which has wiped out all the others: 'Thou shalt not lose thy job.'" The quest for certainty revealed itself in its specifically modern form, the quest for security.

The Clergyman's Daughter contains Orwell's first nightmare vision, in 1933, and it has not changed radically by *1984*. From his first novel to the last, Orwell saw "an evil time ahead." The year 1984 closely resembles 1933. In both years, Orwell describes the winter of western civilization. Both worlds are "desolate," "dank," "windless," "bleak," "colourless," "grey." The "slummy wilderness" of capitalist civilization is succeeded by the slummier wilderness of totalitarianism. There are the same "labyrinths of little dingy-coloured houses," the same "derelict buildings," the same destruction everywhere. The later world is only a political translation of the earlier. What was commercial science in one has become political science in the other. Orwell first tested the great slogan of the new order ("War is Peace") in the business colleges of the old order. Toots Commercial College, in the "desolate suburb" where Dorothy Hare discovers her unbelief, is in fact Orwell's first model of the garrison state. Orwell was Marxist enough to see the new society contained in the old, especially on the ideological level. The first formulation of the totalitarian catechism is contained in the advertising slogans of a business school. "Its watchword was Efficiency; meaning a tremendous parade of hustling, and the banishment of all humane studies. One of its features was a kind of catechism called the Efficiency Ritual, which all the children were required to learn by heart as soon as they joined the school.

Q. 'What is the secret of success?'
A. 'The secret of success is efficiency.'
Q. 'What is the test of efficiency?'
A. 'The test of efficiency is success.'

And so on and so on. It was said that the spectacle of the whole school, boys and girls together, reciting the Efficiency Ritual under the leadership of the headmaster—they had this ceremony two mornings a week instead of prayers—was most impressive."

By 1933 the prayers of Christian civilization and the slogans of capitalism were in any case indistinguishable. Both were directed to the elimination of the differences between things or to the differentiation of identical things. Orwell simply transformed the capitalist catechism into a more political language, but the logic was the same. Two plus two had in any case not equalled an unequivocal four in the bourgeois arithmetic for some time. To learn six of one is half a dozen of the other is perfect training for the new politics. *1984* continued the shabby business accounting of 1933, except that politics had become the world's only business. The grey dying world of Dorothy Hare, the clergyman's daughter, ends in the grey dead world of Winston Smith, in *1984*. Winston Smith not only drinks the same stale, weak, dirty tea of his predecessors in 1933, but his moral problem is curiously the same: the absence of belief and the presence of poverty. The total shabbiness of the inevitable future is Orwell's most comprehensive accusation.

The acceptance of the economic catechism empties Dorothy of her moral energy just as the acceptance of the political catechism empties Winston of his. The clergyman's daughter has been left "in a perpetually low-spirited, jaded state, in which, try as she would, nothing seemed to interest her. It was in the hateful ennui of this time—the corrupting ennui that lies in wait for every modern soul—that she first came to a full understanding of what it meant to have lost her faith." When we meet Winston Smith, he is already jaded. He can only vaguely remember an earlier temper. He is not at all sure just what it is he has lost. His acceptance of the meaninglessness of this world makes him happy, for the first time in his life. Her acceptance does not make Dorothy happy, only determined. She is still too close to the liberal-Christian temper, however exhausted it is in her, to settle passively into a world without meaning. She is too kind, and too frigid, to be bitter; and in any case she is not an intellectual. Gordon Comstock, the thin, always hungry poet (*Keep the Aspidistra Flying*), and George Bowling, the fat insurance tout who is "thin inside" (*Coming Up for Air*), are plainly intellectuals and plainly bitter. As liberals who have not yet accepted and no longer know how to reject the meaningless world around them, they are full of the last fine activity of the liberal: imagining the utter destruction of this commercial world. From his bookshop window in 1936, Gordon Comstock

> gazed out at the graceless street. At this moment it seemed to him that in a street like this, in a town like this, every life that is lived must be meaningless and intolerable. The sense of disintegration, of decay, that is endemic in our time, was strong upon him. Somehow it was mixed up with the ad-posters opposite. He looked now with more seeing eyes at those grinning yard-wide faces. After all, there was more there than mere silliness, greed and vulgarity. . . . 'Corner Table enjoys his meal with Bovex.' Gordon examined the thing with the intimacy of hatred. . . . A spectacled rat-faced clerk, with patent-leather hair, sitting at a cafe table grinning over a white mug of Bovex. . . . The idiotic grinning face, like the face of a self-satisfied rat, the slick black hair, the silly spectacles. Corner Table, heir of ages; victor of Waterloo; Corner Table, modern man as his masters want him to be. A docile little porker, sitting in the money-sty, drinking Bovex. . . . He watched the ribbon of torn paper whirling, fluttering on the Q. T. Sauce advertisement. Our civilization is dying! It *must* be dying. But it isn't going to die in its bed. Presently the aeroplanes are coming. Zoom—whizz—crash! The whole western world going up in a roar of high explosives. . . . He looked at the darkened street, at the greyish reflection of his face in the pane, at the shabby

figures shuffling past. Almost involuntarily he repeated: *C'est l'Ennui—l'oeil chargé d'un pleur involuntaire, Il rêve d'échafauds en fumant son houka!* Money, money! Corner Table! The humming of the aeroplanes and the crash of the bombs. . . . Gordon squinted up at the leaden sky. Those aeroplanes are coming. In imagination he saw them coming now; squadron after squadron, innumerable, darkening the sky like clouds of gnats. With his tongue he made a buzzing, blue-bottle-on-the-window-pane sound to represent the humming of the aeroplanes. It was a sound which, at that moment, he ardently desired to hear.

From his train window, after the unsuccessful attempt to come up for air, George Bowling is equally resentful. Orwell puts his unlikely George in a mood no insurance man could know, "in a kind of prophetic mood, the mood in which you foresee the end of the world and get a certain kick out of it. . . . We're all on the burning deck and nobody knows it except me. I looked at the dumb-bell faces streaming past. Like turkeys in November, I thought. Not a notion of what's coming to them. It was as if I'd got X-rays in my eyes and could see the skeletons walking. . . . I looked forward a few years." *Coming Up for Air* was published in 1939. "I saw this street as it'll be in five years' time, say, or three years' time (1941 they say it's booked for), after the fighting's started." George sees not only the burnt out buildings, but that "everyone's very thin. A platoon of soldiers comes marching up the street. They're all as thin as rakes and their boots are dragging. The sergeant's thin too and he's got a cough that almost tears him open." These are the final pages of *Coming Up for Air.* George Bowling has spanned the entire novel trying to find an escape from the money-world. He goes back to his birthplace, a village Eden of the liberal-Christian era, to inquire whether it still lives. It was a foolish question, although George does not regret spending his windfall money to find the answer, to find Lower Binfield another industrial slum. "The old life's finished, and to go about looking for it is just a waste of time. There's no way back to Lower Binfield, you can't put Jonah back into the whale." But this is only the old whale. The old world can only be recollected from the outside. George's problem is how to live inside the new whale, given the fact that *"it's all going to happen . . .* the bombs, the food-queues, the rubber truncheons, the barbed wire, the coloured shirts, the slogans, the enormous faces, the machine-guns squirting out of bedroom windows. It's all going to happen. . . . There's no escape."

Since there is no escape back into the old whale, the novel ends with George's bitter acceptance of the new. "Why had I bothered about the future and the past, seeing that the future and the past don't matter?" George decides to get back inside the new, transparent whale, passively accepting his place in it, his unbearable wife, his snotty children, the money-god, the next war—everything. He feels a certain comfort he has never felt before. Being inside the whale is, after all, the only place to be.

George Bowling's wife, like Elizabeth (*Burmese Days*), has never revolted against the soul-defacing experience of poverty. Both women are completely hollowed out from the beginning. Some of Orwell's heroes do revolt, but the revolt ends in acceptance. George Bowling goes back to his wife and the money-world, accepting. Gordon Comstock, too, accepts the only comfort available. At the close of *Keep the Aspidistra Flying*, he has gone back to making slogans at his advertising job and is finally seen in an ecstasy of touching all the ugly furniture in the ugly little flat in which he will begin his marriage to the world as it is. In an ecstasy of humiliation, Winston Smith finally accepts Big Brother and is really happy for the first time in his life. Poor Flory, in *Burmese Days*, cannot accept his humiliation and commits suicide. This leaves the clergyman's daughter and George Orwell himself, somewhere between acceptance and suicide, to explain themselves.

The virtue of both George Orwell and the clergyman's daughter is that they choose to remain in the middle, between a rejection made impossible by intelligence and an acceptance made impossible by morality. The old morality seems no longer defensible against the new intelligence. The liberal-Christian civilization is dead. Orwell calls the church a "powdered corpse," sweet-smelling but even more dead for that. Having put Dorothy through her education in a fine exercise in the picaresque tradition of the English novel, Orwell cannot permit her to return to any *credo non quod, sed quia absurdum est*. Orwell plainly despised those modern intellectuals who furnish their souls with what that last liberal theoretician, Max Weber, called "guaranteed genuine antiques." The Eliots and the Greenes, the Waughs and the Huxleys, are disposed of in the character of Victor, the little Anglo-Catholic lover of archaic ceremonial as against modern, in *The Clergyman's Daughter*. Weber summed up the case against the honesty of most of the intellectuals who have "returned." Their religion is simply antique collecting. They have only lost their taste for modernism or futurism. "Of all things religion is what they do not possess. By way of substitute, however, they play at decorating a sort of domestic chapel with small sacred images from all over the world, or they produce surrogates through all sorts of psychic experience to which they ascribe the dignity of mystic holiness, which they peddle in the book market." Victor peddles his religious virtuosity in the *Church Times*, but otherwise he fits Weber's description.

If Dorothy continues to go to Church, it is not as an antique dealer and certainly not out of faith rewon. "There was never a moment when the power of worship returned to her. Indeed, the whole concept of worship was meaningless to her now; her faith had vanished, utterly and irrevocably. It is a mysterious thing, the loss of faith—as mysterious as faith itself. Like faith, it is ultimately not rooted in logic; it is a change in the climate of the mind." When her intelligence makes faith impossible, Orwell has Dorothy assert "the truism that all real happenings are in the mind." Here is Bishop Berkeley, without bringing God around to tie things together in the last chapter. It is not suffering her poverty that has made it impossible for Dorothy to return innocently to the Christian way; it is a change in the quality of her imagination. Her imagination has lost its theodical energy. She is no longer an optimist. The world can only go from bad to worse. "Something had happened in her heart, and the world was a little emptier, a little poorer from that minute." The religious coherence of intelligence and morality was no longer possible. The money-god had made all gods impossible, finally including itself, in a general exhaustion of the theodical capital built up during the Christian era.

The tension of intelligence and morality has always described the liberal imagination. Dorothy, coming at the end of the liberal-Christian era, can only understand the necessity of the connection; she can no longer make it. Having become more liberal than Christian, she can only regret that loss of faith which makes intelligence so painful. Mr. Warburton, who has intelligence without morality, as the earlier Dorothy had morality without intelligence, cannot understand Dorothy's regret. He has never been poor. He has never experienced transition, the loss of something. Instead, Mr. Warburton proclaims the new faith, Efficiency, in its present transitional, antipolitical form, the efficiency of the orgasm.

But Dorothy is frigid. The irrationality of the old moral discipline has left her incapable of accepting Mr. Warburton's offer of marriage. Mr. Warburton's offer is as meaningless as his earlier attempts to seduce her. His mind is naturally impious. His is the post-liberal imagination: he not only proclaims the world meaningless but is very happy to find it so. Dorothy's terrible experience of poverty, which he had caused, means nothing to him. In fact, to the post-liberal, meaning is never a problem. Mr. Warburton is the only happy character Orwell ever describes. "The world's full of amusing things . . . everything." Meaning is a moral term, to be avoided. "I've never seen any meaning in it all, and I don't want to see one. Why not take life as you find it?" But Dorothy cannot make such an acceptance. "A mind naturally pious must recoil from a world discovered to be meaningless." Dorothy recoils from Mr. Warburton, even though she knows he is correct. "Women who don't marry wither up—they wither up like aspidistras in back-parlour windows." Mr. Warburton thinks the lesson is obvious. Since the end of life is only to live, as the aspidistra has no virtue other than persistence (Gordon could not kill the one in his room, however he tried), and Dorothy's only choice is to marry or die—well then, keep the aspidistras flying.

But living is not necessarily being human. The aspidistra is not quite human. Dorothy finds it impossible to accept life for the sake of living. The human may choose to die, like Orwell himself, who might have lived had he followed his doctor's advice. Orwell's mind, like Dorothy's, was naturally pious. He belonged to the liberal-Christian era. But the liberal-Christian is very little Christian. V. S. Pritchett, in his obituary notice of Orwell, memoralized him as "a kind of saint," the "wintry conscience of a generation" (*The New Statesman*, 28 January 1950). But, as Mr. Trilling notices, Orwell's insight into the bleak age was not religious; if religion still implies some doctrine of personal sin and salvation. If for the early Dorothy everyone was innocent and all would be saved, for the late Orwell no one is guilty and none shall be saved (except perhaps the proles by their mindless sexuality).

Orwell thought he lived at the end of the liberal-Christian era, but he did not care to drive his own imagination beyond it. He thought he could discern the post-liberal imagination already, in other writers, but not in himself. He still insisted on joining morality and intelligence, as best he could. He could not accept honest sexuality as a substitute for honest social action. He thought he saw what was humanly necessary, even if it was not explainable. Orwell tried to explain Dorothy's rejection of the world as it is for her, beyond the accident of her frigidity:

> What she would have said was that though her faith had left her, she had not changed, could not change, did not want to change, the spiritual background of her mind; that her cosmos, though it seemed to her empty and meaningless, was still in a sense the Christian cosmos.

Dorothy would do her best to be a useful old maid, as before. She would meet the demands of the day, however futile they appeared. This was all that was left of her "Christian way of life." She would continue in her station, since that was her only commitment. Anyway, the church at least represented something better than what was coming. The clergyman's daughter

> perceived that in all that happens in church, however absurd and cowardly its supposed purpose may be, there is something—it is hard to define, but something of decency, of spiritual comeliness—that is not easily found in the world outside. It seemed to her that even though you no longer believe, it is better to go to church than not; better to follow in the ancient ways, than to drift in rootless freedom. . . . Just this much remained in her of the faith that had once, like the bones in a living frame, held her life together.

George Orwell was a *Left Book Club* man as Dorothy Hare was a Church of England girl. He remained a socialist not from belief but from disbelief in other choices. Socialism was the last form of faith of the liberal-Christian era. The socialist is then succeeded by a transitional figure: a new kind of fellow-traveler, not pink but grey, not crypto-communist but crypto-conservative, defending the good old values even as one reports their decline. These are the liberals who most appreciate Orwell.

The good old value most worth defending seems to be "plain intellectual integrity." As a liberal, Orwell is revered for nothing so much as his intellectual integrity. But intellectual integrity also points up the despair of the liberals, for it shows how meaningless the old style of questioning and searching has become. Intellectual integrity compelled Max Weber, in an essay that rattled the liberal European intelligentsia after the first world war as if it were already a skeleton, to say to those who still "tarry for new prophets and saviors, the situation is the same as resounds in . . . Isaiah's oracles:

> He calleth to me out of Seir, Watchman, what of the night? The watchman said, The morning cometh, and also the night; if ye will enquire, enquire ye; return, come.

The people to whom this was said has enquired and tarried for more than two millennia, and we are shaken when we realize its fate. From this we want to draw the lesson that nothing is gained by yearning and tarrying alone, and we shall act differently. We shall set to work and meet the 'demands of the day,' in human relations as well as in our vocation. This, however, is plain and simple, if each finds and obeys the daimon who holds the fibers of his very life." Orwell obeyed his daimon and met the demands of the day, in Spain and elsewhere as long as he lived. To "meet the demands of the day" is an ethic for liberals in a meaningless world. It is an ethic of action for the morally exhausted, an attempt to hold themselves and the world together.

Orwell was aware of the sources of his ethic of action. When Dorothy prays (unbelievingly) for strength, at the end of *The Clergyman's Daughter*, not God but "the smell of glue was the answer to her prayer. She did not reflect, consciously, that the solution to her difficulty lay in accepting the fact that there was no solution; that if one gets on with the job that lies to hand, the ultimate purpose of the job fades into insignificance; that faith and no faith are very much the same provided one is doing what is customary, useful and acceptable." To do what is acceptable is at least to be doing, to reject that passivity the new world is imposing upon humans. Dorothy again begins to use herself up in her pathetically useful activities. In the liberal theory, only the exhaustion of activity can counter the exhaustion of morality.

> The glue had liquefied. The problem of faith and no faith had vanished utterly from her mind. It was beginning to get dark, but, too busy to stop and light the lamp, she worked on, pasting strip after strip of paper into place, with absorbed, with pious concentration, in the penetrating smell of the glue-pot.

These are the final sentences of *The Clergyman's Daughter*. Orwell's answer for Dorothy is his own. The only available liberal substitute for faith was the action of gluing together what has fallen to pieces. Glue replaces Christian love as the sign of unity in the religion of the exhausted. One has to be completely outside religious experience to conceive of religion as most basically a mode of social cohesion. And, indeed, from Feuerbach to Durkheim, the liberals had known faith was nothing except its function as glue. Unity was the needful thing. (Whether it was called caritas or phallus worship was only an accidental distinction.) It was plain to Orwell, in his intellectual integrity, that the liberal-Christian civilization was irrevocably exhausted, but it was necessary to act as if it were not.

Orwell saw another possibility for the exhausted. The feeling of exhaustion, so pervasive in his fiction, connects him both with the final form of the liberal ethic and with the rise of the post-liberal imagination, exhausted beyond even the possibility of activity. Weber picked up the Efficiency theme in his despair at the growing "bureaucratization" or "rationalization" of western civilization. Orwell thought the post-liberal imagination must accept precisely a meaningless world, accept what he called "the deadly emptiness at the heart of things." This was the lesson "the Warburtons of this world"—finally exemplified in O'Brien—teach the Dorothys of this world—finally exemplified in Winston. Mr. Warburton does not quite succeed in making Dorothy passive to the experience he offers; later tempters do succeed, and Orwell's latest hero does finally accept and get inside the whale.

Orwell discovered his Mr. Warburton, among the novelists. His name was Henry Miller. Like Mr. Warburton, Henry Miller is that rare sight on an Orwellian page, a happy man. Except that Miller's is American, both men have that same "friendly voice, with no humbug in it, no moral purpose, merely an implicit assumption that we are all alike." Miller is surprised that Orwell is going to Spain, and Mr. Warburton is surprised that Dorothy refuses him. But neither is overly surprised. Both take life as they find it.

Henry Miller seemed to Orwell the best literary representative yet available of the post-liberal imagination. It was not that he worshipped the meaningless, as Hindus worshipped the void. To find the world empty of meaning is still a hangover of faith; it is still a search for an answer, even a no. But Miller, Orwell discovered, asked no questions. He simply accepted the world as it is, and thus freed himself to write honestly about it.

Orwell's essay on Miller, "Inside the Whale" (1939), is a brilliant treatment of the problems of his own novels from the perspective of literary criticism. In Miller, Orwell thought he had found a writer who had gone beyond the liberal imagination instead of returning to versions before it. Miller was the most advanced novelist of this period of transition to 1984. "After all, he is a completely negative, unconstructive, amoral writer, a mere Jonah, a passive accepter of evil, a sort of Whitman among the corpses." Miller proposes the only workable ethic for the modern writer, the ethic of irresponsibility. Of course, the man has no talent. He can only publish gratuitously detailed reports on his own trivial life, quite carefree and superficial. Talent had been, in the liberal-Christian society, "being able to care." But now caring drove the writer to dishonesty. The fact that Miller cares for nothing, and suffers no beliefs lost, protects him equally against the exhaustion of those who cannot quite escape caring (Orwell thought this helped account for his own limitations as a novelist) and against the dishonesty of those who have returned to impossible answers.

Orwell explained Miller's blissful unconcern with everything happening in the world, especially with politics, as the source of his greatest literary virtue. The passage is worth quoting in full:

War is only 'peace intensified.' What is quite obviously happening, war or no war, is the break-up of laissez-faire capitalism and of the liberal-Christian culture. Until recently the full implications of this were not foreseen, because it was generally imagined that Socialism could preserve and even enlarge the atmosphere of liberalism. It is now beginning to be realized how false this idea was. Almost certainly we are moving into an age of totalitarian dictatorships—an age in which freedom of thought will be at first a deadly sin and later on a meaningless abstraction. The autonomous individual is going to be stamped out of existence. But this means that literature, in the form in which we know it, must suffer at least a temporary death. The literature of liberalism is coming to an end and the literature of totalitarianism has not yet appeared and is barely imaginable. As for the writer, he is sitting on a melting iceberg; he is merely an anachronism, a hangover from the bourgeois age, as surely doomed as the hippopotamus. Miller seems to me a man out of the common because he saw and proclaimed this fact a long while before most of his contemporaries. . . . From now onwards the all-important fact for the creative writer is going to be that this is not a writer's world. This does not mean that he cannot help to bring the new society into being, but he can take no part in the process *as a writer*. For *as a writer* he is a liberal, and what is happening is the destruction of liberalism. It seems likely, therefore, that in the remaining years of free speech any novel worth reading will follow more or less along the lines that Miller has followed—I do not mean in technique or subject-matter, but in implied outlook. The passive attitude will come back, and it will be more consciously passive than before. . . . Get inside the whale—or rather, admit that you are inside the whale (for you *are*, of course). Give yourself over the world-process, stop fighting against it, or pretending that you control it; simply accept it, endure it, record it. . . . A novel on more positive, "constructive" lines, and not emotionally spurious, is at present very difficult to imagine.

Of course, James Joyce, Orwell thought—one might add Gertrude Stein and Virginia Woolf among others—had already muted the new antipolitical literature. The Joycean novel explored "the imbecilities of the inner mind." The universal mind was an idiot, capable of nothing more than registering discrete perceptions, as in Miss Stein's famous prose poem, "One Hundred

Men," "one and one and one and one" and so on to the quite arbitrary limit imposed by art. In the new literature, Orwell saw, the mind had turned in upon itself, to describe not the objects of reality but only its own perceptions. Reality was no longer a problem. Literature was to be concerned only with internal processes.

Morality, too, was no longer a problem, for it was a creation of the outer world. Only the instincts remain to the new literature as a problem, for reality and regimes are nothing to the instincts. 1984 will not abolish the instinctual life, only the coherence of morality and intelligence. This is Orwell's perverse hope for the proles, that they can live safely inside the new whale precisely because they live most closely to their instincts. The proles, Orwell thought, had never been either liberal or Christian, but sexual. They would persist in any civilization.

When Orwell wrote his essay on Henry Miller just before the war, the antipolitical writers seemed in relative eclipse. But Orwell knew that soon the Eliots and the Wyndham Lewises would displace the politicals, like Auden and Spender. For one thing, they were better writers being freed, he thought, from responsibility. The only honest men were private men. The public writers of the 'thirties had constructed a progressive orthodoxy, and joined "movements" and "countermovements" as if organizations could produce good fiction. But

> the atmosphere of orthodoxy is always damaging to prose, and above all it is completely ruinous to the novel, the most anarchical of all forms of literature. . . . From 1933 onwards the mental climate was increasingly against it. . . . Literature as we know it is an individual thing, demanding mental honesty and a minimum of censorship . . . a writer does well to stay out of politics.

To stay out of politics is not a protest against it, but an acceptance of whatever powers may be. "So far from protesting," Orwell writes of Miller, "he is accepting." If Miller seemed another Whitman, it only pointed up the fact that Whitman yelled "I accept" to a relatively good world; Miller yells to a bad one. Miller's "mystical acceptance of the thing as it is" is an expression of the perfect amorality of the idiot mind. What Miller accepts is not "an epoch of expansion and liberty, but an epoch of fear, tyranny, and regimentation." The liberal imagination is tempted to accept even this epoch. Still trying to protect its dwindling investment in the old culture, it can always point to the constantly retreating horizon and claim rightly it is still there.

If as Orwell wrote, "the democratic vistas have ended in barbed wire," it is still the peculiar talent of many liberals to point unerringly at the breaks in the wire and at the dullness of some of the barbs. Or, the liberal may claim that the instinctual life is still free, and thus turn for the salvation of culture to anticultural forces. (This explains in part the enthusiastic reception of Freudianism as an ethical doctrine among liberals.) Orwell's great insight is to have insisted, rightly, that this instinctualist protest is itself a form of acceptance; and "to say 'I accept' in an age like our own is to say that you accept concentration camps, rubber truncheons, Hitler, Stalin, bombs, aeroplanes, tinned food, machine guns, putsches, purges, slogans, Bedaux belts, gas masks, submarines, spies, provocateurs, press-censorship, secret prisons, aspirins, Hollywood films, and political murders." No doubt "on the whole this is Henry Miller's attitude." At least, it is more honest than the corrupting optimism that says: "Not *only* these things, of course."

The liberal imagination at the end of its optimism is deeply irritable; it would feel better if the whole civilization blew up. Gordon Comstock and George Bowling are always imagining that probability, and here Orwell himself was very close to Henry Miller's temper. He, as Orwell notices sympathetically, is always talking about blowing the place up. (Rejection has become a fantasy.) Orwell is mistaken, however, to think that Miller's autobiographical technique and subject-matter are only accidental to his posture of acceptance. Miller's concern with sex is no more accidental to him than it was to Mr. Warburton. If "Miller is simply a hard-boiled person talking about life, an ordinary American business-man with intellectual courage and a gift for words," sex is Henry Miller's business, and the only really worthwhile racket. It is not exile that made Miller write about "the man in the street full of brothels—of people drinking, talking, meditating and fornicating, not about people working, marrying and bringing up children." Nor, as Orwell thinks, could Miller "describe the one set of activities as well as the other." It is not exile but honesty, not the penalty of leaving your native land and thus necessarily transferring your roots to shallower soil. Rather, all soil has become shallow. As for one's roots, the thing is to be allowed to dig them up; and Miller found that easier to do in Paris than in New York.

Like Orwell, Miller had the experience of poverty; both had been down and out in Paris. Their descriptions of this experience could not be more antithetical. But still Orwell is sympathetic to Miller, even to the point of misunderstanding the necessities of his art, narrowing the gap between the liberal and the transitional writer. It is not so important that Orwell misunderstood Miller, out of sympathy for the common predicament of modern writers, but that he is sympathetic. His sympathy marks the loosening of his imagination from its old liberal forms.

Perhaps it is worth recalling liberals to the traditionally pejorative understanding of the term "imagination." Until the dawn of romanticism in the late eighteenth century, imagination had always been considered a source of error; and it is still true that, as an aesthetic term, "imagination" connotes moral and intellectual permissiveness. Creativity undisciplined by morality and reason is still a dangerous possibility, breaking through the forms in which it must be limited to be art. But Orwell does not consider Miller's art critically. In the final exhaustion of the liberal imagination, it is possible to treat a writer who is neither liberal—Miller, Orwell proclaims, is happily free of moral sensibilities—nor imaginative—Miller's perceptions are as superficial as his subject matter—as representative of the only creative possibility in modern literature.

What drives the liberal imagination beyond itself is precisely the ascendancy of imagination, no longer confident in its liberal-Christian forms. Orwell was the perfect liberal, neither passive nor unimaginative. Yet at the same time there was in Orwell a residual ambiguity typical of the finest liberalism. The sympathetic acceptance of the acceptor of 1984, along with the acutest picture of what 1984 would really be like, is a *caritas* liberalism cannot afford to pay for the sake of improving its imagination. (54:2)

24

On Religion and Power

The powerful are rarely religious. The sacredness of power contradicts the sacredness of religion. Religion assumes a power beyond. Power assumes there is nothing beyond itself, only power after power.

Marx made a religious critique of power when he noticed that it was the fate of ruling classes to have no need of faith. The powerful shed faith as they acquire power. Ruling classes are the least amenable to religion. Anglicanism, after all, was a living for later sons and poor relations. Faith arises out of the poor life. The good life needs no faith. It is for this reason that aristocratic dignity in the Western ethos has always imputed to the aristocrat an emancipation from faith. Aristocrats, as a class, have always treated their religion cavalierly, even when they are cardinals. Enthusiasm, as the highly aristocratic Duchess of Buckingham once noted to her deviant enthusiastic friend, the Countess of Huntingdon, is not an aristocratic virtue. "I cannot but wonder that your Ladyship should relish any sentiments so much at variance with high rank and good breeding."

Excerpted from: "Review of *Lust for Power*, by Joseph Haroutunian," *Journal of Religion* 31, no. 2 (April): 141–42, © 1951 by The University of Chicago, all rights reserved; "Review of *Marsilius of Padua, The Defender of Peace, vol. II*," *Journal of Religion* 37, no. 1 (January): 57–58, © 1958 by The University of Chicago, all rights reserved; "Reviews of *American Freedom and Catholic Power*, by Paul Blanshard; *Essays on Freedom and Power*, by Lord Acton; *The Vatican in World Politics*, by Avro Manhattan," *The Chicago Jewish Forum* 8, no. 2 (Winter 1949–50): 140–41.

People of breeding know enough not to push their religion too far. Enthusiasm, as Bishop Butler said in his famous interview with John Wesley, is a "very horrid thing." It can only end in a commitment beyond power. Thus, the failure of nerve is an aristocratic habit. Failing successfully, the failure of nerve comes to mean the nerve of failure. Aristocrats learn that they need not worry, about either hope or despair. Power, therefore, is freedom from religion. Man is emancipated from religion by power. (51:2, p. 141)

Marsilius of Padua marked the first stage in transposition of roles that has taken place in the modern era between church and state. Against the church, which was in his time still claiming supremacy over the state, with the state merely one agency of a Christian society, Marsilius proposed a state which would, in effect, become a church. For this is the implication of Marsilius's main intent: to strip the church of its political character. For if the church no longer has the prerogative of Christianizing society, then that prerogative—in its generality, the capacity to transform society—belongs to the state.

The conception of the church proposed by Marsilius is very modern, if not both modern and Protestant. To Marsilius, the church refers not to the hierarchy or the ecclesiastical bureaucracy but to the laity, who are also citizens of the state. Therefore, the church itself is a civil institution and subject to judgment along with other civil institutions by the people themselves through the highest agency of popular will, the state. In the Marsilian interpretation of the relation between religion and politics, even Jesus would have to submit himself to Pilate, as to the verdict of divine providence, which speaks now through the administrators of the general will. Power, thus secularized, nevertheless retains its divine character. If Pilate had only conducted affairs according to Marsilian strategy, no doubt he would have released Jesus, on the grounds that His Kingdom was not of this world. Here was a case of which a Marsilian administrator could have easily disposed: to release Jesus would have dealt a blow to the pretensions of power of a theocratic institution. In one sense, indeed, Pilate was the perfect Marsilian administrator, for he recognized the divine character of power—over life and death—invested in his office. "I have power to release thee and power to crucify thee."

Having assigned coercive authority to the state, Marsilius also assigned to the state that divine character now breathtaking in its completeness. With nothing more remaining to it than the freedom to persuade men of what is God's will, the church takes on, in the theory of Marsilius, the character it now cannot alter: it is purely voluntary and associational. If power is truly that which is given by God, then the church as such, being powerless, is no longer a divine institution; that title rather belongs to the state as the agency of the most general will. Marsilius is a very modern theorist of the relation between religion and politics in yet another important sense: he divinizes the state at the same time that he totally ignores that justification of sinful man through which the church was created and state affirmed. In the Marsilian view, the state is no longer a scourge, however ordained, but the best hope of a humanity no longer conceived as sinful but as weak. It is the Roman governor who, in his capacity to choose to crucify or not to crucify, is the virtual founder of the church. And it is Israel, as the first church, that is defeated. Interpreted in a Marsilian way, the Christian tragedy can be made into a paradigm of the legitimate place and use of authority. To the church, nothing remains except to become one civil institution among others.

For his theory, subjecting church to state—indeed, dissolving papacy into a congregational priesthood of equals, both in authority and in jurisdiction—for taking all power to enjoin violence away from the church, except as the state grants it, Marsilius was declared not merely heretic but "manifest and notorious arch-heretic." Marsilius died, unreconciled to the church in 1343. In time, the church has become reconciled to Marsilius. It has learned to coexist and even to take advantage of the modern state and the secular civilization foretold by Marsilius. All over the Western world the church has gone into politics, scrambling with other civil institutions for its share in the divine immanence of power. Nowadays, a church that is nonpolitical is no church at all. In this the churches are blamelessly innocent. Having been drawn into the Marsilian world, they have had to act accordingly or perish for lack of relevance to the essential character of modern society. (58:1, pp. 57–58)

There are two spectres haunting Europe and the world, one rising young with old dreams in Moscow, the other rising old with older dreams in Rome. And Moscow aspires to be a third Rome, while the second has gained a new life from Moscow's aspirations. From the end of the House of Habsburg to the rise of the spectre in the East, the Catholic Church had been isolated from direct political power of the first order in Europe. Now Moscow has given the second Rome back a role, to halt the building of the third Rome. The spectres haunt and are married to each other. Each feeds on the other's successes even more than on its failures. This is always the way of rival absolutisms.

. . . the great Protestant theologian, Karl Barth . . . sees "some connection" between Roman Catholicism and Communism. "Both are totalitarian; both claim man as a whole. Communism uses about the same methods of organization (learned from the Jesuits). Both lay great stress on all that is visible." Nevertheless, Barth concludes, Roman Catholicism is "the more dangerous of the two," at least "for Protestantism." "Communism will pass; Roman Catholicism is lasting." (49:1, p. 140)

The church is neither a collection of heroic turbulent priests holding the sanctuaries against the rush of omnipotent statism. Nor is it a mindless rock sat upon by too many nostalgic men turning passionate eyes upon the past even if Tyrrell thought so at times. Rather, the church will act as all other political organizations must act, expediently to preserve and increase its power. The church has lived too long to martyr itself even to its own principles. It has built up a tremendous structure of casuistry to deal with the expedients of political action. There will be no final struggle between church and state. The descendants of Constantine must know that a *Concordat* with Rome is as possible in the future as it was in the past. Only the romantic disillusioned radicals who hate the state can afford the illusion of loving the church so much. The flight from party animosity can end in the deification of ecclesiastical tyranny as often as flight in the reverse direction can end in the deification of a party. (49:1, p. 141)

25

A Jesuit Looks at Proudhon
Competition in Damnation

Father de Lubac can say anything he wishes about Proudhon.[1] Even more than most seminal tongues, Proudhon said everything. If he became famous with his saying, in 1840, that "Property is theft," later he said property was liberty. If he said "God is evil," he also said God is "the conscience of humanity." It is difficult to say of Proudhon at one time what will be true at another. Thus it has been comparatively easy for each commentator and biographer to build their own Proudhon, in turn. Reading Proudhon, as Herzen said, never furnishes results, only weapons and styles. That may explain how Sorel can possibly be Proudhon's finest extension, in one direction. An entire political spectrum, anarchist to royalist, has been able to claim him, to use him as a weapon and as a style. The thing is to know what remains true for all of the Proudhons, or better, what is true in Father de Lubac's Proudhon.

Proudhon contradicted himself all his life, as readily as he contradicted others. This was not to become famous, although the style brought him his first fame. Some commentators and antagonists assumed he contradicted himself because he had contradictory ideas and loved them all. Others, including de Lubac, understand that Proudhon considered himself always a critic. The function of the critic is to contradict; to play the minority, or better to create one; to be the eternal nay-sayer, the somewhat disloyal opposition, even of himself and of his own criticism. The role of the critic is as conscience in the Protestant tradition, to express a constant protest against

Reprinted from *Modern Review* 3, no. 2 (January 1950): 166–71.
    1. Henri de Lubac, *The Un-Marxian Socialist* (London: Sheed & Ward, 1948).

whatever is. Proudhon knew he could be a critic and nothing else. To be a critic meant he could never quite be a politician, or enjoy a mission, or breed disciples and found a school. Proudhon decided early the role of the critic was the only one he could play. Critics are made by temperament, not by insight. A politician can have insight without being a critic. His own insight into his critical temperament confirmed Proudhon in a lifelong role. "You know that, by temperament," he concluded, "I rather make fun of everything, even my own beliefs, and . . . this constitutes the basis of my conscience."

Critics, at least in ages when there were fewer of them, must become famous. John Selden made the rule of critical fame pointed enough: Preach damnation, he said, in a famous aphorism, "for we love a man who damns us, and we run after him to save us." Proudhon preached a kind of damnation, but never to save men. It was his function to damn, and whatever other men sought to create he sought to destroy. He took *"Destruam et Aedificabo"* as his motto from 32 *Deuteronomy.* Bakunin picked up and polished the motto of his teacher for himself: *"The passion for destruction is a creative passion."* Proudhon would have agreed. He carefully left behind him no disciples, no systems, and no movements; not even Bakunin or anarchism. Syndicalism was a movement, and many men have called themselves Proudhonians. In France, certainly until 1895, even until 1914, when the French trade union movement obeyed the state as it went to war against another state, the working-class movement was Proudhonian. But to be a Proudhonian was to be unpolitical, so far as politics must have always to do with the capture of the state, not with its abolition by some vague supercession of the multiple trade union organs of the working class. Syndicalism is dead for not recognizing what it chose to deny: the persistence of politics as a struggle to capture the state, not to abolish it. Proudhonism did not organize parties, the organ of the political struggle for the power of the state, while it was Marxism that found expression in party organization. Marxism became a *political* movement, as Proudhonism, on principle, could not. This has made Proudhon famous without being important, creative without being politically constructive, in the history of European movements. As it turned out, he simply delayed Marxism. Proudhon did not leave behind the legacy for a movement, to contradict the Marxist, even though he contradicted Marx. Father de Lubac is not concerned with movements. Rather, he wants to know how Proudhon contradicted Marx, after he has told us why.

The answer, in the Jesuit writer's scholarly volume, is that Proudhon could not be politically constructive. As a critic, he joined rarely, and resigned as often, organized nothing, and pretended to resolve nothing. A man who insists he cannot resolve—and that men cannot resolve—problems does not become a politician, or the intellectual father of power politicians. Probably, Proudhon taught Marx socialism. At least, Marx did not take up the concept of the class struggle until after he had read Proudhon. But Proudhon could not teach Marx his fear of power or his dread of optimism. This meant he necessarily contradicted Marx at every step and particularly when Marx said "humanity lays down for itself only problems that it can resolve." On the contrary, according to Proudhon, the only problems humanity has are the ones it can never resolve. Change is not resolution. Neither is progress. Proudhon believed there was change and progress, but not resolution.

Proudhon's thought, as de Lubac notices in the most important chapter 7, is centered upon the concept of *antinomy*. "This word, antinomy," de Lubac writes, "summarizes for Proudhon a whole vision of the Universe." It meant, as Proudhon explained many times, a "contradiction . . . an opposition inherent, in all the elements, in all the forces which constitute the community." Everything, and everyone, for Proudhon, is "two-faced." "The world, the community and man are made up of irreducible elements, of antithetical principles and antagonist forces." God is the first expression of antinomy. Proudhon, who was something of a biblical scholar, and had taught himself Hebrew, thought the Jews summed Him up as such: "The Lord is a man of war." "War is our history, our life, our whole soul. Once more, it is everything." War is Proudhon's poetic summary image of the natural law of antinomy. It is an "inward act" as well as outward, the psychological condition of man, as well as political. It is the nature of all relationships that they be antinomical, the first relationship of God and men, of men and men, class and class. Proudhon does not mean to be paradoxical. He cannot help it if "everything in society is primarily a paradox."

Antinomy is the principle of destruction. But at the same time, Proudhon writes, it makes creation possible. It is the action of forces that must "clash and devour one another that is the only condition on which they are productive."

In many ways, Proudhon is a democratic philosopher of the nineteenth century. Nineteenth-century thought did not deny the principle of antinomy, rather it based its political thought upon it. "What makes freedom possible," wrote Proudhon, is "the opposition among powers." Nineteenth-century democrats agreed. The opposition, as much as the separation, of powers made freedom possible. If Proudhon was a pluralist, then he was a liberal-democrat. Pluralism is the first principle of liberal-democratic thought. Marx was right to call him a bourgeois thinker. Pluralism is inherent in the basic conceptual structure of Proudhon's thought. "Any one who says organism, says complication: any one who says plurality, says contrariety, opposition. . . ." Proudhon feared power, when it was not pluralized, as he feared the masses when they voted together. In power centralized, "man no longer belongs to himself, no longer feels for himself, no longer lives, is no longer anything." Power centralized leads to the dictatorship of the bureaucracy, and that is a late stage of political self-alienation. "You are only a routine and you do not understand yourself."

What is necessary to the creativity of opposition—and here Proudhon is in the nineteenth-century mainstream, still basic to contemporary sociological thought—is that the antinomical forces tend toward equilibrium, as the balance of power is momentarily necessary to political equilibrium. Equilibrium, moving balances, are leading principles of nineteenth-century liberalism, if Spencer and Malthus can be called liberals. For Spencer, a moving equilibrium is the limiting principle in progress (evolution) as it is, in other areas of evidence, for Malthus. Proudhon shared the idea of progress, and its moving equilibrium, with Spencer and with Malthus, to name only two secret sharers. Spencer and Malthus would have agreed with the French "socialist": "Take away the antinomy and the progress of Beings is inexplicable; for where is the force which would produce progress?" If Malthus would object that progress is not infinite, that there are constant antinomical forces pushing toward an equilibrium, Proudhon would have to agree, despite his penchant for disagreement. It would be utopian to think otherwise. The trouble with Marx is that he is a utopian, granted his criticism of other utopians. With Hegel, Marx "states the contradiction to 'rise above' it afterwards." Proudhon, de Lubac concludes, "notes the antinomy, and does not claim to resolve it." The antinomy is persistent. The utopianism in Marx is to think it is not. Proudhon gave up the idea of the synthesis, and this retreat from Hegel meant, as de Lubac and others have said, that he gave up the idea of getting "beyond the antagonisms of existing society." Proudhon turned his principle, and his temperament, to a criticism of the theoretical basis of the analysis of social change in Hegelian thought, and thus, laterally, in Marxism.

What Hegel could not admit was that "an antinomy cannot be resolved, but that it indicates an oscillation or an antagonism susceptible only of equilibrium." The basic illusion Hegelian thought has projected upon the world is its optimism. Optimism, in this case, Marxism, has an eschatological dynamic, as theology and politics have always had. "People would like to see an end to it all, but I tell you . . . *there is no end at all.*" Proudhon had a churchman's mind, not an evangelical's. Eschatological thought must always hope, and its hope must be always that the antinomy will be resolved finally. Proudhon italicized his answer. *"The antinomy cannot be resolved."* The answer stands as his motto, better than the phrase from *32 Deut.* It is, as de Lubac says, even the motto of his "agony," since all his life he wanted to make a revolution. "We must make revolution, damn it! It is the only good thing, the only reality in this life!" Proudhon's "agony," "the persistent antinomy" is very close to the Christian idea of sin. The warfare image is, of course, standard as the symbol of sin in the Christian literature. Sin is the state of war 'in the heart of each.' But Father de Lubac carefully avoids making the connection himself. Good style is never obvious.

The answer Proudhon gave to Marx itself answers the question of why Proudhon's thought has been politically unimportant. Marx promised men they could, in time, relieve themselves of the agony. Sin, he promised, is really an internalization of social contradictions. It has not been very promising politics, particularly in ages of transition, to tell men the agony is immanent. But Proudhon rebutted that his politics were better and truer, however unsuccessful. Marx, like the theologians, is an idolator to promise men such things as an end of history. If the promise is wrapped in God, then "the fight against God is never-ending."

The curious may ask why a thinker in the first rank of Jesuit intellectuals has taken up Proudhon. Obviously, Father de Lubac takes delight in the man, and that is reason enough to write a book. But there are other reasons. Father de Lubac has taken up Proudhon to take him up; to take up a man is to have him serve one's own purposes. The Father understands that the controversy on the left has been much more than a logomachy, and in this situation it is relatively easy to achieve one of the most crucial kinds of polemical victories, the stealing of the symbols and the historic symbol-makers of the opposition. In another place,[2] Father de Lubac has displayed his talent for casuistical stretching around the socialist position to engross it within one that is ostensibly Catholic. He writes that modern man is suffering from "a new ambition," the lust after self-mastery. Humanity, he continues, "means to forge its destiny." This is a "forbidden dream, a diabolical ambition." Man is "once more on the point of eating of the forbidden fruit, of usurping a *role* which is not his." Father de Lubac is parroting the style of his own critical tradition, but beneath the gentle digging there is substantial agreement. He concludes, in his own kind of language, that "Man's present evil cannot be reduced to some fault in the organization of society." But he does not allow Proudhon enough of his usual luxury of contradiction. Finally, for Proudhon, when religion becomes anthropology, and men are disenchanted even of this last ambition, they will achieve precisely what Father de Lubac rises to deny, utter self-mastery. The scholarly priest is unwilling to risk the critic's final paradox. (50:1)

26
Socialism and Sociology

To the ironic critics of the age, the militancy of C. Wright Mills is suspect. Annoyed, as by a gadfly who insists on landing somewhere, Mills's fellow

2. See *The Dublin Review*, no. 442, (First Quarter 1948), 5–36.
Reprinted from *Partisan Review* 23, no. 3 (Summer 1956): 365–69.

critics have fixed on the exaggerations to which his militancy has led—the partisan use of evidence, the unrelieved gloom. In American social letters, Mills is bracketed as a naïf, a pure dissenter in an agreeable time. If this were all, if Mills were accused of nothing worse than being naïve, of remaining narrowly negative in a period of ideological as well as material abundance, the charges should of course be dismissed. He is, however vulnerable to the more serious charge of posturing. As Christianity, following the death of Christian belief, multiplied its armchair apologists in the universities, so socialism has its professional and passionate academics, transforming their socialism into sociology. Mills must be ranked as one of these caretakers of the socialist polemical tradition. He incites without hope; he offers not a single saving myth—no hope from the proletariat; nor from the engineers; and certainly not from a cultivated and responsible upper class, that fantasy-compliment of the conservative critics to themselves. Further, it is hard to see what group of readers Mills can hope to move. Literate *and* committed audiences are as scarce these days as salvation-bearing social classes. Mills's sympathetic reader is, I suppose, that stable *Partisan Review* type, culturally rather than politically committed—the literary son of socialist fathers, who takes over the tatters of liberal belief and becomes the moralizing man in an immoral society.

What confutes the militancy of C. Wright Mills is his marginal relation to both the academy and the doctrinal vacuum of American politics surrounding it. From inside the academy Mills looks like a political man, a polemicist; from outside his commitments look academic. Just this double jeopardy makes it likely that his criticism, despite its genuine cutting edge, will gain public favor. Criticism is part of the largess of American culture, and the critic who bestows it may hope for generous receipts. Even Mills, the angry man of American social letters, may ultimately expect to hitch a ride on the American gravy train, against his personal will, as one of its most celebrated critics. For criticism too is a saleable commodity, as long as it remains professional and sharpens no movement of protest. If Veblen, to whom Mills is often compared when he is being rated favorably, can be canonized by *Fortune*, Mills may expect no less, and probably within his own lifetime. *Time* could render his face iconic for a week. This means no insult to Mills. The mass society which is rapidly overtaking our inherited liberal one has no explicit faith, and its implicit faith is so diffuse that it can digest any virtuoso heretic striking blindly at where dogma used to be.

The dogma at which Mills strikes has become so shadowy that he never locates it explicitly as his target. Briefly, it is the classical liberal thesis that the institutions of government are distinct from the institutions of property. Mills's antithesis, also not stated explicitly in this book,[1] is the classical so-

---

1. C. Wright Mills, *The Power Elite* (New York: Oxford University Press, 1956).

cialist denial: power is not separate from property; corporate property cannot be realistically or legitimately considered private. By submitting the present American situation to an essentially socialist analysis, Mills demonstrates (successfully, I think) how irrelevant to American reality liberalism has become. Property, and the hidden privileges and flow of opportunity that go with it, does not exist antecedently to government. Indeed, in our present social arrangement, the major institutions of government and the major institutions of property tend openly to merge. The primitive stuff of institutions are the humans who staff them, and Mills goes about the theoretically simple but polemically complex task of spotting the men who circulate among the merging institutions, therefore occupying what he calls the "command posts" atop American society.

Mills perhaps credits the old liberal dogma of separate and balancing institutions with too much life, so that he fatigues the reader with lengthy parades of tycoons in Washington, generals at ease in executive suites, and the new hybrid politicians, with business hearts and military heads. But the book is no mere exposé of money lords, or of the vested interests of our military economy. Indeed, Mills says too little of the movement of funds that is sapping the economic potential of America, and talks mainly about the movement of men that is sapping our civic potential. For this alliance, between the high officers of executive government and the chief managers of corporate property, Mills finds a new name: the power elite. Despite the fact that such an alliance is the staple of socialist theory, Mills holds that this new name for it is necessary. For a third institution, the armed services, has become the mortar holding the two familiar old institutions of rule together, and has come to personify for a politically illiterate public the idea of political and economic stability: a permanent war economy based on a negative ideology of an absolute enemy.

Mills has written as fine an obituary notice on liberal society as any lover of the genre could hope to read. Chapters 11 and 12, in particular, survey our liberal inheritance and exhibit its bankruptcy both as political theory (chapter 11: "The Theory of Balance") and political fact (chapter 12: "The Power Elite"). The liberal principles of a government instituted and operated separately from property, against which the propertied classes had rights and toward which the powers of government were limited—these principles have been quietly abrogated. Even granting that the founding fathers, following Locke's *Second Treatise*, enacted a government charged with protecting the natural rights of property, nevertheless according to classical liberalism political institutions were something superimposed upon economic ones and different from them. By gradual extension, the liberal principle retracted the absolute guarantee of property inserted into the very definition of the liberal state. Thus extended, liberalism operated occasionally to check the in any case fragmented interests of the propertied classes.

And in the regime of FDR the liberal principle of an autonomous political order was turned to check the increasingly unified interests of the executive class that had come to be the representative men of property. Having slowly learned the lessons that the New Deal had to teach it, the executive class simply took over the administration of the bureaucratic welfare state and merged its personnel and purposes with it. Thus, when the historical carriers of liberalism were no longer served by it, the liberal principle of autonomous and mutually limiting political and economic orders was scuttled. In America the scuttling is so recent that Mills takes almost all of his examples of it from the Eisenhower years, though of course it began in the Roosevelt war-preparedness period.

To explain why there has been so little serious opposition to the scuttling of American liberalism, Mills resorts to the obvious tautology that American society is, anyway, in process of transition from liberal to mass form. And, as a result of this trend, the classes and the masses grow together. If anything, I should say that the elites Mills studies are farther along toward the psychology characteristic of a mass society than large segments of the population. The elites are incapable of contemplating serious questions steadily; they have a few fixed ideas and no fixed morality. This much Mills confirms. But the intellectual and moral condition of the many is scarcely better than that of the ruling few; chapter 13, "The Mass Society," makes this clear. Being so unsentimental as to label the "people" of nineteenth-century liberalism and socialism alike as a "mass," Mills is at a loss to find a sharp angle from which to criticize the higher immorality of the elite. Unwittingly, he demonstrates that the powerless mass and the power elite complement each other perfectly. The lower immorality differs only in size and import from the higher. Such essential agreement creates a major problem of approach for Mills. As a serious critic, who will allow neither his socialism nor his respect for the liberal civilization of an earlier America to bemuse his vision of the present, Mills is unable to moor the repugnant facts of American public life against the pier of American values. In a manner no critic has yet adequately described, the pier has somehow torn loose and floats around like another fact on the calm, oily surface of American life.

Of course to defend is to be conservative, as Mills points out. But just at its best, as an attack, Mills's performance is purely negative. Against the conservative mood of the liberals, Mills offers a mood of vague resentment. He has looked into the faces of the American elite and realized with dramatic pleasure that they are blank. It is the misfortune of the socialist critic in our time, equipped with better social psychology than his forebears, to look into the faces of the mass and see that these too are irremediably blank. Masses are merely the poorer relations of elites. For all Mills's middle-western devotion to the idea that American power is won on the playing fields of Exeter, and other such eastern places, the fact is that the elites are quite as mindless as the mass and share a similarly empty inner life. False consciousness is here to stay; it is the happy psychic condition of a mature and still dynamic industrial civilization that has worked back through a religion of transcendence to a religion of immanence based on a supra-primitive fetishism of infinitely variable commodities. Criticism, when it serves no religion of transcendence, not even a secular one, such as socialism, becomes another bright and shiny thing, to be admired and consumed. All the same, even if blame can be bought like praise nowadays, he who blames is still to be preferred to he who praises. (56:4)

27

Nineteenth-Century European Positivism

Two great and related motifs appear in the history of nineteenth-century sociological theory: first, theory was developed as an ideological response to the problem of social order after the fall of the *ancien regime;* second, theory was developed as a source of ideals calculated to replace those fatally called into question during the period of middle-class political and social revolution. In this informative volume of intellectual history,[1] Simon sees both motifs converging in the "ultimate purpose" of Comtean positivism, namely, "to alter society according to the laws discovered by sociology."

The "laws" discovered by Comte (which were also the predicates of that which was discovered, according to Comte's own method) were called into question with embarrassing haste and regularity by his immediate disciples, especially the able Emile Littre, who tried to protect the doctrine against itself. But despite Littre, and others who considered Positivism as a methodological advance toward a viable social science rather than a solution to the problem of disorder in European culture and society, the history of nineteenth-century European positivism is chiefly a chronicle of piffling controversies among the religiously inclined, who found in Positivism the "religion without theology" that they sought. Simon notes that his study of various orthodox conventicles yields, as the "most striking element" in their membership, a high proportion of "known cases of religious disorientation prior to contact with Positivism, in other words the degree to which Positivism played the role of a substitute religion."

Simon does not trace the tension, as regularly and clearly as his own published material would allow, imposed by the double Comtean influence on

Reprinted from *American Sociological Review* 30, no. 5 (October 1965): 790–91.

    1. W. M. Simon, *European Positivism in the Nineteenth Century: An Essay in Intellectual History* (Ithaca, NY: Cornell University Press, 1963).

those who were engaged in what they considered an advance toward the scientific study of society: as Comte himself announced, scientific study could not but fundamentally transform society, in the very process of studying it. Although he has written on an important aspect in the history, at once, of sociological theory and of the European intelligentsia, Simon did not penetrate very far beyond the data into its meaning, of which one major aspect is the ambivalence of the social scientist toward his own role as transformer as well as student of social transformations.

Comte's own sociological theory reached a culminating point, fusing methodology and ideology, in his doctrine of the "spritual power," that scientific caste charged by the "law of succession" in history to take up functions superior even to those earlier performed by the Christian clergy—the care of the hearts and minds of a scientifically organized citizenry. That doctrine was not exclusively Comtean, but, in its Comtean dress, it penetrated France, England and Germany until it was met and defeated by more powerful pretenders to the same power: Marxism and Freudianism. (Freud's phrase describing the ideal therapist of the future as a "secular spiritual guide" is very Comtean, and the Leninist-Marxist doctrine of the Party can be interpreted as the doctrine of a successor power to the church.) This book traces the various means by which Comtean method and doctrine diffused through western European culture, preparing the way for "spiritual powers" that would take up the religion of Science in ways only slightly less bizarre than Comte's own.

Specialists in sociological theory would find it useful if an intellectual historian of Simon's high caliber were to specify the "connection between Comte's sociological and religious constructions," which gave "science . . . a religious or quasi-religious authority." In Comte's case, the connection lay in his attempts to institutionalize sociological constructions, for purposes of social control, through the agency of a nonexistent "spiritual power" or Comtean intelligentsia. But one is left to wonder about the "idée maitresse of a spiritual power" as this might be found implicit in the work of sociologists after Comte—in Durkheim, for example. But Simon set himself strict limits of interpretation. Within those limits, his historical chronicle of official and formally stated influences is still useful, and his book will no doubt take its place on the shelves of many professional libraries. But it would have had a more lasting effect if Simon had sought the *implicit* influences of Positivism in the work of some among those he exhibits as having been influenced. As it is, we read some familiar names, with rather ambiguous statements of their indebtedness to Positivism, without coming to grips with the great inner tension still deeply agitating a discipline that once understood itself as a "spiritual power." (65:2)

28

T. G. Masaryk's *The Social Question*

Who reads Masaryk? He is one of the losers in the struggle of titans, a victim of what he himself called our "exaggerated historicism," the logic of practices (commonly passed off by sociologists as "facts") so accomplished that we treat them *eo ipso* as good. From what did the winning titan, Marx, derive his historicism? It followed, the losing lecturer declared, from the winner's "exaggerated love of innovations," his "revolutionism." Marx has imposed the terrible restlessness of his theory upon us, while Masaryk's realism, the alternative theory, is positively unpopular. Who now understands a theory that would put the study of things before that of their development? In Masaryk's realism, "the static rather than the dynamic elements of our world seem . . . the proper and most important object of reflection" (pp. 85–86).[1]

What constitutes the proper and most important object of reflection for the Marxist? Answer: the dynamic elements of our world, by which the theory in one or a few minds becomes the practice that is in many minds. That "becoming" is in revolution. Without revolution, Marxism would remain theoretical, a mere religion; for this revulsion against religion, in Marx's practice, is interpreted as revolution. But that revolution is not only practice but also a violent act, that, for instance, it demands killing, is something about which Marx has no scruples. "The famous proletariat" is constructed by Marx precisely for this purpose; it is Feuerbach's "humanity" transformed into a class, then further transformed by the winners who followed Marx into a mass—more precisely, The Masses. Masaryk has no doubts about how to judge a revolution. It is a blood sport, for would-be aristocrats: "Revolution means killing." Marx extended the blood sport that is politics—man-killing—and gave it a slightly different justification, not a new end but the old means with different enactors. "Marx proclaims a permanent revolution, that is, not only revolution, but revolutionism" (p. 348).

Against the permanent revolution that appeals perhaps more to the dated than to the deprived, what did Masaryk have to offer? "Reformation, not revolution!" How that phrase must have rung out when Masaryk first read to his students in the University of Prague, in the mid-nineties, the lecture notes upon which this book was based. "Revolution today is philistinism.

Reprinted from *Contemporary Sociology* 3, no. 1 (January 1974): 26–27.
1. T. G. Masaryk, *The Social Question: Philosophical and Sociological Foundations of Marxism*, edited and translated by Erazim V. Kohák (Lewisburg, PA: Bucknell University Press, 1972).

. . . Old means will not create the new, and revolution is a very old means. I am opposed to revolutionism because I believe in evolution and progress through work, while revolution is a sport, a gamble. I do not believe in chance and in miracles. I am decidedly a determinist, but not a fatalist" (p. 350).

The hidden dogmatism in the Marxist critique is in its amoral adherence to revolutionism. When they attained power, and defeated the sons of Masaryk, the heirs of Marx merely gave up the negativity of revolution and maintained the amoralism of the Marxist absolute: its negation of the old absolutely. If Marxism was itself, as Masaryk thought in the 1890s, an outdated and worn-out materialism, then Party-organized communism is an up-to-date philistinism. Comrade Brezhnev must pave over the Soviet wilderness and raise indefinitely the Gross National Product of the USSR. Bread and highways: these are the units in which our established rulers measure out political democracy. The heirs of both bourgeois capitalist democracy and proletarian revolutionism have nothing to offer either the deprived or the sated except bigger shares in the GNP. Only those shares guarantee the survival (West) or promise the prospect (East) of political democracy.

The main alternative to these big offers is still not Masaryk's, although he was aware of that alternative, which had already appeared in his time— "unceasing critique, an evil angry critique, thought without heart. . . . Suicide is the delirium of subjectivism, murder the delirium of objectivism, both of egotism—the one because it cannot love, the other because it hates" (p. 358). The two deliriums are interchangeable: the Left, with its furled banners of revolution, can easily become an indifferent, calculating Right. On both left and right, Masaryk saw a gathering emptiness which was supposed to be filled "by gathering every possible thought, in a bright multiplicity."

Where is Masaryk's alternative? It appears to open up the moment he notes, to his students, that it was the old God who created, while we new gods do not know how to create: we can only "criticize the work of the old God." The objectivists among the new gods "criticize the world and society; the subjectivists criticize themselves" (p. 358). The artists criticize world, society, and self. What, then, are we do do? Stop playing the god game, or even the Christ game; instead, we are to work, diligently, like reformed men and so earn some measure of justification, within our various and related particularities. There are to be no completely new societies, only the old ones reformed. Let there be no more ethical than economic centralization. Masaryk supports autonomy and federalization. Communism—economic, intellectual, or sexual—is impossible, "even in the distant future" (p. 251). The fourth way opens up the moment that the social theorist recognizes that any great leap from theory to practice must become a death leap.

All students of sociological theory should be grateful to Professor Kohák for making this fine edition of Masaryk's work on Marx's theory available in a useful English translation. Through this edition, the struggle of titans has been renewed and, despite what has happened politically, I still think that Masaryk's heirs have a fighting chance—if only they would fight on, with all their inherited wisdom, against (1) the permanent revolutionaries, (2) their indifferent calculating opponents, (3) those new elitists who combine in their functions permanent revolution and calculating indifference. (74:1)

29
Aesthetic Functions in Modern Politics

The relations between art and politics have rarely been discussed either in contemporary aesthetics or in political science. Since Hegel's *Philosophy of Fine Arts*, the analysis of art styles as the sensuous objectifications of cultural attitudes has been worked out in detail. But the same method has not been applied to the sensuous objectifications of political action. The removal of art from social life to the museum has also removed it from among the integral concerns of political science. Accepting the popular dichotomy between art and politics, modern political science has long lost its sense of art as *techne*, as a practical instrument of communication and coercion. An older political science did indeed consider "art" an instrument of coercion, curbing what Freud liked to call "the rebelliousness and destructive passions" of the masses and binding them to their rulers. Indeed, perhaps Freud alone among modern masters of social science comprehended art as one of the weapons of coercion in the arsenal of culture. "Works of art," Freud writes, "promote the feelings of identification" and identification is, in the Freudian theory, the modality of authority.[1]

Of course, the finest discussion of art as a political instrument remains Plato's. That first and most astute political scientist understood art strictly as *techne*. Plato's analysis of the subsumption of art to politics is the foundation upon which this discussion of certain aspects of their contemporary relation is constructed. Rejecting the dichotomy of art and politics, Plato viewed politics as itself an art, a craft—*techne*—which subsumed the other arts. The Greek *aesthesis* means "sensation" or "sense perception"; and the term as used today (referring to good taste or to the beautiful) is a recent and considerable narrowing of the original meaning. It is the authentic connota-

Reprinted by permission of Princeton University Press from *World Politics* 5, no. 4 (July 1953): 478–502. Copyright 1953, © 1981 renewed by Princeton University Press.
    1. Sigmund Freud, *The Future of an Illusion* (London, 1928), 23.

tions of "aesthetic" which have the greatest relevance to political science, for the aesthetic or sensuous is a permanent aspect of political action.

More precisely, the aesthetic may be an exemplar of a given form of political action, changing as the political forms to which it is appropriate change. The aesthetic forms expressive of parliamentary democracy or of revolutionary movements may offer significant differences from the aesthetic forms accompanying the totalitarian state or monarchy, just as the aesthetic production of the Protestant Church immediately differentiates it from the Roman.[2] It is my assumption here that there are aesthetic or sensuous objectifications appropriate to various stages and types of political action that may be understood as functions of those stages and types.

Following Tolstoy, I would define the "aesthetic" as that activity in which, by means of external signs, human beings communicate feelings to others, who are thereby "infected by these feelings and also experience them." Tolstoy's definition of art, like Plato's, is political. Both define the aesthetic in terms of its function in uniting individuals to contribute to the enthusiastic execution of the purposes of their community. Art is not simply "the expression of man's emotions by external signs." It is neither "as the metaphysicians say, the manifestation of some mysterious Idea of beauty or God," nor "as the aesthetical physiologists say, a game in which man lets off his excess of stored-up energy." Art, for Tolstoy, is not "the production of pleasing objects; and, above all, it is not pleasure." Great art may produce displeasing objects, and its perception may be something quite other than pleasurable. (*Les Fleurs du mal* are pleasurable only in a very ambiguous sense.) Rather, art is a "means of union among men, joining them together in the same feelings," and indispensable for their community, however that community is conceived.

The political process necessarily develops aesthetic functions. Art is joined to politics as an instrument of unity, unity being considered as the proper end of politics. But having placed art in the service of politics, Tolstoy did not neglect to judge both by an end beyond the purely political—that is, by the "well-being of individuals and of humanity."[3] Thus Tolstoy still submitted to moral criticism the means-relation of the aesthetic to the political. There may be a nonpolitical end, such as freedom or beatitude, in relation to which the political end is only a means. The aesthetic instruments of politics might, therefore, bulwark a unity judged improper from the perspective of an end beyond or contradicting that unity.

The loss of an end beyond the political is perhaps the essential characteristic of modern politics. In opposition to this accelerating trend, democratic

2. See, for example, G. G. Coulton, *Art and the Reformation* (Oxford, 1928), esp. chap. 14 ("The Poor Man's Bible").

3. Leo Tolstoy, "What is Art?" in *Tolstoy on Art*, translated by Aylmer Maude (London, 1924), 173.

politics, like democratic religion, has had a characteristic distrust of unity itself as the appropriate end of political action. Democracy has been disposed to eschew aesthetic devices as instruments of either politics or religion. Art in the service of politics or religion has tended to be magical and authoritarian, rather than critical and democratic—as it is when it plays an autonomous role in a society characterized by autonomous occupations and doctrines operating at best in antagonistic cooperation. Democratic religion, in its anti-hierocratic organization, originally devalued art (especially visual art) as an instrument of unity dangerous to its own discursive form: the "priesthood of all believers." Democratic politics, true to its Protestant origins, also succeeded in devaluing art as an instrument dangerous to its discursive (i.e., parliamentary) form. The doctrine of discursive value was opposed to the use of aesthetic values in Protestant, bourgeois, democratic society.

It is precisely the emptying of discursive values and their replacement by aesthetic that is one of the chief problems of politics in our time. The problem is one a democratic culture needs to recognize as a threat and resolve, if its own aesthetic devices—inherited from an age in revolt against the aesthetics of vision in favor of the aesthetics of hearing—are to survive. Modern antidemocratic politics seems to signal a new functional relation between the aesthetic and the political. The aesthetics of rhetoric is largely displaced by the aesthetics of spectacle as a general device of political unification. The voice itself may become a nondiscursive instrument, engaged not so much in argumentation as in the communication of commands by states of feeling. Individuals may want no longer to talk, or even to listen to argument. In the age after the Age of Discussion, they may want only to see. Seeing, as in an earlier period of authoritarianism, is again believing. The eye again replaces the ear as the sense organ of political action, and spatial forms replace discursive as the structural modes of such action.

The aesthetic devices considered here are mainly visual, since the manipulation of the visual is the most appropriate device of political unity in an age at least in transition from the Age of Discussion. The three sections of this essay attempt to analyze a variety of visual devices employed to create unity in shifting historical contexts. I shall note, first, the changing function of dress fashion as a supplement to political action; second, the spatialization of politics in modern ceremonial; and third, the altered relation of command and obedience implicit in political aesthetics.

I

It can be argued that unity is primarily a rhetorical function, employing those often undemocratic forms that political science has learned to call ideologies, myths, or otherwise discursive symbol systems. Slogans, as condensed vehicles of ideologies, may seem more important means of unifying masses than the relatively superficial spatial and visual means that are the subject of this article. But it is questionable just how discursive a slogan, for example, really is. A slogan is, of course, a combination of words, and words are connected in time and thus have the quality of discursiveness. But it is precisely the characteristic of a slogan that it must strain toward absolute condensation, and in this tendency it approximates a spatial form. A slogan aims at radical concision to gain an immediate and total effect (through assonance, rhythm, rhyming, etc.). It must be remembered as a whole—a spatial, not a discursive, whole.

In the category of spatial forms, perhaps the simplest way of making unity immediate is by that "external sign" most literally worn by all: dress. Dress is, however much or little, an aesthetic function of all social action, including the political. If visual forms are the most superficial signs of unity, they are also perhaps the most elementary.

Fashion in dress, set in the nineteenth century by the unpolitical dandy, articulated social distance in a dynamically stratified society. As Veblen formulated what was to become his most fashionable insight, differential positions according to income could best be represented by competitive emulation in such matters as dress. Competitive emulation implies its opposite: identity by polarization. In order to maximize social distance, dress and other aesthetic representations of the middle-class era were by definition style elaborations dictated by a high velocity of style changes.

But the entry of the masses into politics created a countertyranny to the tyranny of fashion as the basic aesthetic elaboration of bourgeois power. The political uniform is the costume of mass identification, a counterdevice to the fragmentation of identification expressed by the variety of costume in the era of middle-class domination. Twentieth-century uniformity of political dress indicates a new confluence of the political and the aesthetic. The countertyranny of uniformity is enforced as a visual representation of the cleansing puritanism of revolutionary mass parties and movements.

The plain style, as the aesthetic image of all revolutionary uniforms, is initially implemented by "political soldiers," and indicates a reorganization of the components of political unity. The original Nazi party uniforms were donned by what Hitler called his detachment of "meeting supervisors," the bully boys whose function was to distress hecklers. These flying squads later formed the nucleus of the S.A. Roehm, the leader of the S.A., was more revolutionary than Hitler, if his own projection of the future German army is taken as a criterion. He envisioned the new model army of Germany as the school as well as the weapon of the masses, training vanguard elements of the masses in a new value system.

New model armies generally serve as schools (for the new discipline) and experimental vanguards of revolutionary regimes, at least in their early stages.[4] This is the present role of the army in Israeli society. The Israeli army is as much an institution of socialization and ideological training as it is a military force. A distinction between "political soldier" and "soldier-civilian" is necessary to the understanding of mass parties as paramilitary, in contrast to antimilitary middle-class parties. This distinction explains, for example, certain aspects of the early history of the Red Army, and of Cromwell's army when the agitators almost gained control. Revolutionary movements may be described in terms of the assimilation of army and party into an "armed party."

Of course, army and party may again bifurcate. It is only a matter of time before the revolutionary task of the army is accomplished. As it loses its original function as the locus of participation of masses new to the political scene, the army tends to become less relevant as a laboratory of social experimentation. Aesthetic devices shift as functions of political purposes. The dress of regularized revolutionary armies takes on all the distancing ornamentation of the nonrevolutionary type. When political soldiers exchange costumes of principled shabbiness for individually distinguishable uniforms, it indicates their separation from the mass party. If the change appears in the officer caste of an army, it usually indicates the neutralization of that institution.[5] This is obvious in the political neutralization of the Red Army, as evidenced in the contemporary dress of Soviet generals. And one might conclude, comparing the dress characteristics of North Korean high officers with Chinese officer uniforms, that the North Koreans are the leaders of a colonial levy, not of an army with revolutionary *élan*.

The formal function of visual uniformity, as of other aesthetic devices serving a political end, is to unite heterogeneous groups and individuals into a political instrument that is itself determined by the necessity of varying intensities of militancy. There is a direct correlation between intensity levels of militancy and the aesthetic devices of visual uniformity. An image of militancy was as much the source of the principled plainness of the Calvinists and the Orders of the Counter-Reformation—whatever their differential self-images—as of the early Soviet or Zionist armed parties. Doctrinal militants have usually tried to rule against ostentation as displeasing to God, or to history.

But the sociological meaning of uniformity is not only the representation

4. C. H. Firth's classic study, *Cromwell's Army* (London, 1905), is only one example of a rich literature relevant to the problem.

5. There is an antinomical possibility. The appearance of different uniform images within a militant society may indicate a breakdown of controls, pointing toward civil war. In middle-class cultures, different style combinations indicate different social classes in a society without legally sanctioned indicators of stratification. In mass cultures, different style combinations indicate polarized power blocs in a society without traditionally sanctioned images of power.

of group participation and discipline in religiously or politically defined doctrinal groups. A more precise definition of its unique modern function must notice the displacement of discursive meanings of uniformity by aesthetic meanings. The rebellion against the politics of the Age of Discussion[6] is represented as a rebellion against individual fashion, superimposing a mass pattern from below. The ambiguity of mass participation—the great problem of modern politics—has been successfully resolved on the symbolic level, by the manipulation of aesthetic uniformity as a counterimage to the alienation and stratification dynamics of societies characterized by dress fashion and doctrinal competition.

Since Garibaldi's use of the red shirt, the colored shirt has been a typically modern sign not only of solidarization in a militant society, but of the aesthetic displacement of discursive motives. The fact that the colored shirt is a worker's habit points back to the origins of the political uniform as a mass counterimage to hierarchical fashion. Its value is located in the fact that it does not change, no matter what the doctrines of the party may be at any particular moment. The political uniform always tends to maintain itself as principled plainness.

Militancy in a mass society has been emptied of its substantive purposes and become an end in itself. Then, in mass society, principled plainness tends to become principled shabbiness. It creates a visual definition of that form of true service characteristic of militant doctrineless societies: one that does not respect differential claims and expectations. There are only two strata recognized as legitimate in the age of doctrineless militancy—the one (leader) and the many (masses). The new politics has reversed the traditional aesthetic organization of leader and led. Uniform dress maintains the nimbus of the leader's intimate relation to the masses, not his distance from them. In aristocratic or middle-class politics, the leader's dress (for example, top hat and formal or semi-formal attire) asserts his difference from the masses. In mass politics, the leader's dress pledges his identity with the masses. Thus, it is precisely on ceremonial occasions that Hitler and Stalin, as antibourgeois leaders, posed in the deliberate shabbiness of the old party costume. The dress uniform has been abolished precisely for ceremonial occasions.

Even where the second-level *farceurs* go all out for braid, medals, gorgeous uniforms, and other refinements, the leader stands apart from them, identified with the masses in his principled shabbiness. This reinforces the party model of anonymity, and at the same time denotes the whole cloth of authority. Hitler carefully maintained his public image as a mass militant, ornamented only by the Iron Cross, second class, which had become the plainest and most widely held distinction of the German common soldier.

6. The birthplace of the Age of Discussion, Britain, recognized the danger, prohibiting political uniforms in 1939.

Before the war situation, he continued to represent himself, even as the head of the state, as a hatless, demobilized soldier in a trench coat, the universally recognized postwar image of militancy—after militancy had lost its purpose. Stalin, particularly in the annual Red Square ceremonials, usually remained simply the party secretary, clothed in the unrelieved drabness of his high-buttoned tunic. And at Stalin's funeral, Malenkov legitimated his succession to the mass party leadership with visual immediacy by assuming precisely the same dress image. Mao still wears, as his public mask, the shabby uniform of the Long March, and this is the general dress habit of the Chinese leadership.

Political soldiers represent themselves in principled shabbiness deliberately to minimize the social distance between leaders and led. All political militants, so far as they seek support of the masses, affect puritanism of dress. This has been true of the great captains of armed parties from Cromwell to Stalin. Having to manage morale problems similar to those of armed parties, professional soldiers like Generals Eisenhower and Montgomery, who were more distant than ever in function and perspective from the common soldier, had to assume in World War II the protective aesthetic of dress puritanism to close the symbolic distance and remain "close" to their men. President Eisenhower's principled plainness during his inauguration ceremonial was perhaps more than a matter of taste, when viewed in the context of this iron time.

When political soldiers can indulge themselves in disdain of the masses, as Franco may in Spain, they tend to ornament themselves heavily. Spain, however, is not a mass society. Political soldiers in a mass society usually cannot permit themselves the luxury of public disdain of the masses. Morale must be one of their chief concerns. In his public image, at least, a political soldier must play the unknown son of the unknown people. There is, of course, another permutation: where the political soldier wishes to create a nonpolitical image [7] he may wear more ornamental costumes. But this must not eclipse his militant political dress.

In terms of the relation between the aesthetics of the plain style and the command sequences limited in part by social origins, the political soldier cannot move from the top down, from riches to rags. As a leader of the historyless masses, he can only move from enforced plainness to principled plainness. The plain style among the Puritan army agitators of the seventeenth century is not within the purview of this essay. But it is important to notice the common function of the plain style from the seventeenth to the twentieth century: the representation of democracy. Schools of mass agitation cannot permit visual differentiation of dress images. The lowest and the

7. See the Soviet movie, "The Fall of Berlin," part I, where the actor playing Stalin appears first as a refined country gentleman, pruning his rose bushes—white roses to match his rich white tunic and pants.

highest born are to be held together by representational equality, reciprocally in both the electoral and the aesthetic context.

An understanding of the aesthetic strategy of dress in militant "democratic" movements is complicated and refined by the strategy of aristocratic
dress. In middle-class society, deliberate style understatement developed
as an aristocratic defense against the overdress of the parvenu. This is a
counterstyle against competitive emulation that Veblen missed. But aristocratic plainness is not effective in a mass society. The strategy of plainness
can best be operated by the lower-class man identifying himself across, not
by the aristocratic renegade identifying down.

The political soldier, if he is of aristocratic appearance, has no choice
except to play upon his image. There was always something incongruous
about General MacArthur's patrician features framed between his squashed
hat and open-necked shirt. The rank and file of the American army distrusted his image perhaps more than his history. Among high U.S. officers
during World War II, General Stilwell most consistently exploited the morale potential of the plain style. General Patton, at the other extreme, displayed his egoism and his otherwise explicit contempt for the rank and file
in his ornamentation. General Eisenhower, treating the American electorate
to the rhetoric of militancy during the presidential campaign, affected the
plain style in every respect, moving carefully in the image of the political
soldier close to the masses. Governor Stevenson's rhetoric was not so militant, nor his style so plain. "Steve" was somehow incongruous to the style of
the man; "Ike" held no such incongruity.

Yet the secret of Sir Stafford Cripps's uncommon success in the Labour
Party was that he always lectured the rank and file as their lord and schoolmaster. Franklin Roosevelt used his aristocratic image to good advantage in
American politics, although Theodore Roosevelt worked hard to discard his
own. Like Disraeli's use of his psychological Jewishness, F.D.R. turned his
class vice into a mysterious virtue. Sir Oswald Mosely, however, illustrates
the failure of an aristocratic attempt to put on a political uniform. He could
never wear his colored shirt like a man of plebeian origins. Rather, Sir
Oswald always looked as if he were slumming from Mayfair. This was
equally his trouble when he was a Communist. His lack of political success
was due chiefly, no doubt, to the good sense of the British people, but it also
was due to his imaginative failure. Above all, a renegade aristocrat must
remain an aristocrat, if he desires to act convincingly in the mass situation.
There is something approximating an aesthetic law for renegades: to "go
over," the renegade must not look as though he has "gone over." Some measure of honest respect for one's past is expected of all converts. Converts
must not totally obliterate what they have been, even if, like the *conversos* of
Spain, they hate most what they have been.

The totalitarian party, as a commonly uniformed militant community,
narrows the social distance enforced in earlier societies either by aristo-

cratic uniqueness or by middle-class competition in appearance values. This is done in the name of a common ethical goal of fighting effectiveness. There is a parallel in the common dress enforced by armies. The difference between armed parties and armies, however, is that in armies the common uniform is understood as imposed, while in armed parties, the common uniform is understood as voluntary. It is adopted as a felt need, as an expression and index of political unity. The euphoric value of common dress is higher when it is understood as voluntary, solidarizing all levels of the totally mobilized population.[8]

However, the mass party and the army are assimilated to each other insofar as the masses are treated as an industrial army. The distinction between worker and soldier tends to disappear. Both are subject to the same discipline, and play equivalent roles as battle potential. In terms of the new spatial criteria available to political maneuvers, the distinction between "home" front and "battle" front disappears (as the "battleground" has disappeared as the spatial criterion available to military maneuvers), and all elements of social life are treated as "battle potential." Generals must be as interested in the discipline of trade unions and other skill groups as they are in the discipline of divisions. "Labor" must not disrupt logistical schedules. Teachers must not subvert "morale."

It is interesting that the combat dress of American soldiers in World War II was commonly called a "fatigue uniform." The worker becomes a soldier and the soldier a worker. Both are eliminated from the decision-making roles that characterize participation in a democratic process. The armed party cannot be a mechanism for the direct implementation of discussion, any more than can the internal structure of any military organization. Rather, the armed party is a mechanism for enforcing mass discipline in a permanent war situation assimilated to the characteristic situation of professional armies, that is, one demanding militancy undirected by stable, discursive motives.

In totalitarian societies, party debate becomes party ceremonial, with identity of dress as one of the chief aesthetic devices instrumenting the new political unity. Discursive argument is a less efficient basis of identification than nondiscursive visualization. The problem of mass participation, met in the Age of Discussion by the institutions of representative democracy, has been resolved in what might be called the Age of Administration by converting the masses into extras at party spectacles. Militant politicians must become, as Hitler insisted, aestheticians of militancy, as mass politics has

8. The distinction between self-selected armed parties and conscripted populations points, of course, to a crucial difference between religious and modern political armed parties. Total mobilization is a phenomenon which first appears in the French Revolution and is quite antithetical to the ethic of any of the Churches Militant. The sect achieves part of its militancy by uniformity of visual identification. But uniformity of dress is in this case a doctrinal element in a militancy recruited only by self-selection, never by conscription or birth.

become aesthetized and unity *per se* becomes the final rather than the instrumental end of social life.

II

The specific trends of aesthetization in contemporary mass politics operate not only as an internal dynamic of unity, but as an external representation of the doctrineless militant society before a potential world audience understood as equally doctrineless, and thus as equally available to submission before the spectacle of superior militancy. Given the correlate emptying of doctrinal contents from contemporary political warfare, and the development of mass media of aesthetic communication, the staging of party ceremonial may be based upon effects visible to the camera eye as an aesthetic weapon, rather than upon effects visible to the human eye as a critical witness of political processes. Political ceremonial has developed purposes beyond both the immediacy of uniform dress and the stabilization of power relations through spurious mass participation. The technique of the camera eye has broadened the political stage to the level of world-wide visibility. The fact of the absolute control of the leadership over the masses is available to the eyes of everyone outside the structure of control itself and has changed the entire meaning of being an eye-witness from an active to a passive implication.

Political ceremonial thus may be considered in other than its immediate effects upon the actual participants. It is not directed solely, nor perhaps even primarily, at the extras involved. The camera eye, far more selective than the human eye, has introduced new techniques of domination. The aim of the ceremonial itself now transcends its aesthetic immediacy, being organized in terms of future screen projection. Ceremonialization has been united with a phenomenon new to the history of politics, universal theater. When viewed from a seat in a theater—or, originally, by the diplomatic envoys of potential enemy or friendly nations in a theater defined as exclusively political, such as Red Square—the exhibition of the capacity to set masses in motion must impress the viewer. (The distinction between friendly and enemy nations is irrelevant to ceremonial in a mass society. Both need equally to be impressed.)

Empty of discursive content, political ceremonial demonstrates to the widest possible audience that, in the constant war of nerves characteristic of modern society, the viable battle potential that is the masses is an aesthetic instrument in the hands of their rulers. For example, during the Olympic games of 1936, the Nazis transformed the Berlin citizens into stagehands and extras to prepare the city for foreign spectators. The administration issued new city dog-curbing ordinances. The fronts of readily visible areas of depressed housing were redecorated. According to a joke widely told among Berliners, the national slogan had been changed to "Ein Volk, Ein Reich, Ein Theater." There are the same tendencies in every city and in every regime. All life has been politicized, and all politics has taken on the quality and form of theatrical performances. War has become the biggest show on earth, with Gotterdammerung, as Hitler thought, perhaps the final gigantic event in what is to be treated in every important sense as a spectacle. For the rest, the spectators are given programs that identify the actors and the plot during a limited engagement only.

The Nazis did not have the scope for ceremonialization that technology was to provide only a decade later. The possibilities of aesthetization are increased enormously since the home itself has become available as a theater. Through television, political ceremonial is potentially available at all times to the masses, who act as permanent spectators on themselves.

What the spectators see is an anonymous pattern of solidarity. The individuality of any pinpoint in the aesthetic pattern is impossible to discern. All individual participants, except the leader as star and the few supporting players about him, are dissolved into the production of the ceremonial itself. The technology of the reproduction of ceremonials demonstrates the degree to which politics has become a matter of aesthetic experiments in mass mobilization. Indeed, its effects are achieved through a process of mass fixation similar to the star fixation created by the movies as an attention area.

With politics fixated on the visual level, public speech (given the fact that it no longer has any decision-making function) becomes increasingly ceremonial. The vocabulary of ceremonial speech tends to cluster around polar friend-enemy images, for example, *Tovarischen*, *Volk*, Friends, Jews, Capitalists, Communists, etc. This spurious intimacy with the anonymous and patterned mass of extras serves much the same purpose the term "brother" served at revival meetings in the nineteenth century. Except for the centralization of spontaneity in the leader, mass ceremonial and revival meetings share the same aesthetic function: to provide a euphoric or ecstatic sense of community among relative strangers, brought together from disparate ideological, spatial, and occupational situations. (The Soviet use of Youth Festivals may be best described in these terms.) The euphoric focus is the star performer, the revivalist preacher, the Leader.

The comparative absence of friendship vocabulary clusters in ceremonial speech may denote the failure of a movement to capture its potential audience. The decline of the friendship vocabulary in non-Stalinist left propaganda between the wars indicates the privatization of the intellectuals making the propaganda, their growing indifference to the logic of militancy, and their irrelevance to political action. The relation of progressive and radical intellectuals to modern politics has been assimilated to that of artists. And the relation of the artist-intellectual to mass politics is in turn another index of ceremonialization, and of the general aesthetic functions implicated in modern politics.

The art of political ceremonial was borrowed second-hand from business. But business learned its ceremonial techniques from art.[9] Wherever art escaped, business followed, to transform art into advertising.[10] Faced with the universalization of politics in doctrineless militant societies, the artist-intellectual has been polarized between two alternatives: either his work has to be "politically committed"[11] or privatized into strictly delimited esoteric availability. The trend is to allow only such art as can be managed as political advertisement. Examples can be taken not only from the obvious case of Soviet composers and artists, but from the vogue of governmentally commissioned war paintings, or from the renascence of mural painting as an ornament of bureaucratic office buildings. The fresco style must always be the major art form of bureaucracies, ecclesiastical or secular. Works of art are thus made available on a scale commensurate with mass objectives. In contrast, literary art must be privately apprehended. Literary forms, being temporal rather than spatial, can never provide aesthetic instruments of domination in any way approximating the effectiveness of pyramids, open tombs (for example, the Lenin-Stalin mausoleum), statues, etc. But whatever the medium, in totalitarian culture art must be legitimated by official sponsorship. What is not publicly relevant will not be sponsored, and what is not sponsored automatically increases the likelihood of sanctions against the artist.

Art and business have thus suffered a reversal of roles. As art has become more and more privatized, in order to escape, first, the pressure of science,[12] and second, the banality created by the advertising technology of business and politics, private business has become more and more politicized as its art has created public identification with private power symbols. The whole structure of American private business is enveloped in an aura of public legitimation and, indeed, of identification with government.

9. Edward Bernays, in his pioneer study on the aesthetics of advertising, reverses the process and has art following business. Cf. also Harold D. Lasswell's "The Rise of the Propagandist," in *The Analysis of Political Behaviour* (London, 1948).

10. A perfect example of business following the most esoteric art styles is the appropriation of surrealism as the dominant style of window-dressing in American upper-class shops and department stores, imitated from French equivalents. Note also billboards and other forms of visual advertising in France.

11. For example, the "committed" movies of Eisenstein, or the novels of Howard Fast or earlier practitioners of proletarian fiction. Picasso experienced the difficulties of "committed" art when his party disapproved of his memorial drawing of Stalin. Cf., Herbert Read, "The State as Patron," in *University Observer*, I, no. 1 (Winter 1947): 3–9.

12. For the reaction of art to science and technology, see, for example, Paul Klee's satirical painting, "The Limits of Reason." In its esoteric reaction, art treats itself as a mysterious and inaccessible universe, like Klee's sun. There is an autonomous sphere of art which the ladders of science cannot reach. The general aesthetization of the nonaesthetic in modern art (such as abstract painting) may be understood as a reaction to the de-aesthetization of the aesthetic (for example, the reproduction industry). The aesthetization of modern politics may be considered a complement of the esoteric character of the decision-making process.

This is the major function of institutional advertising, which has become perhaps more important than product advertising in the mass circulation magazines. Big business has developed a political aura, and when a family name is the name of the aura (such as Ford, DuPont) the family itself acquires tremendous prestige without being subject to any formal mode of political responsibility.

The stabilization of big business within the political aura has structured national prestige relations on the model of extended families. The image of glamor has shifted from the self-made man to third-generation executives in public institutions. Silas Lapham would be much less interesting today than he was to the reporter whom W. D. Howells dispatched at the beginning of his novel to cover the big story of an earlier American culture. The American dream has developed a dominant scenery of backgrounds. The wish-fulfillment mechanism of the American dream has been reversed from an address to the future to an address to the past. The reversal has given totalitarian regimes the opportunity to legitimate themselves as "real democracies" as against the "pluto-democracies" of the West. American advertising models—such as the "distinguished man" images and the woman as mannequin—have no doubt helped to confirm pejorative versions of the United States as a "pluto-democracy."

American private business has been nationally sentimentalized by its advertising in terms of certain national attributes: freedom, technical efficiency, service, etc. American advertising has glamorized technical efficiency in particular as a political standard. The Squibb corporation, which is perhaps best known for its toothpaste and mineral oil, advertises itself with a picture of a little Austrian boy ecstatically clutching a pair of American-made shoes, "the most beautiful thing in the world." (The ad continues: "Crow, little Hans, beam with delight at your shoes. You make our American leather, and neat, machine stitching, something we never thought it could be. You make of it hope that we in America may use our strength wisely and well . . . hope that in time, with experience, you and your people may learn to have faith again . . . in yourselves, in each other . . . and in us.") The whole effort of American foreign policy necessarily suffers from the identification of politics and business—an identification that is "necessary" because it is rooted in our political culture. Neat, machine stitching is not necessarily equivalent to any political value and may indeed contradict some. Technical efficiency cannot properly be treated as an element of political value. The identification of business attainments with national values is limited by the specific property structure of a nation. Steel is not a battleship. Even highly disciplined industrial armies are reluctant to die for other than noninstrumental values. American policy finds the range of its concerns constantly expanding. In a permanent war situation, it is an important policy problem to review the historic American emphasis on instrumental values. It may be as serious an ideological liability to export economic as to export military aid. A worldwide propaganda system cannot be operated in terms of institutional advertising. America needs to export a radically different value commodity. But this commodity cannot be manufactured, or codified by a governmental agency. This is the ambiguity of America's role in the ideological world struggle.

The preemption of public symbols by private institutional structures is an ambiguity in the democratic process that has been evident since the Reformation, when the sect and its particularist business endeavors were identified as defining the moral structure of a "holy community." In the holy community, business was still subsumed under public morality. But the relation was reversed as capitalism developed. (This is Weber's final theme in *The Protestant Ethic*.) In the next development, the new politics preempted all private moral and public prestige symbols, thus completing the thrust of business. This pre-emption has incorporated all the arts of mass display and salesmanship, and the fine arts supporting them. Finally, all aesthetic skills available in totalitarian culture are focused on the art of politics. Or, put more precisely, the art of politics becomes a more purely aesthetic skill.

Hitler's admiration of the arts of commercial advertising is too well known to discuss here. Certainly, one major criterion for his choice of a party emblem and party flag was "aesthetic effect." Politics becomes a problem of color, of external signs rather than internal doctrine. What is needed is something that carries a simple effect "as great as that of a poster." It must have the resonance of a call to the colors. Therefore, white was rejected for the Nazi flag because it was "not a color that carries people away. It is suitable for associations of chaste virgins, but not for the overpowering movement of a revolutionary time." Black was equally unsuitable. It was not "thrilling enough." White and blue were "out of the question," despite the "wonderful effect from the aesthetic point of view," probably because they were the established Zionist colors. The external sign needed to help create a new political unity, according to the former corporal of the imperial army, was one that could legitimate the party as the true descendant of Hohenzollern glory at the same time that it exploited some racist symbol. Thus, the party colors finally chosen were the imperial German colors— red, white, and black—and the swastika became the emblem.[13]

III

The characteristic aesthetic functions serving modern politics are most clearly described in the relation of the two actors present in the ceremonial situation: the leader and the masses. The leader is the only individual actor. The masses serve as extras. As business art narrowed the attention area of

13. Adolph Hitler, *Mein Kampf* (New York, 1939), 734–35. Goebbels, in his novel *Michael*, writes, "Leaders and masses are as little a problem as painter and color."

the masses by techniques of repetition and ubiquitous poster images focusing on one product, political art has shifted the focus to one man. Concentration on a single personality is an aesthetic function of political action in a mass society. In the single personality of the leader, aesthetic and political necessities fuse.

As in politics, so in art, the optimum psychological power is achieved by concentration on a single personality. The poetic form which produces the most intense aesthetic effect is tragedy. Aristotle found *Oedipus* a model of tragedy (and induced his *Poetics* from it) precisely because of the purity of its focus on a single action and a single hero. Comedy and epic, Aristotle noticed, never sought the same emotional intensity, but rather tried to create a counterpoint of characters and variety of action and scene. Similarly, in the poetics of politics, the democratic process has no image of tragedy. Unlike dictatorships, the optimistic drama of parliamentary democracy can afford a plurality of protagonists and aesthetic detail.

Aesthetic necessity confirms political necessity. The star system achieves the most successful "psychological abolition" of mass apathy. Plainly, the star of mass politics operates quite differently from, for example, the monarchical leader. The monarchical leader excludes all spontaneity and personalization from his public image. Franz Joseph or George V performed as lifelessly as their images on the national coin. The political star, on the other hand, absorbs into his image everything that is spontaneous and personal. In constitutional monarchy, the political star is absorbed in the ceremonial office. In anticonstitutional dictatorships, the political star may be said to absorb the ceremonial office. Representative democracy exhibits a mediate type.

In aesthetic terms, the mass leader may be called an expressionist. He operates, like the artist who preceded him, inventively, as an antitraditionalist. This is the opposite of the monarchical or parliamentary leader. Aesthetic experimentalism, limited to professional art and the private life of bohemia forty years ago, has been transformed into aesthetic experimentalism on the level of mass politics. Perhaps it is no accident that Hitler aspired to be an artist. The nation was treated as his expressionist canvas. A hatred of conventions for their restrictions and regulation of spontaneous aesthetic style has been transformed into a hatred of social institutions for their restrictions and regulation of spontaneous political style.

Hitler called off the mobilization of two million troops as a personal caprice. The order reversals of the expressionist politician create a basic tension within modern militant societies, which are polarized between the free aesthetic star and all-embracing bureaucratic command channels.[14] The

14. This is reflected in the tension between Hitler's personal information channels (which came to reflect his own fantasies and thus systematically misinformed him) and the parallel (and more reality-adequate) information channels of the regular army.

star—viewed psychologically—has an ambivalent relation to bureaucracy. But the competitive tensions within and between bureaucratic organs necessitate precisely that discretion resides in a single figure. A plurality of bureaucratic structures is equally necessary to the star to avoid the threat of personal and clique competitiveness. As sole arbiter of competitive rivalries, the entire structure becomes aware of its fundamental dependence upon his integrating personality. Thus, the star can neutralize any tendencies toward competitive thrusts in his direction.

As caste was once the most perfect spatial elaboration of power relations, the topography of totalitarian ceremonial now mirrors the isolation of the leader become a star—as his dress expresses his spurious intimacy. Symmetry is the universal frame for the leadership situation. Court etiquette was always spatialized in symmetrical designs, to indicate the status locations of various figures and offices. The aesthetics of modern political ceremonial makes use of the same principles. But, instead of having figures grouped around the royal leader, mass ceremonial reemphasizes the emptiness of the space immediately around the star. The space between Hitler and the first ranks of the symmetrically arranged blocs of extras who performed at Nuremberg was quite clearly used to delineate the figure of the leader in a vast topographic allegory, characterized by the general difficulty of discerning personal characteristics.

The star, however else he may be discerned, is immediately recognized by his entrances. Hitler learned early to enter party ceremonials from the rear. The procession up the center aisle served to identify him as coming out of the anonymous mass at the same time it spatialized his separation from them. His entrances were staged with all the skill first-rate technicans of the aesthetics of ceremonial could muster. He marched down the center aisle to the ominous repetitiveness of a military drumbeat. Auditory forms, necessary to the implementation of visual and topographic forms, were always exploited.

On the auditory level, as on the visual, repetition creates expectation through the restatement of the theme in differing contexts and by the cumulative weight of new details. It is a hypnotic device in the sense that it is preparatory. The extras and the larger world spectatorship are prepared, by a certain qualitative progression in the auditory and visual repetition, to expect the uniform dress image and the spatial distance of the star, and to accept them as absolutely right and necessary. Rhythm bulwarks mass discipline by further linking expectation to acquiescence. Coordinated movement—marching, saluting, chanting in unison—expresses the muscular imagination of the garrison state's ceremonial forms. A rhythm is a promise and, as such, a full alternative to political rhetoric. It moves the subject from one state of feeling to another. There remains only to notice that Freud thought that the aesthetics of muscular movement must always describe the movement from life toward death. The musculature, he wrote, was the organ of death.[15] The middle-class novelist Stendhal thought that art was "une promesse du bonheur." The art of totalitarian politics is "une promesse de la mort."

The aesthetic function of totalitarian ceremonial is expressed in the relation between the repetitive progression of the meeting and the expectation of the climax in the appearance of the star. As a form of ratification of the executive's action and prerogative, the progression of the meeting is designed to force the audience to a consciousness of their dependent relation to the single protagonist. The ceremonial of discovering the One among the Many, and the progression of expectation that precedes the discovery, is a standard aesthetic device of totalitarian stage-management. Dramatic effects may be managed with as much sophistication as any technician of melodrama could demand.

The dramatic techniques of political ceremonial—the merging of the meaning of participation and spectatorship, the buildup of spectator expectation around the One—was recorded in a remarkable report of a Wallace rally published in *The Call* on 10 September 1947. It is a first-rate description of aesthetic functions implemented as political ceremonial:

> Offstage stands the director. At his command the audience has been plunged into utter darkness. In the darkness each of the thousands is all alone and waits. The expectant silence and the loneliness grows heavier. If this continues surely someone will cry out. The director gives his sign . . . the corsage of loudspeakers pinned to the roof of the Garden booms out a welcome. At this meeting no chairman presides, the audience is to be its own master— by following the script and responding to the cues. Out of the audience itself, two voices are heard and the spotlight picks out their faces while the mikes amplify their voices. A boy and a girl speak to each other of their devoted love, their words weave a pattern for the night. They tell of their youthful hopes, they linger on their fears. "If only Franklin Roosevelt were here," says the boy. "He would know the answer." Suddenly the spotlight goes out and the two are submerged in the same darkness and silence that have swallowed the thousands around them. In the next moment up on the stage another

15. Sigmund Freud, *The Ego and the Id* (London, 1947), 56. See also George Orwell, *The Lion and the Unicorn* (London, 1941), 20–22: "One rapid but fairly sure guide to the social atmosphere of a country is the parade-step of its army. A military parade is really a kind of ritual dance, something like a ballet, expressing a certain philosophy of life. The goose-step, for instance, is one of the most horrible sights in the world, far more terrifying than a dive bomber. It is simply an affirmation of naked power; contained in it, quite consciously and intentionally, is the vision of a boot crashing down on a face. . . . Why is the goose-step not used in England? There are, heavens knows, plenty of army officers who would be only too glad to introduce some such thing. It is not used because the people in the street would laugh. . . . In the British army the drill is rigid and complicated . . . but without definite swagger; the march is merely a formalized walk."

spot rings the face of a well-built man. "No, I am not Franklin Roosevelt," he says. "I am only his son." He pauses. The impact of the name catches the many-headed ear. The applause becomes a wave lashing through the Garden, mounting. . . .

And so it goes. Each speaker is brought carefully into the spotlight with introductions voiced by the boy or girl. . . . But none of them is the One. They, too, are among the Many, seeking the One.

And then the climax. A voice booms out over the loudspeakers. "Franklin Roosevelt is no longer with us. But there is a man in our midst who wears his mantle." From every side of the great arena, circles of light burst forth. The spotlights flash back and forth across the crowd, roaming, searching among the clusters of white faces. The loudspeaker continues: "Do you want to hear from him? His name is——!" and from the audience comes the roar, "Henry Wallace!" The loudspeaker comes in, its volume rising. "Yes, his name is Henry Wallace, Henry Wallace!" The spotlights move faster through the darkness, as if seeking to find and pinpoint the face of every man in the crowd. The lights move in fast, jerky, excited movements. Faster and faster they turn, seeking out the sadly groping, now twisting and turning mass. The chanted name grows louder and louder. The scattered voices are reaching out toward each other. The threads of sound are merging until they are almost a visible blanket. The uproar crashes on the eardrums, the spotlights hammer on the retina, louder and faster and brighter. The tension mounts and breaks suddenly as the beams retreat into the darkness, leaving one strong light from above focussed directly on the lectern. Behind it is the man. . . .

Henry Wallace received better stage management than any other political leader in American history. Never before was the progression of expectancy managed so well. Unfortunately, a buildup is not enough. In this case, the man never matched his staging. There was always a fatal letdown soon after Wallace stepped into the halo.

In general, the United States has not developed the art of political ceremonial, although it lies ready at hand in American sport. The potentiality of sports events as a model of political ceremonial was long realized in the famous Sokol demonstrations. The aesthetic effect of the massed gymnastics resulted precisely from the fact that the maneuvers were a collective nationalist gesture.

An excellent example of an American sports event as a potential model for political ceremonial is furnished by the strategy of mounting spectator tension at the annual All-Star football game in Chicago. Each star is introduced by a loudspeaker blaring his name and school. Massed bands play his school's anthem as he trots out majestically into a darkened stadium filled with 100,000 people. One lone beam from a powerful searchlight in a stadium tower haloes the hero as from heaven, until it is time to pick out the next one. In American college football massed cheering and giant poster sections made up of students organized in desired colors and patterns of light and darkness share many of the elements standard to European mass manipulation. If future political aestheticians need to develop American political spectacle, they have the material prepared for them in college football.

One might generalize that night ceremonials are psychically more coercive than day ceremonials (as Hitler reported), that open-air ceremonials have a greater aesthetic immediacy than those held indoors. The manipulation of light, of course, is a definitive frame of all ceremonials, no less important than the organization of space. The uses of light have been fully developed in totalitarian politics. The star, when he appears, must be haloed in an aura of light. The aura, as Walter Benjamin has pointed out, will legitimate him as unique. Hitler carefully managed the uses of light in his own appearances. His theatrical abilities are worth noting in detail:

> In his good hours [Hitler] exerts a power of suggestion which would be surprising if shown in an experimental demonstration, but we must always remember that a mighty suggestive power precedes [him] before his actual appearance. . . . We must remember the extreme impressionability of crowds under sustained influence. . . .
>
> The German people is already transformed into a mechanical chorus, for it is no longer its mental attitude that counts, but only its technical approval. The symbol of this mechanization is the extraordinary desk or lectern from which Hitler speaks. . . . This desk, of which at that time, the spring of 1936, there were five examples, has a number of buttons, by means of which Hitler gives certain signals while he is speaking; he gives the sign for film photographs to be taken[16] and for the dimming or brightening and the direction of the searchlights. By thus regulating the mood of the audience he increases the will to applaud until at another signal the Storm Troops by clapping and shouting let loose general applause. . . .
>
> Under the glare of searchlights, thus controlled by his suggestion machine, human beings are lost to sight and nothing remains but the inchoate mass, the mechanical chorus. . . .[17]

The masses have become a mechanical chorus, spectators in an aesthetically organized self-exhibition, mobilized for whatever purposes an unaccountable decision-making process demands. Political ceremonial aims to elicit only the technical approval of the masses. In mass politics, as in all other aspects of modern culture, spectatorship has become the method of participation. Spectatorship stabilizes power relations; participation disrupts them, or at least provides a possibility of disruption.

16. F.D.R., during the war years, exercised similar prerogatives, personally captioning all news pictures of himself and censoring those he found unsuitable. See an unpublished Ph.D. dissertation: William McKinley Moore, "FDR's Image: A Study in Pictorial Symbols," University of Wisconsin, 1946.

17. Konrad Heiden, *One Man Against Europe* (London, 1939), 41.

The principle of the mechanical chorus has triumphed in every area of modern culture. Heiden's terminology points to the ultimate problem in a discussion of the aesthetics of power. Modern instruments of domination can be understood by an analysis of the parallel rise of mass audiences for the fine arts and sport, and for politics. The great romantics, like Goethe and, in a new context definitive for the modern temper, Nietzsche, thought life itself had to be lived as a "work of art." Modern morality, as it has become aesthetized, has become profoundly anti-political. The unique contemporary challenge to democratic policy is to develop specific devices for redirecting spectatorship from spurious to genuine participation, to displace aesthetic by discursive criteria. Whether this is possible in a culture that has lost contact with its characteristic doctrine and its constraints is a problem beyond the limits of this essay. (53:3)

30
The Culture of Unbelief

What a gorgeous event it must have been: this "First International Symposium on Belief held at Rome, between March 22–27, 1969." Other symposia have been recorded as events worthy to be held in perpetual recollection; there was, to name the most memorable example, if not the first, that one recorded by Plato, at which Socrates was present. In our tradition, the symposium begins as a feast of love—not the desire of men after women (or of women mad for men), but of that love which is felt by men for one another, differing mainly in respect of age. How appropriate to the inner meaning of the symposium under review here that it should end in a vision of a new "community of love." The vision was conveyed by professional sociologists. How it must have alarmed the professionally religious present. In his foreword to this record of the symposium, Professor Berger refers to that alarm. He remarks on the "ambivalent impact of [the sociologist's] views, particularly Luckmann's and Bellah's . . . on the participant theologians. The ambivalence was one of initial relief and subsequent new alarm—a little like the reactions of a man told not to worry about his ulcer, since he does not have an ulcer, but rather has cancer" (pp. xiii–xiv).[1]

Before I try to illuminate Berger's dark reference to this terminal case in the history of love feasts within our tradition of spirit inseparable from flesh,

Reprinted from *Contemporary Sociology* 1, no. 6 (November 1972): 505–7.

1. *The Culture of Unbelief*, Studies and Proceedings from the First International Symposium on Belief, Rome, 22–27 March 1969, edited by Rocco Caporale and Antonio Grumelli with a foreword by Peter Berger (Berkeley, CA: University of California Press, 1971).

I feel moved as a sociologist to mark the banquet scene. Berger does not tell us what main dishes there were, nor what delicacies for dessert. All of it reads like caviar for the general, absolutely ready for testing by all those with a taste for the most important and most questionable things.

No doubt our sociological colleagues and their clerical hosts, were men of the mean, unlikely to inflame their passions with meat and drink. But there are new ways of feasting, new techniques of the endless expressional quest. Where cooks and waiters once were and boys to pour out the wine, there let television teams be, and journalists to pour out the hot copy. Looking at the symposium from the cold vantage point of my immense sociological distance, I can see how exactly right-on Berger was to make his first observation, "obvious and yet essential . . . , that the symposium had the character of an historic occasion." He says nothing of victuals. He passes by the grandeur that is still Rome with a passing acknowledgment of the "ecclesiastical and scholarly Roman ambience." Although he does not say so outright, Berger's keen sociological eye, trained perhaps by a Protestant ambivalence in the presence of opulence (Is success graceful? Are saints ever to be known by externals?) fixes on the real flesh of the occasion: the mass media. Imagine the eyes and ears and nostrils of all these mainly American, largely "backsliding" (Parsons' self-description), Protestant, and Catholic sociologists at the "opening session in the tightly packed great hall of the Gregorian University," the "sense of excitement that quickly communicated itself to the participants." The real meat and drink of the symposium, its inner erotic meaning, must have been the mass media. Berger records the subtle debauch, neither approving nor disapproving, keeping his own distance: "Throughout the symposium, the participants were surrounded by the press, by observers from various ecclesiastical agencies, by television teams originating in places as far apart as Canada and Yugoslavia, and last but not least by the technological apparatus (simultaneous translation systems, visual and audial recording devices, and so on). . . ." Here was the technological equivalent of the insatiable erotic greed criticized by earlier religious professionals when they reconsidered the Platonic or Xenophonic accounts of symposia. Here, too, I suspect, is some indication of the point driven at by Bryan Wilson (and treated rather dismissively by Talcott Parsons) in his remarks on the domination of the modern world by technological apparatus. That apparatus is alive with sociological meaning and not entirely with the agapic effect Parsons implies.

This first symposium on the culture of unbelief was sponsored by the Agnelli Foundation, the University of California at Berkeley, and the Vatican Secretariat for Non-believers. If there is to be a second symposium, then perhaps it ought to be on the beliefs of sociologists about their religion, with most of the talking done by churched theologians and historians of their faiths. Of course, there were many ceremonious gestures of disagreement among the social scientists present: scholars will be scholars. Behind the ceremonies of disagreement, however, our colleagues were so agreed that, being expert and authoritative as well, their discussions amounted to an implicit faith. But no implicit faith can be made explicit, without rousing furies of disagreement among those who have implicitly agreed. In the interest of the irenical movement in sociology, of which I am leader and sole follower, I forbear any effort to make explicit what is better left implicit. There only remains to list some of the propositions that might conceivably be considered implicit in the sociological faith. I refer to each piece of the body of faith by the name of the celebrant who raised it at the feast; I have picked those succulent pieces out of the record to please my own taste for caviar and other fish dishes, of course:

> *Luckmann:* We live in a period of transition in which a particular social form of religion, institutional specialization, is on the wane. Belief . . . is undergoing a radical transformation. Unbelief, on the other hand, is about to disappear entirely as a social fact. If this hypothesis is correct the only way to study the socio-psychological phenomena that were traditionally designated by the concept of unbelief will be by a technically and theoretically very difficult analysis of various kinds of highly privatized subjective *belief* systems. The notion of unbelief may be heuristically unproductive even today (p. 37).

> *Isambert:* Unbelief can only be defined with reference to a given belief (p. 148).

Reviewer: In sum: this means that, given the characterization of emergent contemporary 'belief,' there is less and less to which 'unbelief' can refer. How can this less and less, and those who carry it like an invisible shibboleth, be studied?

> *Bellah:* The effort to maintain orthodox belief has primarily been an effort to maintain authority rather than faith (p. 44).

> *O'Dea:* Internalization is not the opposition of objectified institutionalization (p. 168).

Reviewer (agreeing with O'Dea): Creeds and syllogistic arguments may have been someone's or some group's expressive gesture and inner experience. We sociologists need to look to our own anti-credal interpretations of religious phenomena.

> *Bellah:* If internalization has been the main direction, . . . this might argue in favor of . . . increased privatization (p. 47). [A] nascent [world] religion of humanity [has its] roots in many traditions. [The stress of this religion is on] inner authenticity and autonomy; [in the] present situation, all cognitive structures have been rendered provisional. . . . Though I know that most men are still caught in archaic or traditional modes of consciousness, I speak of

the innovating vanguard, and I know that this will create problems for survey research (p. 156).

Glock: It would seem advisable to think in terms of a set of [survey-research] instruments rather than a single one. The final products might comprise: an instrument capable of being administered cross-culturally; a set of instruments each designed to be used across the board in particular cultures; and a still larger set of instruments, each designed for use among subgroups within cultures. A virtually infinite number of instruments of the last variety are possible, of course. The ones to be actually constructed would be decided by the research questions to be addressed.

The construction process would require at least one test, but more probably a series of empirical tests, of the evolving instruments. These would presumably include some effort to establish the reliability and validity of what we have been calling the culture-free instrument. To make this test we can administer the range of instruments to equivalent samples in a number of settings. The culture-free instrument would be administered uniformly in all settings. At the same time and with the same samples, the culture-bound and group-bound instruments would also be administered but, of course, only in the appropriate setting and group. This procedure would allow intra-setting comparisons, to establish consistency between the ordering produced by the culture-free and by the culture-bound data (p. 62).

Wilson: Let us concede the immense diversity of the belief systems in the modern world and of cultures, and abandon for the present the attempt to develop a conceptual framework that encompasses this diversity. In investigating crime, which is a much more elaborately investigated subject by sociologists than is religion, we accept at least provisionally the specifications of the law without anyone thereby suggesting that the law is immutable and should not be changed. In investigating nonconformity, even within our own field, we accept orthodoxy as an appropriate base line from which to look at nonconformist belief. In inquiring into nonbelief, we might accept the broad cultural concept of belief as we know it in our culture (p. 122).

Parsons: The current new movements, of the 'Christening' of which Bellah so eloquently spoke, seem to have one very important kind of relation to early Christianity, namely their immense concern with the theme of love (p. 232). Probably . . . the most important motivation for an avoidance of theism concerns the desire to emphasize the this-worldly location of the valued objects and interests. From one point of view, then, the new movement may be a kind of culmination of the trend of secularization we have traced which has sanctified, by inclusion, and moral upgrading component after component of what originally was conceived to be the world by contrast with the spiritual order. If, as Weber stressed, the order of secular work could be so sanctified, why not the order of human love? The immediacy of this orientation pattern, however, is too oblivious to the need for a transcendent anchorage which must somehow include both affectively adequate symbolizations and some elements of cognitive belief. So far the dominant tone seems to be the repudiation of the inherited symbols and beliefs, but that may well prove to be temporary (p. 233).

[It] does not seem that a major prophet of the new religion of love has yet appeared. Perhaps, in retrospect, Gandhi will appear as a kind of John the Baptist (p. 234).

Therapy . . . is the first cousin of creativity. New creative developments in the personality or the cultural or social system are overwhelmingly associated with phases of regression (p. 235).

[The] new religious movement, which I feel will almost certainly prove to be largely Christian, cannot define itself as a separated collectivity outside of what has been called secular society, but must be defined as an integral part of the latter which hopes to permeate its moral and spiritual qualities. Not only the love component—which is not the same as the moral—of solidarities, but the erotic component, is too deeply intertwined in the texture of society, especially at the level of the interpersonal intimate relations which are coming to be so highly valued, for it to be extirpated. If, indeed, this extirpation were possible, which I doubt short of major convulsions, the price would be the postponement of any new community of love, probably for many centuries (p. 239).

If we love a person—or a group or a symbol—we must at the same time understand and empathize with his difficulties and his conflicts, including those which from our point of view are destructive of our values, and still love him, not only in the sense of particularized affection, but of giving him support for the implementation of the value of universalized love (p. 245).

If, as many of us feel, there is enormous creative potential in the emerging religion of love, the danger of lapsing into aggression and violence, along with that of moral absolutism, which are of course related to each other, seem to me more serious than the danger of regression into eroticism (pp. 240–41).

Reviewer: So some of our colleagues see humanity progressing by regression to the cities of refuge (Numbers XXXV, 9–28). What is nowhere explicit in the sociological faith, as I read it in the record of this symposium, is that in order to get to the final city, of love, it may be necessary first to inhabit the nearer city, where the negative commandments of law are practiced, because they have been authoritatively preached. Perhaps the theologians might convene the second symposium, definitely in Rome, the mass media excommunicated, under some such charmingly archaic title as "The Self-Justifications of Sociology," or better "Love's Body Sociologized Without Law Divinized."

Paul: What follows? Is the law identical with sin? Of course not (Romans VII–7). (72:4)

Intellectuals and Education

31

Max Weber's "Science as a Vocation" [1]

Weber argues that the sciences cannot ask questions of value. Neither philosophy nor theology is now competent to ask, let alone to answer. The arts, if they could make an answer, would only point narcissistically to themselves. No new answer sounds, and the old ones bore us, for they are no longer directed to apparently relevant questions. Perhaps, Weber hints, we ought to abandon such questions and treat every aspect of life as a work of art, something worth while so far as we respond to it. But other minds, not less keen than Weber's, are still at work formulating the questions. And it does not help, as Weber agrees, to dismiss the questions as unscientific; that would be to ignore the complicity of science itself in creating our main embarrassment, to raise first questions long after they had been laid to rest with their ancestors, the gods.

Men became religious when they had to approach and rationalize the chaos of powers by which they were moved and their destinies sealed. But from Hobbes to Weber there has been an insistent, ironic voice saying that religious man is really, at bottom, political man. All theologies are metaphors of politics. Thus, from the primitive notion that God is power we have advanced to the notion that power is God. Now, as once in some mythic time mankind tested the limits of God, the limits of power are being tested. Whether we shall end with a real Fall is not yet certain, although some testers imagine such things in their most expert dreams. Weber shared in the

Reprinted by permission of *Daedalus*, Journal of the American Academy of Arts and Sciences, Science and the Modern World View 87, no. 1 (Winter 1958): 111. Cambridge, MA.

1. Rieff introduced the reprinting of Weber's essay in *Daedalus* in a section "designed to convert those among us who have lapsed back into the comforting uncertainties of our own disciplines to the larger uncertainties." In this brief summary, Rieff remarks upon Weber's "profound and illuminating despair" and suggests that only from such despair "can any affirmative doctrine of man, as seen from the shattered perspectives of the modern arts and sciences, again arise."

scientific imagination of disaster. In this essay he sketches the model of all our present disasters. Weber was an honest and passionate scientist; when he had finished constructing his model and found himself enclosed in it, he stayed. To his way of thinking there is no way out. (58:3)

32
The Case of Dr. Oppenheimer

It has become a habit among thoughtful Americans to see the handwriting on the wall. What indeed suggests nothing but mean times ahead is not so much the events themselves as the official explanation of them. Thus the case of J. Robert Oppenheimer has been judged entirely on the basis of his character and social conduct. Psychology has masked politics, victories and defeats essential to the future course of American history have gone largely unremarked in the general curiosity over twists in Dr. Oppenheimer's character and over questions of his behavior. These are important enough; Dr. Oppenheimer's soul was searched for its deceits, its contradictions, its dubious soul-mates, and a goodly number were found. But even granting that the scientist, like the poet, is uniquely neurotic, and that therefore he must be judged more leniently than ordinary men (as some of his defenders have foolishly urged) the position held on the hard issues of American politics by Dr. Oppenheimer cannot be collapsed into his character or even into his associations. His position, his place and influence in the political order, were rarely touched in the thousands of pages of published testimony and opinions. In the end, after an inquiry dating from 23 December 1953 to 30 June 1954, he was condemned in an appellate decision by the Atomic Energy Commission (AEC) for "fundamental defects of character" and for social relations with Communists extending "far beyond the tolerable limits of prudence and self-restraint."

Dr. Oppenheimer's soul being searched and his private conduct surveyed, the findings were reviewed by two separate boards of inquiry—the Personnel Security Board and the parent Atomic Energy Commission. In both decisions, with only the one scientific member of each panel dissenting, it was found that his personality was too 'complex' to carry the responsibilities his scientific position and access to restricted data inevitably entailed. He lied in order to protect friends, and some of his lies were so elaborate and unnecessary that they alarmed the normal people by whom he was judged; above all, he dined with the translator Haakon Chevalier in

Reprinted from *On Intellectuals, Theoretical Studies/Case Studies*, edited by Philip Rieff (New York: Doubleday, 1969): 314–40.

Paris, in December 1953—the very man who once approached him with a treasonable proposition. The entire case was a triumph of psychological over straight old-fashioned political warfare. The charge sustained in the first decision by Gordon Gray[1] and Thomas J. Morgan,[2] as the majority members of the Personnel Security Board, that Dr. Oppenheimer showed a notable lack of 'enthusiasm' during the early stages of hydrogen bomb research, was carefully excluded from the appellate decision. Oppenheimer, the man, the neurotic scientist who did not have sense enough to know that M. Chevalier might well have acted for Soviet agents who would spirit him away to the Soviet Union, was tried. Oppenheimer the spokesman for an alternative military and political policy for the United States never once emerged for public judgment.

The decisions of the Gray Board and the AEC merit careful examination. It is something of a landmark in American political history that a man can be officially condemned for his private associations. But behind this inquiry into the character and conduct of one man lay a long battle over the facts of American military strategy. It was Oppenheimer's misfortune that he had lost the battle many months before; his lost case was a public parody of his lost battle. The open decision on his character masked the hidden decision on his policy; his exclusion from 'restricted data,' whatever the fears about his past associations, was, objectively, a savage act of revenge for the long fight he waged against established American military policy.

The public was never allowed to look at the real issues. When the government chose to make a public examination (the release of the decisions and testimony amounted to that) of Dr. Oppenheimer's character, his political role was already thwarted and with this the persistent effort of his profession to gain a voice in the councils of state. The bitter five-year struggle between science and military politics in the United States was carried on mainly in the privacy of bureaucratic offices and in the secrecy of research laboratories. And the official version of the case, as involving simply the character and personal conduct of Dr. Oppenheimer, was the way in which modern victors in the secret wars of state rewrite history. Losing sides never get their position written clearly into the record; they are forced to argue on grounds chosen by the winners, and the issue is staged for public edification after the real battle is over. It is like an internecine party struggle, of which the rank and file knows nothing until the defeated leader is brought before some tribunes of the people, his person condemned and his great contributions to the cause expunged from the official histories.

1. Subsequently, President of the University of North Carolina, formerly a Cabinet member in the Truman Administration.

2. A Southerner; once President of United Negro College Funds; retired head of Sperry Gyroscope, a company contributing greatly to the American arsenal.

Dr. Oppenheimer's contribution to American history is in no danger of being forgotten or denied. If only he had remained within the ambience of scientific research and organization the entire case might never have been aired, although it is unclear how Senator McCarthy could have been kept from airing it. But the line between science and politics has grown very shadowy. Neither Dr. Oppenheimer nor his fellow scientists knew, after they had by their inventions added another long arm to the body of the state, how to remain within the limits of their technical capacities. The scientist has, since World War I, achieved a new place in the political order—a place that has given him enormous public prestige and involved him in the most serious decisions of government. The Oppenheimer case signals not merely the personal defeat of a leading scientist, but the removal of the American scientists as a group from their high place in the political order. Dr. Oppenheimer's personal humiliation covers the failure of American scientists as a more or less corporate body to play a role in shaping an American military policy they themselves have made possible.

Between the first and second world wars, the relation of science and politics in America entirely changed. Newton Baker, Secretary of War in Wilson's Cabinet, found *one* chemist adequate to the needs of the military forces. Charles Wilson, Secretary of Defence ('War' is an unsophisticated word) in the mid-fifties, had an Under-Secretary in charge of research. From 1941 to 1954 the government spent some eighteen billion dollars for mainly military research and development. Of 155,000 persons who might be classed as natural or physical scientists in the United States (about two-thirds of one percent of the working population of sixty-three millions) some 32,000 work for the government, and many of the remainder are indirectly dependent upon the government through industrial and university research on official projects. The importance of the scientists' connection with the government cannot, however, be rightly measured by their involvement in such work, although this is in itself of great significance; above all there is the fact that the scientific élite creates the weapons of offence and defence upon which the political and military élites depend. Along with the concentration of control over the material apparatus of society, as described by Marx and later by Max Weber, has come the concentration of scientific skills. Science has forged great new weapons and therefore the scientific élite is absolutely necessary, especially at the creative stages, to the political élite—the military and the high policy planners. This brings the scientists directly into politics, for the planning and execution of new elements in the arms race is inseparable from other parts of the political process. And as the scared rabbits of the arms race, the scientists are continually urged to provide a lead that the military can follow to new advantage in the struggle for power within and between nations.

Élite politics characterize all mass societies, totalitarian and democratic alike; indeed, the élites may have greater importance in democratic societies. Thus the real decisions in the United States tend to hang in the balance between the competing aims and skills of small groups. Into this sort of politics, demagogues such as Senator Joseph McCarthy may intrude as representatives of popular forces, breaking through the matrix of élite formations and capturing some measure of power by the public intimidation of one or another group. Nevertheless, despite these intrusions, the élites, or *service classes*, usually make, or fail to make, history without benefit of much public discussion or awareness—which is why their increased dominance is a threat to the liberal principles of democratic politics. Thus, the United States was on the verge of unlimited intervention in Indo-China, but the public knew almost nothing about it; there was not even a spurious debate on intervention, such as that preceding Pearl Harbor. Until the recent counterdevelopment from below of street politics, the American public might wake one morning to hear over the car-radio that the nation was in yet another conflict and immediately accept the *fait accompli* as the necessary logic of higher powers.

With the explosions over Hiroshima and Nagasaki, the physical scientist had made an auspicious entry into élite status. Willingly or no, the scientists found themselves beyond the realm of technique and in politics; they responded with that balanced concern for both the nation and the world that is the special virtue of the scientific morality and, in their special knowledge of the atomic bomb, with the almost Messianic fervor of men who had seen hell and wanted to do something to save the rest of us from it. The nuclear scientists organized themselves into regional and national groups, and set up a lobby in Washington. The Federation of Atomic Scientists, with advisors from among America's most astute and sophisticated social scientists, was an unprecedented political organization of American scientists, concerned not only with the protection of the scientist in his new political environment, but with the larger disposition of atomic energy, the great new transformation of nature that could affect the social order for good or evil.

Tension between the scientific élite, on the one side, and the military on the other, began almost immediately. Some tension between such different personality types and levels of intellection was inevitable, but the issues ran deeper than psychological difference. Some early battles (1945–46) were won by the scientists; the McMahon bill setting up a civilian commission (the Atomic Energy Commission, which ruled Dr. Oppenheimer a 'security risk') was their victory, against the May-Johnson (Administration) bill which would have continued military control of the atomic energy project after the war. This was no personal victory for J. Robert Oppenheimer, who in fact supported the May-Johnson bill. Nevertheless, in the immediate post-war period his authority and prestige increased. From being merely scientific head of the Manhattan District and director in the construction of the bomb at Los Alamos, Oppenheimer became a symbol of the new status of science in American society. His thin handsome face and figure replaced Einstein's as the public image of genius. Less charismatic, although equally important figures among the atomic-researchers took lesser parts in the new pantheon. Behind this scene, in the bureaucratic labyrinth of Washington, Dr. Oppenheimer's importance was greater than his public image showed. He had actually become the priest-scientist of the Comtean vision, transforming history as well as nature. His place as advisor in the State Department on matters of atomic strategy during the tenure of Dean Acheson was bound to bring him further into contact with the makers of policy. He began to play a leading role, perhaps the first scientist in American history to achieve so great an influence in government. The Acheson-Lilienthal[3] plan for international control of atomic energy, which the Russians rejected, was largely his work.

Dr. Oppenheimer's hope was for some sort of *modus vivendi* with the Russians, to avert an atomic catastrophe. But as the cold war grew hotter and the Russians proved intransigent, the post-war flutter of public campaigns to reach diplomatic agreement was stilled. World government organizations of all sorts lost motion; the American public had in any case maintained its vigorous disinterest in international proclamations, including those by the atomic scientists. The latter's efforts to play a role in deciding American policy shifted out of public view to the operations of the élites themselves. Struggles over the future course of American strategy were to take place, for two decades, over the heads of the public, and any shots that were fired in the open were aimed deliberately high, so that only the instructed reader could understand. A major dispute arose within the scientific group itself, over the problem of constructing a hydrogen bomb. Edward Teller, a Hungarian-born scientist, had proposed as early as 1945 a theoretical solution that would permit the construction of an H-bomb. Oppenheimer, and men such as Conant, DuBridge, Rabi, Bethe—great names in science— disagreed for technical reasons, although plainly they also considered the construction of the H-bomb a political and moral error. But in 1947, in a seminar at Los Alamos incidentally attended by Klaus Fuchs, Dr. Teller came within one final step of working out the theoretical mechanics of exploding an H-bomb; the theory of the fusion of hydrogen atoms, worked out by Hans Bethe, had been long accepted. Lewis Strauss,[4] then a member of the AEC and afterward its chairman, decided with Senator McMahon to

3. David Lilienthal, first chairman of the AEC and former head of TVA.

4. Admiral Lewis Strauss, investment banker, devout Jew, Taft Republican, former Secretary to Herbert Hoover, and valuable naval bureaucrat.

push construction of the H-bomb. Lilienthal, then chairman, opposed it, as did almost all the leading scientists on the advisory council. H-bomb research dragged for various reasons, none of which can be laid at Oppenheimer's door. The Air Force wanted it, because it would mean a greater slice of appropriations, although they had no clear idea of its special usefulness. Not only were there technical and moral doubts, but the problem of recruiting personnel without injuring other atomic bomb work presented itself. Finally the Air Force, then under the Secretaryship of Thomas K. Finletter, a liberal lawyer, forced the AEC to establish Dr. Teller in his own laboratory (by 1952) and the production of thermonuclear weapons, having proved feasible, began in earnest.

The decision to go ahead with the H-bomb marked the official adoption of a new military policy built around the Strategic Air Command (SAC) of the Air Force—a policy of immediate and massive retaliation from the American stockpile of atomic and super-atomic weapons as a deterrent against any Soviet aggression. As the vehicle of delivery, SAC, commanded by General Curtis Le May, became the essential unit of American strategy. As stated to a Los Angeles Chamber of Commerce meeting in October of 1953 by Gordon Dean, a former member of the Atomic Energy Commission personally friendly to Dr. Oppenheimer, the United States' policy takes on the therapeutic value of a shock treatment:

> The time has come . . . to make Russia understand that if she moves in any quarter of the globe, she will be struck and struck hard, not simply at the front line of her aggressive troops but at every element which supplies these troops. Let's make it plain that if Russia moves directly or indirectly . . . we not only will, but we must, destroy the vitals of such a movement—every marshalling yard, every supply depot, every contributory industrial population.

The established policy[5] of immediate and massive retaliation—hard to distinguish in theory or practice from the doctrine of preventive war—was necessarily total, for every population in modern warfare contributes something to the war effort. Against this conception, embodied in the perpetual readiness of the SAC to strike at targets from one end of the Soviet Union to the other, or anywhere else in the world, Dr. Oppenheimer raised the possibility of a tight defensive ring around the American continent. Thus his opposition to the H-bomb reflected his feeling about the futility of the arms race as such, if it was not balanced with an equal concentration on defence. The sporting belief of Americans that "the only good defence is a good offence" (a phrase popular in every sport and essential to understanding the American style of play and politics) militated against the Oppenheimer conception

---

5. The missiles program is a further development of the same strategy.

as 'Maginot Line' and as the defeatist psychology of a hand-wringing scientist, perhaps even of a neutralist with no stomach for fighting Russia. As against him, the official school held that

> the surest way to prevent bombs from falling on American cities is to destroy those bombs, and particularly the enemy carriers designed to take them to their objectives, before they leave their bases. Offensive air power, to strike against enemy atomic facilities and stockpiles, and particularly against enemy airfields and submarine bases, is the first element of sound air defence.

Yet the position taken by Dr. Oppenheimer was not a clear-cut 'defensive versus offensive' strategy, but aimed at greater emphasis on defence. Dr. Oppenheimer argued that in order for the United States to negotiate from strength a far more elaborate continental defence system than the offensive-mindedness of established strategy allowed was needed. He further argued that the major problems of defence against total attack in a democracy needed the participation and understanding of the public and that this was impossible to achieve under the heavy cloak of secrecy wrapped around all military strategy. The basic Air Force argument was that no adequate defence against atomic attack was foreseeable. The late General Vandenberg, when head of the Air Forces, thought that American air defence might bring down twenty or thirty percent of an attacking force. But even if by 1957, after a substantial national investment, the air defence system should be able to bring down fifty percent of a Russian force, the damage from the other half that got through could cripple America's industrial capacity for war and produce millions of casualties; night attack would cause even larger havoc. It should be noted that, when the argument between the scientists and the air officers was at its height, it was assumed that a Russian attack with 100 atomic weapons would destroy well over one-third of American industrial power and cause about thirteen million casualties. The defence apparatus of the U.S. against air attack at the time consisted mainly of interceptors and anti-aircraft artillery, with some World War II style radar coverage along the continental approaches. The anti-aircraft batteries, consisting predominantly of World War II batteries of 120 mm. guns and other types, were token weapons, ineffective above twenty thousand feet. In darkness the interceptor wings would lose much of their accuracy, few of them at that time being equipped with radar devices. A comparable study by the British authorities of their air defences forecast that an all-out attack on the British Isles would take a toll of two million lives.

Both sides used these grisly figures for their own purposes: the military to demonstrate the need to keep the SAC's retaliatory weapon always sharp and enlarging, the scientists to demonstrate the futility of the entire arms struggle and the need for a greater scientific and financial expenditure on defence research. The scientists' argument was really a technical elaboration of George Kennan's 'containment' thesis, which affirmed that the democracies must hold the line and wait for disintegrating forces to operate within the Soviet sphere. A greater emphasis on defence, however, cannot be called static any more than the policy of containment; and plainly a retaliatory thesis must veer ever closer to a preventive war thesis, which was abandoned at least by the executive arm of the Government. In any event, the scientific élite moved to test their own defence theories. In 1951 the scientists of Project Vista, who had been recruited by the Air Force to study tactical and field use of atomic weapons, came up with a report that supported the Oppenheimer thesis. Contradicting the Air Force conception of a huge heavy atomic stockpile carried by intercontinental bombers, Project Vista concluded that short-range tactical air forces with small atomic weapons, in addition to a small ground force, could check the Red Army in Europe. The struggle over atomic strategy soon involved General Eisenhower, who as an old ground soldier showed some inclinations toward the scientists' view when the Project Vista report was presented to him in Paris during the last period of his NATO command. But General Norstad, then head of the NATO air forces, opposed the report with its underlying thesis of a "mutual forswearing of strategic air war," and it never received serious consideration. The argument then shifted to the strategy of air defence, which appeared to the scientists to leave the American continent virtually open to intercontinental attack. An actual increase in the American capacity to negotiate with the Russians was predicted if the United States could build a defence network that would also act as a deterrent to aggression. The Air Force strategy counted on the instinct of self-preservation among the Soviet leadership, the rational recognition on the part of the potential enemy that the retaliatory price of atomic attack on the United States would be too high. Clinging to a policy originally adopted before the Russians had developed in their own atomic stockpile weapons between four and five times more powerful than those used at Hiroshima and Nagasaki eight years before, the Air Force continued to concentrate on offensive weapons immune from annihilation, rather than on defensive networks.

As if again to demonstrate the feasibility of their own conception of defence, the scientific *élite* gathered a remarkable task force, drawn from the leading university centers of research. The controversial Lincoln Summer Study group of thirty scientists played war games for three months in 1952 at the Massachusetts Institute of Technology and demonstrated, to their own satisfaction at least, that with an early warning system of interlocking radar stations, guided missiles, 'mother' aircraft launching smaller interceptor wings, Russian bomber penetration could be reduced to mere 'leakage.' Of course the retaliatory striking force would continue to be shielded; thus the present retaliatory-deterrent strategy would not be scrapped, but in the scientists' view actually increased in effect. The novelty of these proposals lay in plans for the defence of the ten thousand miles of American frontier available to the Russians. Existing radar equipment could not keep such a territory under accurate surveillance. The Summer Study group, organized by friends and disciples of Dr. Oppenheimer, advocated a new system of radar surveillance along the Arctic circle as close to the Soviet frontiers as possible, increasing the margin of warning from an hour or less in the present system to four and perhaps six hours. The Air Force objected to the cost of such a warning system, to its drainage effect on the remainder of the air budget, and its consequent effect on American striking power, which still seemed the primary weapon of defence. Technical doubts also arose and some resentment at the aura of originality around the scientists' proposals.

The Summer Study had its effect in sharpening the conflict between the scientists and the military. Faced with a good motion, the standard riposte of the politician is to shelve it and get the entire problem reviewed; shelving has the value of a clinch in boxing—a chance to recover from a blow, study the opposition and learn how to meet it. The Summer Study findings did not reach a formal stage of discussion in the National Security Council (the President, Secretary of State and Chiefs of Staff), which is now the body ultimately responsible for the strategy of the United States. But it did push the argument into such a state of intense controversy during the final months of the Truman Administration that a new special committee of investigation (under Mervin Kelly, vice-president of the Bell Laboratories) was appointed to review the entire problem of vulnerability. The Kelly Report substantially confirmed the established military thesis that the best defence was the retaliatory-deterrent theory of offence. In direct criticism of Dr. Oppenheimer's attempt to alter the pattern of American military strategy, the Kelly Report

> expressed concern . . . about the recent public advocacy of a programme which would purportedly give nearly perfect protection against air attack. . . . Any such level of protection is unattainable and . . . completely impractical, economically and technically, in the face of expected advances in [Russian] capabilities.

In rebuttal to the Summer Study, the report urged "continued development of a powerful United States atomic offensive capability, reasonably invulnerable to initial attack." The deeply ingrained American view of offence as the best defence remained invulnerable to the complicated alternative suggested by the scientists.

The Oppenheimer affair involved far more than uncertainty about the political and personal attitude of a leading scientist; in fact the whole complex of American military strategy in the atomic age was involved. The first full-length journalistic account of the scientists' efforts and the position of the military was given in an article in *Fortune* magazine, May 1953, headlined

"The Hidden Struggle for the H-bomb: The Story of Dr. Oppenheimer's Persistent Campaign to Reverse U.S. Military Strategy." The writer fairly reports the history of the struggle, despite his clear animus against Oppenheimer and the scientists for their meddling in military affairs. The last sentence formulates concisely, from the military point of view, the present tension between science and politics in America: "There is a serious question of the propriety of scientists trying to settle grave national issues alone, inasmuch as they bear no responsibility for the successful execution of war plans."

Dr. Oppenheimer's own position was best summed up in his famous article in the quarterly *Foreign Affairs* of July 1953, a rewriting of a speech he delivered before the Council on Foreign Relations, which in turn grew out of his State Department disarmament report. Here he reviewed his challenge to the foundation of American strategy: the "rather rigid commitment to use (atomic weapons) in a very massive unremitting strategic assault on the enemy." The Air Force strategy depended on maintaining a larger stock of weapons than the Russians. But "the very least we can conclude is that our twenty-thousandth bomb . . . will not in any deep strategic sense affect their two thousandth." The futility of stockpiling and retaliation as the basis of American strategy was accented by the "relatively little done to secure our defence against the atom." There was also the unsolved question of how we would defend our Allies and behind this the agonizing logic of the present strategy which would make it necessary for the United States to atomize the cities of Western Europe if they came under Soviet control early in the next world war. As a final—technical—point against the stockpiling-retaliatory strategy, Dr. Oppenheimer foresaw a "time when . . . the art of delivery and the art of defence will have a much higher military relevance than supremacy in the atomic munitions field itself." This restated the conclusions of the Summer Study group.

But perhaps the major point Dr. Oppenheimer had to make was not technical but political. At the end of his article he suggested a reform in official behavior, in order to make "available to ourselves, in this tough time, the inherent resources of a country like ours and a government like ours." Especially, in view of the alarming tendency of the Air Defence command to concentrate on the protection of the nation's striking arm rather than on the protection of the country itself, Oppenheimer was worried about what he called the 'political vitality' of America. Of one source of political vitality— "the interplay, the conflict of opinion and debate, in many diverse and complex agencies, legislative and executive, which contribute to the making of policy"—he had seen a great deal. But the other resource—a "public opinion which is based on confidence that it knows the truth"—was "not available today." Public opinion was the great factor which the government had bypassed. In the field of atomic strategy public opinion cannot exist." Se-

crecy veiled the "important conditions." For the survival of democracy, for
the preservation of its will to fight in the unparalleled tests to come, Dr.
Oppenheimer recommended 'candor' as the first reform to which the new
Republican Administration should attend. Against this, the military insisted
that only the Russians could possibly benefit from candor, that the American people could not understand the technicalities, and that to frighten
them was dangerous from the perspective of morale.

Certainly one *Foreign Affairs* article by Oppenheimer, and the rebuttal of
Oppenheimer's position in *Fortune,* was not enough to bring the struggle into
the arena of public debate. And even in the open, the military and governmental élites would have held a profound advantage. Air Force strategy was
deeply rooted in the American ethos. The 'fortress' or 'Maginot Line' strategy could never have evoked the same appeal; it was a complicated argument, led by a 'complicated' man. In the press, only the Alsop brothers (in
the New York *Herald Tribune*) carried the Oppenheimer position to their
readers, and even their perceptive and sometimes hair-raising frankness
failed to develop any public pressure on the scientists. The issues seemed
too strategic, not moralistic enough to attract a sufficient number of do-
gooders. The aloofness of the scientist from even the educated and liberal
portions of the public is evident in America, for this public tends to moralize
a great deal about the 'ethical failure' of science, as well as about all other
ethical failures. The humanist intellectual in the United States has been retreating at a remarkable pace from his earlier interest in politics and science. This increasing isolation of the scientific élite is an important factor in
the crisis of culture that has overtaken liberal democratic society in America. The main fact of political life in American during the fifties was that an
Oppenheimer could never operate in the open with any expectation of significant public support. Not only was there no party that might conceivably
have supported him, but no constellation of public opinion could form near
him. The autonomous cosmopolitan community of science is necessarily
alienated from the American public and gains no advantage in taking an
argument before it. The distance between the scientist with a liberal ethic
and even the educated public is perhaps greater now than in the Protestant
era of American culture, when 'science' was more popular and the educated
classes could more easily confront it. No significant segment of American
public opinion exists to appraise or even interest itself in 'technical' problems. The ignorance of the public no longer keeps it away from politics, but
it does keep it away from science. In a technologically mysterious culture
even the educated take the magic of their electric toasters and their atomic
strategy for granted; they are more helpless before it than the primitive before the unorganized powers of nature, for modern man has no magic to
exert. The magic is left to the scientist, and therefore in a technologically
recondite age more and more issues become magical and are considered

outside the orbit of public competence. This is a problem of democratic life which no argument for candor can easily turn.

It was cruelly appropriate that a battle fought so secretly should end not with private dismissal but with public humiliation. For the basis of attack was not the one still unknown to the American public, but the one familiar now through years of public investigation by Congressional committees. Dr. Oppenheimer was accused not for the policy to which he had bent his science, but for his past and his associations which remain unmendable—all family 'relations' being in the official definition 'associations.'

Dr. Oppenheimer's past was well known to the government: a number of friends, a dead sweetheart, his wife's first husband, his wife, his brother, his brother's wife—all at one time or another Communists. Nevertheless in 1942 he was asked to organize atomic bomb research. The same past could be again in question, not because new evidence had been offered, but because a conspiratorial tedium had settled even more heavily upon American institutional and élite life than upon the public. The Administration could not decline to compete with Senator McCarthy in the art of demonstrating its fixation on the past. Such fixations—like the revived spy charges made against Harry Dexter White, who died in 1948—provided the nation with relief from the frustrations of the present. Dr. Oppenheimer's former military superior, General Groves, pinpointed the paranoid tendencies of the security drive—ironically, as I think—when he replied to a question about Dr. Oppenheimer's trustworthiness: "I don't know. How can you always tell if your own husband or wife is trustworthy?"

Dr. Oppenheimer's past had permitted the government to display all sorts of cleverness in catching him out, not only in the final cross-examinations but in the earlier investigations. He was exposed not so much in the few obvious lies he told to protect friends, but in the more subtle possibilities of treason. A dialectic the more resembling that of the Communists in the very fervor of opposing them had seeped into the American official mind. In the 1951 report of the California State Senate Fact-Finding Commission used by the AEC to prepare its original charges against Dr. Oppenheimer, this dialectic is marvelously strung together out of gossamer inference. Since it was discovered that he was classified in secret Communist Party communications as unsympathetic to Communism, the California report suggested that the Party was really counting on Dr. Oppenheimer and that his known antipathy to them might well be a "deliberate ruse." Starting from this plausibility, American security forces found the facts "quite plain that [Russian agents] were unanimous in picking Dr. J. Robert Oppenheimer as the most suitable man to contact." They judged him as a "potential traitor."

The case broke on 4 March 1954, when Oppenheimer released to the press his reply to a letter of charges from Major-General Nichols, general

manager of the AEC. It was then made known that since the previous summer, on the personal order of the President, a 'blank wall' had been placed
between Dr. Oppenheimer and all 'restricted data.' For almost a year he had
been barred from government work and consultations. The letter listed an
unsorted number of charges, most of them held over from the previous investigations of Dr. Oppenheimer in 1946 and 1948. The only new accusation, that of opposing the hydrogen bomb, seemed the most ominous.

But this was not the charge singled out as decisive in Dr. Oppenheimer's
reply. He did not choose to defend his policies but his past and person—the
old charges on which he had already been cleared. His letter to the Atomic
Energy Commission (4 March) avoided the homiletics on "the god that
failed" we have come to expect in such cases, for he was never a believer
but only a friend and relative of believers. Nevertheless, if he did not indulge in any theoretic recantations, Dr. Oppenheimer did in another sense
exceed the limits of defensiveness. His response to the rehash of his past in
the changed climate of America was if anything too appropriate to the pattern of attack. Dr. Oppenheimer did not discuss the objective political argument which was responsible for his present humiliation. The effect of his
language was to transform his case into a case history, as if a clinical understanding was the best one he could reach with his accusers (and the public).
Read against the nasty brieflike letter from the Atomic Energy Commission,
Dr. Oppenheimer's reply was too long and too intimate for a political accounting. Such a letter is in itself an act of penance, for the total man can
never be innocent. In modern politics it is not resistance but the fullness of
revelation that is the standard act of guilt. A chilling sense of confession
could easily be read into the letter.

Dr. Oppenheimer exercised the intellectual's right of introspection in
coming up against power. But the self-portrait he drew was uncomfortably
general, a portrait not of an individual but of a stock academic American.
When not suspect, the professor in America is invariably located a little
outside the main realities. Piano-players in the brothels of Storyville (New
Orleans), where jazz was born, were for their fine art and eunuchal functions
honored with the title 'Professor,' a considered opinion of the few relatively
sexless males at the gate to the plenitude sexuality. The mass media are full
of mad professors. The academies are full of men who, despite the ruthlessness of university politics, are convinced that they could not survive in the
'real' world outside. Many of them accept even now, despite student instruction to the contrary, the popular definition of reality as practically anywhere
outside the academy, and Dr. Oppenheimer could not be expected to escape
the air he breathed. It was inevitable that his self-criticism should appeal to
our sense of comedy. His letter reports how friends "chided" him with being
too much of a "highbrow," and how his fault was the fault of the world in
which he moved, for his friends were "mostly faculty people . . . and art-

ists." Thus he studied and read Sanskrit; "Led Abnormal Life," ran some newspaper headlines when the case first broke. Forwarded to clarify "the context of my life and my work" by the self-examination of "character" as well as "associations and loyalty," Dr. Oppenheimer's letter even hinted at some sort of hereditary highbrowism. Although his father was a successful businessman, his mother "before her marriage was an artist and teacher of art." One is left to wonder what his mother's premarital talents had to do with the case, unless it is part of the case history.

There is also a more specialized cliché evoked by Dr. Oppenheimer's defence. Although he identified himself as an intellectual (poetry and protest), in another sense he removed himself from membership of the cultured classes in general. It is not simply the joke about the absent-minded professor to which his letter appealed, but specifically the popular image of theoretical physicists confused by a short circuit in the basement, of mathematicians helpless before this week's grocery bill. Dr. Oppenheimer stood finally as the practitioner of what used to be an unpolitical science. He reports that he

> read very widely, but mostly classics, novels, plays, and poetry; and . . . something of other parts of science. I was not interested in and did not read about economics or politics. I was almost wholly divorced from the contemporary scene in this country. I never read a newspaper or a current magazine like *Time* or *Harper's*; I had no radio, no telephone; I learned of the stock market crash in the fall of 1929 only long after the event; the first time I ever voted was in the Presidential election of 1936.

The familiar plea of innocence by dissociation marred Dr. Oppenheimer's defence. The highbrow—especially the physical scientist—breathing only the rare realities available at his heights, develops a special brand of political innocence. It is from the abstractedness of his perspective that Dr. Oppenheimer denominated his past. Such an account seems to request that the physical scientist, dealing in nature not history, should be treated with a special clemency. *Nolo episcopari.* But this logic makes life a little harder for those less specialized intellectuals who always did read papers and political magazines (perhaps other than *Time* and *Harper's*), installed telephones, knew all about the stock market crash, and yet also—as Dr. Oppenheimer did—sympathized with the Popular Front against the rise of Fascism in Spain and elsewhere.

To understand why Dr. Oppenheimer's defence was so accommodating to the means of attack chosen by his political enemies, one must understand the deep and broad acceptance of psychology in America. The popular myth of the treason of the intellectuals is now widely reinforced by the myth of the special neuroticism of the 'scientist,' as well as the artist. Dr. Oppenheimer was thus at once condemned and condoned as too 'complex' a personality.

After all those years of great responsibility, he had been washed out of government service, like a young officer candidate in training school, for showing unstable tendencies. This test of character, as distinct from 'association,'
in American politics indicates to some extent how the idea of the neurotic
has been fused, in the official as well as in the popular mind, with the idea
of the treasonably inclined. Sickness and health are fast becoming political
categories, as once they were religious categories. 'Security' is after all a
significantly psychological term, and by the awful weight of psychological
accusation one's opposition can be crushed even more thoroughly in public
encounters than in private.

The viciousness of the psychological accusations does not of course discount the real problem which is today compromised and manipulated by the
language of 'security.' The tightening anxieties expressed in the Oppenheimer opinions have to be understood against the background of shock
among many of the nation's leaders at the size and depth of Communist infil-
tration. In response to the incomprehensible challenge of ideological betrayal, the honorable and old-fashioned men at the head of American affairs
reacted with renewed and calculated suspicion of those within the nation
who appear so different in their habits of thought and in the range of their
loyalties. Fear of the scientist, as of the politically cultured, becomes more
understandable as a reaction to the strange new political culture in which
old-line American political and military leaders find they must operate.
Since it has been discovered that there are strange creatures without and
within who have no price, make no deals, and talk a language of morals and
tactics foreign to the popular culture which the leadership shares, Red-
hunting easily incorporates highbrow-hunting. The attack upon radicals as
intellectuals, and upon intellectuals as radicals, is a standard item of popular resentment since the Dreyfus case; and anti-intellectualism appears especially ominous when it is compounded with psychological investigation.
Nevertheless, no criticism of the rhetoric of the attack, either in its simple-
minded or vicious forms, argues away the closeness of belief and action, nor
the traumatic betrayals already known.

These considerations have not yet, I think, been taken seriously enough
by liberals. Despite Dr. Oppenheimer's somewhat overcooperative admissions of political ignorance and the allusions to neurotic braininess, there
was some optimism about the outcome of the case. Since Dr. Oppenheimer's
past associations had always been known to the government, many did not
expect to see condoned, even in the fifties' climate of 'hysteria,' such a
"breach of faith on the part of the government" (the words of a May, 1954,
editorial in the *Bulletin of Atomic Scientists*)[6] that calls upon a man "to as-

6. The Editorial Board, "Editorial: The Oppenheimer Case," *Bulletin of the Atomic Scientists* 10, no. 5 (May 1954): 173.

sume such heavy responsibilities in full knowledge of his life history and
then, after he has demonstrably done his best and given the most valuable
services to the nation . . . uses facts which were substantially known all
the time to cast aspersions on his integrity." Some defenders of Dr. Oppenheimer privately considered it a pity that his case was tried long after that of
Alger Hiss. If only Oppenheimer, and not Hiss, had represented them when
their generation was put on trial, liberals might have felt less guilty. Yet the
Oppenheimer case portended something more sinister than that of Hiss. If
Hiss was condemned for his acts and admired for his strong character (set off
against the neurotic Chambers who had accused him), Oppenheimer was
condemned for his character and praised for his actions. The latter may
stand in history as a form of condemnation far more dangerous to liberal
society than any straightforward condemnation for acts of treason.

The decision of the Gray Committee was issued on 1 June 1954. Its members had met for eight weeks and heard 500,000 words (992 pages in fine
print) of testimony; of the forty witnesses who testified, the majority (including
Gordon Dean, former chairman of the AEC in 1950–53, James B. Conant,
and Vannevar Bush, director of the Office of Scientific Research and Development during World War II) were favorable to Oppenheimer. The decision
was in the light of the later appellate decision of the AEC, a heavily quali-
fied one. Gray noted that if they had been able to use common sense rather
than the harsh requirements of 'security,' the decision might have been different. Oppenheimer's 'loyalty' was reaffirmed, but in the light of his associations and his opposition to the hydrogen bomb, he was judged a 'security
risk' and denied renewal of access to 'classified material.' The decision of
the AEC board made public four weeks later, on 29 June presented a more
formidable majority (4–1 instead of 2–1) against Oppenheimer and a more
severe and consistent verdict, solely on the basis of his character and associations. In a separate concurring opinion, one member of the commission,
Thomas E. Murray,[7] found Dr. Oppenheimer 'disloyal' for failing to show
'exact fidelity' and 'obedience' to the government's security regulations. As
the editorial in one major newspaper ran, Dr. Oppenheimer

> can clear himself. To do so he will have to forsake suspect companions. He
> will have to work independently in his chosen field. He must prove that
> he can learn under this painful pressure, that he can be discreet in his
> friendships.

Thus while Dr. Oppenheimer was not asked to change his mind, he was
encouraged to change his heart. Perhaps this is a more insidious demand

7. The majority voters of the AEC, aside from Admiral Strauss and Mr. Murray, were
Eugene M. Zuckert, a former Assistant Secretary of the Air Force, and Joseph Campbell,
former vice-president and treasurer of Columbia University. Strauss and Campbell were Re-
publicans, Murray aned Zuckert Democrats.

than any the state could make upon his mind. It is a demand higher than any but recent totalitarianisms have yet made. There is already a touch of this in the original verdict, in the place where the Gray Report congratulates itself on its human tenderness and psychological delicacy. "We believe," wrote Gray and Thomas J. Morgan, representing the majority, "that it has been demonstrated that the Government can search . . . the soul of an individual whose relationship to his Government is in question." Not his scientific decisions but his lack of the proper spirit made of Dr. Oppenheimer a political danger. For these reasons he was denied further access to secret information and his role as adviser to the government terminated. Although there was no question of his having committed any act prejudicial to national interest, Dr. Oppenheimer did not have properly fervent emotions about his Communist relatives and friends.

The case for special restrictions on the life and habits of certain classes of the skilled and informed within a garrison state was brilliantly developed in the concurring opinion of AEC Commissioner Murray. "The American citizen in private life, the man who is not engaged in Governmental service, is not bound by the requirements of the security system." Only certain persons are subject to this "special system of law." A man in Dr. Oppenheimer's position should "relinquish the right to the complete freedom of association that would be his in other circumstances." It is not a matter of action or even omission contrary to the national interest. "What is incompatible with obedience to the laws of security is the associations themselves, however innocent in fact." Thus the friend-enemy relationship (chiefly the dinner meeting with M. Chevalier) is the key to the Oppenheimer decision. Dr. Oppenheimer cannot have for a friend anyone who can, by any stretch of the imagination, be considered an enemy of the state. No relation is unpolitical, no level of dining politeness can continue between the Oppenheimers and the Chevaliers, even if all they did together was to go and see M. André Malraux. As a government scientist, Oppenheimer would have to live under special restrictions and must observe the friend-enemy relationship in his personal life. In his case the tragic impossibility of this demand on his person is obvious: he would have had to deny his brother (whose career in physics was then ruined and who turned to ranching in the West) and divorce his wife.

Among the scientists there was a great public outcry against the Oppenheimer decision. From the beginning they cried 'Shame' and 'Ingratitude' at the excommunication of so great a figure among them. In both hearings the dissenting opinion came from a representative of science on each board, the chemist, Evans, on the three-man Gray Commission and the physicist, Smyth, on the five-man Atomic Energy Commission sitting as an appellate board. Yet within the scientific élite there was much the same fear, mutual suspicion, whispering, shamming, and discarding of powerful leaders, once they are beaten, as besets other élite formations in modern politics. Although the scientists know each other intimately and have great corporate feelings, in the atmosphere of American culture during the fifties they were rent by a variety of schisms and hatreds caused by their new relation to political power.

Particularly among the younger scientists there were many who found it agreeable to combine their technical functions with a technical morality, and for whom the Oppenheimer policy wars were simply intrusions on their established honorific relation to the political order. Actually the Oppenheimer case marked an end to the unique and necessary theoretical work related to atomic weapons. Oppenheimer's services were no longer indispensable, and the fulsome thanks he got with his kicks only made the cries of 'Ingratitude' the more bitter. Another element in the scientific élite, the engineers, who are more tractable than the theorists, increased in value as the arms race neared a saturation level in point of destructive capacity. Reacting to this trend, some theorists, unwilling to submit to the aims of policy, advocated retreat from government service. If, between the established Soviet reality and the American reaction to it, there then appeared to many scientists a shrinking difference, retreat from direct or indirect government employment takes on prudent as well as moral aspects. This position was advanced by the celebrated founder of cybernetics, Professor Norbert Wiener. Immediately after Oppenheimer was put on his long trial, Wiener wrote an editorial for *The Nation* asking the rhetorical question whether those who play with fire ought not to expect to get their fingers burnt. No doubt it was as a man of high moral as well as intellectual qualities that Oppenheimer could not submit to policy as a technician does. And with his figure the urgent alternatives of doom or grace were bound up in a way sensible to Americans otherwise even more indifferent to ultimate urgencies. Oppenheimer spoke for 'science'; as the American inheritor of the mantle of Einstein no one else could have played this role and hoped somehow to reach public opinion. Before the emergence of the militant blacks, the prophetic thunder, so far as in America it sounds at all, sounded from the scientist agonizing over his entrapment in a final politics. The design on the cover of the monthly *Bulletin of Atomic Scientists* (Dr. Oppenheimer was the chairman of its board of directors) is a clock whose hands pointed some minutes to midnight. It is the scientist who has consistently prophesied, in however small and censored a voice, the real probabilities of Judgment Day. To have such a prevision is not calculated to make a scientist with keen moral sensibilities comfortable in his connection with any régime. Modern régimes in particular do not take suggestions of the Apocalypse seriously and, with perfect political rationality, seek to translate them into logistical terms or terror propaganda.

In the liberal vision, science carried along with it belief in progress (through science) toward the apotheosis of humanity. It was, no doubt, this liberal vision that brought Dr. Oppenheimer into some sympathy with the Communist movement, as he understood it, in the 1930s. The scientist's confidence in his capacity to transform nature fitted in perfectly with the Marxist confidence in a new political capacity to transform society. Sophisticated scientists could thus become naïve Marxists, for there appears little transfer of training from scientific to political skills. But nowadays, for reasons inherent in the logic of science as well as in the logic of politics, the scientist is troubled by a decline of optimism concerning the consequences of scientific knowledge. A loss of that confidence which is an inseparable part of the priest-scientist role has made it far more difficult for the contemporary scientist to assume a position in relation to politics more positive than alarm. Science appeared not to remake the world, but to be remade by it. Men like Oppenheimer did indeed hold the keys to the arms race— thereby becoming figures of immense political relevance. But when they tried to enlarge their function and influence policy, with only fragments of the old progressivist scientific faith upon which to fall back, they were left peculiarly vulnerable to attack and internally divided. Plainly, Oppenheimer had none of the self-confidence of the Communist that comes with the convergence of personal and movement identity. No doubt qualities of personal impatience did offend a number of the highly intelligent administrators with whom he dealt, but the scientists' criticism of American strategy was never offered by Oppenheimer with any theoretic arrogance that he held the secret of victory and peace. It was advanced hesitantly and with careful qualification, as befits the condition of the modern liberal who has shed any residual Marxist certainties. The immediate postwar calls of the American atomic scientists for world government were nostalgic evocations of an earlier optimism, now held in trust by dwindling numbers of liberals. As the realities of living in a world that includes Russia and China impressed themselves on the scientists, such grand solutions to the world's ills were rapidly dropped.

Nevertheless, despite a loss of surety, the faith of the scientist remains liberal. The liberal conception of intellectual and political life depends on assuming the virtue of an 'antagonism of influences'[8] in which no defeat is total; decisions should emerge out of a never-ending discussion in which, soon or late, all would have their say. It was the duty of participants in such an ongoing discussion to revive those positions which they noticed had been neglected for any considerable time, so that all the truths could be available in the public market place. Not Dr. Oppenheimer's certainty that he had a correct answer, but his liberal impulse to have an alternative so as to clarify

8. The summary notion of society as a "balance of countervailing forces" by Professor Galbraith, of Harvard University, is a recent and no doubt unconscious rendering of Mill's phrase.

the issues in public (for the public and by the public) motivated the preliminary argument for 'candor,' beyond which he never got. The surprise and
disappointment among the scientists at the rough treatment of Oppenheimer
reflects their illusion that they still lived in a liberal society. The scientific
élite never dreamed that it would be so defeated and humiliated publicly.
The gratuitous raising of ten-year-old issues in the Oppenheimer case confirms their sense of shock that the rules of fair play by which controversy in a
liberal society is governed were scrapped. But the shock was too great to be
accepted and there was great emphasis laid on the fairness of the entire
procedure.

So far as this liberal conception of politics and culture emergent from an
antagonism of influences persists, it has led to a newly trivial social role for
the intellectual, who becomes the perpetual minority member moralizing for
lost causes. In scholarship especially the tendency is well established:
whole fields are preoccupied with marginal or safely empirical problems that
cannot be taken seriously, nor leave any serious impression even on the academic world. The present revival of interest in the theory and practice of
religious heresy, for example, is not a symptom of intellectualized revolt but
simply an intellectual safety valve, for history has fossilized heresy and orthodoxy together. It is therefore safe to make great play with protecting
'heresy,' for it has no political relevance. Dare the 'heresy' become political,
the game turns vicious. Still liberated in their civic pride, the scientific élite
did not foresee that they would be defeated in such a way that they would no
longer be able to argue their case—indeed, in such a way that their case
could never be presented.

It is tragic that the American scientists did not have a passion more positive than horror from which to elaborate their opposition to the drift, not only
of military policy, but of American politics in general. When the warfare
was chiefly between science and theology a more positive emotion was
easier to develop. Theology took special pains to keep science from developing along its own logic, and science resisted this in the name of freedom
and progress. Now that warfare is ended. A subtler enemy faces science: for
the state is without any dogma it cannot abandon overnight to catch the
shifts of power. The freedom and progress of science are not necessarily in-
terfered with by the state. On the contrary, the state is zealous for the most
advanced scientific knowledge and for its practical application. The scientist is free to work, urged to work, recruited, honored. But the opinions of
the scientist may interfere with the prosecution of policy. The scientist and
his élite may go into opposition to the other élites. Neither science nor the
scientist, when they serve the state, can be expected to stop short of exact
obedience without inviting investigation and reprisal. What was heresy
when science was under theology becomes disloyalty when it is under politics. Scientists have never held power anywhere; they have never been able

to command. But as a reward for their skill and conscientiousness they thought to reserve the right to advise, persuade, withdraw, suffer defeat, and stay on. The Oppenheimer case signified that these rights were no longer theirs. Scientific opinion cannot claim that immunity from political discipline won for it by nineteenth-century liberalism.

The social ambition of science was based on quite another image of the technological society, with the scientists as masters, not as the magicians of new masters. In a scientific age, scientists were to have duties like those of priests in the old society—duties superior to those of the warriors. By the twentieth century it was expected that in the scientist the Greek prophecy of society governed by philosopher-kings would at last be fulfilled. But something went astray, even while the expectation was at its highest in the mid-nineteenth century. With the Oppenheimer case the modern relation between science and politics in America was painfully revealed. Great social consequences are bound to follow from this revelation. Such an interference with the scientific élite, thwarting their free associations with undesirable social and political types, may alter the social conditions of its development. The élite is transformed into a service class, technically still supremely competent and much rewarded, but no longer so attractive to the most creative minds of the succeeding generations. (69:3)

33
Kelly Miller's *Radicals and Conservatives*

Kelly Miller was one of the dominant intellects of black America from the turn of the century to the 1930s. In 1934, Miller retired from his alma mater, Howard University, after long and distinguished membership in that institution, first in mathematics and then as professor of sociology—and, from 1907 to 1918, as Dean of the College. He died in 1939.

Miller was born in South Carolina, in 1863, the son of a free Negro tenant farmer and his slave wife. A paternal uncle served in the state legislature during Reconstruction. The young Kelly Miller was lucky, in a classical way: the bright, doomed peasant boy was given a chance to raise himself by a churchman, who, correctly reading the signs of intellectual promise, helped him into a better school. By 1886, Kelly Miller had worked his way through Howard, meanwhile saving enough money from his outside job in the United States Pension Office to buy his parents a farm as *his* graduation gift to them. Miller thus inverted the customary ritual exchange between parents and children of higher social strata; here, upon the occasion of the

Reprinted from *Radicals & Conservatives and Other Essays on the Negro in America*, by Kelly Miller (New York: Schocken, 1968), 7–24.

graduation gift, the child gave to the parents. Further details of Miller's life and career are easily accessible in the article on him, in the *Dictionary of American Biography* (Supplement 2), pp. 456–57, by his even more distinguished successor to the chair of sociology at Howard, E. Franklin Frazier; I refer the reader to that article.

The essays in this volume were written by Miller for various magazines or as polemical pamphlets published separately and first collected by him in 1908 under the main title, *Race Adjustment*. This book has been out of print for more than a generation.

As Miller himself realized, I think, W. E. B. DuBois was the supreme intellect of black America during his own time. DuBois was Miller's superior both as writer and scholar. In the leading (and now titular) essay of this book, Miller acknowledges DuBois's "extraordinary scientific and literary talent." However, part of Miller's analysis of DuBois's early career should be read against the history of rivalry between men equally passionate in their devotion to that justice and welfare which they knew, with equal subtlety, their people would have to acquire for themselves, through continuing struggle with the American experience. In the first years of the twentieth century, the leadership of the new militants, gathering around that fascinating Harvard contemporary of DuBois, William Monroe Trotter, editor of the *Boston Guardian*, might have fallen to Miller. But Miller was no 'radical'; the mantle of militancy passed swiftly from Trotter to a figure no less angular and aristocratic, DuBois.

The earliest excellence to appear in this book is Miller's own reflection on radicals and conservatives, as types, among the leaders of black America in Miller's own time. I shall concentrate the main part of this introductory essay upon a brief analysis of what radicalism and conservatism may mean, when drawn along the color line, then and now. In part II, as a coda, I shall draw some implications for the rise of black militancy within the context of the larger and deeper revolutionary crisis of western culture. After the titular essay, many other pieces of wisdom remain here to be found by the reader: Miller's reflections on "Surplus Negro Women"; the iron courtesy with which he frames his irrefutable denunciation of a white racist literary gent, Thomas Dixon, Jr., who was the author of that *Birth of a Nation* upon which D. W. Griffith based his great and vicious film; Miller's passionate reading of Whitman; his "Brief for Higher Education." In fact, all the essays following "Radicals and Conservatives" remain usable sources for the contemporary reader's knowledge of the inner history of black America.

I

As Miller tells us, it is nonsense to imagine that any reflective Negro can be satisfied with the condition of his existence in American society. In this sense, there are no conservative blacks. Precisely in the face of white caste defensiveness and racial ambivalence, how could any self-respecting Negro be conservative? "Every consideration of enlightened self-respect impels him to unremitting protest." The latent thought behind this manifest truth is constantly present in this volume: protest is itself, in the oppressive condition of Negro life, a function of self-respect. Yet there remain two major questions: first, the *form* of protest, whether lawful or unlawful (Miller is straightforwardly for lawful protest); second, the *ubiquity* of the oppressive condition. Miller and his generation of black leaders were quite clear about the terrible condition of the Negro people. Yet none adopted some apocalyptic fantasy-theory of a deeper disorder, in which Negroes, as the prisoners of a racist social structure, rattle their chains also against high culture, oppressive somehow even in its most sublime expressions. There was no disagreement in *theory* among the Negro leaders of Miller's time: all must protest and seek a fundamental change in the order of black and white America. But such protest had nothing whatever to do with apocalyptic theories of a saving disorder or a liberating chaos of destruction. The black leaders were deeply committed, in their own persons, to high culture, and to its ideas of law and order. Their disagreements were mainly, then, about the *tactics* of orderly change.

About the tactics of orderly change, based, as all tactics must be, upon estimates of one's own weaknesses as compared with the enemy's particular strengths, there were, in Miller's time as in our own, continuing disagreements. Miller refused to take a dogmatically rigid position, militant or moderate. Tactics have to be adjusted, as he rightly said, "to the dictates of prudence." The radicals of the Trotter-DuBois school were embarked, with the second manifesto of the "Niagara Movement" (called into being by DuBois in 1905), on a course of "verbal vehemence void of practical power to enforce demands" against the strongholds of racism. On the other hand, the dominant conservatives, led by Booker T. Washington, were not vehement enough, too prudent before the structured impulse cruelties of white society, too accommodating before racist fantasies passed off as recondite science or common knowledge about the permanent (because inherent) inferiority of blacks in a high culture that was never to be their own. To the radicals, these Negro conservatives looked like sycophants, court jesters without courage and wit enough to goad the ruling race in the right direction—toward a society freed from racist grotesquerie.

In Miller's long view, the tactical range of opposition to white racism must include both radicals and conservatives. There was no doubt in his mind that the "Niagara Movement" would grow out of its "declamatory stage" and become "tempered by dealing with the actualities of the situation." Miller's expectation was justified by historical developments. To be truly creative, militant movements must institutionalize the newly released energies. By 1909, the "Niagara Movement" invested its new energies as the NAACP. Thus the militants contributed something vital, as Miller thought they would, to the "many agencies working together for the general cause."

Miller did what he could to push Washington and the conservatives, beyond their programs of racial self-strengthening, toward the necessary risks of antiracist demands and programs. He rightly judged and accepted Washington as a "practical opportunist, accepting the best terms which he thinks it possible to secure." But there was a tactical trap into which a conservative leader such as Washington might fall all too easily: a permanent acceptance of the best terms of one encounter with racism as necessarily the best terms of subsequent encounters. Miller took it upon himself publicly to urge Washington, who was vulnerable from the black side of the color line because of his obvious usefulness on the white side,[1] not to be content with the constricting "practical" achievements which, even if they succeeded, would cut off the Negro from his just chances of leading the life of the mind. At a banquet, in proposing a toast to the greatness of Booker T. Washington, in the very face of the great man himself, Miller included an implicit threat that Washington's leadership was far from unconditionally acceptable. On the contrary, it was important for Washington not to take too seriously the "sycophantic adulation" with which he liked to be surrounded. In some phrases hard with Miller's usual iron courtesy in criticism, Washington was advised that he would do better to "invite candid criticism." Nor did Miller spare the great black father the central criticism. Wrapped inside the velvet tributes of the banquet toast, there was an unyielding demand for more militant action. "Pursue policies," he urged Washington, "that are commensurate with the entire circle of our needs, and which are broad-based upon the people's will, and advocate the fullest opportunity of Negro youth to expand and exploit their faculties." This was certainly the radical line, couched in terms that Washington could not rebut.

Throughout Miller's career, and practically until our own time, radical and conservative Negro leaders agreed on antiracist theory, the end in view; but, specially in view of the historical remoteness of that end, they differed mainly on race tactics. The generals of opposing tactics were DuBois and Washington. It was true that Washington could be interpreted as a monumental time-server to the white racist establishment. This interpretation of Washington did not alarm Miller. As a sophisticated participant-observer of all the internecine struggles that accompanied the struggle with the real enemy, white racism, Miller knew the universal rules of the political game and tells us, flatly, that there is something of the time-server in "all truly useful men." At the same time, militancy was equally necessary and practical, de-

---

1. Washington established his national preeminence with his famous separate-but-equal metaphors of the hand and fingers, in his Atlanta Exposition address of 18 September 1895.

spite the self-indulgent passion of militants for 'verbal vehemence' and the dangers of raising the ideological temperature of the white racists. Such risks were worth taking in order to raise the ideological temperature of the blacks—to make them more active on their own behalf.

What was the theory agreed among the black leadership of Miller's era, radicals and conservatives alike, even as they disagreed about tactics? That theory referred to an eventual reality upon which all students of the race problem must agree, in reason, although the reality to which the theory referred was not yet fact. On the contrary, far from being accomplished fact, the trouble with the theory was that it pointed to a tragically remote eventuality, a future fact toward which present fact would continue to work itself—but with painful reluctance. In the following passage, Miller summarizes the theory that framed all tactics, radical and conservative, up to the most recent period: he held the *"intellectual conviction that two races cannot live indefinitely side by side, under the same general regime, without ultimately fusing."* (My italics.)

Now, there is an important sense in which a theory can be a hypothetical prediction. Since a 'fusing' or amalgamation of the races, as a social phenomenon, must, like other social phenomena, take its real existence from the subjective meaning attached to such an eventuality by the social actors themselves, Miller understood perfectly that his hypothetical prediction was no prediction at all. There were necessary conditions without the operation of which such an outcome as an ultimate 'fusing' was not assured. Patently, the necessary conditions were not present and the prediction remains, for our time as for Miller's, merely hypothetical.

Massive fusing had taken place, of course. It was the most visible sign of the degradation, the concubinage, to which black Americans had been subjected—and in that forced amalgam, a new racial type, the Negro American, unknown elsewhere, was being created. However, under the present and foreseeable conditions of race relations in America, Miller's theory as a hypothetical prediction, carried neither "the utterance of a preference nor the formulation of a policy." He could safely say that he knew of no Negro "who advocates amalgamation as a feasible policy of solution." White racists are mistaken. "The Negro does not 'hope and dream of amalgamation.' This would be self-stultification with a vengeance."

The validity of a theory may be distinguished from its practical applicability; it may, indeed, explain tactical limits and also, in its validity, be so different from the observed facts as to stand in transformative judgment over them. In their historical situation, black radicals and conservatives held to the theory, as Miller phrased it, that the "amalgamation of the races is an ultimate possibility, though not an immediate probability." The theory remains true. It is imperative, I think, that antiracist theory be held fast, nowadays; only by holding onto it can blacks and whites rightly assert their common humanity. Here is the ultimate question answering itself: rightly asserted by the directive theory, all racial tactics will remain subordinate to it.

"But what have you and I to do with ultimate questions, anyway?" Miller asks, in careful irony, of the white racist to whom were addressed the passages from which I have been quoting.[2] What, indeed! Without keeping the ultimate theoretical questions in mind, as Miller did in the courageous act of insisting upon their validity—and, moreover, precisely in view of the fact that the main racist frenzy is about just this theory—immediate tactical answers lose all sense of direction. Through all the tactical struggles between radicals and conservatives, Miller kept his sense of direction, of what tactics we may and may not use—which *is* the theoretical sense. He rejected color line and caste, constantly breaking anyway under the historic arrangements of racial life in America, as principles of social organization. The Negro must organize his own corporate identity in both tactical moods, radical and conservative, precisely in order to break beyond racial forms of social organization. Beyond all tactics, then, there was no conflict of principles, of ultimate questions, of theory. Miller kept clearly in mind, I suggest, the difference between theory and tactics. He did not allow antiracist theory to become confused in his mind with racial tactics. Precisely this confusion of theory and tactics—and, moreover, a conflict of theories—is now occurring, with a vengeance for the failure of antiracist theory to overtake and transform more swiftly the facts of racial life in America.

There appears to be developing within our contemporary Negro leadership a split in theory as well as tactics. Proudly, and without the slightest trace of anxiety in the acceptance of it, Miller did accept the great truth that there were neither 'white' nor 'black' values, neither white nor black properties in cultures. A culture, Miller proclaimed, is "the equal inheritance of anyone who can appropriate and apply it." Shakespeare and Whitman belonged to him; they were part of his inalienable life; they did not belong to butchers in London or slobs in Camden simply because they happen to be white men. Race is the most terrible cultural simplification of all; in his wisdom and learning, Miller rejected the fatal simplicity that the provenance of a value determined membership in it. "The Negro enters into the inheritance of all the ages on equal terms with the rest." Here, I think, is another truth of which we are reminded by a reading of these essays. That there have been modes of African cultural genius is also true and urgently needs teaching. But this is only to amplify the basic theoretical point: that "the white man has no exclusive proprietorship of civilization." There are no values for whites only and none are black, whatever their origins. Our moral demands stand or fall on the proposition that they belong to those who enact those demands in their own lives.

Nevertheless, it appears to me that a new generation of Negro radicals

2. See "As to the Leopard's Spots," 42–70.

has all but abandoned antiracist theory, as, under the accelerating force of its failures, they pursue racial tactics. Although they are still intended, mainly, I think, to raise the ideological temperature of Negro communal life, to motivate movements of self-help, militant declamations on 'black values,' if they are offered as expressions of racist theory, can only damage the dignity and restrict the range of the Negro's own infinitely human capacities. What are 'black values' anyway? A culture has no color; it belongs, as Miller insisted, to him who lives and enacts it. A high culture is a living and active faith. Blood cannot civilize. Even vague as they are at present, 'black values' sound suspiciously like an inversion of that kind of racist theory which even asserted Shakespeare for WASPS only, once used to keep Jews from teaching in English departments. Will black militants insist on artistic parity for LeRoi Jones, in English departments, alongside Shakespeare, with black teachers for Jones and white for Shakespeare? And what of all the Jewish literary dancers who, opposing the historic faith of Israel, make their protests in the name of the new Baal of Sex-Revolution? Are they to be constrained to the Song of Solomon? Will Pushkin become required reading in the original Russian, as a 'black' writer? Or will he have to be translated, first, into the language of the slave-traders, Swahili? There is something phony about the present talking up of 'black values.' I hear in this talk the characteristic hysterical tones of racist theory, except this time, in counterpoint to Miller's, the racist hysteria is also black.

II

Perhaps the current radical Negro turn to racist theory—at least to racist declamations that imply a theory—represents a desperate adaptation of the ideological movement by which our common culture is destroying itself from within. Black racist theory may be a desperate kicking at the old white womb of Negro consciousness. But the white womb has felt these self-same kicks before, from earlier children of its own making. Morally revolutionary whites have been kicking inside that same womb for more than a century. I suspect that, its ancestry traced back far enough, revolutionary black racist theory includes some great white fathers—Marx, Nietzsche, and D. H. Lawrence, for example—all those persuasive white haters of 'ideals' who wrote and acted in opposition to a culture high precisely in the creative discontent of its identification with ideals. In the racist context of modernity, ideals are easily associated with inhibition of the black power of impulse and self-gratification. "Away with ideals!" Lawrence declaimed. Who does not now know that 'white' is uptight? But this also implies that 'black' is slack. In the symbolic of western cultural modernity, dependent as it is upon racist prejudices shared by some blacks, 'black' is associated with those efforts to reject the faltering interdictory motifs that must dominate this (or any other) culture, by asserting its remissive motifs—more direct sexuality; spontaneity; the impulse life; personality as the flash point of will; gaiety; playfulness; arrogance. These are the kicks of the therapeutic through the womb of repressive, idealizing (but not white) culture in order to reassert the remissive part of that very same interdictory-remissive culture under an inverse order. The spreading collective violence of western life is explainable, I think, as a massive and long-prepared experiment in a remissive culture of play and self-gratification. We are witnessing a sociological freak of western cultural development, what might be called 'Revolution as therapy.' Revolt may be treated as an end in itself, the therapeutic heightening of a sense of personal well-being.

In this theoretical perspective, here briefly indicated,[3] the racist declamations of our contemporary black militants become understandable as one aspect of the remissive motifs integral to our culture; into the thrust toward interdictory dominance of these remissive motifs, the archetypal threatening figure of the black is welcomed, with a shiver of *Schadenfreude*, as an all-purpose subversive of culture itself. This expressive side of our inherited cultural ambivalence is quite as dangerous to the humanity of Negroes as the repressive side was in Miller's period of race psycho-history. The racist structure of modern cultural ambivalence can never be adapted, by an inversion of the established but failing interdictory-remissive contents, to serve the cause of racial justice.

Why not "chaos and disorderliness"? that moral revolutionary, Lev Shestov, once asked. The black has long served as a figure of chaos and disorderliness. By their willing loan of the archetypal violent black to revolutionary (as well as defensively hostile) whites, as a counter-ideal of themselves, the new Negro militants have been sucked into a white revolutionary movement that cuts across the path of their own, diverting them from their antiracist normative theory. That white revolutionary movement has made nonsense of the old political distinctions between Left and Right. Hitler's armed bohemians made serious, anti-establishment noises even more loudly than the students of the New Left nowadays. On the one hand, the most radical voices of the nineteenth and twentieth centuries have shouted for a destructiveness that goes far beyond politics. On the other hand, in the perspective suggested here, merely political Marxism appears now as a conservative cultural force, quite at odds with the deeper current of moral revolution in the West. Caught now in this deeper current, the militant black leaders, in their declamations of violence and free-floating racial hostility, have become archetypal Americans; I suspect that many whites se-

3. For a more extended perspective, see the main theoretical chapters beginning and ending *The Triumph of the Therapeutic*, 2d ed., by Philip Rieff (Chicago: University of Chicago Press, 1987), 1–27 and 232–61.

cretly envy them their American freedom from the constraints of civility. All men long for this freedom. As their frontier culture was so much a form of escape from the constraints of civility, Americans have learned to enjoy living on the brink of that flash point of will we like to call 'personality'; just this flash point threatens our compensatorily rigid collectivities, from within, with chaos.

The culture of economic man is a jungle of barely suppressed hostilities anyway. Perhaps its putative inheritor, the remissive culture of psychological man,[4] will not be much worse. But successive evaginations of the American moral order, raising to the superficies of thought and behavior what were once more deeply installed inhibitions of impulse and hostility, promise a terrible harvest of free-floating hostility in our future even within a more and more manipulable technological culture. Blacks have ample reason to be doubly hostile. For centuries they were constrained to be uniquely and universally subject to the flash points of white will. With blacks one could do what was otherwise not done. Thus enhanced, white Americans could falsely celebrate their racial submissions to interdictory civilities and restraints.

The opening up of possibility, the liquidation of that which is 'not done,' represents the long revolution of modernity at its most basic level. Our revolution cannot be described in the received terms—Left or Right, Red or Black. As I have said, the moral revolutionaries of white modernity have been, often enough, fascist. Some variety of black fascism cannot break the racist structure of that modernity. Any effort to harden that structure with a racist theory derived from the black side of the color line is an evil to be fought in the name of all God's children. A victory for black racism would be tantamount to a defeat for black humanity. The counter-ideal of the moral revolutionaries is to make 'niggers' of us all—and this would be the deepest defeat of all to the real blacks, of America or Africa, past or present, different as they are from white racist-libertarian fantasies of them. I consider the implicit use of the black as the new storm-trooper of the white revolutionary movement against its own failing interdicts as another grave threat to the dignity, self-respect, and ultimate triumph of black men over all racist theories. Under this latest and most subtle inversion of white racist theory, not the black man but chaos will triumph.

I think it is possible that, in the complex internecine warfare of modern western culture against itself, chaos and destruction will emerge as the real victors. The most militant black dream, of a racial state carved out of America, can only lead to full-scale racist wars of extermination, for racist theory is always and everywhere an instrument for the release of that sadistic impulse by which one self or a corporate self can demonstrate its existence

---

4. See Rieff's considerations of "psychological man" in chapter 1 of this volume. See also 59:1a, 329–57 [ed.].

only by overpowering another. In the heart of darkness, a Kurtz or a Hitler can only assert himself through his power to destroy others.

In their own peculiar version of racist tactics, preempting the antiracist theory of Kelly Miller and his generation of Negro leaders, the new radicals of black America are repeating a revolutionary call to the worship of chaos that has enchanted the modern white mind. That terrible enchantment has now spread to the militant black leadership. On your knees before the New Disorder: bourgeois, old folks, men of taste and women of refinement— white and black! The modern worship of chaos has had its successes, drawing to itself the naïve and sophisticated alike. Our black revolutionaries are captives of the white revolutionaries. Being black, they are assigned the horrific role of negating white history with black values; they are to supply the myth and madness by which the logic of the past is to be cut short.

The success that would come out of such chaos certainly has the power to draw new worshippers. After all, success is the longest-lived of the gods. Perhaps white history has this chaos coming to it. The white establishment has itself worshipped none other than that self-same god, success, but always in the name of order. At once thus enchanted and disenchanted with success-chaos in its two faces of power, black and white, the new radicalism is very different from the old radicalism that Miller reviews for us in this volume. The new Adam that the black racists seek is really the son and heir of the old Adam of white racism. Away with all thought of new, innocent Adams; they will grow up to be even more evil than their guilty fathers.

As a special type of modern revolutionary, psychological men are trying to teach themselves how to be honest enough to enjoy the experience of self overpowering some other self, how to take pleasure straightforwardly in the experience of smashing the face of authority. But this is a pleasure and an honesty no culture can afford to admit openly. Violence cannot become a way of life. A violent culture is a dying one. In order to survive, a culture must endure the guilt it necessarily produces, for it is a structure by which certain possibilities are closed off, made impossible to conceive, repressed— but not eliminated. No culture can long endure massive and open violence, because violence is the principal means by which the impossible is made possible and nothing is 'not done.' In order to break the fatal modern symbolic of therapeutic violence that has overtaken the historic effort to cope with racism, antiracist theory must be maintained superior to, and judge of, all racial tactics. Here is a humane book, to help preserve us to the necessary antiracist theory, in control over the welter of racial tactics—however tragically necessary those tactics may be. Only under the name of right theory can we preserve our saving sense of what is not to be done. (68:1)

34
Education and the Priestly Lie

Professor Counts is usually a teacher—indeed, a teacher of teachers. The function of the teacher is to help students to know the truth, even if they cannot love it. The teacher, if he respects his students as potential equals, ought to try to strip them of their illusions and of their loves—if their loves are illusions. When the teacher tries instead to bulwark illusions, he becomes a priest, and education a priestly lie.

Plainly, Professor Counts thinks of himself as a democratic educator. He thinks everybody can be and ought to be educated. In this, he is quite opposed to the tradition of the priestly lie, which would educate a few and control the rest by carefully manipulating their illusions to serve the purposes of high policy. But democrats have had their own priestly lies. Professor Counts subscribes to the myth of the common man. Even John Stuart Mill, whom Professor Counts would include in his pantheon of democrats, noticed that common men were "generally liars." Professor Counts notices nothing wrong:

> Faith in America has always been faith in common people. . . . If the age of
> the common man is in truth opening throughout the world . . . we should be
> well prepared by our history to play a great and significant role in this
> new age.[1]

Somehow, preparedness is the clue to Professor Counts's linking of education and American civilization. His argument is that, since America is the greatest power on earth, American civilization must be able to wield that power to good use at home and abroad. Education is the instrument he favors to express our civilization and justify our power. Enviously aware of the advertising charm of the great books in a civilization gone nostalgic for its moral patrimony, he proposes instead a "great education" to inculcate "a great conception of our civilization." But our civilization is not great, whatever it was, and a "great education" could only criticize it. The trouble with American education is not that it does not reflect American civilization enough, but that it reflects it too much. Professor Counts knows this. Embarrassed by the present, his book is divided between lyricism on our moral patrimony and manifestos on what education needs to do to be great in the future.

What education needs to do is to develop among the common men "such

Reprinted with permission of *The New Leader* 35, no. 43 (27 October 1952): 26. © 1952, the
American Labor Conference on International Affairs, Inc.
1. George S. Counts, *Education and American Civilization* (New York: Teacher's College,
1952).

a conception" of American civilization as will "prepare [the American people] to discharge with honor and strength the heavy responsibilities which history has placed firmly on their shoulders." Professor Counts has made education an agency of political policy. Dogmatic liberalism shares with totalitarianism the notion of education, not as free and critical, but as an agency of a given "civilization" in preserving itself. But self-preservation, or the honor of world power and responsibility, is not a proper end for education. Education is precisely the freedom and capacity to speculate that aristocracy or monarchy or totalitarianism may possibly be better than democracy. Otherwise, neither democratic values nor any others can ever be clarified. (Actually, Professor Counts is well behind the times. American education is already being converted into an instrument of national policy. Almost everybody has joined the love-feast of American civilization.)

Professor Counts is very lyrical. His book contains no analysis, for analysis kills love. It is full of references to our "glorious heritage" and to "north, south, east and west." But Professor Counts is also very ambivalent. The common man is somehow not up on his glorious heritage. "Whatever our present merits, whatever our future may hold, we possess a glorious heritage." But the glorious heritage is also not entirely adequate to "meet the needs of the times." Professor Counts is all for more "science" and more "technological advance." He is also for more "group living." "The schools lag far behind the march of events." They need more contemporaneity.

Fortunately, there is one part of our heritage we can continue to use without much modernizing: the doctrine of progress. Professor Counts is pleased to note that "even our most conservative interests always claim to be battling in the name of progress." Again, he is behind the times. The schools are up on progress, and science is the only thing a student is encouraged—even allowed—to take seriously aside from sports.

Professor Counts is a more innocent lover of American civilization than most. His cheerfulness is not posed; he is an old believer in progress, and his love is predicated on that belief. The new believers, however, have a more certain faith, for they do not expect progress. Indeed, for their infidelities they expect reaction and receive it without surprise. Professor Counts will always be surprised, and for that we must thank him. (52:4)

35

Emile Durkheim's *Education and Sociology*

All the great educational reformers have died disappointed men. On the very year (1808) in which Fichte proclaimed to the German nation that edu-

Reprinted from *American Sociological Review* 22, no. 2 (April 1957): 233–34.

cation was the only means of raising themselves, as a nation, and that
Pestalozzi was the only educator worth importing, Pestalozzi himself had his
coffin made and placed in his school; standing beside it, he delivered
gloomy speeches on his failure to wretched disciples. Friedrich Froebel
ended no more happily. He was associated with the wrong, or losing, side in
1848 and spent his few remaining years defending himself against official
suspicions of socialism. John Dewey, the inspired schoolmaster of America
in its Wilsonian interlude, might well have died a disappointed man. For his
pedagogical reforms only obscured his surpassing importance as a philosopher, while little of the subtlety of his philosophy passed over into his pedagogical reforms. Rousseau set up *Emile*, a seductive little straw child, who
would become a philosopher while all the while he was having fun becoming
an artisan. But no education in arts and crafts has ever produced a philosopher. And Rousseau, when he was honest, knew better; his pedagogy was a
revenge on philosophy. Nothing pleased him more than to fancy education
as a revolutionary instrument, destroying the intellectual and social order by
which he had decided to be exquisitely hurt.

Emile Durkheim was no educational reformer.[1] The great reforming theorists of education had been misled by their conception of it as an instrument
with which to alter the structure of authority in society. Rousseau and his
sort of enthusiast for education are revolutionary *manques*, children are
their proletariat, love is their ideology, and the schoolroom is the good society in microcosm. Durkheim had the sense to see microcosms are never
the models of macrocosms; on the contrary, in social life, it is the macrocosm that serves as a model for the microcosm. The school cannot dictate to
society; rather, society always dictates to the school. It is a pathetic, and
historic, error to treat the school as GHQ for any movement toward the new
society.

As a sociologist, Durkheim could not be a revolutionary mind, not even
an educational reformer. Where the revolutionary would see conflict of contents, the sociologist tends to see dysfunction. Thus Durkheim, as one of the
greatest of sociologists, understands education not in terms of content, but
of function: as the main institution communicating the modes of authority
from one generation to another. This is what Durkheim means when he
writes that "education is a socialization . . . of the younger generation."
Thus, in contrast with most of his predecessors, Durkheim emphasizes education as the conservative functioning of society. Treating education as "essentially a matter of authority," Durkheim is free from the characteristic
utopianism that renders so much otherwise first-rate literature in education
obsolete—and even foolish. Durkheim tells the reader of this small volume
that there can be no 'ideal' system of education. With Durkheim, and

---

1. Emile Durkheim, *Education and Sociology*, translated and with an introduction by
Sherwood D. Fox. Foreword by Talcott Parsons (Glencoe, IL: Free Press, 1956).

granted the further development of a sociology of education, the philosophy of education, as a more or less disguised form of utopia-building, finds a logical terminus.

Durkheim raises subtle and important problems, for which this collection of his writings in educational theory and pedagogy offers points of departure rather than discussions. For the contemporary sociologist, his brief references to the teacher as the necessary, exemplary, social type in a secular civilization opens one avenue of discussion; his reference to humanist, or literary, culture as merely another area of specialization points down another important avenue. In short, the book is full of hints at answers, if not full of answers. Perhaps most important of all, the sociologist of education in a mass democracy will want to submit Durkheim's book to the main question pressing upon the entire community of educators: if, as Durkheim says, education is a function of social authority, then what shall we make of the decline of authority that characterizes modern educational institutions on every level, from primary grades to graduate schools? Perhaps the school, the system of education entire, is losing its historic social function? Perhaps, in a mass society, the school cannot be the transmitter of civilized values but only a complex of training programs for various skill groups?

Durkheim cannot be expected to help us with questions of the above sort; he lived just a little while before questions relating to the fate of ancient institutions (or their functions) in a mass society became all too clear. Nevertheless, *Education and Sociology* contains discussions of continuing import. For one thing, Durkheim definitely wedded his sociology of education to a viable social psychology. As Talcott Parsons puts the matter in his useful Foreword: Durkheim grasped the essentials of the educative process in terms of the "internalization of culture as part of the structure of personality itself, not simply as providing an 'environment' within which the personality . . . functioned." To Talcott Parsons thanks are due for vindicating at last Durkheim as social psychologist and moreover for encouraging the translation and publication of these essays in the sociology of education. These fragments from the Durkheim canon are well placed within the reach of American sociologists and educators. (57:2)

36

From Clergyman to Don [1]

For seven centuries, from mid-twelfth to nineteenth, the teaching office in Western culture was largely adjuvant to the priestly. *Studium* illuminated

Reprinted from *Contemporary Sociology* 14, no. 3 (May 1985): 347–48.
1. A. J. Engel, *From Clergyman to Don: The Rise of the Academic Profession in Nineteenth-Century Oxford* (Oxford: Clarendon Press, 1983).

sacerdotum and advised *imperium*. In this cautious historical record, A. J. Engel reviews the facts in an important case in the larger history of the separation—the sociological word spells "secularization"—between the teaching and priestly offices.

Engel's case is Oxford in the mid-nineteenth century. Then it was the clerical academic began to lose his grip on the university. That secularization by commission and omission is important because Oxford is Oxford, the most venerable and prestigious of academic place names in English and American culture. That secularization is important, too, because the case, like a neurotic on Freud's couch, can be used to see something otherwise hidden in the nighttime dynamics of secularization as it operates in younger cases and less prestigious places.

Without the theory of secularization, the facts in this case might not interest even a historian of Oxford. But the historian's facts are so manifestly restricted that they tempt the appetitive sociological theorist with their latent meanings. For example, early in chapter 1 (pp. 14–54), titled "Emerging Concepts of the Academic Profession 1800–1845," after only eight pages spent tracing early nineteenth-century proposals for recognizing college teaching as a life career instead of a station on the way to a parish church, Engel explores the unintended consequence, for Oxford, of Oxford's greatest and last religious movement before the religious parodied themselves in the very last Oxford Movement.

The Tractarian Movement aimed to save Oxford's piety; and, with piety, to revive learning and the soul of England. But Tractarianism led its greatest theorist, Oxford's Newman, to Catholicism. Catastrophe followed success, as night day. Newman's conversion to Rome meant, to the powers that were in Westminster, that "Oxford could no longer be regarded as a reliable defender of the Church of England" (p. 23). So, with Engel's fastidiously drawn facts, we arrive the more swiftly at an absurd truth: that England's last great movement of religious revival helped break the near-monopoly of Oxford teaching by the religious.

Sociologists of education and sociologists of religion, both, can flesh out their skeletal typologies with Engel's quintessentially Oxford type, the college tutor. After 1850, the college tutor, who had been a temporary don before he became a permanent parish priest, became "an Oxford don whose academic work was a career for life" (p. 280).

There is also, for sociological taste, the delicious issue of celibacy and "the general restriction of [College] fellowships to unmarried men" (see chapter 3, pp. 106–14). Taking on flesh, Engel's temporarily academic clergyman grew the more temporary and temporal with every desire to marry. Here is a paradox to amuse the gods in some other heaven: the academic clergyman could marry when he left Oxford for a parish church. In order to have both Oxford and a wife, some farsighted academic clergymen fought to change the old statutes; they succeeded, first at New College (founded 1379), in 1869. It is not within the historian's jurisdiction to tell us when New College went, as they say at Oxford, "mixed." That secularization took only just over a century.

The pace of secularization increases. Next we shall have, I predict, women priests and antiacademic academics. But first we will see the secularization of liberal education, with the latest research where the oldest wisdom has departed long since. But I grow incautious in my historical visions of total secularization: by which time the priestly and teaching offices, both, will have become dead matter in historical records as distinct from living historical memories. (85:1)

37

The Function of the Social Sciences and Humanities in a Science Curriculum [1]

Introduction

The sciences in which a college of technology is primarily interested have developed only since the beginning of the seventeenth century. No such college, nowadays, can avoid plunging its students into the hot crucibles of meaning that science—and its muscular sibling, technology—has constructed for the new cultures it has thus helped to make; nor can a science of technology avoid confronting the student with the still hot crucibles of meaning characteristic of cultures that science has helped to unmake.

If a college of technology is successfully to prepare students not only for their professional function as scientists and engineers, competent to handle the body of knowledge existing at a certain moment in time, but also for science as an activity worthy for its own sake, and often irrespective of any practical results which may follow from that activity, then this preparation must admit the religious motif into the student's idea of science and possibly even the scientific motif into the student's idea of religion. Science, like religion, is constantly changing; the science or engineering student needs to be prepared to exercise his intelligence and sensibilities in a trained and responsible way not merely upon changing scientific but also upon religious

Reprinted from *Religious Education* 54, no. 2 (March–April 1959): 156–63, by permission from the publisher, The Religions Education Association, 409 Prospect St., New Haven, CT.

1. A version of this paper was first presented to the Curriculum Committee of Harvey Mudd College, the newest of the Associated Claremont Colleges, at Claremont, California, 24 July 1958. The author wishes to thank the College and The Fund For The Advancement of Education for making possible this invaluable experience in college administration.

problems. The two categories of problems have never been entirely separable, and they grow less so under the impact of science and its method.

Science is not only an activity and a body of knowledge, but a method. Whatever his activity, however his body of knowledge changes, the science student ought to be trained to apply his critical judgments and creative intuitions to those morally ambiguous situations of crisis that always arise in the course of life—both public and private.

The role of the scientist and engineer in modern society, his function in the culture, is itself more ambiguous than at any other time in the relatively brief history of these professional men. Although the activities of the scientist and engineer have increased in relevance and import to societies everywhere, this is not to say that the scientist has acceded to power. Other trends—for example, the bureaucratization of professional and scientific life, the integration of scientific personnel into totalitarian democracies dominated by state party machines—indicate without exaggeration and only partially the multiple crises which confront the scientist in his function as scientist. The student in a science and engineering college will in time confront these crises in his double capacity as scientist and citizen; to understand their genesis and feel the necessity of contributing to their solution in a way that will preserve and augment the values of a free society is a vital part of scientific education—unless the scientist is to resign himself to the status of an unselfconscious instrument of the successive crises that have all but overwhelmed modern civilization. Unless the student in a science and engineering college is put in pursuit not only of knowledge, through his developed competence as a professional man, but also of the higher pleasures, as a man of culture, he will continue however unwittingly to destroy the conditions that make possible the pursuit of higher pleasures.

The Nature and Aims of Technological Schools
in Historical Perspective

Universities were first founded to pursue objectives religiously (or legalistically) defined. As late as the late nineteenth century, in most places, the laboratory and the scientist were still on the fringe of the academic community. Slowly and often reluctantly the colleges attached science faculties to themselves. The two have not lived easily or always successfully together—even to this day. Now the initiative for reform must come from those who hold power in the universities: the scientists and technologists themselves. The mission, in this age of technology, of the technical school is to reformulate, to encompass from the other end of the intellectual spectrum, the intellectual and moral questions once formulated by our religiously founded institutions of higher learning.

Some Limiting Conditions Upon the Formulation of the Social Sciences-Humanities Program at a Technological College

No one can underestimate the pressure of the science curriculum, or the covert pressure of more definitely articulated vocational motivations, upon engineering and science students. The resistance to a social-humanities program is likely to be greater in an engineering college than in other educational institutions. Add to these pressures the present apparent uncertainty about the nature and aims of the liberal arts curriculum, and there are the ingredients of a major crisis in scientific education. In this crisis, the aim of the social scientists and humanities faculties ought to be to transform this latent resistance (built into the situation) into manifest involvement in the liberal arts programs.

Certain Permitting Conditions

It is, I suggest, especially necessary for a technological school to build a logically structured and coherently interrelated social sciences and humanities program, one that will comprise a significant (thirty-three percent) part of the total educational experience, transferable and negotiable by the student as scientist and citizen. There is a perhaps spurious issue that will always be raised about the degree to which an undergraduate ought to be allowed to pick his own program. With particular reference to a science and engineering college, and with further particular reference to the complex and opaque but nonetheless worldwide crises in which the scientist finds himself, I suggest that it is the responsibility of the college to offer the student a program that will make him competently self-aware as a scientist. In this sense, given the distance between the problem and adolescent consciousness of the problem, it seems to me any educational revolution must be a revolution from above. The student interested in achieving competence in the narrower sense for purposes of a career cannot be legitimately expected to have the kind of long-term concerns that at present trouble the more sensitive parts of the scientific and educational communities.

Aims of a Social Sciences and Humanities Curriculum: The Widening of Horizons

As a primary aim, I would list the training of better scientists who will see their science as part of the culture, its relations with other disciplines, apparently remote, its interaction with the social and intellectual forces at work historically and contemporaneously: not simply as consumers of cultural tid-bits, but as potential producers at the frontiers of knowledge. A social science and humanities program that merely "exposes" the student to some of the best books and most firmly established thoughts in the welter of disciplines that make up the social sciences and humanities would not accomplish the training of better scientists and certainly would not accomplish the training of scientists better able to defend themselves and a free society against those totalitarian encroachments apparent not only in the political but also in the cultural realm.

It is not contradictory to aim at the transmission of tradition, both as process and as product. By tradition as *product*, I mean the best, and respectful attentiveness to the best, that has been written and thought. I am not above wishing to see a certain piety, a certain sentiment, developed for our masterworks and leading ideas, especially for students training professionally to confront current problems. The greatness of the past, and the continuity (as well as discontinuity) of present problems with the past, needs to be communicated. I would suggest the transmission of tradition as product as one aim of the liberal arts curriculum as a whole.

This aim is stated against the background of a problem I should like to call that of "scientific barbarism." This barbarism characterizes not merely the physical and material scientist, but also the social scientist. We have made the error of assigning the transmission of tradition too much to our specialists in the humanities, treating them as secular preachers of exhausted words. In fact, the task of communicating tradition as product ought to be shared by the entire faculty. It was Leibniz who suggested that the scientist had to extricate himself from his limiting and often conflicting cultural tradition and build a supracultural tradition in a supranational community. This aim has been largely achieved, but at a cost which must now be reassessed, in particular with reference to the education of future generations of scientists. A memory-less people, as Jacob Burckhardt once pointed out, is a barbaric people, whatever their level of technical competence. Here, I am consciously denying the still influential dogma of the late nineteenth century positivism, which presumed that we had passed through the "theological" and "metaphysical" stages of societal development and were now at last in the "scientific stage." If one rejects this doctrine of progress, then the attitude toward past truths will be quite different from the positivist attitude.

By *process*, I mean emphasis on the dynamic characteristics of the tradition represented in the product studied. Tradition needs analysis, not merely respectful appreciation but analytic and critical scrutiny—*in its own terms.* I emphasize "in its own terms"; first of all, our aim ought to be to train science students in a usable awareness of other realities. I wish to quote a famous passage from Yeats:

God appointed Berkeley who proved all things a dream.
That this preposterous pragmatical pig of a world, its

Furrows that so solid seem,
Must vanish on the instant did the mind but change its theme.

The student ought to be trained in the capacity to analyze and appreciate the beauty as well as the utility of other constructed realities. I should like to introduce here a passage with which I both agree and disagree, but one which I consider so significant as to merit quoting in this particular context. Hobbes writes:

> The end . . . of philosophy is not the inward glory and triumph of mind that a man may have for the mastery of some difficult and doubtful matter, or for the discovery of some hidden truth. [This] is not worth so much pain as the study of philosophy requires; nor need any man care much to teach another what he knows himself, if he thinks that will be the only benefit of his labor. The end of knowledge is power; and the use of theorems . . . is for the construction of problems; and, lastly, the scope of all speculation is the performance of some action, or thing to be done.

So far as a technological college transmits major portions of our cultural legacies, its purposes—in the liberal arts program—are not different from that of programs in any liberal arts college. But too often there is an impulse to encourage liberal arts students to start, for instance, "first questions"— as if there were not, as in the sciences, broad and steady shoulders upon which to stand in order to see ahead. In a social sciences and humanities program, the primary aim ought to be so to teach the leading formulation of problems and the splendid variety of solutions thus far suggested in our intellectual trades, that a student will emerge trained in a basic competence to analyze and master said formulations (including the very language used so far as possible) carrying with him throughout life the capacity so to integrate this competence into his own intellectual and emotional life as to use it in ways that amount to personal reformulations. Such integration for personal use throughout life I would consider a major criterion of a successfully executed liberal arts program. After all, science students do not start from scratch, asking "first questions." They are taught, I take it, that physics or that chemistry generally conceded to be the correct one as presently understood by the appropriate professional community. This is dogma: a consensus of authoritative opinion.

To accomplish its aims, both as a college and especially as a college of science and engineering, with the aid of a generous allotment of time and concern to the social sciences and humanities, a technological college should, I suggest, establish certain basic and required courses as well as an integrated elective program. But before I offer these fledgling chicks of courses for the reader quickly to devour, let me say what brand of tender meat this is not.

These are not survey courses in which the aim is to provide the broadest possible nodding acquaintance with a wide variety of material, gathered from all the major disciplines and as many reputable writers as one can squeeze into such a course. The broad survey often lacks logic, structure and a unified theme. On the other hand, I am aware that a minimum structured and unified course runs the risk of losing students by the wayside. I should like here to distinguish between the structure of the curriculum, on the one hand, and the pedagogic conditions under which that curriculum is executed on the other. No student should be sacrificed to the "tough courses." It is the task of the faculty so to teach the "tough course" that it challenges and exhilarates even the relatively weak student. We are aware that no course reaches every student in its entirety. I would prefer a course, however, that may be reviewed by the student as a turning point in his intellectual development long after he has left the college. If the alternatives are to aim above or slightly below the student's head, then for the student's own sake I prefer to aim above his head.

The broad survey course may be organized in various ways. The student may hear something about the Second Punic War, the Industrial Revolution, read part or all of the *Republic*, all of *Brave New World*, *1984*, a selection from Margaret Mead, et cetera. Or the course may be put together from the various departments all exercising a temporal jurisdiction under a part of the survey. Thus, anthropology (if the department is strong) may get six weeks of the survey, while economics gets only three. Many survey courses operate in just this way, with younger departmental cadres stationed in them like soldiers in some dreary outpost, serving time before being allowed to return to the departmental capitol. Neither kind of survey seems to me desirable. Nor is the first kind of survey made more reasonable by a constant moralizing reference. The perennial attempt to read Plato in terms of contemporary authoritarianism, for example, seems to me to misdirect the student's intellectual energies and to freshen up a subject not in need of such misleading freshening.

An alternative to the types of survey courses rejected above might be courses with specific problem themes, aiming to train the students in the use of certain concepts, generally agreed upon as established and as important in our intellectual culture and which the science and engineering student in particular, ought to have had practice in confronting. I do not want to separate form and content in these courses; I consider form to be the implementation of analytical tools upon major and persisting problems. I consider the content of the courses to be these problems. In a sense, therefore, form and content merge. The student ought to be skilled in pulling apart the structure of an argument as well as in the recognition of alternative argument. An engineering student ought to have the experience of studying the topography of Dante's Inferno, so to say, with an intensity and closeness that he would give to more material topography. He ought to have the experience of studying the mechanics leading from faith to right conduct in Christian doctrine, for example, as seriously as he studies mechanisms closer to his own vocational interests.

One final remark before describing the specific order of basic courses I have in mind; these courses all have a Western orientation and can be easily criticized for saying little or nothing about the Orient or Africa. But I suggest that our own culture in many of its aspects, and with particular reference to its development, is as foreign to the student as the Mohammedan. To introduce the student to the fitness, as well as the familiarity of Western culture may, I believe, serve to obviate the objection stated above.

Order of Basic Courses

Required freshman course titled *Social Sciences—Humanities* ("Athens and Jerusalem")

The aim of this course would be to introduce the student to the methods and organization of the sciences, and, in a parallel way, to the methods and organization of religion in western culture. Central to this aim would be study of the place of science and scientific communication in various historic periods in the development of our culture and, in a parallel way, the study of the place of religion and religious communication. It is fair to speak of the origin of the scientific spirit in Greek Philosophy. Therefore, the first readings would consist of appropriate Greek thought, with special reference to the development of concepts, such as that of the nature of the universe, the religion of the one and the many, the basic circumstances that constitute matter and upon which all life is dependent, et cetera, as formulated by various Greek figures and schools. Here too, there would be readings and discussion of the early organization of scientific and philosophic communities and also study of their religious character. This theme could be carried through to recent formulations as given, for example, by Dewey in the last chapter of *Philosophy and Civilization*. There are ample and even brilliant readings, not only in Dewey, but in Whitehead, Santayana, et cetera. The emphasis throughout would be on problems and analytic concepts—for example the relation between myth and science. Here, secondary readings, such as Cassirer, can be available, but my own inclination is to keep the student working on more primary texts. Preliminary to this study of the origins and development of the scientific spirit in the west would be a study of the origin and development of the religious spirit. Here I would concentrate on three rich and fundamental terms:

1. *Faith* (which even within the Christian tradition meant something so different as, on the one hand, the hearing of the word and on the other, eschatological existence).

2. *Knowledge* (as either following or preceding faith, or as independent of it).
3. *The religiously organized community*—the idea of the church. Here one can introduce concepts of social organization, leadership, types of social discipline, the concept of a doctrine as ideology, that is, the church's understanding of its bureaucratization, et cetera. Such concepts can be brought into the specific problem or context of dominant, current Western religion. The readings here would be in the Old and New Testaments, with special emphasis on Paul, the Fourth Gospel, and then on St. Augustine, selections from the Fathers and St. Thomas.

On the other hand, I should like to see some of the later scientific readings so selected as to point up to the student the philosophical and theological background of Newton's genius or Kepler's worldview.

This basic course would be a joint venture of the social sciences and humanities faculty. In addition, I would consider it of the greatest importance that every member of the science faculty teach at some time in one section of the course, not alone, but paired with a social sciences-humanities colleague. This would serve to give the college population as a whole a shared intellectual experience in an analysis of the problems fundamental to the student as a potential scientist.

In the second year, the social sciences and humanities faculty would bifurcate to teach a course entitled, respectively, *Social Sciences* I ("Social Systems" or "Society in Transition") and *Humanities* I ("Culture in Transition"). In the *Social Sciences* I course, given in the second year, one might begin with a survey of what is conceptualized in the social sciences as "problems of social organization." Thus, by way of introduction, the course would survey types of fundamental social organizations and their ideological concomitants on the one hand; family, primary group, "primitive" social organization (extended family, clan, tribe, et cetera) caste, class, status, social role. On the other hand: magic, myth, ritual.

Once this unit of the course, with appropriate reading from the literature of anthropology, had been completed, attention would focus on the major problem of the course—the shift from feudalism to capitalism in Western society. Here, secondary readings, such as Ganshof's little book on feudalism, are quite useful. I am not insisting throughout this sequence of courses on the reading in primary texts; nor is the exegetical talent, I believe, what would be sought, even in a secondary way, in this particular course. Nevertheless, once having reached the problem of the rise of capitalism and the social organization implied in that term, certain readings would demand exegetical skill. For example, a key reading would be Marx's *The Communist Manifesto*, a work which certainly demands the closest textual scrutiny, as does the selection of some of his other writings I would think appropriate to the course.

Moreover, in this course, the religion-science thread, never completely broken in the introductory phase of the course, would reappear closely in the reading and discussion of the impact of religion upon science and technology (and vice-versa). Further readings within this section would include selections from Malthus, Weber's *Protestant Ethic*, Tawney's *Religion and The Rise of Capitalism*, selections from the works of R. K. Merton on the relationship between scientific endeavor and Protestant faith in seventeenth- and eighteenth-century England; selections from Luther, Calvin and certain Catholic writers, and selections from such key secondary reference works as Mantoux or Toynbee on the industrial revolution and perhaps one work of modern monographic scholarship, such as John Nef's brilliant study of the rise of the British coal industry.

Major themes in the development of this larger part of the course would be:

1. The decline of a civilization of authority.
2. The rise of "modern civilization."
3. The development of technology and technological classes as well as the "middle classes."

Of necessity, I must describe the *Humanities* I course more briefly. My aim in this course would be to select three or four major epochs in Western culture and closely examine the literature, art, philosophy and social structure of these epochs. To enumerate:

1. The culture of Southern renascence, beginning perhaps with Petrarch and emphasizing development of a secular as contrasted with sacred literature.
2. The culture of the Northern renascence, focusing exclusively on Elizabethan culture—the Elizabethan drama, Elizabethan audience, other aspects of Elizabethan culture.
3. Victorian culture, in particular reactions against and responses to the new intellectual civilization. Here, I would include not only some of the great Victorian novelists, but figures such as Ruskin.
4. The culture of the American renascence, with special reference to the figures so denominated in F. O. Mathiessen's book of that title.

In the third year, the social sciences-humanities staff would again merge to teach a required course titled "Personalities and Culture" or "Modern Personalities and Modern Culture." Here, the major thematic unity would be achieved around the emerging theme of identity as suffered by modern man. The major subsidiary theme would be worked around the concept of the "burden" or "problem" of modern civilization. For readings I would begin with Rousseau, who first influenced formulation of the concepts of civilization as a burden, and go on to such reading as Freud offers, including *Civilization and Its Discontents*, and his great essay on "'Civilized' Sexual Morality and Modern Nervousness." Further readings in contemporary

SUMMARY OF PLAN

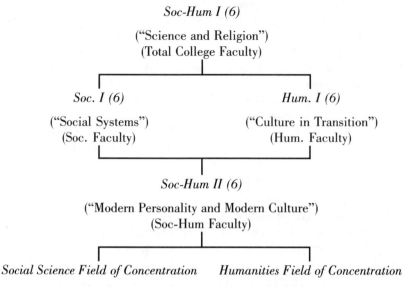

Soc-Hum I (6)

("Science and Religion")
(Total College Faculty)

Soc. I (6)   *Hum. I (6)*

("Social Systems")   ("Culture in Transition")
(Soc. Faculty)   (Hum. Faculty)

Soc-Hum II (6)

("Modern Personality and Modern Culture")
(Soc-Hum Faculty)

Social Science Field of Concentration   *Humanities Field of Concentration*

I. Economics   I. Aesthetics
   a. —   a. Industrial design
   b. —   b. Introduction to art
   c. —   c. —
II. Industrial Sociology   II. ——

depth psychology might include Erich Fromm's *Escape From Freedom*, et cetera. (*The Future Of An Illusion* or *Escape from Freedom* would permit the course again to continue to analyze in yet another way the supposed conflict between religion and science.)

On the humanities side, I would have an equal, if not superior, number of readings, including novels, poetry and criticisms, not excluding critical study of the impressionist and expressionist movement in the world of painting. Certainly, on the problem of identity, Kafka, Joyce, Eliot, Forster, Yeats and others have had, perhaps, a more profound and certainly more moving thing to say than has been said by anyone that could be even remotely a social or behavioral scientist.

In the fourth year, there would be no required course in either the social sciences or the humanities, but two major areas of concentration within which a student could elect to study.

Within the social sciences concentration, I would put such clusters of electives as economic analysis, money and banking, et cetera; or, group dynamics, business administration, et cetera. In the humanities area of concentration, the student might elect to take a course in art and technology, in which he could pay specific attention to problems of industrial design, the aesthetics of the factory, et cetera. My intention here is twofold:

1. To give the student who has completed the basic courses in the social sciences-humanities division, a chance to concentrate on one or another problem area raised during his three years of work in the integrated program.
2. I should like to see every member of the social sciences-humanities faculty able to teach within his own special areas of scholarly concentration. A significant part of the area of concentration program would thus be shaped by the social sciences-humanities faculty and offered on home ground and point forward to the selection of courses on the graduate level that might continue the specific programs within one or the other areas of concentration as developed by a social sciences and humanities faculty primarily concerned with undergraduate instruction in a technological college. (59:3)

38
The Cultural Economy of Higher Education

I

Matter and Manner. The matter of higher education has always been vocational; the manner has always been suppressive and repressive. In matter and manner, until almost our own time, the purposes of our colleges and universities, as teaching institutions, were derived from the order of authority more or less explicit in the culture.

II

Colleges as Cultural Institutions. By "cultural institutions," I mean those specially attendant upon teaching the more or less complex order of authority by which a culture becomes operative. The family is, in this meaning, a cultural institution; its teaching functions are usually more operative than illuminative. The teaching functions of colleges are usually more illuminative than operative. Conduct does not follow insight. Colleges and universities must depend upon cultural institutions operatively prior to

Between October 22 and 24, 1982, Philip Rieff participated in the Liberty Fund, Inc. Seminar on the Political Economy of Higher Education held by the Law and Economics Center at Emory University. This paper is published here for the first time. Citations to various quotations have been added by the editor.

themselves in order to enact their illuminative functions—to cultivate a reasonably knowing, articulate, and accommodating membership in the culture. (That John Dewey found it necessary to rediscover—even reconceive—American education as an adaptation to the social environment signifies something more than the banality of Dewey as a theorist of education; that the "adaptive" function could have been taken as a fresh truth—or as a new betrayal of the purpose of higher education—may tell us something more about the order of authority from which colleges and universities derive their purpose.) The operative institutions in our culture appear to be doing their job less and less well. The university as an illuminative institution appears to create a crisis of authority that must threaten its place in the larger cultural economy.

III

The Hierarchical Structure of Culture and the Place of the University in That Structure. A vital culture exists as a highly stipulative and complex order of authority. The latest teaching (and research) institutions, like the earliest (such as the family) illuminate, and therefore confirm, the operative order of authority.

IV

The Meaning of Authority. By "authority" I mean an order of accredited facts, and the corresponding beliefs in their commanding truths, by which life is conducted within the range of that authority. The range of authority is always and everywhere interdictory, remissive, and transgressive in respect to what is possible; a primacy of possibility is the first impossibility. So far as humans are uncultivated characters—whether that want of personal cultivation (in the old German word, *bildung*) or "graven character" (Kierkegaard), be titled "instinctual" or "impulsive" or "natural," as if opposed to "cultural"—they are transgressive. The function of all teaching institutions, early and late, illuminative and operative, is to accredit the belief of members in that order of authority as a commanding fact in their lives. Education is the higher the more certainly it achieves the truth of making belief and fact correspond. A higher education has the task of installing the correspondence theory of truth. It is this truth that makes humans free and gives them such liberty as they may then have. Belief tests fact quite as much as fact tests belief.

V

The "Correspondence Theory" of Truth. In any order of authority, higher education is the inevitably chosen instrument of its theoretical truth. That truth implies not only a certain correspondence between belief and fact and a certain opposition between affirmation and negation. "A belief is true when there is a corresponding fact, and is false when there is no corresponding fact."[1] Russell's famous statement of the correspondence theory of truth does assert that judging or believing is a "complex unity"[2] of which our minds are only "a constituent." What makes a belief true or false is not for minds to "create." "Nevertheless, it moves," murmured Galileo, in an inspired moment of modernity. The fact of the earth's motion did not in any way revolve around the mind of the person who believed or did not believe. A mind "believes truly when there is a corresponding complex not involving the mind, but only its objects."[3]

VI

The Order of Authority and the Direction of Truth. His ecclesiastical judges reckoned Galileo had elaborated, before his recantation, an objective falsehood; but, also, he had committed a transgression. Galileo's "truth" had committed a fundamental offense against the ruling direction of Yes-feelings and No-feelings with respect to the motion of the earth. Quite characteristic of what is vital in a culture, if not a truth that maintained itself as complex enough in its unity of subjective belief and objective fact, the champions of ecclesiastical and scientific truth asserted their "No-feeling" against the Galilean "Yes."

VII

The Order of Authority is a Complex Unity of Interdicts (No thoughts and feelings) and *remissions* ("Yes" as exceptions to the No); to the verge of *transgression* or that thought or act in which the interdict is broken without excusing reason and is therefore utterly wrong.

VIII

The Development of the Modern University. That development parallels the triumph of the therapeutic[4] with its endless reasons for doubting the interdictory level of authority (the No-feelings) while excusing with apparent rationality the transgressive levels. Thus, the strange place of the "deviant," the "revolutionary," and the "criminal" in the pantheon of remissive rationalists.

1. Bertrand Russell, *The Problems of Philosophy* (Oxford: Oxford University Press, 1954), 129.
2. Ibid.
3. Ibid.
4. See Philip Rieff, *The Triumph of the Therapeutic*, 2d ed. (Chicago: University of Chicago Press, 1987), 1–27 and 232–61.

IX

The Millenarianism of an Archetypal Remissive Theorist: The Case of Bertrand Russell. He stands for armies of lesser minds in the academic world. Russell carried on the remissive rationalist assault upon orders of authority in which the interdicts are highest in any order, as they must be. His life-long confidence in "rational doubt," the exercise of excusing reasons, amounted to a form of millenarianism. "Thus rational doubt alone, if it could be generated, would suffice to introduce the Millennium."[5] All dogmas have fallen except the antidogma of the remissive intellectual elites who now dominate higher education. They attack the interdictory (No) level of every order and thus open the way to resurgences of the transgressive (Yes) level.

X

An Illuminative Attack on the Interdictory Feeling (The No-Level of Any Right Order of Authority), Calling It False.
    "Every belief which is not merely an impulse to action is in the nature of a picture, combined with a Yes-feeling or a No-feeling; in the case of a Yes-feeling it is 'true' if there is a fact having to the picture the kind of similarity that a prototype has to an image; in the case of a No-feeling it is 'true' if there is no such fact."[6]

XI

No Such Fact. The "No-feeling," as truth, refers to the crucial civilizing function of repression. A "No" refers to that process of denial of what is fundamentally offensive, by which the fact is distanced and distorted, until it is rendered acceptable to consciousness and rationality. The rationalist doubters have never grasped the repressive activity of teaching as fundamental to it. Conscious suppression of the "No-fact," the fundamentally offensive and therefore inadmissible, is based upon unconscious repression and then upon the delicate balancing of interdicts and their remissions—to the verge of transgression.

XII

A Moving and Delicate Balancing. Interdicts and their remissions, in an unconsciously repressive mode rendered by higher education in part consciously suppressive and rational, constitutes, inseparably from vocational

    5. Bertrand Russell, *Let the People Think* (London: Watts & Co., 1941), 27.
    6. Bertrand Russell, *Human Knowledge: Its Scope and Limits* (New York: Simon & Schuster, 1948), 154.

teaching, the civilizing mission of all educational institutions. That civilizing mission was carried out by a repressive elite that followed minds that would be virgin, fleeing to virgin lands which could be raped without giving fundamental offense to the custodians of old No-feelings.

XIII

The Growth of the Colleges in the 1880s. That growth can be best understood as the effort of the repressive elite to contain the "impulse" life of those who fled westward, for land and their ego's autonomy, from the inherited order of authority, itself never static but constantly recreating itself as a complex unity. Professor Horace Bushnell of Yale, who was also the pastor of the North Church in Hartford, Connecticut, and author of *Nature and Nurture* and other treatises on the control of the populace, delivered in New York, Boston, and other places, in 1847, a discourse characteristic of the repressive elite: "Barbarism—The First Danger." A migrant America "cannot carry its roots with it."[7] The colleges of the 1800s were to work upon tastes that would otherwise grow wild, upon resentments that would escape into violence, and upon enjoyments coarsened by the wilderness. Bushnell wrote:

> The salutary restraints of society being to a great extent removed [from the westward migrants], they will think it no degradation to do before the woods and wild animals what, in the presence of a cultivated social state, they would blush to perpetuate.[8]

The colleges, along with the churches, were home missionary institutions designed to recreate among the migrants a cultivated social state. Of course, the state could be assumed to help in preventing the rise of a "bowie-knife civilization." Bushnell could not conceive of bureaucrats who were themselves enchanted with the notion of abolishing the repressions and constantly doubting the No-feelings. Those little colleges, having lost their sense of direction and purpose, are lost, for they were not centers of vocational training, but centers of final preparation for that training. It is in this sense that the colleges were "religious institutions"; they shared with their churches the elaboration of those repressive and suppressive symbols within which liberty represented itself. The learning of the colleges and universities could not be conceived as ends in themselves. Subsequent vocational training, like doctrinal learning, formed a defensive ring of thought and action around the unthinkable primacy of possibility—the will to transgression of which "life-style" is a current euphemism. The bureaucrat and the

7. Horace Bushnell, "Barbarism—The First Danger." Reprinted in *On Intellectuals*, edited by Philip Rieff (New York: Doubleday & Co., 1969), 170.

8. Ibid., 170–71.

professor are chairpersons of the same cloth. In the society of which the modern university is a part, the temporal and spiritual realm have been largely united in a new remissive elite that staffs both the universities and the government. This remissive elite is the key to our understanding the cultural economy of higher education in America.

XIV

The Key to the Remissive Elite. Its defense of the rights of minorities throughout society is rarely if ever in defense of any minority thought superior. "Superiority" can scarcely be said to exist except as a pejorative. The defense of the rights of minorities, thought unjustly made "inferior" by the inherited order of authority, expresses that leveling process which is the single greatest expression of the aim of the remissive elite in the modern university.

XV

Where the Remissive Elite Has Led: The remissive elite has led to a glacial shift toward identification downward in the social order, especially by the more pious among the student populace of rational doubters who doubt that any of the interdicts are true. Until the explosion of post-Christian sentimentalism in the university, during the so-called student revolution of the late 1960s, there was always a student identification upward in the social structure, even if that identification was, among the small but noisy minority of students, with a Marxist elite. The unprecedented identification downward is visible in the language as well as in the body gestures and body imagery of students. The universities have failed to address the question of language and body imagery, and the reality of modern college and university life is an ever-widening gap between professional skill and personal grace.

XVI

Reason Can Always Find Excusing Reasons. What can literally be seen as a generational, but more than generational, as indeed a massive and by now institutionalized identification downward is the work of armies of educators, the successors of the pastorate as a guiding elite. Yet the most influential culture class in American society is the black underclass; that class constitutes the functional equivalent of Christ's publicans and sinners, as against the Pharisaical white middle class. This is a post-Christian symbolism, representing truth as the remissive elite would teach it, the significance of which cannot be overestimated; so important is this symbolism, yet so infinitely fragile, that the symbolic can scarcely suffer criticism. This is not surprising, since the remissive elite must live in two worlds, this world of identification downwards, and the other world of their identification upwards: toward the seizure of power in the state as it has seized power in the university, the mass media and the popular culture industry.

XVII

Can the Matter of Learning (even in that politest fiction of it as an apparent end in itself) Be Separated from the Manner? The answer to this question is a feeling No. The skill and grace that is achieved by such learning as becomes an end in itself must become characteristic of those who have retained such learnedness. It is a matter of character as well as of intellect. The rightful complaints from contemporary students about the impersonality of the university are not directed primarily to the size of the university so much as to the default of the university so far as it addresses the intellect without addressing the character or the body imagery of the student. That character and body imagery must be graven in the refinements of learning that are transmitted, whether that learning be in the humanities or in the natural sciences. The authority of the university, so far as it is intellectual, cannot be separated from the persons being so minded. The ancients understood this and, consequently, moral and bodily disciplines were as much a part of pedagogic concern as training in particular bodies of competencies and what we would call professional skills.

XVIII

The Personal Character of Truth under the Authority of the University. The much boasted search for truth as describing the authoritative purpose or end of the university cannot be separated from the subjective character of truthfulness. Aristotle rightly understood that truthfulness is a matter of character and cannot be abstracted from the truth. Belief and fact join in the truth of character. I remind you of that passage on the character of truth, in the tradition of Athens, upon which the academy depends still:

> Truthfulness is a mean between self-depreciation and boastfulness. It has to do, of course, with words, but not with all words. For the boaster is he who pretends to have more than he has, or to know what he does not know; while the self-depreciator, on the other hand, lays claim to less than he really has and does not declare what he knows, but tries to hide his knowledge. But the truthful man will do neither of these things. For he will not pretend either to more than he has or less, but will say that he has and knows what as a matter of fact he does have and does know.[9]

9. Aristotle, *Magna Moralia*, translated by St. George Stock (Oxford: Clarendon Press, 1915), Book I, 29, 1193ª.

This relates truthfulness, in the Aristotelean doctrine of the mean, to the moral virtue of modesty. Therefore, Aristotle prepares us for the stipulation of what truthfulness means by the stipulation of what modesty means.

> Modesty is a mean between shamelessness and bashfulness, and it has to do with deeds and words. For the shameless man is he who says and does anything on any occasion or before any people; but the bashful man is the opposite of this, who is afraid to say or do anything before anybody (for such a man is incapacitated for action, who is bashful about everything); but modesty and the modest man are a mean between these. For he will not say or do anything under any circumstances, like the shameless man, nor, like the bashful man, be afraid on every occasion and under all circumstances, but will say and do what he ought, where he ought, and when he ought.[10]

It remains the function of the educational arm in any order of authority to inculcate these moral virtues. Intellect without character is bound to make too much of itself.

XIX

Like the death of Satan, the intellectualization of the world has been a tragedy for the Western imagination. That intellectualization describes our present incapacity to transmit character with intellect; or even worse, the transmission of character, in covert and implicit disciplines of endless unprepared criticism, of an intellectuality that is relentlessly remissive. The remissive elites of our universities are "radicals" in their singular skill of pulling up roots in a manner that must kill them: this skill seems to be motivated, as Aristotle would have it, by "a mean state between enviousness and malice." More precisely, our armies of academic intellectuals seem to combine the teaching of envy with the practice of malice.

XX

Vocational Training: Better than Nothing. In default of the legitimate purpose of higher education—the repressive and suppressive discipline coordinate with the culture—primacy has been assigned to vocational training. The opposition so easily constructed by the humanists between learning as an end in itself and the provision of vocational training in the colleges and universities, has been and remains, however enchanting, false. From their mediaeval origins, the colleges and universities provided a vocational training for clerics in the broadest sense of the term—that is, for notaries, secretaries, and other minor members of the pastoral institution of the church; for civil and canon lawyers; for medical men and for the intellectual elite,

10. Ibid., Book I, 32, 1193ᵃ.

theologians and philosophers. That learning as such was an end in itself would have been foreign to the universities at their origin or during their various renaissances. Universities always have participated fully, even at times participant as places of retreat, if not downright somnolence, in the life of their societies. Within each university there were many voices that spoke from the university rather than for it. The university has always been more of an arena than a cloister. It rarely spoke with a single voice, when it spoke at all.

XXI

One voice expressed brilliantly the repressive nature of the university, its inseparability from the No feeling at the height of every order of authority. Listen to Newman's voice as it spoke of what happens when that No-feeling, and its knowledge, is denied on behalf of the young by their teachers. Then, again and again, as Newman said in his sixth lecture on the idea of a University:

> The first time the mind comes across the arguments and speculations of unbelievers, and feels what a novel light they cast upon what he has hitherto accounted sacred; and still more, if it gives in to them and embraces them, and throws off as so much prejudice what it has hitherto held, and, as if waking from a dream, begins to realize to its imagination that there is now no such thing as law and the transgression of law, that sin is a phantom, and punishment a bugbear, that it is free to sin, free to enjoy the world and the flesh; and still further, when it does enjoy them, and reflects that it may think and hold just what it will, that "the world is all before it where to choose," and what system to build up as its own private persuasion; when this torrent of willful thoughts rushes over and inundates it, who will deny that the fruit of the tree of knowledge, or what the mind takes for knowledge, has made it one of the gods, with a sense of expansion and elevation,—an intoxication in reality, still, so far as the subjective state of the mind goes, an illumination? Hence the fanaticism of individuals or nations who suddenly cast off their Maker. Their eyes are opened; and, like the judgment-stricken king in the Tragedy, they see two suns, and a magic universe, out of which they look back upon their former state of faith and innocence with a sort of contempt and indignation, as if they were then but fools, and the dupes of imposture.[11]

XXII

The Dupes of Imposture, Nowadays, Accept a Post-Christian Sentimentalism. That "ism" dominates our elite universities, so far as they are not what they must be: vocational training schools.

11. John Henry Cardinal Newman, *The Idea of a University* (1852) (London: Longmans, Green, 1910), 132–33.

Post-Christian sentimentalism can be studied in such recent specimens of it as the following: "All social primary goods—liberty and opportunity, income and wealth, and the bases of self-respect—are to be distributed equally unless an unequal distribution of any or all of these goods is to the advantage of the least favored." [12]

XXIII

The Origins of Post-Christian Sentimentalism as Modern Social Science. See, for a specimen of the original post-Christian Yes-feeling, "The New Christianity" by the Count de Saint-Simon. In that dialogue, there is but a single supreme command: that humans shall "organize their society so that the poorest class may be guaranteed the most prompt and complete betterment of its moral and physical existence." [13]

XXIV

The university, both past and present, does not derive its strength from endowments and from social prestige; nor does it derive its strength from tranquility. The university, both past and present, derives its strength from its own turbulent life; not least, the life of struggle over how to stipulate the symbols of No and Yes, interdicts and remissions, in an order of authority which cannot be abolished. From Saint-Simon to Rawls, the dominant symbolists, now installed in the major colleges and universities, have been emphatically remissive. Not that any culture can maintain its vitality without its excusing and equitable reasons for doing what is otherwise not to be done. But, for the sake of the truth and its vitality, remissive motifs can never grow dominant. There is that which must remain inexcusable, unpardonable (and punishable by death).

XXV

The Remissive Establishment. Its great sanctuary, the modern university, has been made a prison of its own increasing fortunes, by promising various prompt and complete interventions into private lives, in exchange for more and more dependence upon cognate remissive establishments—interventionist bureaucracies.

12. John Rawls, *A Theory of Justice* (Cambridge, MA: Harvard University Press, 1971), 303.
13. See Henri de Saint-Simon, "New Christianity" (1825) in *Social Organization, The Science of Man and Other Writings*, edited and translated and with a preface and introduction by Felix Markham (New York: Harper & Row, 1964), 81–116.

XXVI

The modern university will protect itself, of course. Unlike its mediaeval predecessor, the modern university cannot fold its tents and pitch them elsewhere. It cannot conduct its business in hired rooms or in private houses. It is no longer a place which possesses few books and little money. Its scholars will not beg from house to house, and its students expect the university to fulfill a number of functions that must be called luxuries. The "problem-solving" and project-developing university is hostage to its own endless promises or hints of success. The more "successful" the university has become, the more hostages it must give to that success. Therefore, the more timid it becomes, especially in view of its growing distrust in the notion that it does have its own inner life and inner resources, however turbulent those inwardnesses may be. The American institutions of higher education in particular have not been tested by adversity and serious persecution. Those elements of persecution that individuals have suffered have been greatly exaggerated. The European universities, in their periods of persecution during the 1930s and again nowadays, not least in Germany, have not performed in ways that encourage us to believe that we can live up to the honor implicit in the dignity of "academic freedom."

XXVII

Applications of Marxist and Weberian Theory. The character necessary for success in the business domain opposes the teaching character of the university, so far as that teaching must be of deeply prepared traditions of knowledge and wisdom.

The Marxist Analysis of the Character Necessary for Success. This analysis can be summarized best by quoting from the "Communist Manifesto." The passage has not lost its shock value, I think; nor, perhaps, its truth: that our propertied classes are anything but culturally conservative.

> The bourgeoisie has played a most revolutionary role in history.
>
> The bourgeoisie, wherever it has got the upper hand, has put an end to all feudal, patriarchal, idyllic relations. It has pitilessly torn asunder the motley feudal ties that bound man to his 'natural superiors' and has left no other bond between man and man than naked self-interest, than callous 'cash payment.' It has drowned the most heavenly ecstasies of religious fervor, of chivalrous enthusiasm, of philistine sentimentalism, in the icy water of egotistical calculation. It has resolved personal worth into exchange value, and in place of the numberless indefeasible chartered freedoms, has set up that single, unconscionable freedom—Free Trade. In one word, for exploitation, veiled by religious and political illusions, it has substituted naked, shameless, direct, brutal exploitation.

The bourgeoisie has stripped of its halo every occupation hitherto honored and looked up to with reverent awe. It has converted the physician, the lawyer, the priest, the poet, the man of science, into its paid wage-laborers.

The bourgeoisie has disclosed how it came to pass that the brutal display of vigor in the Middle Ages, which reactionaries so much admire, found its fitting complement in the most slothful indolence. It has been the first to show what man's activity can bring about. It has accomplished wonders far surpassing Egyptian pyramids, Roman aqueducts, and Gothic cathedrals; it has conducted expeditions that put in the shade all former migrations of nations and crusades.

The bourgeoisie çannot exist without constantly revolutionizing the instruments of production, and thereby the relations of production, and with them the whole relations of society. Conservation of the old modes of production in unaltered form was, on the contrary, the first condition of existence for all earlier industrial classes. Constant revolutionizing of production, uninterrupted disturbance of all social conditions, everlasting uncertainty and agitation distinguish the bourgeois epoch from all earlier ones. All fixed, fast-frozen relations, with their train of ancient and venerable prejudices and opinions, are swept away, all new-formed ones become antiquated before they can ossify. All that is solid melts into air, all that is holy is profaned, and man is at last compelled to face with sober senses his real conditions of life and his relations with his kind.

The need of a constantly expanding market for its products chases the bourgeoisie over the whole surface of the globe. It must nestle everywhere, settle everywhere, establish connections everywhere.[14]

Just as Marxist theory imagines "the executive of the modern state is but a committee for managing the common affairs of the whole bourgeoisie," higher education may be viewed as that institution for legitimating the relentlessly antitraditional and unstable culture of the propertied classes.

XXVIII

Weberian Theory Argues the Opposite Case to the Same End. In Weberian theory, as against Marxist, the spirit of modern capitalism was originally religious and specifically Calvinist; that spirit is now lost. The loss must be seen in our universities, so far as they are of the Western capitalist world. Weber's peroration is not less worth full display; it is a gem, still. It endures and therefore requires regular rereading and reconsideration.

One of the fundamental elements of the spirit of modern capitalism, and not only of that but of all modern culture: rational conduct on the basis of the idea of the calling, was born—that is what this discussion has sought to dem-

14. Karl Marx and Friedrich Engels, *The Communist Manifesto* (New York: International Publishers, 1948), 11–12.

onstrate—from the spirit of Christian asceticism. One has only to re-read the passage from Franklin, quoted at the beginning of this essay, in order to see that the essential elements of the attitude which was there called the spirit of capitalism are the same as what we have just shown to be the content of the Puritan worldly asceticism, only without the religious basis, which by Franklin's time had died away. The idea that modern labor has an ascetic character is of course not new. Limitation to specialized work, with a renunciation of the Faustian universality of man which it involves, is a condition of any valuable work in the modern world; hence deeds and renunciation inevitably condition each other today. This fundamentally ascetic trait of middle-class life, if it attempts to be a way of life at all, and not simply the absence of any, was what Goethe wanted to teach, at the height of his wisdom, in the *Wanderjahren*, and in the end which he gave to the life of his *Faust*. For him the realization meant a renunciation, a departure from an age of full and beautiful humanity, which can no more be repeated in the course of our cultural development than can the flower of the Athenian culture of antiquity.

The Puritan wanted to work in a calling; we are forced to do so. For when asceticism was carried out of monastic cells into everyday life, and began to dominate worldly morality, it did its part in building the tremendous cosmos of the modern economic order. This order is now bound to the technical and economic conditions of machine production which today determine the lives of all the individuals who are born into this mechanism, not only those directly concerned with economic acquisition, with irresistible force. Perhaps it will so determine them until the last ton of fossilized coal is burnt. In Baxter's view the care for external goods should only lie on the shoulders of the "saint like a light cloak, which can be thrown aside at any moment." But fate decreed that the cloak should become an iron cage.

Since asceticism undertook to remodel the world and to work out its ideals in the world, material goods have gained an increasing and finally an inexorable power over the lives of men as at no previous period in history. Today the spirit of religious asceticism—whether finally, who knows?—has escaped from the cage. But victorious capitalism, since it rests on mechanical foundations, needs its support no longer. The rosy blush of its laughing heir, the Enlightenment, seems also to be irretrievably fading, and the idea of duty in one's calling prowls about in our lives like the ghost of dead religious beliefs. Where the fulfillment of the calling cannot directly be related to the highest spiritual and cultural values, or when, on the other hand, it need not be felt simply as economic compulsion, the individual generally abandons the attempt to justify it at all. In the field of its highest development, in the United States, the pursuit of wealth, stripped of its religious and ethical meaning, tends to become associated with purely mundane passions, which often actually give it the character of sport.

No one knows who will live in this cage in the future, or whether at the end of this tremendous development entirely new prophets will arise, or there will be a great rebirth of old ideas and ideals, or, if neither, mechanized petrification, embellished with a sort of convulsive self-importance. For of the last stage of this cultural development, it might well be truly said: "Specialists without spirit, sensualists without heart; this nullity imagines that it has attained a level of civilization never before achieved."

But this brings us to the world of judgments of value and of faith. . . .[15]

XXIX

I conclude that, seen through Marxist or Weberian prisms, the university was the last surviving institution of a Church civilization; that civilization has only just ended, as historical time drags. Much remains of the university, even as little remains of the church.

XXX

The College as an Institution of Traditionalist Critical Authority. Noah Porter, in his inaugural address as president of Yale University, expressed the self-understanding of the college as such an institution. His address continues to merit our affection, so far as we continue in search of an institution within which to reconcile the training of our critical powers and the continuity between successive generations in those social orders of authority within which those critical powers can be expressed other than transgressively. What more do we academics really want than Porter's thought?

> Let any reflecting man think for a moment of the trickery of business, the jobbing of politicians, the slang of newspapers, the vulgarity of fashion, the sensationalism of popular books, the shallowness and cant that dishonor pulpit and defile worship, and he may reasonably rejoice that there is one community which, for a considerable period, takes in its keeping many of the most susceptible and promising of our youth to impart to them better tastes, higher aims and, above all, to teach them to despise all sorts of intellectual and moral shams.[16]

XXXI

The College as the Critical and Traditional Authority of American Society. In Porter's address, the aspiration of the American college to become such an authority is made explicit. This aspiration appeared settled about a hundred years ago. Is it still the settled aim of the university? I think not. What aim has replaced it? Traditionalist critical authority, located in the college,

15. Max Weber, *The Protestant Ethic and the Spirit of Capitalism*, translated by Talcott Parsons (New York: Charles Scribner's Sons, 1958), 180–82.

16. See Professor Noah Porter's Inaugural Address, in *Addresses at the Inauguration of Professor Noah Porter, D.D., LL.D., as President of Yale College, Wednesday, October 11, 1871* (New York: Charles Scribner and Company, 1871), 45–46.

identical with the college, represented high culture, better tastes, "higher" aims; above all, the despising of intellectual and moral shams.

XXXII

The Civilizing Mission of the College. The tradition of critical authority, passing almost unremarked from church to college, its mission to all our internal migrants, fleeing to the liberties of the latest humbug, was accepted by literally millions of youth for whom this institution and this institution alone appeared to have some residue, however irrational, of this traditionalist critical authority. Of course, the American college was also very much a place to go to in order to climb the social ladder from one class to another. Good taste is always class-bound. Even so, bound to the propertied classes, the American college and university became the focus of what survived in the traditions of critical authority. Criticism cannot be released from authority—except to another authority. Radical criticism organizes itself into a party, or a counterculture, with known results. Sensualists without heart abound in the counterculture.

XXXIII

The Spiritual Burden of Higher Education. Such a spiritual burden, laid upon the American colleges and universities, the tremendous charge of emotion shifted to it in the long default of our church civilization, was bound to be too heavy. Academics have never been *Spiritualers*. Colleges were— and are—nothing like monasteries, except in the incidence of *accidie* common to both. Nevertheless, the spiritual charge of American youth demanded something—an impossible something—of our educational institutions. This demand, endlessly aggrieved by the late sixties, and convenient to draft-dodging as well, subjected the university to an inverted spiritualizing pressure—the identification downward. It is pressure that the American university has never borne well, even in Porter's time. The pressure has eased for the moment. Yet the promise of a higher life remains; where but in our university is intellect and character to merge in a grace so studied as to appear unstudied. That study cannot disappear altogether unless the university change its character entirely and become nothing but mass trade schools—including the literature and philosophy trades. But why should "trade" carry such an odor?

XXXIV

The Academic's Trade in the Traditions of Critical Authority. The academic, to continue in his unique trade, cannot but continue to tell serenely con-

fident stories against himself. As one of those stories, Oxford born, goes: A
. patriotic lady sees a don browsing at a table in Blackwells. It is a time of
war. The lady approaches our don indignantly. "Why aren't you fighting
for civilization?" The don replies, "Madam, I am civilization." All too
often, nowadays, the best such a don can think to do is teach—usually in a
vulgar Freudian way—*Civilization and Its Discontents;* with the discontents
emphasized.

XXXV

A Post-Freudian Reflection by Civilization Incarnate.

> The most important thing about a liberal education, you see, is what it makes
> impossible: certain things don't go with it, and that's that. A man of educa-
> tion, a man of culture, will for instance never eat gravy with his knife. Heaven
> knows why! It's not as though he learnt it at school. That's where breeding
> comes in, and that's based on the existence of a privileged class to which what
> we call Culture looks up—an example to Culture—in short, if I may say so:
> an aristocracy. I admit that our own aristocracy hasn't . . . lived up to this.[17]

XXXVI

Breeding a Privileged Class. In Eastern Europe, teachers are known to be
the "proletariat of the intelligentsia." The Western intelligentsia, and especially its teaching cadres, are among the least trustworthy, among those
least likely to show breeding and instinct; that character to which the less
cultivated were once taught to look up to. Children of our educational system have nothing to which to look up to. It is for this reason that they reject
all heroic and romantic attitudes: rightly so. The mendacious moralisms that
older generations foist on them are met with forms of responsive mendacity
which consist of regurgitating the stock answers to stock questions. Nevertheless, the preoccupation of all such institutions of transmission of authority, whether of the party in the Soviet world, or of the school, from bottom to
top in the Western world, is quite rightly preoccupied with its young people;
and those young people are quite rightly constantly seeking those responses
that will free them from the kinds of doctrines that are available in both the
party in the East and the school in the West. The young of the West distrust
the university and the schools, as in a parallel way the young of the East
distrust the party.

17. Robert Musil, *The Man Without Qualities*, vol. III "Into the Millennium (The Criminals)," translated by E. Wilkins and E. Kaiser (London: Secker & Warburg, 1960), 212.

XXXVII

Living Up to Our Privileged Condition. This entails, in the academy, opposing, in the detail of our disciplines, the modernist tradition of rationalist
doubt. To admit nothing sacred is to accept the primacy of possibility. That
way has led to a barbarism of which Bushnell never dreamt.

XXXVIII

Piety Never Dies; It only Shifts from Object to Object. The antidogmatic dogma
of rationalist doubt cannot have avoided becoming a parody of dogma: the
will to power of those who have the will to believe in the remissions and to
impose that belief. Through the universities the remissive elites have expressed their will to believe and have imposed their beliefs. But in the process, their capacity to inculcate those repressive modes that function to
reject what is fundamentally offensive has been weakened by a false doctrine of tolerance in which there is no stable touchstone of truth in the organization of one's own taste. The dynamics of distaste and taste have been
made shallow to the point at which what is attacked is the very dynamic of
repression itself, as if repression could somehow be abolished. But the only
really stable and deep-lying truths are founded upon repressions that themselves are not subject to critical examination. This is the dilemma faced by
every educator, beginning with the youngest child and continuing through
the educator himself. Signs of the failure of the repressions, and yet of their
survival, are all about us in our high arts and in our social sciences. Collec-
tivist absolutism and the acceptance of transgressive behavior as a matter of
life-style are among the high prices that we have had to pay for the beliefs
of the remissive educators regarding the refutability and unproveability of
those repressive predicates upon which the transgressive motifs themselves
are established. The assaults of modern education, the "liberalism" of it,
have been almost entirely upon the interdictory level in every order of authority and not upon the transgressions attached to those interdicts. The
doctrine that there is nothing sacred enshrines an order of authority that enshrines the will to believe in a fact that cannot endure itself.

XXXIX

Sacrilege Is a Fact. Our trouble is that we no longer believe sacrilege as a
fact. It may be true, as Nietzsche said, that "the best and highest possession
mankind can acquire is obtained by sacrilege."[18] But sacrilege, the fact we

18. Friedrich Nietzsche, *Basic Writings of Nietzsche,* translated and edited by Walter
Kaufmann (New York: Modern Library, 1968), *The Birth of Tragedy,* section 9, 71.

scholars must again contrive to study and teach, entails yet another consequence upon it: the fact that each and every sacrilege "must be paid for
with consequences that involve the whole flood of sufferings and sorrows
with which the offended divinities have to afflict the nobly aspiring race
of men." [19]

XL

*Those payments, when we think not to make them, bankrupt our intellects as
well as our characters.* The cultural economy of American higher education
would be greatly strengthened, I reckon, if we would study, yet again, how
to declare bankruptcy and begin the painful business of repaying our way.

19. Ibid.

Character and Culture

39

Reynard the Fox: A Preface for Parents

"Next to *Aesop*," wrote Joseph Jacobs, the editor of the original edition of this book, first produced near the turn of the century, "*Reynard the Fox* is the best known of the tales in which animals play the chief part." As with *Aesop*, Jacobs, a sound folklorist as well as a masterly editor, produced yet another charming text which could be read by children—or read to them by adults, with even greater pleasure. *Reynard the Fox* is one important piece of folklore that has made its way into literature for children; this literature of the best kind, fit for this and any other conceivable time—for all ages.

Beast tales have an eternal appeal. The genre is far from being played out. For example, American culture has produced in one century the stories told by Uncle Remus and the animated cartoons (such as Bugs Bunny) in which the world of the all-too-human is still being mirrored, to our entertainment and instruction, in the world of the animal. *Reynard the Fox* is still around, in person and in various literary offspring, still cunningly unprincipled if not so victorious as in this original of the tales. Not his cunning but his victories render Reynard superior to his descendants, who are made to lose in the end by the false moralization of Hollywood cartoon strip and other slick writers.

Reynard is a winner. His history remains delectable because it expresses the extraordinary wisdom of rather ordinary people: their knowledge of endless culpability, their pleasure in these admissions that in the world as it is even justice can be made to serve the interest of those who are intent on nothing except winning. In Reynard there is no test of human justice against divine justice, no divine wrath nor mercy, nor any prophecy of a life transformed. There is only the universally and commonly human, which children share with adults. Carlyle knew what this book, with its tricks and trials of

Reprinted from *Reynard the Fox (The Most Delectable History of)*, edited by Joseph Jacobs (New York: Schocken, 1967): ix–xi.

the strength of cleverness, means in Western culture. "The story of *Reynard the Fox*," he concluded, "is more than any other a truly European performance." Here we have a universal household guide and, in Carlyle's wonderfully apt phrase, a "secular bible." What more can be asked of children's literature than that it is "a true World's Book which through the centuries was everywhere at home, the spirit of which diffused itself into all languages and all minds?"

Reynard acts out our cunning, when the rules inhibiting cunning in our corporate life are weak. He is, as we say, a fox. Along with stories of the Gods, anthropomorphic myths, out of the genius of unliterary people who could not but reflect on themselves and the conduct of their lives in the Middle Ages, there developed, in many varieties and a number of European languages, this immortal expression of the continuous and unique effort of humans to understand themselves. Reynard effectively conveys the Christian effort to understand the underside of European spirituality. By deliberately ignoring spirituality in the telling, these stories ease the imagination toward an understanding of what life is like if we would be our "animal" selves. The theriomorphism of such folklore as this provided a refuge, I think, for ordinary people suspicious of a spirituality which demanded too much of life. In the world of Reynard there are no saints, only litigants. European spirituality is the precondition of European animality. So our culture was prepared, in the great age of spirituality, for a remissive expression in the Beast epic, as a pendant to God epics.

The Beast epic develops remissively, as a genre of tactics, for the sake of winning, rather than morality, for the sake of being good or right or blessed. *Reynard the Fox* is about the violence inherent in winning; it has nothing whatever to do with being good or holy. Reynard acts his nature in a world which some philosophers wrongly described as "state of nature," characterized by the war of each against all, in which life may well be nasty, brutish, and short.

In such a world there must be a court and kings who have the power to legitimate Reynard's winnings. Of course, as the people who first began to develop the telling of these tales knew, there is no "state of nature," except the human parody of one. And in that parody there must be personages of power, anointed by past victories dimly but deeply remembered. These personages hold the offices of justice to which the other animals can appeal, in temporary settlement of their differences.

I am far from suggesting that *The Delectable History of Reynard the Fox* needs to be taken seriously. This is children's literature, but as such it will interest adults on just that ground they share with children. Behind the archaic, hieratic air of these medieval tales everything important is contemporary: and most contemporary of all, the supremacy of the rascal.

Reynard may appear, on first reading, one of our earliest antiheroes. In fact, he is the hero of a truly pagan text, in which not even the victims long to be saved from their humiliations in any sense more profound than that of living to fight Reynard another day on his own terms, which they accept for want of any more exclusive creed. This is to say that the victims here are no better than the victors.

Notice the pictures. They are charming; quite as charming as the tales themselves. For it is the charm with which a hard and still familiar world is invested that raises this text from folklore to literature. (67:1)

40

A Character Wrecked by Success

No one has yet improved upon the peroration delivered by Max Weber against American culture. In the final paragraphs of *The Protestant Ethic and the Spirit of Capitalism*, Weber writes of the Protestant—read "American"—who has pursued salvation and won wealth. Having created, through his energy, a world of abundance, the moral athlete grows flabby and complacent in it. His prosperity, stripped of its religious and ethical meaning, becomes a plush cage. "No one knows who will live in this cage in the future, or whether at the end of this tremendous development entirely new prophets will arise, or there will be a great rebirth of old ideas and ideals, or, if neither, mechanized petrifaction, embellished with a sort of convulsive self-importance. For of the last stage of this cultural development, it might truly be said: 'Specialists without spirit, sensualists without heart; this nullity imagines that it has attained a level of civilization never before achieved.'" No Catholic, no socialist, has launched a more prophetic attack on the moral foundations of Western industrial culture than this German liberal. Of course, a Catholic polemicist would find Weber's thesis perfectly compatible with his own anti-Reformation bias. For it is Weber's thesis that the restless, anxiety-ridden Protestant, always in quest of evidence of his salvation, was transformed by the very success of his quest into a very different, and now dominant, type—the competent technician who becomes, after hours, the dull sensual man.

Thus, the Protestant, having discovered how to snatch plenty out of a world of scarcity, and even how to produce a world of plenty, nevertheless lost himself amid his goods and buried his culture under it. It is "this nullity" of the capitalist spirit, now entirely divorced from the Protestant ethic, that William Whyte explores.[1] He is a brilliant and chivalrous journalist,

Reprinted from *Partisan Review* 24, no. 2 (Spring 1957): 304–10.
    1. William H. Whyte, Jr., *The Organization of Man* (New York: Simon & Simon, 1956).

and he withholds censure wherever he can. Whyte has written a sympathetic and remarkably full account of the American moral athlete in premature middle age. But his unfailing generosity as a critic cannot hide the fact that the American character has been fatally damaged. After three centuries of heroic struggle against an economy of scarcity, the American character has caved in just at the threshold of an economy of abundance. It is a national character Freud would have delighted to analyze: a character wrecked by success. Whyte's Organization Man is still mainly Protestant on Sundays, but without the moral egoism, the heroic self-centeredness that once characterized him on the other six days. The pious smile of sociability, once reserved for women and younger children and ministers, has frozen on the American face. Americans smile too readily. And when they smile, it is no longer to bare their teeth in fraternal greeting to a competing athlete met in the race. The smile does not crack our faces, for the remainder of the American face has been composed around the smile. Sociability, like predestination, is an iron creed. The American must smile, or risk challenging the sacramental bond that unites him in one overpoweringly friendly people. In that wide, ever-ready smile the material abundance of America may be said to be transsubstantiated into the personality of the American.

It is well known that the American is a joiner of organizations. He works for them, he plays in them. In a culture of joiners, the line between 'community' and 'organization' grows vague, particularly as the joiners move more and more frequently from one community to another while remaining in the same organization. Thus one's native organization receives some of the reverence once reserved for one's native community. That the subjects of Whyte's study tend increasingly to remain in the same organization while becoming geographically ever more mobile is one of the many interesting correlations he adduces in a convincing way. Regionalism may be ignored as a factor in shaping the new American character. Suburbia, and the employees of the great oligopolies that people it, knows no Yankees, no Southerners, no Plainsmen. Park Forest (Illinois) and Levittown (New York) are enough alike sociologically to make the geographic difference unimportant.

The sanctity of the organization derives from the fact that it is the trustee of American prosperity. And prosperity is, in turn, the historical successor to the Protestant conscience. (Americans do in fact believe that what is good for General Motors is good for the country. Secretary Wilson simply cannot learn that private truths must not be spoken in public places.) The organization—the business organization in particular—leads the American male firmly up the mountain of temptation, and trains him to accept, with thanks, all the suburban kingdoms of this world. Salvation has been worked out in the personnel office; one need only conform to the benevolent will of the organization. With patience and prudence (and an expanding economy), the organization man may confidently expect to arrive at his final destination— the home office and the senior dormitory suburb.

Whyte is half admiring, half shocked at our imaginary fall upwards into the good life. In this respect, his ambivalence is similar to that of other fascinated reporters of this curious fall—David Riesman, for example. It is not the good life that Whyte suspects. Like Riesman, he cherishes a secret nostalgia, not for scarcity, but for that contentious moral athleticism of the Protestant type. From the vantage point of this nostalgia, Whyte gauges the supine hedonism of the American temper today, implying that some higher temperature is still possible in our present-centered culture. Perhaps it is, in rare cases. But because, like Riesman, he is a hopeful man, Whyte does not emphasize how thoroughly unfit the American environment is for a re-creation of Protestant ruthlessness—personified as 'autonomous' man or under any other guise. The world-rejection that underlies the Protestant style of individuality is not a viable attitude today. Even the ongoing religious 'revival' in America is a further world-acceptance—the acceptance of 'religion' as another national good to which all Americans are entitled. Having begun to get religion, the American is reaching toward the point where he has everything.

To Whyte, as to Riesman, the future of American culture revolves mainly around the question of rehabilitating the individual. Whyte assumes, with the old Protestant ethic, that there is a core in every person—unique, incommunicable, indestructible. Further, he assumes that, thus endowed, the person is not exhausted by the social relations into which he must enter, no matter how exhaustively these relations enter into him. Here Whyte has the authority of contemporary social science against him. For every prevailing science of society contains, built into it, a denial—however implicit and unexamined that denial may be—that there is a self which exists prior to, and is not a derivative of, social experience. It is at least questionable whether such an authentic individual still lives, secretly, inside the organization man, except perhaps in the not very helpful way that a thin man may be said to live inside every fat man. Whyte may be appealing to a mythological creature, not merely to one which harkens back to a different mythological environment.

To profit from a reading of Whyte's book, however, one need not believe that an invisible church of individuals still exists. His assumptions about individuality seem to me, as a sociologist, somewhat dubious; yet once past his assumptions and into his descriptions, his book remains very sound sociology. He has a fine eye for noting those suburban social disciplines—the *Kaffee-klatches*, the amateur psychologizing, the institution of the open front door—which repress individuality in the name of democracy. And he describes equally well the organizational glad hands that hover, with a power like that of apostolic succession, over the heads of the young ordinands entering the corporate hierarchies.

Whyte does not attempt to say why the aura of sanctity around big business organization has enlarged in the postwar decade. Nor does he explain why all organizations, in particular the trade unions, have tended to take on this aura. A correct answer to this sort of question would, I think, erase much of Whyte's neat analytic line between the sociable organization man and the Protestant egoist. The social ethic is not so different from the Protestant ethic as Whyte makes out. In both instances, the practical aim is the same: success. The conditions of success have changed, and therefore the character traits that are at a premium for success have also changed. But the end has not changed. That same sensual man against whom Weber inveighed, able to work as devotedly as the Protestant without the same incitement, has been further organized into new methodical routines of self-advancement. The ethical egoism of the Protestant has flowered into unremitting sociability, under the sunlight of an expanding economy. And it is not at all clear that the organization man does not have a certain ethical advantage over his ruthless Protestant predecessor. He mixes more pleasure with his business, and takes his pleasures in a less furtive way. He has regard for his health. He is kind to his children. He is reasonably happy. He is a far more civil creature.

Perhaps the most interesting material in Whyte's book is on the straitjacket of tests into which applied psychology is trying to fit the organization man. Here, with good reason, the author grows vehement and polemical. It is difficult to remain even-tempered when regarding the tyranny of applied psychology over the American business community. Yet, as I have implied, Whyte's is no simple-minded work of protest. Puritanism had a moral theology that left open the possibility of purchasing Christ with money; against this possibility, which opened into a secular and sensual culture, the great divines of New England thundered futilely. The organization man has a moral psychology, wrapped inside the flag of science, against which the moral critics of our time may thunder with equal futility. Whyte senses this futility of moralizing with the system. He does not recommend that his readers fight the application of psychology directly. Instead, he offers some lessons in how to deprive this pseudo-science, not of its capacity to label us, but of its capacity to persuade us that its labels are true.

Industrial psychology represents the supreme ambition of modern science: it carries technology into the inner world, to transform and control it as the outer world can now be transformed and controlled. What the American once did to the wilderness of physical nature, he now moves to do to the tameness of his human nature. The pursuit of power is an integral part of the American's creed, informing his pursuit of happiness. This covert part of the creed illuminates the national eagerness for education. In America, knowledge as such has never meant power. Rather, the Baconian idea has been turned upside down. In the pseudo-science developed in university departments of psychology and applied in the corporations, we see power masquerading as knowledge. Industrial psychology represents power trying to transform itself into knowledge—in order to achieve more power.

It was a bold idea to end the book with an analysis of psychological tests and detailed instructions on how to cheat on them. Whyte's recommendations are genuinely subversive—that is, they are practical, not rhetorical. The free man must learn how to cheat power masquerading as knowledge. He must cultivate that double consciousness which permits the organization to mount a plausible version of himself in the bureaucratic showcase without for a moment believing that the mounted creature is really he. This is an unending task, I think, one requiring more than shrewdness and perhaps beyond the resources of individuality latent in organization man. But if Whyte is not entirely successful in supplying a new hero, there is no doubt that he has correctly spotted, in applied psychology, the new villain for our national success story. (57:1)

41

The Impossible Culture: Wilde as a Modern Prophet

I shall begin by quoting at length from Edward Carson's [1] cross-examination of Wilde during the first of the three trials when Wilde was still plaintiff in that ruinous case of libel he brought against the Marquess of Queensberry.

Reprinted from *Salmagundi* 58–59 (Fall 1982–Winter 1983): 406–26.

1. Edward Henry Carson, Q.C. (1863–1928), later Lord Carson. Carson had been Wilde's contemporary at Trinity College, Dublin, in the seventies and probably shared a general reluctance to take Queensbury's defense. The case taken, he attacked, through Wilde's art, the doctrine of life celebrated in that art.

All three trials of Oscar Wilde were of a man who "stood in symbolic relations to the art and culture of my age." Knowing himself to be a "symbolic figure," always on stage in a life representing the art of brilliant comedy, Wilde rightly took as the vital issue his justification of life as an aesthetic, rather than moral, phenomenon.

Edward Carson, too, was a symbolic figure. The philistine barrister represented life justified as a moral phenomenon. With the instinct of a great advocate, Carson took aim at Wilde's artistic acceptance of all experiences. That acceptance required a tone of subtlety and nuance, a nobility of manner that would limit the danger of moving in strange perspectives. The tone of Wilde's homosexual affairs, not least with Queensberry's son, Lord Alfred Douglas, appears ignoble. Lord Alfred was a bad actor and made ugly scenes. In the Bosie affair, Wilde found no brilliant comedy; rather, "a revolting and sinister tragedy . . . stripped of that mask of joy and pleasure" behind which he saw, too late, the horror of that carnality we, with him, have learned to call 'hatred.'

Through Carson's questions, we may see represented articulate old suspicions of the truth of masks that have all but lost their voice in our culture. Carson stood square for those external sanctions and sacred commands that Wilde would not admit: unadmitted even as necessary fictions of limit upon his search for modes of "self-realization" so fresh that they aspired to self-creation. For all his cold questioning, the victorious philistine kept a merciful sense of fair play. "Cannot you let up on the fellow now?" Carson asked Sir Frank Lockwood, the Solicitor-General. "He has suffered a great deal."

So far as he realized himself in the Wilde affair, Lord Alfred Douglas, too, rises to the rank

Then we shall see at once the quality of Wilde's wit, his view on certain aspects of culture and how far we have come toward Wilde's view in the three-quarters of a century since he became something less than a martyr and more than a victim.

Wilde: 'I do not believe that any book or work of art ever had any effect whatever on morality.'

Carson: 'Am I right in saying that you do not consider the effect in creating morality or immorality?'

Wilde: 'Certainly, I do not.'

Carson: 'So far as your works are concerned, you pose as not being concerned about morality or immorality?'

Wilde: 'I do not know whether you use the word "pose" in any particular sense.'

Carson: 'It is a favourite word of your own?'

Wilde: 'Is it? I have no pose in this matter. In writing a play or a book, I am concerned entirely with literature—that is, with art. I aim not at doing good or evil, but at trying to make a thing that will have some quality of beauty.'

Carson: 'Listen, sir. Here is one of the "Phrases and Philosophies for the Use of the Young" which you contributed: "Wickedness is a myth invented by good people to account for the curious attractiveness of others." You think that true?'

Wilde: 'I rarely think that anything I write is true.'

Carson: 'Did you say "rarely"?'

Wilde: 'I said "rarely," I might have said "never"—not true in the actual sense of the word.'

Carson: '"Religions die when they are proved to be true." Is that true?'

Wilde: 'Yes; I hold that. It is a suggestion towards a philosophy of the absorption of religions by science, but it is too big a question to go into now.'

Carson: 'Do you think that was a safe axiom to put forward for the philosophy of the young?'

Wilde: 'Most stimulating.'

Carson: 'If one tells the truth, one is sure, sooner or later, to be found out'?

Wilde: 'That is a pleasing paradox, but I do not set very high store on it as an axiom.'

Carson: 'Is it good for the young?'

Wilde: 'Anything is good that stimulates thought in whatever age.'

---

of a symbol. It was from this nemesis that Wilde suffered the hatred of father figures complicit in "the love that dare not speak its name."

Suppose Wilde's love life, with both sexes, exemplified a law in which this self-proclaimed "born antinomian" believed: the enlightened modern law of continuity, rather than opposition, between evil and good. Then might "all men kill the thing they love." It was under this profanation of "thou shalt not kill" that Wilde became the victim of his lover and, in turn, Constance Wilde became his victim.

Carson: 'Whether moral or immoral?'

Wilde: 'There is no such thing as morality or immorality in thought. There is immoral emotion.'

Carson: 'Pleasure is the only thing one should live for?'

Wilde: 'I think that the realization of oneself is the prime aim of life, and to realize oneself through pleasure is finer than to do so through pain. I am, on that point, entirely on the side of the ancients—the Greeks. It is a pagan idea.'

Carson: 'A truth ceases to be true when more than one person believes in it'?

Wilde: 'Perfectly. That would be my metaphysical definition of truth; something so personal that the same truth could never be appreciated by two minds.'

Carson: 'The condition of perfection is idleness: the aim of perfection is youth'?

Wilde: 'Oh, yes; I think so. Half of it is true. The life of contemplation is the highest life, and so recognized by the philosopher.'

Carson: 'There is something tragic about the enormous number of young men there are in England at the present moment who start life with perfect profiles, and end by adopting some useful profession'?

Wilde: 'I should think that the young have enough sense of humour.'

Carson: 'You think that is humorous?'

Wilde: 'I think it is an amusing paradox, an amusing play on words.'

Carson: 'What would anybody say would be the effect of *Phrases and Philosophies* taken in connexion with such an article as *The Priest and the Acolyte?*'—

Wilde: 'Undoubtedly it was the idea that might be formed that made me object so strongly to the story. I saw at once that maxims that were perfectly nonsensical, paradoxical, or anything you like, might be read in conjunction with it.'

Carson: 'After the criticisms that were passed on *Dorian Gray*, was it modified a good deal?'

Wilde: 'No. Additions were made. In one case it was pointed out to me—not in a newspaper or anything of that sort, but by the only critic of the century whose opinion I set high, Mr. Walter Pater—that a certain passage was liable to misconstruction, and I made an addition.'

Carson: 'This is in your introduction to *Dorian Gray:* "There is no such thing as a moral or an immoral book. Books are well written or badly written." That expresses your view?'

Wilde: 'My view on art, yes.'

Carson: 'Then, I take it, that no matter how immoral a book may be, if it is well written, it is, in your opinion, a good book?'

Wilde: 'Yes, if it were well written so as to produce a sense of beauty, which is the highest sense of which a human being can be capable. If it were badly written, it would produce a sense of disgust.'

Carson: 'Then a well-written book putting forward perverted moral views may be a good book?'

Wilde: 'No work of art ever puts forward views. Views belong to people who are not artists.'

Carson: 'A perverted novel might be a good book?'

Wilde: 'I don't know what you mean by a "perverted" novel.'

Carson: 'Then I will suggest *Dorian Gray* as open to the interpretation of being such a novel?'

Wilde: 'That could only be to brutes and illiterates. The views of Philistines on art are incalculably stupid.'

Carson: 'An illiterate person reading *Dorian Gray* might consider it such a novel?'

Wilde: 'The views of illiterates on art are unaccountable. I am concerned only with my view of art. I don't care two-pence what other people think of it.'

Carson: 'The majority of persons would come under your definition of Philistines and illiterates?'

Wilde: 'I have found wonderful exceptions.'

Carson: 'Do you think that the majority of people live up to the position you are giving us?'

Wilde: 'I am afraid they are not cultivated enough.'

Carson: 'Not cultivated enough to draw the distinction between a good book and a bad book?'

Wilde: 'Certainly not.'

Carson: 'The affection and love of the artist of *Dorian Gray* might lead an ordinary individual to believe that it might have a certain tendency?'

Wilde: 'I have no knowledge of the views of ordinary individuals.'

Carson: 'You did not prevent the ordinary individual from buying your book?'

Wilde: 'I have never discouraged him.'[2]

Wilde correctly said: "A great artist invents a type, and life tries to copy it, to reproduce it in a popular form, like an enterprizing publisher." He also agreed that "Literature always anticipates life." Nowadays, the type Wilde created, not least in himself, has been reproduced in very popular form. I like to think that Wilde would have despised all the cheap reproductions of his prophecy, especially among the young. Perhaps Wilde might have agreed that there should be limits, not on a great artist's invention of a type but, rather, on the enterprise of reproducing it in popular form. Certainly, Wilde was suspicious enough of the ways in which new character types are commercially exploited and, in their success, cheapened almost to the point of contradiction.

Can invention and reproduction really be separated? I suppose the imaginative invention of a type, and its reproduction, inseparable from the cultural process of choosing a pastoral guide for the conduct of life. This

2. See *The Trials of Oscar Wilde*, edited by H. Montgomery Hyde (London: W. Hodge, 1948), 122–24.

supposition on the changeable character of human types in any society specifies the power of art, even as Wilde wanted to use it—and even as others, at least since Plato, have wanted to censor precisely that power.

There are no neutral powers in the permanent war of culture. In his own way, representing the ordinary and established hypocrisies, Carson knew he was attacking one of the great commanders of the forces subverting his culture. Now Wilde's subversive spirit has been made obsolete by the cheap and massive reproduction of that spirit throughout the educated and televisioned strata of Western society. It is the Carsons, now, who are on the defensive. But Wilde can never win. For he imagined an impossible culture, one inhabited by consummate individualists, freed from the inherited inhibitions necessary, at least until our own time, to culture itself. As a guide through the future maze of choices, leading nowhere but attractive in his activity of choosing, Wilde named a type he imagined opposing all conformities: the "artist." In certain great artists of the past and present, including himself, Wilde found intimations of a future at once socialist (universally rich) and free (universally expressive). This artistic dream is, perhaps especially in advanced technological societies, more revolutionary than the dream of Marx.

For Wilde, the artist is the true revolutionary figure. Only the artist is fit to play the role of guide in the next culture. He is fit because "he expresses everything." Wilde italicized that sentence. The artist, radically different from any revolutionary figure preceding him, precisely by his special freedom to express everything, plays the prophetic role in Wilde's entertainments. Indeed, in the artist, revolutionary and entertainer merge.

Nothing is more contemporary than Wilde's imagination. Almost a century after his time, young revolutionaries in advanced industrial orders conceive themselves more artists than proletarians: their aim is to express everything.[3] But here the resemblance between Wilde and his epigones begins to fade. These latter-day epigones are, mainly, failed artists, relying on their assertions of freedom to express everything rather than upon the wit, grace and reticence with which Wilde believed everything should be expressed. Yet, precisely as failed artists, his successors follow Wilde in asserting the primacy of the artist as a guide to the next culture. What separates them from Wilde may be fatal to their art but vital to their success in a society increasingly uncertain about what it will, and will not, permit. Indeed, some confuse this uncertainty with civilization itself.

In every culture, guides are chosen to help men conduct themselves

3. In America, the allegiance of these young revolutionaries has shifted from proletariat to black *Lumpenproletariat*, because in blacks they believe they see a culture even less inhibited than their own parental one. I consider the Negroes, at least in the young white artist's understanding of them, by far the most powerful influence in contemporary American culture.

through those passages from one crisis of choice to another that constitute the experience of living. Once criteria of choice are established, guides are often self-chosen. Shamanry becomes hereditary; priesthood becomes an institution of those who would be ordained. The bandwagon effect operates in every culture. Men enjoy best those roles in which they can exercise an authority which is not their own and yet does not belong to the people they guide. Power may come out of the barrel of a gun; but authority comes out of the projection—and introjection—of ideals.

The rank-and-file members in idealizing institutions of guidance used to be called "laities": laities were those who listened to whatever the mouthpieces of idealizing institutions had to say. A crisis in culture occurred whenever old guides were struck dumb, or whenever laities began listening to new guides—new, because they encouraged their laities to do what theretofore they had not done (and not do what they had done). The crisis of modern culture adds something new to the history of such crises: the defensiveness and guilt of those who now know that they have nothing to say is compounded by the ascendancy of those who say that there should be no guides. Wilde is one of those permanently putative guides, ordained by his art, who have helped our culture advance beyond its unsuccessful Protestant phase in which every man would have been his own priest.

In the next culture, there are to be no priests, not even secular ones; we are not to be guided—rather, entertainment, stimulation, liberation from the constraints drawn around us by narrowing guidelines become the functional equivalents of guidance. Where creeds once were, there therapies will be. Oscar Wilde was a brilliant herald of therapeutic culture, when, near the turn of the century, the promise of it seemed dazzling. Neither the design nor implications of Wilde's heraldry are obvious to the naked eye. Wilde entertains so well that a guest at one of his feasts of words may easily forget these pleasures have a purpose beyond entertainment. The philistines wanted only entertainment, to be reassured by him in an amusing manner. And Wilde used his talent to entertain, precisely in his most popular plays, such as *The Importance of Being Earnest*. It is in his best essays that he tried to achieve the other purpose of art, which is not to entertain but to insinuate alternative prophecies of how men ought—and ought not—to act; and to make these insinuations at a level of character deep enough to help transform a culture. Plato was the first to acknowledge the seriousness and power of art in the transformation of character and society. Wilde denied this penultimate power only when he was in the public dock; there he defended the purity of art in a vain effort to save his life from the vengeance of philistines. But the philistines, who had him cornered, knew almost as well as he the power of art and its differences from entertainment. As entertainer, Wilde threatened nothing; only as an artist was he a threat to established culture. There is pathos in the separation of Wilde's talent as an entertainer from his genius as an artist; that genius appeared more in his life and essays than in his plays. He was a relentless performer, intent mainly upon himself and the impression he made. It was only upon those who knew him that Wilde made his greatest impression. We who come long after his performances are left with his supreme talent as an entertainer. But there is that other side of Wilde: his subversiveness as an artist.

A culture survives the assault of sheer possibility against it only so far as the members of a culture learn, through their membership, how to narrow the range of choices otherwise open. Safely inside their culture—more precisely, the culture safely inside them—members of it are disposed to enact only certain possibilities of behavior while refusing even to dream of others. It is culture, deeply installed as authority, that generates depth of character; indeed, "depth" is an edifying word for the learned capacity of rejection and acceptance. Members of the same culture can expect each other to behave in certain ways and not in others.

As culture sinks into the psyche and becomes character, what Wilde prized above all else is constrained: individuality. A culture in crisis favors the growth of individuality; deep down things no longer weigh so heavily to slow the surface play of experience. Hypothetically, if a culture could grow to full crisis, then everything could be expressed and nothing would be true. To prevent the expression of everything: that is the irreducible function of culture. By the creation of opposing values [4]—of ideals, of militant truths— a seal is fastened upon the terrific capacity of man to express everything.

Priesthoods preside over the origins of a culture and guard its character. If they did not preside, then a culture could be established without the mixed blessing of authority. A priest is whoever guides men by teaching them truths, or ideals. Sociologically, a truth is whatever militates against the human capacity to express everything. Repression is truth. God is not love, except as he is authority. When Wilde declared himself against authority, he did not know how he weakened what he was for: love. Authority will not be separated from love. To be for love and against authority is a paradox upon which no institution, socialist or otherwise, can be built.

Wilde tells a different story. In a culture without authority—Wilde called it "socialist"—the artist would teach each man, even the least talented, how to become more like himself. Freed by technology from labor, and by socialism from bondage to private property, each man would become what he can be: an individual, enjoying his own life, not degraded by poverty, not absorbed by possession. Imagine: not an art which has become popular, but a

---

4. "Values": whenever I hear the word, I reach for my pillow. It is a poor, misleading word and belongs to a marketing culture. In order not to expand the argument with my search for a better word, I beg leave to use "values" sparingly in this essay.

populace become artistic. We would entertain ourselves; self-entertainment is the final human autonomy.

> Is this Utopian? A map of the world that does not include Utopia is not worth even glancing at, for it leaves out the one country at which Humanity is always landing. And when Humanity lands there, it looks out, and, seeing a better country, sets sail. Progress is the realisation of Utopias.[5]

We will have to tease out this new kind of prophet, the artist as every man who would inhabit Wilde's Utopia—until he spies a better country.

Certainly, the new prophet will be more witty and less serious than any who came before him. This is not a small point toward the understanding of Oscar Wilde. The artist is he who can take all God-terms lightly. Because Wilde's new prophet possesses the comic spirit, he is self-possessed—as no other man has been before him. The alternative to self-possession is to be possessed by some God-term.

By "God-terms" I mean values that forbid certain actions and thereby encourage others. "God-terms" express those significant inhibitions that characterize us all within a culture. They are compelling truths. To take God-terms unseriously, while admitting their existence, seemed to Wilde the main, saving "pagan idea." Wilde put himself entirely on the side of the pagans, against Jerusalem, because he knew that the terms in which our particular God was conceived could exist only so long as they limited the capacity of man to express everything; the "pagan idea" was treated, in the nineteenth century by a small group of supremely talented European minds, as the refusal of this limit.

That Wilde had a most inaccurate notion of any actually pagan idea is beside the point. Like others gifted with revolutionary imaginations, Wilde meant by "pagan" some ideas that he considered would release men from their impoverishing inhibitions. To believe that man is the supreme being for man—supreme even over those primordial powers to which real pagans submitted—this is a subversive idea of modernity without precedent in any "pagan" culture. Like Marx, or Nietzsche, Wilde is a very modern man. What characterizes modernity, I think, is just this idea that men need not submit to any power—higher or lower—other than their own. It is in this sense that modern men really believe they are becoming gods. This belief is the exact reverse of the truth; modern men are becoming antigods. Because, as I have said earlier, the terms in which our God was conceived can exist only so long as they limit the capacity of man to express everything, our old God was never so uninhibited as young man. Our God was bound, after all, by the terms of various covenants.

---

5. Oscar Wilde, *The Soul of Man Under Socialism and Other Essays* (New York: Harper Colophon Bools), 246.

Thus, we can imagine all too easily Wilde's parody priesthood of de-inhibitors pitted against the repressive elites left over from the God-terms and institutions of the past. In Wilde's time, the struggle was still unequal; and Wilde himself has been considered a martyr in the struggle. That martyrdom, the trials and jail sentence, was due less to the repressive elite of English culture, which was more than willing not to have its hand forced, than to Wilde's own imperfect artistry. He intruded deeply into a struggle of son against father—Bosie Douglas against the Marquess of Queensberry—without realizing what it was about. More important, Wilde may have been led into the fatal step of prosecuting Queensberry for slander (the Marquess was naive enough at first to accuse Wilde merely of *posing* as a homosexual with his son) by his own sense of guilt. A more perfect artist of life should have been able to shatter the connection between guilt and culture. But the repressive culture was still enough alive inside Wilde, I think, to destroy him when he blundered into a direct confrontation with its official inhibitions. Wilde lost his personal battle, in 1895, the moment he went to court against his own knowledge (not admitted to his lawyers) that he was a practicing homosexual. That battle lost, Wilde's side appears now to be winning the war, even in the courts.

In the history of Western culture, churchmen have played the leading role of pastoral guide. By Wilde's year of success and wreck, 1895, all except the obtuse understood that the clergy had lost whatever sense of direction they once may have had. The office of guide, the most important in any culture, was vacant. Why should not literary men, artists, scientists try to step in? Wilde commended this seizure of moral power. Such a seizure was in no way bizarre or out of the question; the modern political struggle appears to urban sophisticates an enlargment of their own personal struggles: over distributions of the privileges and deprivations that determine differences of style.

Of course, at the turn of the century, many churchmen were still unaware of their default. Ibsen's Pastor Manders is an immortal characterization of a guide upon whom it never dawns that he has nothing to say. Mrs. Alving twice appealed to him as her figure of authority only because her own conversion to the art of life is bookish, a matter of idle chatter; deep down, she still submits to the old authorities. Oswald is doomed by the fact that he is her son, the child of a destructively fictionalized past. The culture that Ibsen denounces so heavily, and that Wilde dismisses so wittily, must be called neurotic. But Wilde, and his circle, are products of that very culture. They are examples of posh bohemia, deviant entertainers whose subversive attitudes can be at once supported and denounced by the philistines in imperial cities. Posh bohemians become a pseudo-elite, easy to sacrifice and replace if they go too far out of line and forget that they are not really heralds of a new culture but entertainers of a society in search of kicks.

What has changed since Wilde's time? First, the artist has become a popular type, reproduced now in massive numbers among the young in Western societies; second, the philistines are less self-confident and more easily persuaded that the bohemian life-style is something more than shocking entertainment, exhibitions intended chiefly for their embarrassed pleasure. The philistines can now read *The Soul of Man Under Socialism* more sympathetically than in Wilde's time. Even so, he remains the kind of figure who attracts philistine hostility precisely by asserting a near relation between artistic genius and deviancy.

Not only respectable philistines feel hostility to those who challenge their established sense of limit, particularly on the range of allowable deviancy. Prostitutes danced outside the Old Bailey, and lifted their skirts in mock salutes, when Wilde was convicted. Were they mocking Wilde alone? The respectable philistine prosecutors of Wilde might well avert their eyes; they too were being mocked, I think, for reaching up to the talent of their own most celebrated entertainer and destroying him for a deviancy he had kept quite private.[6]

A culture in control needs first of all to preserve that control by not reaching its legal arms too far into the labyrinths of private life. The guardians of any culture must constantly protect the difference between the public and private sectors—and encourage forms of translation between the two sectors; that is the meaning of ritual in all traditional cultures. Wilde never advocated his private deviancy through his public art, as it is done nowadays. On the contrary, stage Bunburying masks and transforms very different home truths. Wilde dealt brilliantly with the relations between art, lying and truth. (See his duologues on "The Decay of Lying.") It is the stage honesty of his successors that makes them failed artists. Their failure to realize the superiority of stage Bunburying, in all its forms, is a subversion of art itself and inadmissable in any culture. By their failure to respect the rights of privacy and its sovereign deceits, respectable philistines have played into the hands of the new revolutionaries who, unlike Wilde, use honesty to oppose culture itself. For the very life of every culture depends upon its powers to mask and transform private motive into something very different, even opposite, when it appears in public. In this sense, art, including Wilde's art, ought to function as an equivalent in modern culture of our lost opposing values. Art should be expressive and repressive at the same time. This, after all, is what is meant by sublimation.

In Wilde's time, as a side effect of their humorless insistence upon honesty, the philistines (this was what Wilde called the great propertied public)

6. Wilde was punishable under a bill that almost casually included a section which created as a new offense indecencies between male persons in public *or private*. The clause making deviant behavior in private an offense had become law only in 1886.

had created a high-mindedness that they mistook for culture. In this kind of culture, with the space between public and private sectors of feeling too narrow, anything of beauty was likely to give its viewer a case of what Wilde once called the "Protestant jumps."[7] Early in his life, Wilde determined to escape high-mindedness. The philistines, even those who called themselves socialists and engaged in good works,[8] were his natural enemies. The one difficulty with this ethic of escape is that it has become so easy; it can be achieved without the slightest talent. To be an escape artist without talent contradicts the meaning of art, installs things that are ugly as equal with anything beautiful and smashes up those structures of conformity from which alone art can emerge. This helps us understand why all those failed artists among the contemporary culture revolutionaries shout as one of their favorite words, "Smash." On walls everywhere in Western societies, graffiti invite us to smash this and smash that—solemn calls to an iconoclasm undignified by the slightest hint of alternative achievements of public meaning. Our young revolutionaries might learn from Wilde the real worth of wit. His genius lay in doing away with both the solemnity and incipient violence of serious argument. What should a free man, an artist, do when he is arguing against authority as such? Wilde's wit and good humor, his style, are the essence, not the ornament, of his case.

Under the needling of such wit, under those comic revelations of the Tartuffery of ideals that come from the best writers of the nineteenth century—Marx, Freud, Nietzsche, Wilde among the more strictly literary—we moderns have fled all militant ideal conceptions of our own character; those conceptions once supplied bridges between the private and public sectors of our experience, without abolishing the difference. On the contrary, a bridge of militant ideals functioned to establish and maintain the difference between what is private and what public, although the price was certain necessary tensions, now variously called "guilt," "alienation" and other current curse words. Against those separations of public and private, installed inside ourselves as our good name, we once learned to fear even the faintest dispraise and willingly put up with a diet of admonitions as our earliest form of moral nurture. Personality was identified with an idealized image of itself.[9] Wilde was an early modern opponent of militant ideal conceptions of the self, despite the fact that by such conceptions the private and public

7. *The Letters of Oscar Wilde*, edited by Rupert Hart-Davis (New York: Harcourt, Brace and World, 1962), 30.

8. The highest-minded socialists have also been philistines; the Webbs, and other fighters for humanity in the abstract, come most easily to mind.

9. In contrast, modern children are often educated early in a rejection of authority and hear little about themselves except praise. At the same time, militant ideal conceptions of character are mocked as injurious to the creative potential of the child. This revolution in childrearing has occurred mainly among the educated classes in Western societies.

sectors of experience are kept discrete and in order, the one a transformation of the other. That order cannot be established, as art or society, if no dialectic of translation occurs between private motive and public experience. Without thereby eliminating what is an eternally renewable difference between culture and morality, the point at which they meet and become inseparable is wherever a transformation of private motive occurs. A culture that does not moralize is no culture at all.

Militant ideals are not another name for public poses; if they are that, then they become the outward and visible signs of some private hell. A transformation forbids what would otherwise be allowed. A deceit, so far as the joke is not on the deceiver, allows precisely what it would forbid. Tartuffe was a poseur, immediately comic, at least to maid servants and theater audiences. But not all poses are comic. Kurtz, for example, made "Civilization" to mean "exterminate the brutes." The best way to read every cultural translation is backwards, from public experience to private motive. Thus read—backwards—too many translations evoke laughter, if only in order to avoid tears. Wilde chose laughter. As a guide, his artist is deliberately intended to suspend belief; he must ensure his own harmlessness.

To emphasize the harmlessness of the new man, Wilde shifted from the artist to the more traditional image of the child. In his greatest essay, *The Soul of Man Under Socialism*, Wilde offers for our guidance both the artist and the child.

> It will be a marvellous thing—the true personality of man—when we see it. It will grow naturally and simply, flower-like, or as a tree grows. It will not be at discord. It will never argue or dispute. It will not prove things. It will know everything. And yet it will not busy itself about knowledge. It will have wisdom. Its value will not be measured by material things. It will have nothing. And yet it will have everything, and whatever one takes from it, it will still have, so rich will it be. It will not be always meddling with others, or asking them to be like itself. It will love them because they will be different. And yet while it will not meddle with others, it will help all, as a beautiful thing helps us, by being what it is. The personality of man will be very wonderful. It will be as wonderful as the personality of a child.[10]

This is one of Wilde's more sentimental passages. Nothing in it hints how human personality can stabilize its ambivalences except by installing oppositional ideals. Wilde's sentimentality derives from the ancient logic of so-called antinomian thought: if nothing is prohibited, then there will be no transgressions. But in point of psychiatric and historical fact, it is *no*, rather than *yes*, upon which all culture and inner development of character, depend. Ambivalence will not, I think, be eliminated; it can only be con-

---

10. Oscar Wilde, *The Soul of Man Under Socialism and Other Essays* (New York: Harper Colophon Books), 237.

trolled and exploited. Ideal self-conceptions, militant truths, are modes of control. Character is the restrictive shaping of possibility. What Wilde called "personality" represents a dissolution of restrictive shapings. In such freedom, grown men would act less like cherubic children than like demons, for they would disrupt the restrictive order of character and social life.

Anyone who so disrupts a restrictive order is performing a demonic function. Just such disruptions seemed to Wilde the mission of the artist. The main, sociological question is never whether such disruptions occur but only whether they occur in the public or private sector of behavior. Wilde understood this difference between public and private disruption; we must understand the difference between public and private therapies—and, moreover, understand the dynamics by which every powerful private therapy tends to become public. In public, the art of Bunburying meant one thing: in private, it meant quite another.[11] Like any pastoral guide, the artist is a bridge between the private and public sectors of a culture. Therefore, by Wilde's implicit argument, the artist becomes a dangerous and necessary figure— dangerous because he disrupts the established order by casting doubt upon it, necessary because through such doubt progress occurs toward another mode of expressiveness.

We are now better placed to understand the precision of Wilde's wittiest and most famous interpretation of himself. André Gide had asked him how it happened that Wilde had failed to put the best of himself into his plays. Wilde replied: "Would you like to know the great drama of my life? It is that I have put my genius into my life—I have put only my talent into my works." Wilde understood that in the established society this was an inversion of the energies appropriate to the private and public sectors. In our culture, any man who exercises a genius for intimacy is bound to find it becoming public and therefore scandalous; he may be rewarded by public martyrdom. If some rare individual should be cursed with genius, then the safe course, in any society, is to put that genius into work, while reserving his talent, which can reassure friends and entertain associates, for living. So Kierkegaard arranged his life, after all, in the critical case of his genius versus Regine. In this way are preserved the sacred distances between desires and their objects. Ordinary men will rarely tolerate, except occasionally in politicians or prophets, a steady confusion of the public and private spheres. Yet it is precisely men who aspire to confuse the public and private sectors, putting genius into their lives, that become putative guides toward a different way of life. Following Weber (but with Freud's help) we now title such men "Charismatics." This merely argues the uncharitable character of

11. Just as in public the word "artist" might mean one thing and in certain private circles another. In one of Wilde's circles, the word "artist" also meant homosexual; "renter" was yet another term Wilde used with the same meaning.

charismatics, for they will not leave people alone in their privacies. Western society is again crawling with would-be charismatics; and they have a ready-made audience. With all their experience of default among candidates for the office, ordinary men still crave guides for their conduct. And not merely guiding principles. Abstractions will never do. God-terms have to be exemplified in order to be taught; or, at least, vital examples must be pointed to and a sense of indebtedness (which is the same as guilt) encouraged toward the imitation of these examples. Men crave their principles incarnate in enactable characters, actual selective mediators between themselves and the polytheism of experience.

Until recently, it seemed true that without imitations of compelling characters, *character* itself could not develop. Morality abhors impersonality. In this sense, so far as science develops through a transfer of truths impersonally, there can be no such cultural phenomenon as a scientific morality. In science, a truth ceases to be ideal and militant. Wilde had some premonitions of the dissolving effect of science upon culture and, as an artist, declared the amity of art and science—and both with socialism. Only under this triumvirate—art, science and socialism—could the New Man exist as anything more than an occasional rebel sport of the world as it is. But under the triumvirate of art, science and socialism, Wilde looked forward, with a messianic smile, to a culture of many truths, none of them set up as ideal and none militant. In this way, authority as such—not merely this or that authority—would be defeated.

There are counter arguments. What Wilde dismissed as mere imitation of authority, as well as authority itself, may turn out to be the one way necessary to decide questions of internal development; culture must always come to each man with certain claims ready-made, to set deep within him answers that can prevent disorganizing questions from arising. To conceive of an individualism that "does not come to a man with any claims upon him at all" destroys the established meaning of culture. Wilde could accept this destruction because he conceived of authority as completely external, like the cross he had heard of being carried through the streets of Jerusalem by some madman imitating Jesus. That madman seemed to Wilde acting out all "lives that are marred by imitation."

Wilde's attack on all authority is too easy. When authority becomes so external, then it has ceased to be authoritative. The heaviest crosses are internal, and men make them so, that, thus skeletally supported, they can bear the burden of themselves. Under the sign of this inner cross, a certain inner distance is achieved from the infantile desire to be and have everything. Identification is a far more compelling concept of authority and includes imitation. True individuality must involve the capacity to say no, and this capacity is inseparable from the genesis of no in authority. A man can only resist the polytheism of experience if his character is anchored deeply enough by certain God-terms to resist shuttling endlessly among all.

Wilde uses the traditional, God-term-determined rhetoric of the inner life against the inner life itself. The logic of Wilde's opposition to all authority depends upon his prototype of a new prophet, the artist. He imagined himself and others, each with his sovereign calm, self-centered, submitting only to the authority of experience—never predisposed by the experience of authority. By the grace of his opposition to militant truths Wilde helped lead an aesthetic movement away from the dominance of inwardness and toward an externalization that works against all our received conceptions of character. The genius of modernity is in Wilde's cleverness. That genius is only now being caricatured by a culture which produces revolutionaries who are less oppressed proletarians than failed artists.

The history of the struggle to fill the vacant office of guide to what men may not and may do has taken a remarkable turn. There are powerful movements which proclaim some version or other of the doctrine that the new guiding character must make his presence felt only in order to abolish himself. By virtue of his essays, Wilde belongs in the pantheon of this movement.

Of course, there are larger figures in the pantheon. But they are faced in the same direction. Nietzsche's future philosopher, as a humorist, is not far from Wilde's artist. The New Man for whom Marx was so impatient, and without whom the revolutionary process that he found in the hands of the unprincipled bourgeois could not be complete, is another near relation to Wilde's artist. Freud made a different and more cautious case in the character of the therapist, who is inseparable from his theory. I shall review the Freudian case briefly, for the background lighting it casts upon the Wildean case of the artist as our New Man.

For Freud, the power of decision over the internal redevelopment of a crippled, or arrested, individuality could be acquired, or extended, in that last phase of therapeutic suffering which constitutes the psychoanalytic relation. In correct Freudian time, after necessarily protracted resistances against his own opportunities, a patient should become able to sieze on the opportunity presented by the fact that the sources of his suffering are evaginated. Those sources are uncovered precisely in the patient's relation to the analyst. In the resolution of the transference, certain internal guides lose their authority and the patient therefore becomes that much freer to be his own guide. The analyst played a virtually silent critic without whom a patient could not recreate his own character, at last to say something on his own behalf. Psychoanalysis may be viewed as much a branch of moral letters made over into a unique process of therapy as it was of medicine.

But, with all his interest in the relation between case and collectivity, Freud never made therapy a model for culture. On the contrary, therapy can be understood as the model for anticulture. Precisely here is the tension between Freudian therapy and his theory of culture, of which authority, incarnate in character, is a necessary part. Freud never dreamed that his genius would be used to assert a culture in which there would be no figures of authority against whom youth could react and thus achieve their own sense of the limits that define any truly human existence. Such a dream, if he had it, would batter against Freud's own colossal creation of himself as a figure of authority locked in immortal combat against his final rival, Moses.

Wilde shared with the other most sensitive spirits of the late nineteenth century what is now public knowledge: that whatever makes authority incarnate in our culture is no longer available to it. No creed, no ramifying symbolic of militant truths, is installed deeply enough now to help men constrain their capacity for expressing everything. Wilde understood that internalizations from an earlier period in our moral history no longer held good. Western men were sick precisely of those interior ideals which had shaped their characters. The New Man has no choice except to try and become a free character. Viewed from within any among the precedent cultures of commitment, the character of the New Man must be anticredal. Wilde's artist is another version of the anticredal character around whom other, more notable heralds of the future have announced their designs. No less than Marx's New Man, Wilde's artist is anticredal because he too is conceived to live free from ideals. All the most important revolutionary movements of our culture, including the Marxist, represent various strategies of attack upon the inwardness of the Western character. They are efforts to evaginate those militant truths, functioning mainly as inhibitions, around which men learn to negotiate their elaborate dodges toward pleasure. Freud, Marx, Nietzsche, Wilde: these are some of the chief evangels associated with new ways toward the realization of self.[12]

A new way has to be shown, at least until laities are so practical in it that they can find the way for themselves. But contemporary culture is in such a turmoil of new ways that none of them can show to advantage. The field is too crowded. Even more in the era of anticreeds than of creeds, prophecy and deviant performance have become closely related and lucrative arts. Where individualism is so highly prized, charisma can be reproduced cheaply and becomes a highly profitable product. Wilde reckoned that, until the advent of socialism, full expressive individuality could occur only "on the imaginative plane of art." He reckoned without the cultural effect of the mass media—and without an alliance of art with the most philistine commercialism. Bohemia is more posh than ever, and more inclusive, in a society that will buy everything. The revolutionary arts are now mass entertainments.

By standing the artist "outside his subject," Wilde tried to make the artist revolutionary in a less easily corrupted manner. Such a lack of identification with his subject implies that the artist is a very special kind of personality. In Wilde's conception, the dissent of the artist becomes a kind

---

12. New ways, in order to appeal the more readily, can be supported by intimations from an ambivalently rejected past. Wilde considered Jesus as a forerunner, rather as Marx considered the utopian socialists. This branch of literature once came under the rubic "apologetics."

of deviance. It is because he is detached from his subject that the artist can be trusted to defy authority. Such a mistaken conception of the relation between dissent and deviance permitted Wilde to indulge in some very sentimental writing, about criminals as well as artists. It helped him locate the revolutionary animus in psychological rather than social relations.

This is not to dismiss all thought on the psychological origins of revolution. The animus of all revolution may well be summed up in one passage from Marx, where he invokes that "revolutionary daring which throws at its adversary the defiant phrase: 'I am nothing and I should be everything.'" No phrase could be more defiant, and none could better express the infantile unconscious—if the infantile unconscious could express itself. But animus is not action. The artist who stands outside his subject is himself a subject. He is neither nothing nor everything, but, like all other men, a significant something. Culture is a tremendous articulation of compromise between equally intolerable feelings of nothing and everything.

The claim of the artist to express everything is subversive in one especially acute sense: the claim to express everything can only exacerbate feelings of being nothing. In such a mood, all limits begin to feel like humiliations. Wilde did not know that he was prophesying a hideous new anger in modern men, one that will render unexcited, peaceable existence even more utopian than before.

To criticize Wilde's prophecy of the soul of man under socialism is not to defend a dying culture. Indeed, men who aspire to express everything can exist only in a culture grown so superficial that it can no longer perform its proper preventative functions. A culture that penetrates deeper into the interior, creating its own interior space rather than growing ever more disposable, is not made to order. Professors do not renew a culture. The sources of renewal are no less irrational than the sources of revolutionary death sentences against it. We can only wait and see which character will dominate the future: the credal or anticredal.

Wilde would have had the future liberate itself from the authority of the past. But, in the absence of sustaining opposition from its credal parent, the anticredal character compounds for its own defeat, as Wilde's did; that character, instinct in his and all comic art, proved tragic to the life.

Near the end of his life, Wilde reaffirmed its aesthetic justification: "Whatever is realized is right." His homosexual realizations had a pyrrhic air about them. From the affair with Lord Alfred Douglas rose a miasma of ugliness. Wilde's laudations of the paederastic glory that was Greece, its pedagogic eros, bore little upon his relations to homosexual prostitutes. His feastings with those "panthers," as he called them, appear to have been nothing like Plato's *Symposium*, in which he must have read, expertly in the original: "diseases of all sorts spring from the excesses and disorders of the elements of love."

On his own report, Wilde's homosexual affairs were lowering. Low life mocked high art. Wilde transgressed in life against the one god-term, Beauty, to which he would have remained faithful. We Pharisees of culture know the world is justified neither morally nor aesthetically. Yet we need trouble no more than Wilde about Leviticus 18:22; or any other of those sacred commands to disobedience from which we may acquire our own compassionate understandings of faithlessness. Wilde's homosexuality is condemned by his own aesthetic, which he took too seriously, as if it were his true religion.

In his great confession, *De Profundis*, Wilde almost realized what had "lured" him from the "beautiful unreal world of Art . . . into the imperfect world of coarse uncompleted passions, of appetite without distinction, desire without limit, and formless greed." His aesthetic justifications of life scarcely survive their translations into life.

Asked how he endured prison, Wilde's riposte plunged deeper than any other he ever delivered: "I was buoyed up with a sense of guilt." That sense true, it is more spiritual than legal; it is more trustworthy than ego; it is more profound than reason. If shallowness is the supreme vice, as Wilde believed, then his true guilt began in the clever insolence of his approach to art as if it were supreme reality. The most insolent and contemporary of cleverities must follow: an approach to life as if it were an endless choice of styles; modes of fiction contrived by any with wit enough and will for such contrivances.

Tragedy reminds us that true condemnations of the self cannot be pronounced by the self alone. I shall end by quoting two sentences that may be taken to constitute Wilde's verdict upon his life as work of art. Taken one after the other, they show a movement inevitable as that in a tragedy.

What the paradox was to me in the sphere of thought,
perversity became to me in the sphere of passion.

Everything to be true must become a religion.

(70:1b)

42

Michel Foucault's *Madness and Civilization*

Madness and Civilization[1] is truly an important book, one of those rare events in the history of the social sciences—a book that merits not only

Reprinted from *The Annals of the American Academy of Political and Social Science* 371 (May 1967): 258–59. © 1967, The American Academy of Political and Social Science.
    1. Michel Foucault, *Madness and Civilization: A History of Insanity in the Age of Reason* (New York: Random House, 1966).

reading but rereading. Dr. Foucault has taken as his subject the history of the treatment of madness from, roughly, 1500 to 1800. This is cultural history at its most penetrating, not so much an effort to report what actually happened, which is futile, but rather an analysis of what contemporaries felt about what was happening: specially with reference to those strange figures in Western culture, the insane; and not only the insane, but with them, the other transgressors against what is safe and acceptable among men: the idle poor, the witch, the heretic, and the criminal—all those who, in their very existence, incarnate danger. The radical solution for three centuries was to put away—to confine first in special institutions which had once housed lepers and later in penal houses for the once human conquered by the "beast" in them—all the dangerous, lest the contagion of their animal-like behavior spread to others struggling to control themselves. The implicit assumption behind the treatment of the insane was that the prohibited impulses which had broken through the crust of law and religion could only be broken; thus, the mad had to be treated severely, shocked, in penal and therapeutic response to their shocking behavior.

The mad were, therefore, a kind of counterelite; and the madhouse was an uncivilization to which the civilized could repair on Sundays and holidays, to see, for a modest price of admission, what the entertaining and frightening alternative was to their own way of life. Thousands of sane and solid citizens visited Bedlams, as places within which unreason was concentrated. In this way, the Age of Reason explained to itself precisely what unreason was. There was no dialogue with the mad; no hidden wisdom was to be listened for among these pathetic and dangerous fools. Western culture awaited Freud to re-establish what Foucault calls the "dialogue with unreason."

By the time of Freud, the rationalist culture that had devised "the Great Confinement" as the singular anti-institution by which the institutions of reason were affirmed was itself disorganized to the point where all the arts and literature pointed toward the imminence of a fundamental change. The slightly mad man, aware of his madness, appeared not only in the best of families but in the highest and most respectable places. The rather-mad could not be confined or isolated; the contagion seemed everywhere, diffuse and inseparable from what was to become the exception—health and safety. Foucault does not bring his history all the way into the present culture. Had he done so, this book would surely have instructed contemporary social scientists on the "neurotic" and the historical meaning of his appearance at the end of the civilization of authoritarian rationalism. Madness had condensed the meaning of sin and animality—sixteenth century—and of distance from nature—eighteenth century. By the twentieth century, men were ready to perceive madness as mere instances of a general social condition. At mid-century, the perception has again changed: whatever the causes the "cure" is perceived to be chemical. (67:4)

43
The Life and Death of Death

Were he not dead, Lord Clark would have a lot to answer for. His famous television series, *Civilization* (first broadcast in the spring of 1969), has led other scholars to imagine themselves teaching and guiding mass audiences through the changing meaning of their subject, so far as inward meanings can be discerned behind their outward and visible signs.

In this book,[1] Philippe Ariès aspires to guide the reader through various meanings of death in Latin Christian and post-Christian culture. Ariès plays Virgil and guides the viewer to no Inferno of the high and low, famous and infamous, but rather to graves, cemeteries, tombs, charnel-houses, death masks, paintings; at the end, to Ingmar Bergman's film, *Cries and Whispers*.

Because this is a book on the social aesthetics of the buried life, the reference to Ariès playing Virgil means his reader-viewers are unbelieving Dantes, who can make precisely nothing of death. Yet, even so, there remain at the edges of modern culture that mortally "dark wood" of fear to which Dante referred in the second line of the *Inferno*. Ariès tries to guide the reader through the dark wood by following a path along which there are, marking the way, funerary expressions of changing attitudes toward death. His images of cemeteries and tombs begin at the threshold of the Christian era, in a Roman or Romanized world, and continue to the present world.

From that two-thousand-year survey, no doubt for methodological reasons, images of dead Jews are excluded. Yet it may be argued that images of death are best studied, in their most contemporary meanings, by illustrating the recent experience of European Jews. Mass graves, in which none of the dead maintain their individual identities, occur in the earliest images Ariès exhibits. The book would have come, with the mass graves of the Jews of the Holocaust, full circle. What a pity Ariès did not consult me. Closure lends meaning.

With the ending modern belief that death means nothing, that unbelief taken up in the hurried last chapter (pp. 266–68), Ariès stops. As a scholar, he appears to accept that the death of God means, by our time, the death of meaning in the death of human beings.

To have nothing to say about the dead may be tantamount to saying that they never existed. It is not simply that the dead are nothing now; rather, in our unremembrances, that they have achieved the lowest status: of never

Reprinted from *Contemporary Sociology* 15, no. 4 (July 1986): 510–11.
1. Philippe Ariès, *Images of Man and Death*, translated by Janet Lloyd (Cambridge, MA: Harvard University Press, 1985).

having been. What can be lower than the has-been who never was? That may be the lowest status sociologically conceivable. Of all classes, those under the earth are the most wretched. It is, Ariès believes, a new culture that lives in the never-having-been-nor-to-be of the modern dead.

If it emerges first in the dead who go unremembered, then the new culture of the living unbound reveals Ariès (p. 267) as an oppositional and scholarly incarnation of the prophet Elisha (2 Kings 4:34). In his *Images*, Ariès tries to stretch himself down upon the childish body of this new culture of radical and endless contemporaneity, resolutely dead to the meaning of death and the past. Ariès tries to administer eye-to-eye resuscitation by remembrance.

Every historian must be a remembrancer. Historians are collectors of certain debts we in this present life owe the magisterially dead past. Ariès' images of humans in their habitats of death, various as they are, serve to show, I suggest, the various artifices by which we the living fasten on or free ourselves from what were once thought the artifices of eternity. Not all artifacts of eternity are equal or equally moving. Early and late in the history of our culture, there have been dismissive images of those dead who do not count, those without rank or fame or wealth, jumbled in mass graves unedifying as garbage dumps. By contrast, Ariès shows tombs, from the same cultural epochs, of the elite and individual dead: those higher dead respected in effigies and epitaphs and in tombs like palaces.

After the establishment and expansion of Christianity, a turning point in the cultural history of the dead in those habitats made for them by the living came in the expiring Middle Ages, in the fourteenth and fifteenth centuries. Here, Ariès appears to agree with one of his masters in cultural history, Huizinga. The prevalent imagery of death at the close of the Middle Ages is macabre. Death dances a dance to which the living are issued an invitation they cannot refuse. And a ruthlessly egalitarian dance it is. In the charnel house, too, captive audiences were taught, by everyone in general so housed, the mortal lesson of equality. Equality, without fraternity or liberty, may constitute the reality of all deaths.

Ariès treats death imagery with a subtlety appropriate to his sociological, historical, and aesthetic mastery of the images, if not of the subject. He makes delicate and even oblique approaches to the sociology of priesthoods. It can be inferred, from his text, that clergies sign their own death warrants when they surrender their prerogatives over the meaning of death and the practices of interment and commemoration.

If modern clergies appear hopeless about their second most signifying subject, then Ariès is not. He seems to see that Elisha's God is dead but that the body of Elisha's love is not. He tries to see some little cinematic signs of a new and erotic symbolism emerging that may help us defeat not death itself but at least our own macabre vision of it as an abstract nothingness.

Upon this resurrection of extremely ancient meanings, Ariès is prudent enough to spend only the three closing pages of his book. About that inverted guardian angel, death by nuclear holocaust, which compelled Lord Clark to hint, in the conclusions of his *Civilization*, that civilization itself may die entire in the light of a thousand suns, Ariès remains silent and dark as the grave; no doubt, for the good methodological reason that he can find no image yet with which to capture the meaning of such a death; no more than have the Jews an image for their Holocaust, which was not to God but for The Nothing.

Ariès cannot be expected to see what is not to be seen except by prophets and other heroes of faith. In the end, Ariès can see only pathetic hints of hope for another Elisha, perhaps this time in the ample spirit and flesh of a motherly woman. (86:1)

44

Charles Horton Cooley's *Social Organization*

Individualism is a mature and calm feeling, which disposes each member of the community to sever himself from the mass of his fellow-creatures; and to draw apart with his family and friends; so that after he has thus formed a little circle of his own, he willingly leaves society at large to itself. . . . Amongst democratic nations . . . the interest of man is confined to those in close propinquity to himself. . . . Aristocracy had made a chain of all the members of the community, from the peasant to the king; democracy breaks that chain, and severs every link of it. . . . Thus not only does democracy make every man forget his ancestors, but it hides his descendants, and separates his contemporaries, from him; it throws him back forever upon himself alone, and threatens in the end to confine him entirely within the solitude of his own heart.

Tocqueville, *Democracy in America*

Charles Horton Cooley's reputation is established, high and secure: in *Social Organization* (as before in *Human Nature and the Social Order*) he produced a classic text of American sociology—classic because it continues to give its readers something permanently important about which to think and, at the same time, adds to their intellectual equipment. My aim, in this introductory essay, is to exhibit one major aspect of Cooley's subtle response to the problems American culture presented not merely to him but also to the sociology that has followed after him. For, despite occasional rebellions

Reprinted from *Social Organization: A Study of the Larger Mind*, by Charles Horton Cooley (New York: Schocken, 1962), v–xx.

against its inevitable subject, American sociology continues to cope with the moral quality of American life, and in ways for which Cooley set a superior standard. He came to a series of understandings with his subject that make him a representative American sociologist.

Cooley lived between the years 1864–1929, just that time during which, except for the Wilsonian interlude, Americans settled into the attitude Tocqueville first noted. In this time, sympathetic critics of the national attitude appeared, trying to lure the American out beyond the safe limit of his self-concern. Of these philosophical doctors, pacifying the American ego in order to retrain it, Cooley remains one of the most adroit, taking up sociology as once men took up theology or socialism: in order to resolve the perennial issue of whether men can live well for themselves and their intimates alone.

In America, where theology was, there, in the latter third of the nineteenth century, sociology appeared, to argue the perennial issue in a new and revealing way, often against the officially religious preachers, mainly of Calvinist persuasion, who had transformed their God into a likeness of themselves—rugged individualists, without the slightest sense of responsibility to the community. With the exception of William Graham Sumner, all the American converts to sociology—Ward, Small, Cooley and their company—made cases against the prevailing individualism. There was something unintentionally subversive about that first generation, in the very choice of sociology. The nature of the discipline itself dictated a struggle against what Small once called "the preposterous initial fact of the individual"—in sum, against the American's most reverent conception of himself. Cooley was attracted to sociology from economics, in which he had taken his doctorate, and from government service, in which he had been bored for the brief time he spent away from his place of birth and breeding, the campus of the University of Michigan, at Ann Arbor. But Cooley was attracted to sociology less by the size of its achievement than by the size of its target, as he came to see it, that false antinomy between self and society by which men improved themselves at the expense of others. "We must improve as a whole"—Cooley jotted down the subversive notion in his diaries. *Social Organization* makes the prior point that each exists only as a member of all. It is at once a book of analysis and recommendation, as sociology at its best must always be.

Unlike some among his successors in the discipline, Cooley never worried whether, as a sociologist, he would look acceptably scientific to his academic neighbors. But then, Cooley worked before the period when envy of the scientist's power to actually transform his subject matter had eaten the heart out of sociology. He did not choose to caricature the scientist by imitation, but to respect science the more by cultivating the necessary artist in himself, as his discipline required. The conditions of his science, Cooley believed, were irremediably different from those relating to the material world. Statistics might be used, in an ancillary way. But, as in all sciences, in sociology interpretation is all. A science may be loaded down with too many facts, its vision blurred by peering too intently at the machinery for collecting them. The selected facts can be brought to life, as the statisticians themselves agree, only by a compelling vision of their meaning. Untouched by the magic of a sufficiently powerful and trained imagination, data play dead. No exactitude will bring them to life. Nor are statistics the sole language of precision. For his special purposes, Cooley practiced sociology with an old, but precise and difficult weapon: *le mot juste.*

There is moreover, the question of who is to be compelled. Cooley wrote for an audience larger, and more important, than his own profession, while the audience of the physical scientist is usually his own profession. The function of the sociologist is both scientific and pedagogic; dealing with moral problems, he must teach moral lessons—otherwise, his sociology fails to be social enough. On the other hand, since Leibniz, it has been the ambition of the scientific community to divorce itself from all others—national, cultural, political. The special language of the physical scientist enunciates an act of emancipation that, when imitated too strenuously by the social scientist, deprives the latter of his proper audience. Jargon is a curse; it permits professional groups to turn in upon themselves, thus helping them evade their pedagogic responsibility. Cooley remained readable because he knew that, given his subject matter, he was obliged to communicate like an artist, intimately, by the personal force of his vision.

Yet, although inherently pedagogic, sociology is not itself bound to any doctrine but can transform them all—Marxist, Freudian, Thomist, Durkheimian, Platonist, Weberian, Lucretian, any—into cues for prompting into presence and voice the otherwise silent and invisible actors of social reality. Sociologists may try on New Yorkers perspectives first applied to Samoans, so long as they remember that they are thus experimenting with angles of vision that may, in time, significantly alter what is seen. No more than the physical sciences can sociology evade responsibility for transforming its subject matter. Even the most complex analytic perspectives may develop into ideology. More important, sociological analysis always carries with it a polemical implication. Who are scientists, that they should be, in their peculiar work, without passion, for and against their subject? Indeed, the analytic perspective may have been trained, in the first place, by a reaction against some established doctrine, which once itself may have been a polemically useful analytic perspective. Cooley judged that "behaviorism reflects mysticism." It is a new style of mystification, suitable for those who hated the old religious mystifications with such passion that they needed new ones to set against the old. Much "scientific animus," Cooley observed, is in this way "subservient to theology."

Only by multiplying analytic perspectives, shifting from one to another with a permanent tentativeness, can sociology avoid slipping over into ideology. That a unified sociological theory now may be emerging, from the varied and often conflicting analytic perspectives available, does not alter the case: this unity is unlikely to be more than a systematic presentation of multiple perspectives. And for such systematic presentation, a canon is necessary, from which students can expand and deepen their analytic competence. Cooley's *Social Organization* has canonical status; it has helped the discipline grow to its present strength.

Cooley was even harder on the polemicists than on the data-mongers. "Conspicuous radicals," he thought, are "likely to be contradictors," incapable of balancing their analyses, giving it that symmetry of yes and no which is a similitude of truth. In the Cooley tradition, a sociologist would learn to be generous to the beautiful, complex ugliness of things as they are.

Himself a theorist, yet Cooley was hostile to theoretical system-builders. It seemed to him that they made gratuitously hard reading; they are "seldom worth the trouble," he concluded, in a rare ungenerous mood. More important, systematic theory departed too far from the jurisdiction of common sense. "An enduring philosophy must appeal to everyday, human modes of thinking." But precisely modern scientific theory ignores—and may even contradict—everyday modes of thinking. Common sense has no place in modern science, no more than in modern art. By placing a limit on the abstract and systematic character of theorizing, Cooley too closely fused pedagogic appeal and analytic value. He thought those writers appealed most and saw most deeply who were "not very systematic." Thus Cooley rationalized a certain disconnectedness in his own style. At the same time, by his discursive manner, Cooley knew exactly what he was trying to achieve: he aimed to shift perspectives regularly. "From every new point of view, new forms are revealed." I would take this as a usable motto for a statement about sociological method. For a sociologist must, I think, wield multiple analytic perspectives across actions and ideas that are themselves thus rendered multiple, and perhaps even contradictory, in meaning. Without this intellectual-aesthetic capacity, which includes quantitative procedures as one tool of vision among others, the sociologist cannot deal, as Cooley put it, "with life in its fullness." Instead, as has happened, the discipline is broken up into many little sciences of detail, never to be brought together into a larger art of interpretation. It is only from confrontations of diverse theories, supported by obedient armies of fact, that the social sciences can hope to achieve something like unity. Perhaps that unity can only exist in the capacity of the social scientist himself to use multiple analytic perspectives, and not in an apparently more substantial unity—which is merely another name for doctrine.

In the absence of a unifying doctrine, the social scientist needs to experiment permanently with multiple perspectives. For this experimental skill, he needs training in the history of abandoned doctrines and current methodologies—the latter being styles of analytic address in which the doctrinal motive has been repressed. More important, the social scientist, doctrinally uncommitted, needs the aesthetic gift, without which his analytic powers remain trivial. Cooley has the aesthetic gift. What he understands is beautifully understood, because for him "visible society is, indeed, literally a work of art . . . of inexhaustible beauty and fascination." Yet, throughout *Social Organization*, Cooley's intellectual-aesthetic capacity strains against his pedagogic intention. On the one hand, he communicates the complex and contradictory nature of his subject matter; on the other hand, he tries to use his gift to compel the reader to share in his uniting and serene vision of the self lying peacefully in the maternal bed of society. The picture is too pious for contemporary taste. There is too much warmth and security, not enough cold and desolation, precisely because it was Cooley's intention to bring his reader in out of the solitude Tocqueville described. Thus Cooley's projection of the concept of the "primary group" swiftly takes on a doctrinal cast. As an American sociologist, he could scarcely avoid constructing some mode of analysis that would substitute for beliefs that had once regulated conduct but now could not organize the basic human need to choose. It was Cooley's business to teach his readers that, in one important respect, they did not have a choice. In the old theology, God chooses man, no matter how man hides. In the new sociology, society creates the self in its own image, however autonomous the self believes itself. The primary group is Cooley's God-term, at once the principle of analysis and that which is the object of analysis. As a work of doctrine, *Social Organization* is an effort to overcome the "discontinuous life" that had broken the connective tissue of community in urban, industrial America. Cooley was himself a village intellectual, trying to save city civilization from an historic incapacity to generate emotional warmth.

In the concept of the primary group, Cooley created another of those formal symbols in which American sociology abounds, at once the vehicle of address and that which is being addressed. By thus identifying social reality with its own analytic devices, sociology does what it can to alleviate the shortage of symbols that has impoverished American culture since the passing of the age of doctrine. Symbolic impoverishment, in the midst of material plenty, characterizes all post-religious cultures. Or, put differently, the symbols must grow more and more concrete, with specific powers assigned to them, as in primitive cultures. In modern culture, power has again passed into things; the world is again a pantheon of weapons, with science where animistic belief used to be. Against these idolatrous practices, sociology, like psychiatry, has succeeded to the preaching function. Books such as *The*

Lonely Crowd, The Affluent Society, The Power Elite communicate warnings against this technological primitivism: as works of social analysis, they are at the same time modes of moral chastisement.

Cooley is a more sanguine writer. His primary group is an image of hope rather than of foreboding; it is thus an authentic God-term, the symbol from which his entire analysis derives, which may itself be symbolized but cannot be displaced by a superior unit of analysis. Sociology is a collection of such analytic symbols. They help unify and enrich a symbolically impoverished world, enabling the secular to become the shadow of what once the sacred was. The subtle functional *oughts* of societies replaced the simple *isness* of gods. Salvations give way to controls. An ounce of prevention is worth a pound of redemption. Thus sociology "tends to cure pessimism," not in the old messianic way, "by promising a bright future," but in the new pan-social way, "by showing each one's life as member of a great process."

The great process is industrialization. Cooley insists that a culture on wheels, talking perpetually on the telephone, might bring together the selves set wandering by the whirring machine of an industrial civilization. He could still hope that the radio, and the automobile (and all that has followed since his time), would reestablish local culture on a national scale— as if television were the opportunity for a gigantic town meeting. Nothing of the sort has happened. On the contrary, Tolstoy's fear that a Genghis Khan would learn to use the telephone seems more realistic than Cooley's hope that many Thomas Jeffersons would be trained through the use of it. Cooley indulges in the paradoxical hope that precisely the spread of "mechanical conditions" into everyday life would create the "organic society." It seems more reasonable than ever, now, to assume that mechanical conditions tend to create mechanical societies. Television in the bedroom helps the members of even that sticky primary group ignore each other.

Furthermore, in a free society, the delicate capacity for making free and rational choices among the plentitudes is not trained when the alternatives are so much alike as "Laramie" and "Cheyenne." Nor are genuinely different alternatives themselves enough. Plenty of great books and good thoughts are available. But a corrupt audience can corrupt even the finest work of art. Being a democrat, Cooley never considered the problem of how to train a public to accept the authority of the good, true, or beautiful.

People draw together, not to see the show, really, but because they prefer any company to being alone. In the concept of the primary group, into which all men are born and which they always seek, Cooley proposed the eternal and unchanging form that would save the American individualist from demoralizing belief in himself alone. Togetherness, it seemed to Cooley, rendered the content of the getting together quite secondary, a mere occasion for the chance to exercise the primary ideals, the chief of which is

togetherness itself.[1] The social good follows from sociability: "The improvement of society does not call for any essential change in human nature, but,
chiefly, for a larger and higher application of its familiar impulses"—that
is, the ideals of truth-telling, kindness and loyalty bred in the primary
group. A larger togetherness is now possible, thanks to the mass media.
Indeed, according to Cooley, if only the mass media would be reasonable
and truthful, thus confirming the native moral sense, a good society might at
last be created, quite without any special creed. He assumed that it would
be sufficient to present the best abundantly and well. His trust in the mass
media reflected a deeper disinclination to take into account the demonic in
man. Cooley's sociology was a variety of the religion of culture to which the
cultured resort after all other religions fail them.

Cooley found in the modern potential of social organization that "differentiated unity of mental and social life" which, to him, defines the good
society. Indeed, social organization is the very form of love, giving to human
nature its specific quality of humanity. The entire first part of this book con-
centrates on demonstrating the classical proposition that man is a social animal, against the profound American sentiment that opposes self and society.
The primary group is thus an analytic symbol forwarding a case as old as
Aristotle. Man owes the form of his individuality not to his own creative ego
but to the creative collectivity. The self is the creative act of others. "I imagine your mind, and especially what your mind thinks of my mind, and what
your mind thinks about what my mind thinks about your mind. I dress my
mind before yours and expect that you will dress yours before mine." From
this tight erotic weave of reciprocal imagining, both self and society achieve
their unity; without this reciprocity, both self and society disintegrate internally, lacking the sense of obligation that makes life worth living. Yet the
ethic of responsibility that Cooley derives from the mingling of self and other
has no special content. There is no criterion of judgment beyond the group.
Cooley's worry about this problem can be expressed in a question he once
asked himself: "The group disciplines its membership, but who will discipline the group?" It is the question of a man who still hankers after some
authority larger than his own group writ small. Rarely does Cooley resort to
the exhausted rhetoric of conscience; he was too fine a social psychologist
for that.

In the second part of *Social Organization*, Cooley tries to show the ways

1. Simmel expresses the notion of the intractable sociability of individuals in the following
passage: "above and beyond their [specific] content, all . . . associations are accompanied by
a feeling for, by a satisfaction in, the very fact that one is associated with others and that the
solitariness of the individual is resolved into togetherness, a union of others." See Georg Simmel, "The Sociology of Sociability," translated by Everett C. Hughes, *American Journal of
Sociology* 40, no. 3 (November 1949): 255–61.

in which the symbolic form of everyday life is diffused and complicated in order to meet the exigencies of less intimate contacts among selves. It is the point at which all selves can be analyzed as others that the task of the sociologist begins. Cooley tried, by the personal force of his analytic understanding, to help extend the "primary ideals" (that is, the sentiments generated by primary group living) into areas of society where they cannot be carried directly by primary groups themselves. Cooley's essential conservatism—and, indeed, the essential conservatism of sociology—is most evident here. Implicit in all his intellectual work is the purpose of preserving the ideal values of small, preindustrial communities in the period of massive, industrial societies. Cooley defended the old values of his idealized America, no less than Orwell defended the values of his imagined old England.

In the third part of this book, titled "Social Disorganization," Cooley tried to cope with the breakup of the basic form and also with its inherent deficiencies. He is aware that the primary group does not appear cohesive enough to sustain its ideals even for itself. Yet he has nothing to offer as a substitute for the primary group, as Marx did, for example, in the symbolic form resting upon his mystique of class struggle. In consequence, the third is by far the weakest part of this book. The liberal sociologist, hoping for the extension of truth-telling, kindness and loyalty through the remote psychological space of the great society, depended entirely on his esteem for democracy as a self-correcting convergence of private sentiments into a reasoned and socially concerned public opinion. Cooley's belief in social democracy—in a culture effectively improving itself despite the absence of an authoritative set of moral standard-bearers—no longer elicits quite the same response of confident agreement as it did in 1909, when his book first appeared. The "enlightened public" appears now, more certainly than ever before, a figment of Cooley's sociological imagination, his edifying mass media pathetic reminders of what might have been. *Social Organization* is a book full of such beautiful hallucinations. All the fragments of the American dream are there arranged in a way that was perhaps, in Cooley's time, still a possible truth. The dream has become a futile wish, protecting the ugliness of the American reality. From the warmth of Cooley's Primary Group there is a sinister short way to the stifling creed of togetherness.

No more than individuals can societies live without love. Having been trained in this true belief, Americans have taken on, as their second job, the search for love. Searching thus, self-consciously, they have found sex, personality, and other similar creeds which render them incapable of loving. Yet Cooley's fundamental point, in his sociological version of the truth that societies cannot live without love, is that the usefulness of creeds has long passed. In the future, as Cooley envisioned it, American unity would consist not in agreement, or creed, but in "organization." The very form of our private experience, if judiciously diffused, would supply us with our sense of unity. In the form Cooley gave to it, love is an antidoctrine, opposing all relations of power, an enactment that needs no symbolism. The most ordinary life is always and everywhere the most extraordinary demonstration of love. All social action expresses devotion.

Perhaps the final weakness in Cooley's argument can be located in his assumption that men perfect themselves in acts of devotion—whatever the varieties of purpose to which they may be devoted. But this describes the action of only one among many possible personality types, once dominant in western culture: the ascetic. Cooley's entire sociology depends upon the persistence of the ascetic, as the dominant personality type. Early in the book, he assures his readers that "the fullest self-realization will belong to the one who embraces in a passionate self-feeling the aims of the fellowship, and spends his life in fighting for their attainment." Here is a straightforward sociological reading of the Christian injunction that he who loses himself in God will find himself.

Cooley's conception of love remains the ascetic one of sacrificial action. "One is never more human, and as a rule never happier," Cooley asserts, in the traditional way, "than when he is sacrificing his narrow and merely private interest to the higher call of the congenial group." The primary group offers the individual an introductory course in self-sacrifice, without which he can never advance to full participation in the city-state, the Germanic *comitatis*, the New Jerusalem, the working-class movement, American democracy. "It is a poor sort of individual that does not feel the need to devote himself to the larger purposes of the group." Yet, just that poor sort has learned, the hard way, to suspect all larger purposes and higher calls. More precisely, the American individualist demands of all higher calls that are not merely conscriptions that they demonstrate their usefulness to his personal sense of well-being.

There are other, easier points of criticism that might be directed against Cooley. His faith in the binding quality of face-to-face relations is difficult to sustain, once the ambivalence of personal experience becomes as clear as Freud has made it. And, of course, "larger purposes" can be made to look rather ugly by reviewing them too close up. Nevertheless, knowing all this, Cooley refused to contribute to the immense and popular literature of disappointment, both in the self for continuing to make sacrifices and in society for continuing to demand them. Cooley had the rare insight that in a democratic culture the self could live only through a series of sacrifices. To the dominant, individualistic view this is a doctrine of "anti-life," as D. H. Lawrence once called it. But then, significantly enough, Lawrence was no democrat. So, to Lawrence, for example, "the greatest democrats, like Abraham Lincoln, had always a sacrificial, self-murdering note in their voices. American Democracy was a form of self-murder, always." *Social Organization* is a book seeking to protect the life of American democracy against its members. No more gently resolute argument for the superiority of what Lawrence called "self-murder" has been made by an American writer. Conservative and democratic, advocating the moral bind in a fresh and subtle way, Cooley is a very American sociologist. His successors have been more energetic collectors of empirical data, but none are more clever advocates of the search for community built into the analysis of society. (62:4)

45
Cooley's *Human Nature and the Social Order*

"The imaginations people have of one another," Cooley wrote, "are the solid facts of society." *Human Nature and the Social Order* is a classic examination, first published in 1902 and then again in a revised edition in 1922, of the flash point at which the human imagination ignites to produce the infinitely adjustable social temperature without which man has not yet learned to live. That flash point may produce the cold of the concentration camp or the warmth of the family. Cooley can account for both; his theory of human nature predicates no ontology but only the social order itself. In this brilliantly written work, Cooley, pushing the modern genius for social analysis against all ontological traditions of human nature, destroys, in a way that has persuaded generations of readers, the belief that human nature has some content and meaning superior to the social order of which it is the representative conception.

That there is a human nature,[1] mirroring in each man the social order in which men act out their lives, seemed to Cooley something more than an article of faith, a *fides quarens intellectum*. It is the very language of faith, supplying every culture with its self-revelation, and therefore with its self-understanding. The social order requires some such faith. And yet this too may have become an article of faith, for those who, following Cooley, have been systematically autobiographical enough to recognize the changeable contents of their symbolic interactions.

What distinguishes Cooley, as sociologist, from all those philosophers, psychologists, theologians, artists, novelists, poets and holy men who have written on human nature before him, is that he does not propose a position

Reprinted from *Human Nature and the Social Order*, by Charles Horton Cooley (New York: Schocken, 1964), ix–xx.

1. "Shewing the two contrary states of the human soul," as Blake puts it.

but rather examines the dynamics which make this mode of self-understanding socially necessary. *Human Nature and the Social Order* contains no maneuverings for moral position. Cooley does not strive to gain that high symbolic ground from which the great forgers of human nature have organized the egos of others, as, in the act of seeing the nature of the human, they must organize their own.

Primarily by linking doctrines of human nature to social orders, Cooley asserts how widely diffused and varied both are, inducing terror and consolation among men about themselves, in ways that facilitate their particular habits of action for and against each other. Doctrines separating human nature from social order, for all their brilliant complexities, belong to those great dead cultures in which men knew chiefly what they believed. In doctrines of human nature(s)[2] they found a way of putting a face on their group identity, thus forging the missing link between self and society. That link broken, there is the privacy of madness or a more social disorder. Without an imagery of self, a common consciousness, a culture would be characterized mainly by doubts about its own existence, as ours is nowadays.

Culture survives. Every social order produces a doctrine of human nature, an imagery of individual development (as from original sin to ultimate salvation), implicit in that order. Thus warmth is achieved, great communities founded. Every doctrine is an internal fix, from which each man must depart and yet maintain, by virtue of his graduated membership in the life-plan of that order, his self-esteem. Departing, each man achieves his mandatory sense of guilt, a motor for the driving in of social demand thus rendered moral. Granted a working balance of self-esteem and guilt, each man, collecting himself from elements of the social order, according to its ethos, measures the manner and distance of his drift through existence. There are combinations and complexities of fix and drift that have to be treated historically, empirically—treated finally, in Cooley's view, by a sociology united, in its highest style, to "systematic autobiography."

The intellectual ancestry of Cooley includes all those for whom autobiography is the highest science—that science being the least likely to freeze into a permanent truth. Montaigne understood the pathos of modern autobiographies; they render individualities endurable by rendering them problematic. Pulling up anchor, making autobiography itself the object of his ironic address, Montaigne set himself adrift on the sea of modern self-consciousness. From this voyage no one has yet had the genius to return, except as to some port of call. "If my health smiles on me and the day is clear," Montaigne remarked, "I am a worthy person." Here we have described, in one self-reference, the plan of the autobiographical culture to

2. In Western societies, these doctrines are dualist, characteristically.

which we ourselves belong. Montaigne's "health" Pascal called sickness—but the issue has been settled, in Montaigne's favor, by successors like Cooley, who made society the subject of autobiography.

To the professional students of society, living as they do under the duress of life plans that have cracked up, or, perhaps, of non-plans not yet compelling enough to serve an equivalent function, doctrines of human nature, in all varieties everywhere, may be known, but only at the expense of belief. They appear as the embarrassing expedients with which every social order, until our own, has given shape and color to the emptiness that might otherwise expand inside and shiver the ego. When doctrines of human nature hold, like centers, the panic and emptiness may even be therapeutically elicited and contained, sending vicarious shivers through the *I* in the middle of everyone's head. Better than any sociologist or psychologist, Forster described in *Howard's End* the function of high culture. Leonard Bast goes to a concert, listens to Beethoven's *Ninth*, and, in its resonance, catches the silence around which every culture gulls every man into producing an appropriate insulation of experience. Of course that experience which is encouraged in the culture must also be mastered; otherwise, it is not insulating. In some cultures, the insulation of experience mastered may be more producible in the arts; in others, warfare or a theology may supply the functional equivalent. Thus, in Buddhist doctrine, the panic and emptiness can itself be experienced and rendered an integral part of the religious tasks set for mastery from earliest childhood.

Mastery is usually taught from earliest childhood, in a magnificent variety of modes, beginning always with the parental and sibling pedagogy. In the period after Cooley's, in the history of American social science, the study of children became a field of the first importance, not only because of Freud but also because of insights into the development of social communication supplied by Cooley, Mead, and William James. Those insights, adumbrated in this book, remain important for understanding how the naked ego is clothed and thus protected from the ontological emptiness.

Of course, the social order does swiftly clothe the actors born into it in the self-understandings they are, thereafter, reluctant to shed even for the rare privilege of a glimpse of themselves in their nothingness. The clothing, it may be argued, tentatively and in an exploratory way, has been tailored to make every man assume the role of emperor. But in a nation of emperors, who is to play the child? On the other hand, by this time in the history of Western culture, the child, or naivete about the sanctity of our social sentiments, may be superfluous. The emperors do not believe. They do not disbelieve. In the world of the nude, who is nude?

In the subtle business of detecting how emperors are clothed, none was more subtle, or more sympathetic to the enterprise, than Cooley. In this book he argues, beautifully and with full knowledge of the dangers inherent in the argument, the classical case that every society produces, out of its own structure, the myth within which it is thus empowered to live. It is required that "self-feeling" be thus fused, with enough social strength to keep the individual in that "middle-road" of civility and self-respect where Cooley found all truly civilized men, able to communicate and disagree—and yet maintain the social peace.

It is the "control of hostility by a sense of allegiance to rule," the social necessity of vetting all lasting animal angers that has led Cooley's successors in sociology to covet the possibility of a place in the new symbol industry. With both hostility and allegiance growingly inaccurate general terms from which to begin a description of the popular mind, alarmed students of our own social order call for the mass manufacture of emperor's clothes, advertising them all as rather useful and nice. They will give warmth, they look good, if not looked at too closely. But men like to look closely. Boredom supports animal curiosity; fashions of doctrinal denials come quickly on the heels of doctrinal affirmation until naivete is exhausted and all understand that it is a necessary game, a dressing-up of the ego. There is nothing, really, to believe—except the utility of belief itself. We are all Anglicans now, going to church because it is the civil thing to do on Sunday morning. Some old philosophers may continue to argue seriously on the nature of man, but that is because they are poorly educated in the new learning and ignore, in plain self-defense, their logical successors, the interior decorators.

Among our present cadres of interior decorators, the psychiatrists are probably the most widely remarked. The best of them know that our ego models have a long history of contradiction. Therefore, they build a model of nature that is contradictory. The natural is an idealization of the social. It is, perhaps, conflicting ego ideals that lead to contrary states of the soul.

Read a reputable book on modern interior decoration, titled *Understandable Psychiatry* (I choose it mainly because of the title—the point can be reproduced from a thousand texts) by Hinsie, published in 1948. This book demonstrates, to my satisfaction at least, what a hard time dying the idea of human nature has had. In fact, it is still alive and excessively popular nowadays, putting on the fashion of the time. Psychiatrists, in the late forties, being unembarrassed by the slightest training in philosophy or theology, not to mention sociology, went so far as to distinguish "first nature" from "second nature." First nature turns out to be "the undiluted and unmodified instincts," primitive "drives" emanating from the bodily tissues. This first nature distributes itself in the body and is also taken up, so to say, into the mind. "Second nature" refers, of course, to the "super-ego." It is a term that is equivalent to "inner conscience," derived, of course, from parental management. First nature is somehow organic; second nature social. Here is perpetuated the myth that man has two natures, one supervising the other. In this way does psychiatry make itself understandable in the Western tradition. Just as the Jesuits forwarded education precisely to the point where it served their object of restoring the authority of the Church, and no farther, so the contemporary psychiatrist forwards a doctrine of two natures so far as it buttresses his therapeutic authority. The idea of human nature has always been thus associated with polemical and institutional uses. The rhetorical problem of contemporary dynamic psychiatry is how to put "instinct," which is hypostasized as the raw limit of social order, on the loftiest pedestal and yet keep it in subjection, like a beautiful and dangerous woman.

Exploring the Jesuits on intellect, or the psychoanalysts on instinct, the social psychology of knowledge (by which I would understand the sociological discipline to which Cooley's work was propaedeutic) exemplifies in itself the polemical uses of the doctrine of human nature, those purposes served by its particular conceptualization within this present social order. Certainly, Cooley was entirely opposed to any variety of ontological argument, whether human nature is the predicate of society, or vice versa. Like the philosophers Mead and James, the sociologist Cooley was too hard-headed an American to be interested in the European shadow play of the dialectic between essence and existence. To meddle thus with philosophical terms is no part of sociology. That ontology returns regularly to distract the social sciences is therefore only a measure of their faulty self-understanding.

I do not say that ontological argument ought to be summarily dismissed. Contemporary psychiatry conceives of anxiety, for example, not merely as something we *have* but also as something we *are*. Perhaps there is a healthy residue of philosophical tradition in the persistent tendency of modern psychology to treat every event or symptom (in appearance) as a correlative of a real personal subsistence (in reality). A particular symptom therefore becomes related to its hypostasis, although the relation is rarely more than assumed. Freud assumed an "organic" repression, although the relation between "organic" and "symbolic" repression is never worked out. Thus some shred of ontology makes its strand even in Freud, who was so impatient with what he called the "abstractness" of philosophy.

Human Nature and the Social Order is a sociological, as opposed to a philosophical, piece of work. It is, of course, subject to further sociological analysis. Cooley's book is itself a chapter in the doctrinal history of human nature. Referring to the chapter in this book on "The Social Conscience," Mead remarks that it is an "admirable ethical treatise" in the American style. "His sociology," Mead concludes, "was in a sense an account of the American community to which he [that is, Cooley] belonged, and presupposed its normal healthful process." My point here has been that, in face of the evidence, Cooley's successors need no longer make this presupposition. Cooley represented a limited constituency, with a limited history. His small-town doctrine of human nature may appear as archaic now as that of the philosopher-aristocrats of Greek culture, in the context of Greek political theory and institutional practice. The intelligent and gentlemanly Cooleyan symbolic of human nature—White, Anglo-Saxon, Protestant and Liberal—may no longer serve to build up that controlling consensus which once constituted the specific genius of American culture. It is not yet clear what the new symbolic is, nor whether, in a technologically advanced and bureaucratically organized mass society, a controlling consensus, in the classical mode, is required for social order.

To say how a doctrine—or doctrinal element—functions is to exhibit the consensual purposes it serves in the social order. Thus, the main component elements of the doctrine of human nature among upper-class and upper-middle-class Unitarians in the nineteenth century indicates that they meant by "reason" and "progress" (as the twin elements of human nature) to include the prerogatives of private property. "Reason" functioned differently for the leadership of the Paris Communards. In this sense, the question of truth, in sociological analysis, is limited to the truth of a specific consensus. No doctrine of human nature has yet indicated its independence from the social order in which it has appeared. These doctrines may be treated as salient ways in which societies organize their systems of moral demand.

All doctrines of human nature are subject to what Durkheim rightly called the "laws of collective ideation." In *Human Nature and the Social Order*, Cooley composed a psychology of cultural forms. His analysis of American culture, in the ideal form it took in his imagination, exhibits the modes of control and release by which our moral consensus was once achieved. Because "collective psychology is sociology,"[3] this work on the American collective psychology remains an exemplary display of sociological competence.

I have tried to indicate the way in which *Human Nature and the Social Order* is something more than an admirable ethical treatise. It is also a classic work on the process of social communication as the very stuff of which the self is made. To the study of this process both Cooley and Mead contributed insights that have become the trustworthy basis of contemporary social psychology.

Both Cooley and Mead went beyond the Wundtian concept of the gesture. A gesture is, as Mead would have it, that part of a social act which serves as a stimulus to other forms involved in the same social act. To both Cooley and Mead, the Darwinian notion of gesture proved mistaken. Gestures do not

3. Again, according to Durkheim.

have as their primary function the "expression of emotion." They are, rather, parts of a complex system of social communication in which many different forms are involved. *We* observe animals and assume emotional attitudes which lie behind acts; they have that meaning *for us*. No consciousness is necessary for animals—animal communication does not necessarily involve consciousness. When, however, a man shakes his fist in another's face, we assume not only a hostile attitude but that *meaning* of hostility for him which it has for us—a fist is a significant symbol. We have a symbol which answers to a meaning in the experience of the first individual and which also calls out that meaning in the second individual.

Thus gesture may become language, or a significant symbol. The gesture *as such* merely makes adjustment possible; the significant symbol makes meaning possible—and a truly social order. Sociology begins with this assumption of action meaningful to the actors. Only when we have significant symbols are mind and society, in the human sense, possible.

"Taking the attitude of the other" toward one's own conduct is, for Mead and Cooley, the essential characteristic of social conduct. Even the body is not a self, *as such*; it becomes a self only when it imagines itself in relation to others; without social experience, therefore, the self cannot develop. Social communication is thus fundamental to selfhood.

The theory of imitation, like the theory of gesture, proved an inadequate basis for modern social psychology. Meaning is something different from mocking. Intelligibility is something more than intelligence. A computer may exhibit intelligence without producing significant symbols. If a gesture calls out an appropriate response in others, it is possible to get complex cooperation, as in the case of ants or bees; but an imitation of another is not necessarily a significant symbol. In fact, imitation really depends on the individual influencing himself as others influence him, so that he undergoes the influence not only of the other but also of himself insofar as he uses the same vocal gesture. There is, therefore, no imitation *as such*; but if there is already present in the individual an action like the action of another, then there is a situation which makes so-called imitation possible. The critical importance of vocal gesture lies in its reciprocal character; it immensely facilitates role assumption. It is largely owing to language that we "see oursel's as ithers see us," for from infancy onward we address ourselves as others address us.

Extreme behaviorists like Watson held that all our thinking is explicit or implicit vocalization. In "silent thinking" we are simply starting to use certain words. Even so, the extreme behaviorists overlook the fact that these words, as stimuli, are essential elements in elaborate social processes and carry with them the other components of those processes.

The meaning of "calling out in oneself the same response as in others" is illustrated by asking someone to do something. It becomes difficult to keep from doing it oneself; the prophet is stirred by his prophecy. The categorical imperative might be reinterpreted in this way, not as a sublime ethical doctrine but as routine philosophical dynamics. And this was Cooley's polemical intention: so to reinterpret the categorical imperative that it became the inescapable meaning of social life. (64:1)

46

Cooley and Culture

Of all the mentors I have found in our discipline, Cooley is the one who speaks to me, through his writing, in the most intimate and formative way. I return regularly to readings of him, as to conversations with a wise colleague and older friend. He is permanently capable of a conversation in which our agreements and disagreements are passing incidents. I think this capability places him high in the permanent order of professionals in the field. For myself, there is no substitute for Cooley, no superseding him, no danger of obsolescence; he is a truly humane sociologist, a sagacity worth confronting well beyond his own time. I can think of no higher praise than to recommend such a sagacity as a model teacher of aspirant sociologists.

I am not a follower of Cooley, in the sense some of my students intend when they ask whether I am a "Freudian," "Weberian," "Durkheimian," or something or other. My debt to Cooley is too personal for this kind of labeling. Rather, he is an old and trusted ally, who preserves me from feeling a greater sense of certainty than our subject allows, and, I hope, instills in me that sense of the otherness of human actors that, possessing it himself to a serviceable degree, he never hesitated to call "sympathy." (See especially chapter 4 of *Human Nature and the Social Order.*)

Perhaps mainly because his writings are so full of this sympathy and thus provoke anxiety, if not downright hostility, among the professional sociologists of today, Cooley is not now read as seriously or as often as he should be, I think. He has not quite joined the army of the distinguished but ignored, like Albion Small, or Lester F. Ward. But I see the sales figures on the paperback editions, to which I wrote introductions, of two major products of his life's work, *Human Nature and the Social Order* and *Social Organization;* those figures warrant the publishers' keeping his work in print, but barely. When I assign one of his books entire in courses on sociological theory, as I invariably do, many students resist. Ours is a discipline suffering

Reprinted from *Cooley and Sociological Analysis,* edited by Albert J. Reiss, Jr. (Ann Arbor: University of Michigan Press, 1968), 32–47.

from a widespread belief in its own radical contemporaneity. Cooley appears out of date. The rank and file among my students prefer to read snippets of Cooley's thought; his slow inward wisdom has not survived—only some strong and sticky external labels of wisdom, like "primary group." Graduate students are, too often, busy people; they have less and less time to read entire books, not to mention time to sit contemplatively over them. Grants and projects keep them very busy. But Cooley is best taken slowly; the student should linger long enough in his presence to appreciate some of his nobility of mind and rare gift for analyzing society as a whole, yet without oversimplification. (Cooley did not, however, claim to be a systematic theorist in the traditional sense; rather, he made systematic use of what I have called "multiple analytic perspectives." Introduction to *Social Organization*; see p. 297 in this volume.)

Cooley is not the only sociologist whose works communicate a nobility, a magnanimity of mind. But there are not so many that students can be permitted, without cost to their development as sociologists, to spare themselves the experience of confronting him. What troubles them is that the experience of reading a whole book by Cooley does not readily transfer into usable research formulae. The experience seems diffuse. Cooley will not boil down: there appears nothing unequivocal and thus easy to use.

Of course, the fault lies less with the students than with their teachers. Our too strictly departmental training of sociologists leaves little time or incentive to acquire personal culture. To the well-adjusted graduate student, Cooley appears dangerously speculative. Even worse, he was simultaneously a sociological and introspective writer, whose mixed visions of self and society can easily confuse and even bore the candidate social engineer, with his almost exclusive emphases on structure rather than idea. It is a vision maintained tentatively, of inner meanings that are not simply reflexive, without assurances to the reader that even this subjectivity is truth—let alone a sound method for explaining social reality. Cooley saw social reality as something "organic"; this, for him, was a way of conceiving what he felt to be the integrity of social phenomena—a unity of interior meaning and social action that any less than sympathetic approach could not but fail to discover. (See especially pp. 48–50 of *Human Nature and the Social Order*, Schocken Books edition.) Once personally envisioned, the organic structure of social reality appeared to Cooley to be the primary sociological fact; only those for whom sociology remained a set of analytic instruments external to the self—impersonal—could deny the organic character of social reality and abstract from it all the inwardness of social life.

Abstractionist sociology expresses something more than a misguided labor to be a natural science; it demonstrates how far a great intellectual tradition has gone to pieces, to a point at which "quality" is simply an archaic word for that which has not yet been quantified. The present antiqualitative mood of sociology may well open up new possibilities for the elaboration of sociology. But such an opening up of some possibilities may be at the intellectual cost of the discipline, closing down others. As teachers, some of us, in the tradition of which Cooley was a practitioner, must keep open the possibility that sociology is a personal, normative—even transformative—discipline.

One of Cooley's didactic purposes was to help counterbalance the influence in sociology of what he called, in another context, "routine methods" that turn out "cheap work in large quantities."[1] "Use diagrams, by all means," he once wrote, "use classifications, use maps, curves, statistics—and forget them!" There was no substitute, he thought, for "trained sympathy." His answer to all "methods" is not yet another method but "sagacity, insight, breadth of knowledge, humble honesty and real love of truth."[2] Can such virtues be taught? At least the discipline need not go so far in its search for objective and systematic methods that it falls into the opposing vice of teaching methodology as if it were a substitute for what may be missing from the personal culture of the student.

Some readers of Cooley appear hostile to him for another, though related reason: they are offended by his ready way with what they are still pleased to call "value judgments." Passage after passage seems to them downright unprofessional. How can he write of "higher" and "lower" individualisms, of "ruthless self-assertion," of "a lack of that high discipline which prints the good of the whole upon the heart of the member"? Cooley regularly offends the young in their idea of scientific neutrality; and he equally offends the sophisticated in their skepticism about any moral order of social reality.

Of course Cooley was aware of the basic cultural situation of which sociology was both expression and diagnosis—". . . it is a question whether we are not, in some degree and no doubt temporarily, actually relapsing into a kind of barbarism through the sudden decay of a culture type imperfectly suited to our use but much better than none." He could not permit himself to be entirely pessimistic. On the contrary, he suspected that "we may be participating in the rise of a new type of culture which shall revise rather than abandon the old traditions, and whose central current will perhaps be a large study of the principles of human life and of their expression in history, art, philanthropy and religion. And the belief that the new discipline of sociology (much clarified and freed from whatever crudeness and pretension may now impair it) is to have a part in this may not be entirely a matter of special predilection."[3] Here speaks the sociologist, concisely, of his puta-

1. *Social Organization* (New York, 1909), 345.

2. *Life and the Student* (New York, 1927), 156–58.

3. *Social Organization*, 388–89.

tive role in resolving the crisis of modern culture. Taking Cooley seriously could lead to a view of sociology as a normative discipline.

I cannot enter here into a discussion of Cooley's theory of personal culture: that "common ideal life," that "higher discipline which prints the good of the whole upon the heart of every member," the "slowly built traditions of a deeper right and wrong which cannot be justified to the feelings of the moment." He worried about that "relapse to impulse" which signals great traditions going to pieces. Another system of culture, he concluded, was developing—and the demoralization he observed merely incidental to its development. The next culture would express, he thought, a "higher kind of life," simpler in creed and less authoritarian in manner, of which "personality" would be "the best symbol of all."[4]

Sociology must live inside the symbolic world it is itself constantly examining. The fact that, even for a mind as cautious as Cooley's, personality was to become the "best symbol of all" ("The nearer you can get to universal human nature without abandoning concreteness, the better . . . The less intellectual a religious symbol is the better, because it less confines the mind. Personality is the best symbol of all; and after that music, art, poetry, festivity, and ceremony are more enduring and less perilous symbols than formulas of belief." *Social Organization*, p. 379) helps me state the problem of sociologically interpreting our emergent culture—that is, of interpreting our self-interpretations. I shall devote the second part of this paper not to the drawing out of Cooley's implicit theory of personal culture but rather to one aspect of the sociologist's involvement in cultural change.

Cooley, like other theorists of culture, did not escape unharmed from the ancient and continuing quarrel between science and religion. Let us restate the issues in that quarrel, using terms appropriate to our understanding of the processes of cultural change.

Every culture system organizes the tension of two types of thought-worlds, one type *technological* and the other *religious*. There are ways to mend a canoe, to keep it afloat, rendering existence on the water both possible and ordinary; all this is a part of technology. There must also be ways to "mend" what is directly not yet mendable—death, for example. To do so is obviously the task of religion.

I propose to call everything that falls within some technological thought-world "minimal culture" and everything that falls within some religious thought-world "maximal culture." This distinction resembles, though it is not equivalent to, the traditional one between "secular" and "sacred."

But while some theorists speak of "secular-culture" and of societies become "secularized" as if the sacred can become wholly swallowed up in or reduced to the secular, I, on the contrary, wish to emphasize that secular, or

4. Ibid., 379; see below for the context of this remark.

technological, culture is never anything but a minimal solution to the problems faced by a particular society, because *by its very nature* such culture can deal only with a limited segment of these problems. In other words, certain problems posed by the simple fact of human existence at any time are *inherently* insoluble in terms of technological culture. These insoluble problems, of which death is still the greatest, form part of the "brokenness" of existence, which has also been called the problem of nothingness, of the void, of nonbeing.

Minimal culture, then, refers to those thought-worlds by which men are driven to ameliorate and/or adapt realistically, and for the sake of the system of satisfactions that is the continually changing product of such coping, the environment conceived as objects of desire. Of course, technological societies have always existed. We cannot conceive of a society in which there is not transmitted from generation to generation accretions of know-how, practical knowledge, the skills by which existence is rendered ordinary in the sense that we know we can cope with it predictably on a material plane. All technological societies—that is, societies characterizable in terms of their minimal cultures—are constituted as the external forms of those thought-worlds that are, in their variety, the universal culture of ordinary existence. And all societies may be said to survive, in a physical sense, by means of their secular traditions, be they codified wisdom on stalking game, or on storing food supplies, or on conducting a chain-store operation, or on building a floatable ship. By maximal culture, on the other hand, I mean those thought-worlds that organize our sense of the *extra*ordinariness of existence. Maximal culture is a response, elaborate enough in its own fashion, to the brokenness of existence, to problems with which men cannot cope in the other way.

Most nineteenth-century sociological theory—which, we should remember, was far more concerned with history than is sociological theory today— accorded with the spirit of the age in being prejudiced in favor of minimal culture. Comte's "law" of civilization's three stages—theological, metaphysical, and positive—was a general account of the inroads made by minimal on maximal culture, to the point at which the latter was supposed to be overwhelmed and finally vanish into history. Spencer's theory of societal adaptation had the same emphasis: every "real" success of man in coping with his environment expanded the jurisdiction of minimal culture. Maximal culture was an expression of society's failure to cope more directly with its problems; for this reason, the transformations worked by maximal culture, though surpassingly important in the history of mankind, were thought to be continually superseded by technological thought-worlds.

Comte had argued that history should be interpreted in terms of the gradually expanding jurisdiction over human behavior and events of those thought-worlds that he called "positivist" and that we, with good reason, prefer to call technological. Cooley was not at pains to deny this; on the contrary, he welcomed the secularization of previously sacred institutions, confident that whatever they contained of value to the modern world would be preserved:

> The church is possibly moving toward a differentiated unity, in which the common element will be mainly sentiment—such sentiments as justice, kindness, liberty, and service. These are sufficient for good-will and cooperation, and leave room for all the differentiation of ideas and methods that the diversity of life requires.
>
> With whatever faults the church is one of the great achievements of civilization. Like the body of science or our system of transportation and manufacture, it is the cumulative outcome of human invention and endeavor, and is probably in no more danger of perishing than these are. If certain parts of it break up we shall no doubt find that their sound materials are incorporated into new structures." (*Social Organization*, pp. 381–82)

But maximal, or, as he called it, "higher" culture was for Cooley at least "of a kindred spirit with religion."[5] This was only natural in one whose view of social culture was paralleled by a view of personal culture as a product of something like spiritual discipline. (See *Human Nature and the Social Order, passim*, but especially pp. 396–400.)

Cooley's defense of maximal culture before the aggression of minimal culture was an agile and courageous intellectual performance for a sociologist of his time. But it seems now that even he may have been retreating more than the aggression warrants. Such defenders of maximal culture did not indicate how the "sound materials" were to survive those transformations that accompany incorporations into new structures. How can we sketch the thought world that is the prevailing inner condition of the modern, western social order? To be able to do so would be to characterize the quality of our lives, and to indicate the shape that the emergent culture is taking.

In the system of culture preceding our own, men were haunted by the words: "If thou wilt be perfect . . ." (Matthew XIX:21). To live one's life in the workaday world was clearly something less than a striving for perfection. But the thought-world that organizes modern technological society now assigns the possibility of perfection to none other than men themselves. "If thou wilt be perfect . . ."—the words drove Antony, the founder of monasticism, out of ordinary existence into the desert, and ordinary existence was, in terms dictated by this thought-world, well lost. Withdrawal was the highest style of life, restriction of need its observable ethic. Thus did maximal culture penetrate minimal. The good life was a drawing of limit around sheer

---

5. *Social Process* (New York, 1926), 75.

possibility. In such a culture, the thought-worlds of the then minimal culture were severely restricted. To be a creature of power and wonder, a holy man and God's initiate, was to successfully deny oneself and surrender one's will.

I cannot, in this brief space, try to account for the historic reversal in the positions of maximal and minimal culture. Perhaps it will be enough to suggest that modern men can imagine themselves perfect only in a perfectly ordinary existence; indeed, the extraordinary is just that which threatens technological "perfection." A perfectly ordinary existence is a consummation which sociological theorists less sensitive than Cooley to the brokenness of existence, or perhaps more impatient to act against it, seem devoutly to have wished. Some of the founding European fathers of sociology elaborated theories of progress according to which science was not only undermining religion but setting up new and superior values in its place. "Progress," noted Spencer, "is not an accident but a necessity. Surely must evil and immorality disappear; surely must man become perfect."[6] Successor to the *ascetic*, what I have called elsewhere[7] the *therapeutic* type, incarnates the thought-world of modern society; he is the hero of a minimal culture rendered maximal. Men must become perfect in their instrumentalities, not in themselves. It is not enough to see our fascination with gadgetry and procedural strategies of living as a conspiracy of hucksters and psychotherapists. Such fascination expresses the thought-world of a technologically advanced society in which men must have and use up things, including themselves, in order to become perfect. Only in this way, in using ever more varied things, can they accelerate that change of condition, favorable or unfavorable, which appears the established purpose of modern men and of their different, even contending, social systems.

Unfortunately, men have not become perfect in the sense Spencer and other advocates of minimal culture had in mind. This may be to say that our gadgets and procedures for obtaining satisfaction and social stability are not yet perfect. Even so, within the newly dominant culture, men remain obdurately unwilling to become perfect instruments. Neither psychiatric techniques nor any others more or less advanced have succeeded in mending the brokenness of existence from which high culture used to derive its presence and power. The basic experience of life is still extraordinary; existence is still broken and therefore in need of something other than techniques that merely elaborate the ordinariness of existence.

But one can be too pessimistic a theorist of minimal culture triumphant, as Spencer was too optimistic. In a technological society, men more at their

6. See Herbert Spencer, *Social Statics* (London, 1892), 32.

7. See *The Triumph of the Therapeutic: Uses of Faith After Freud*, 2d ed. (Chicago: University of Chicago Press, 1987).

leisure may have more time and energy to confront—even as play is organized to develop ways of avoiding this confrontation—the brokenness of existence. Technology itself may provide the time men need to discover that the mirrors by which they are made to look larger and more varied have not succeeded in making them feel more the masters of their various selves. Already, therapeutic culture is producing more and more individuals who protest against the false perfection advocated by a therapy that cannot rise above a mechanical version of the self.

I am far from persuaded, however, by my own brief argument against pessimism. Thought-worlds are cages, more or less ample, within which men learn to organize their lives and like it. The famous cage to which Weber referred is ample indeed: its very existence is an interdiction of even the motive of escape. Yet all cages must have escape hatches. We know that our culture has not always been as it is; high culture has not always shrunk at the touch of the practical.

We need a theory of social change that will account for cultural phenomena, a theory that will state the principles by which we can describe the transition from one dominant thought-world to another and the external forms thereof. The best that sociological and cognate theories have so far been able to do with the problem of conceptualizing change is (1) to appeal to the dynamic tension between minimal culture and maximal, in the manner of technological determinism,[8] as I have indicated above; (2) to suppose that when high culture "works" it is ameliorative in the same way as minimal culture, another way of mending the human condition by making existence ordinary. Maximal culture, in this view, becomes viable only as a fantasy technology, an interim ethic, good enough until method catches up with this or that particular madness.

This is not to deny all validity to the admittedly polemical notion of a dialectic between minimal and maximal culture, but rather to suggest that no culture, not even the therapeutic, is immortal. It may do itself in, of course, and in ways obvious to all of us. But it is more important to us as sociological theorists to note that therapeutic culture may be building into itself remissive components that will shorten its own life span. The technological thought-world externalized in mass societies encourages the most bizarre expectations of success, change, breakthrough; it generates its own popular temper of impatience in a huge mass of those who have not know-how but entertain quasi-eschatological daydreams of what they can receive. Our civilization is rapidly producing what is in effect a cultural lumpen pro-

8. "Cultures have changed tremendously, and these changes are basically traceable to new adaptations required by changing technology and productive arrangements" (Julian H. Steward, *The Theory of Culture Change* [Urbana: University of Illinois Press, 1955], 37).

letariat of unsophisticated therapeutic types, intensely demanding benefi-
ciaries of the sheer plenitude, material and otherwise, promised by the
folklore, the *popular* thought-world of technology. Such a hankering for instant satisfactions increases that aggressiveness which threatens to destroy
the therapeutic thought-world with its own handy gadgets. Heightened aggressiveness, combined with impatience, can produce terrifying breaks in
the ordinary routine of existence. Moreover, as therapy succeeds therapy,
therapeutic cultures very quickly go emotionally dry and may even explode
in flashes of personal protest.

I am aware that the modern style of personal protest may subserve the
dominant thought-world rather than subvert it. In what order has a clown-
genius been so honored as Dali in ours? Boredom is indeed the fundamental
ill in a therapeutic culture. It may even be that this style of recalcitrance is a
creative area of relaxation, a truly subversive form of play. But it is not at all
clear to me that most current protest styles have any other than a recreative
significance. Protest styles often strive, I think, mainly for aesthetic effects;
they are branches of modern art rather than of politics. In any case, therapeutic culture in the West may be developing new ways to incorporate and
neutralize irrationals and deviants.

To know what is sacred is to know what is impermissible, what must *not*
be done. In the nineteenth century, as the disintegration of Christian culture
became increasingly obvious, art, music, and literature established themselves as the successors to dogma as a means of telling the educated classes
what was and was not sacred. The romantic movement spearheaded the
counterattack of maximal culture on minimal; for a while, it forced men to
recognize the terrifying shadows cast by their inventions as more real, more
meaningful than the inventions themselves. But the thought-world of a therapeutic culture is shadowless: Therapeutic culture is without demons or
terrible villains. Conrad could not have set *Heart of Darkness* in a bureaucracy or a laboratory. The horror of a thought-world in which anything can
be *made* to happen is far more difficult to oppose with dogma-surrogates,
logico-verbal structures arguing what must not be made to happen. Art and
literature failed as the inheritors of a function once performed, however
poorly and at great cost in human suffering, by dogma; they never succeeded
in taking on the interdictory functions of high culture that have dominated
every system of social order except the therapeutic.

In the culture of the therapeutic, criticism tends to subserve rather than
subvert. The typical modern purveyor of words praises technological progress to urban masses as the mysterious workings of providence were once
praised to ignorant peasants. The few word-mongers who still appear in opposition to the therapeutic thought-world can think of nothing better than to
idealize the instinctual life, which is conceived of as in opposition to all

culture and all thought-worlds, not merely the therapeutic. But such doctrines are not to be dismissed as mere verbalisms. After all, to develop ways
of making life under minimal culture more acceptable is to do that form of
culture a service. A technologically sophisticated society, unlike its predecessors, requires no crises for purposes of system change because its interdictory modes are not deeply internalized and are therefore easily replaced.
Every good citizen of the therapeutic commonwealth can now enjoy a "revolutionary" personal life-style—a strange fulfillment of Marx's vision of the
bourgeoisie as a revolutionary class. Today's bourgeois is continually engaged in a "cultural revolution" not dreamt of in the philosophy of Mao Tse-
tung. The emergent therapeutic culture system must develop and stabilize a
much wider subsystem of subserving releases than existed in the culture
system it has replaced. That is why modes of amusement are becoming the
dynamic of the emergent high culture. And, in the process, the descendants
of the old cultural elites are being reduced to entertainers paid more or less
well to stave off boredom in the lives of still imperfectly socialized members
of the social order.

How can we cure ourselves of this therapy? Can we even imagine a culture that would replace the therapeutic? Am I not, too, a mere critic, another one of those gifted with some capacity for giving us the horrors to no
effect—except, perhaps, some slight diversion? I hope not. I believe that
theory must fight for its vision of the entire sociocultural dialectic, including
those higher orders of interest which pervade the lower. Sociological theory
can become constructive if, and only if, it uses its critical powers to plan a
cultural reconquest of the therapeutic thought-world.

We have lost our way. Maximal culture has finally become what some
sociological theorists in the nineteenth century conceived it to be: a means
for the maintenance of social order, not the level from which that order can
be judged and reordered. If maximal culture is still of use, it is only in the
perverted sense that it subserves the present social order, even in its apparently unstable superficies, by freeing the individual to take his recreation in
areas where minimal culture cannot guide him. Thus the self-limitation of
ascetic culture is replaced, in therapeutic culture, by self-entertainment;
the protest style is the leaven in the cultural mix of an affluent society. I
classify psychotherapeutic devices as belonging in the ambiguous ground
between self-entertainment and political control.

The social functions of entertainment are not viewed here as unimportant;
on the contrary, they have taken over those of religion. As I said, therapeutic culture—especially in affluent societies—must develop and stabilize
modes of release that will permeate the entire social system. It is not a mean
function to protect men against boredom, perhaps the major problem with
which a perfected minimal culture must cope. And it is to defend itself

against boredom and the ills for which boredom is responsible that minimal culture becomes the realm not of the ascetic but of the therapeutic. For this reason, the culture of the therapeutic appears to salvage all previous cultures and can mount a new mood of indulgence even toward the untalented irrationals in its midst.

Because therapeutic culture is indefinitely expansive, it will, I suppose, be mindful even of the "classics." School children will more and more be respectfully aware that the values taught by their own culture are no more "true" or "false" than any others, that, indeed, the various components of maximal culture in their own lives and in that of the community function independently of truth or falsity. Thus truly progressive school children are already set to acting out being ancient Athenians, complete with Greek food and tragedy. So perhaps there is reason to hope that formal education in a therapeutic thought-world will teach our successors to imitate the distant thunder of prophets, and other character types out of the past—teach, in sum, the *amusement* of admitting a wider variety of personality types to the present. In the culture of the therapeutic, inherited criteria of good and bad, right and wrong, are dissolved into the new criteria of well and ill, interesting and uninteresting; there is psychology where there used to be religion, morality, and custom.

And yet, there remain experiences with which we cannot cope, and for which the only mastery, still, lies within the jurisdiction of maximal culture. We are just beginning to control our beginnings, and there is as yet no technique for mastering death. Doctrines of eternal life have lost currency, and so the fact of death stands unmitigated, terrorizing modern man differently, although no less deeply, than it did his predecessors. Until there are techniques for mastering death, the old inviolate dynamic of maximal culture may yet generate the power to return, and penetrate minimal culture, limiting its power to render life ordinary and trivial.

But is death the sole surviving ally of maximal culture? Fortunately, there is also the possibility implicit in the theory of culture adumbrated in this paper: that the very opportunities for release that every moral demand system is bound to permit itself place limits upon that system's capacity for adaptive change. Therapeutic culture may be no less committed to its own destruction than were its predecessors. It is still too early to say whether the modern age will see a breakdown in that internal dynamic of culture by which the mechanisms of release themselves develop power enough first to challenge the superordinate interdictions and then to become interdictory themselves.

Finally, religions, the art, law, and the other elements of maximal culture may still revenge themselves upon a minimal theory of culture that sees no condition that maximal culture may return to claim its rightful supremacy because men cannot long look unblinking at themselves or at what they have done without feeling that particular kind of dissatisfaction which drives them to seek something other than new techniques for coping with the plagues and necessities of the human condition. The brokenness of existence may be a condition that no social order, however methodologically sophisticated, can meliorate, even if this fact drives members of the most advanced technological society to destroy themselves. It is possible that even the inhabitants of a therapeutic culture will learn to preserve themselves by accepting things as they are. Such acceptance may lead to the construction of a maximal culture that disciplines the raging interest in doing everything that can be done. Cooley thought such discipline right and inevitable; this belief was part of his equipment as a sociologist. And it is as a sociologist that I commend the same belief regularly to myself. (68:2)

47

Toward a Theory of Culture:
With Special Reference to the Psychoanalytic Case

But in general we have no cause to deny the hostility of analysis to culture. Culture involves neurosis, which we try to cure. Culture involves super-ego, which we seek to weaken.

—Gez Roheim, *The Riddle of the Sphinx*

Among the absurd little difficulties that Freud carried patiently in his person was what amounted to a 'Rome' phobia. We know that, like others among us, he had anxieties about catching trains; taking a train to Rome was the most postponed, and yet desired, trip of his life. For years Freud wanted to visit Rome and yet could not bring himself there. He achieved northern Italy; he achieved Naples; he skirted Rome. As Freud himself fully understood, this failure of desire had its own significance. Finally, in September of 1901, his own life turned at last in its immortal direction; the *Interpretation of Dreams* achieved, Freud achieved Rome. It was a triumph about which he wrote to his confidant of those long years of interior struggle, the Berlin nosologist, Wilhelm Fliess:[1]

Reprinted with the permission of Faber and Faber, Ltd. from *Imagination and Precision in the Social Sciences (Essays in memory of Peter Nettl)*, edited by T. J. Nossiter, A. H. Hanson and Stein Rokkan (London: Faber & Faber, 1972), 97–108. First read, in an earlier draft, as a lecture at the University of San Francisco, California.

1. *Letters to Wilhelm Fliess, Drafts and Notes: 1887–1902*, edited by Maria Bonaparte, Anna Freud, Ernest Kris. Translated by Eric Mosbacher and James Strachey (New York, 1954), 335–36.

My dear Wilhelm, I received your card a few hours before I left. I ought to write to you about Rome, but it is difficult. It was an overwhelming experience for me, and, as you know, the fulfilment of a long-cherished wish. It was slightly disappointing, as all such fulfilments are when one has waited for them too long, but it was a high spot in my life, all the same. But, while I contemplated ancient Rome undisturbed (I could have worshipped the humble and mutilated remnants of the Temple of Minerva near the forum of Nerva), I found I could not freely enjoy the second Rome. I was disturbed by its meaning, and, being incapable of putting out of my mind my own misery and all the other misery which I know to exist, I found almost intolerable the lie of the salvation of mankind which rears its head so proudly to heaven. I found the third, Italian Rome hopeful and likeable.

This letter, this personal manifesto against the second Rome, the Rome of faith, plunges us directly into Freud's response to one revolutionary condition of his time—and of ours. As a doctor, and, by 1901, as a therapist, Freud was responding, beyond his own misery, to historical conditions he saw carried unconsciously, by diverse people become patients, into his own consulting room. The grotesque inner lives of modern men were literally laid down before his averted eyes, demanding diagnosis and surcease; and yet his patients were unwilling to part precisely from their own profound wretchedness, that true counterpart of a false and superficial spirituality they could not claim truly as their own. The 'lie of salvation' no longer worked. First and foremost, the response of Freud to this historical condition consisted, in great measure, of analyzing that useless lie, in microcosm through the patient, in macrocosm through the culture in which the patient lived.

Much nonsense is talked about the special Viennese culture of Freud's time. In its main characteristics, Freud's culture bore all the marks that have grown more visible in our own. He too was a patient, even like ourselves, in a society that has come to resemble, more and more, one vast emergency ward. I shall be interested, here, not in the mind of Freud as revolutionary, but rather in the revolutionary character of the culture to which, for his own survival and ours, he created his immortal response. Freud's letter to Fliess introduces us directly, and most succinctly, to the culture that had failed and yet, remaining established, produced the condition to which a revolutionary response became necessary, in Freud's mind, as therapy is the necessary response to neurosis. The 'lie of salvation' had become 'intolerable,' not only to Freud but to significant numbers of others. A misery had developed which at once functioned, like a neurosis, as an escape from misery. My references to Freud's critical response are intended to illustrate some aspects of the revolutionary crisis of contemporary western culture.

I must say, briefly, how I intend the concept 'culture.' As individuals, we

live, those of us who may be said to belong somehow together, as unique
subscribers to a common symbolic. By a 'symbolic,' I mean, first of all, a
pattern of moral demands, a range of standard self-expectations about what
we may and may not do, in the face of infinite possibilities. The great Western symbolics, Jewish and Greek, have been constituted by repressive, militant ideals opposing the destructive splendor of human possibility; those
symbolics seemed to Freud embodied in the 'second Rome.'

Culture, our ingeniously developed limitations, is constituted by two
motifs which are dialectically related. These two motifs, which have shifting
contents, I call 'interdicts' and 'remissions' from interdicts. Every culture is
so constituted that there are actions one cannot perform; more precisely,
would dread to perform. (Despite the influence of Freud upon my discipline,
sociology has not paid attention enough to what is not done, to the closed
possibilities, to the negatives, the suppressed.) There are remissions specific to interdicts. These interdictory-remissive complexes are more or less
compelling; human action is organized in their terms. To the degree that
they are imperative, interdictory-remissive complexes are observable specially by those who do not feel compelled by them. For the imperative thrust
of an interdictory-remissive symbolic is into character, the more imperative
the deeper a thrust into the unconscious, beyond reason and capacity deliberately to change it.

A symbolic contains within itself that which one is encouraged to do and
that which one is discouraged from doing, on pain of whatever animates the
interdict. Permit me to cite a trivial example from the everyday life of an
academic. At a certain faculty club I used to frequent, horse steak was
served. It may be still on the menu, and considered by some a delicacy;
why, then, did it provoke such anxieties in me? I could feel my gorge rising
at the thought of eating a horse steak; yet horse steak was precisely what I
came to eat. I was aware of that ambivalence which sometimes complicates
and heightens pleasure. A certain tension had been created; excellent as
they were, horse steaks were difficult for me to eat, just as some 'assimilated' Jews, for example, still find it difficult to eat shellfish. Crustaceans,
not to mention pork or bacon, provoke certain anxieties. I think the 'culturo-
logical' fact is that inhibitions early installed prevent my enjoyment of the
flesh of horses. Some significant time during my boyhood was spent reading
books that were quite sentimental about horses and dogs; I recall Albert
Payson Terhune and other authors of my boyhood, not to mention Black
Beauty, a horse for which I used to care passionately. The interdict upon
horseflesh, shaping my pleasure and pain in a remissive occasion in the
Harvard faculty club, originated in the eighth century. Perhaps it was the
great Boniface, himself from a family not long removed from the Roman
ghetto, who enjoined a superficially Christian peasantry against killing or

eating horses, the animals specially relevant to the power and status of aristocrats.

Of course, horse meat is eaten by other peoples. Thus, in what they may and may not do, on pain of feeling ill, the price of a transgressive breaking of a moral command (the remission thus became subversion) are members of one culture distinguished from another. Worse for me than eating horse meat would be the possibility of eating dog meat. In China dog meat is a common and acceptable delicacy. Anthropological literature abounds in examples, equally elementary, that might provoke anxieties in members of other moral demand systems. In every culture, whether one does or does not cross a certain line, whether one does or does not eat dog meat or horse meat, shell-fish, pork, fish on one day or another, in short, interdictory-remissive complexes, open and close the possibilities of ordinary life activities, differently or universally, to enactors of what is thus rendered a meaningful social structure.

Everything is possible to human beings; we are members of a culture in the sense that everything is not permitted to us, nor even conceivable by us. Every culture is constituted as a moral demand system of shifting interdictory and remissive contents. When significant, profoundly anxiety-producing shifts occur, then, at the most fundamental level, a society is undergoing revolutionary changes. Not all changes are equally significant; indeed, not even the most violent activity is necessarily revolutionary.

As I understand the phenomenon, 'revolution' is a significant discontinuity in the moral demand system, an interchange in the relation of interdictory-remissive contents, by which men may well do what they have not done before—and do not as they have done. Contradicting the older, now archaic, meaning, a 'revolution' implies a definite break with the past. By the efficacy of revolution, the impossible becomes quite possible. In this sense, Hitler, with his dictum that "the impossible is always successful," was a true revolutionary—a permanent revolutionary. On the other hand, most political 'revolutions' in Latin America, consisting in the displacement of one set of military politicians by another, are not revolutionary. Shifts of political authority may not transform the moral demand system, what can and cannot be done. A change in regime is not a revolution, no more than violence necessarily means revolution.[2] Freud, Darwin and Marx may be far more profoundly revolutionary than any mob on a rampage.

Is the 'Negro revolution' a revolution? I doubt it. It may become so, when it is linked to a subversive symbolic, but it does not appear so now. The

---

2. There is a question whether wars, terrorist activities and certain types of violence are not always revolutionary, so far as they close the established distances and role relations between vastly different men, reducing them to a sameness. But this is a problem into which I cannot go here.

black American does not aim to transform the white moral demand system but only to find a larger place in it. The Negro still wants 'in,' not 'out.' Even looting does not necessarily represent a radical break from the white moral demand system; looting may represent an ardent desire to enter and to share in that same American plenitude, to be full receivers in it. Yet, in the process of breaking into the American society more fully, the black American may create a fundamental break away from it; that eventually remains to be developed by blacks themselves, and by those whites who imagine they see among the blacks an erotic alternative to the ascetic traditions of western (white) culture. The white discovery of 'soul,' the noble savage returned yet again to harass high culture, has a far more dangerous revolutionary potential than any of the fighting, politicized gangs within the black ghettoes.

A 'revolution,' then, refers to some radical and significant discontinuity[3] in the moral demand system; what is permitted, so to say, becomes interdicted and what is interdicted is permitted. Revolutions may be defined as reversals—violent or nonviolent—of significant behavioral contents. The Christian movement in Roman culture was revolutionary, although nonviolent in a culture that encouraged official (state) acts of violence. With respect to sexual behavior, the early Christians appear remissive to the dominant establishment Romans. The established interdictory-remissive motifs of Roman culture were reversed in significant ways. In turn, the Christian motifs did not triumph without partially incorporating the defeated Roman motifs. Cultures rarely die; they merely marry.

There are two kinds of remissive motifs. First, those remissions which subserve—that is, support—the moral demand system of which they are a part; second, those same motifs, expanding their jurisdiction in the system of action, can become subversive of that system. This says nothing about any intrinsic meaning of a motif. The question of what an interdictory-remission complex means can be elaborated empirically only with respect to its purposes and effects in a system; no complex means, intrinsically, one thing or another. Even as it functions within a system, an interdictory-remission complex may be significantly differentiated. Thus, Bolshevism may remain in the realm of aesthetics, remarkably conservative. Oppositional elements in a culture are not uniformly conservative or revolutionary; none represent a universal break from what is and is not enactable.

A truly revolutionary movement must penetrate, through the symbolic and beyond it, to at least two other structures: first, the social order of privileges and deprivations; second, the intrapsychic order of character, of impulse and inhibition. Freud has helped sociologists understand the dynamics of change on all three levels, but in particular on the levels of culture and

---

3. Exactly reversing the classical meanings of *evolution* and *revolution*.

personality. He understood politics as the middle level, its shape and thrust mediated through the interplay of culture and personality; thus Freud conceived politics as a more dependent, or reactive, level. *Political* change interested Freud least of all, for theoretical reasons that should now be clear. What interested Freud much more than social structures was the degree to which a symbolic penetrates into the depths of character, organizing what men like and would be like. It may be said that for Freud the most fundamental politics are the politics of desire, always ambivalent, suppressed and suppressing.

To assess the depth at which a new set of moral demands penetrates character structure, in some specific ways altering it, is a task of great difficulty. Freud made efforts, on scattered occasions, to illustrate such assessments, the more to enlighten himself, I think, about what he was doing; for this was by no means always clear to him. For example, in Christian cultures, just beneath the surface where the Christian symbolic had been absorbed, there was lurking the particular organizations of impulse and the control of impulse that preceded Christendom—'pagan' behavior. In Freud's assessment of the quality of Christian life, the Christian symbolic had not penetrated Christian character deeply enough to prevent 'un-Christian' conduct. On the contrary, because the symbolic had not penetrated very deeply, so-called Christians were capable of the most un-Christian behavior, under a Christian institutional veneer.

On the other hand, we may note that within the Christian symbolic there were dominant particular interdictory-remissive motifs. By its original terms, for example, Christianity—more precisely the Christian symbolic or religion of love—encouraged hatred of Jews. In the illogic of Christian culture, there is an unresolved ambivalence toward those who are closest and yet remain furthest apart. Jew-hatred is thus a built-in remissive element of the Christian moral demand system. Here is an example of a remissive motif which has penetrated a variety of social structures; without this motif certain acts fall into disuse.

But my main interest, here, is not in elaborating upon the dynamics of Jew-hatred in Christian and post-Christian cultures. (In this culture, ironically, since the late nineteenth century, the Jew has been reassociated with the Christian system, which is itself under attack. This may help to explain the nature of Nietzsche's anti-Semitism.) My point is more general to the revolutionary potential in all cultures rather than to the relation between cultural and social structures. I suggest that interdictory-remissive complexes, like motifs of hatred in religions of love, can be found in all systems of culture. The normative structure of personal and social reality is characterized by *ambivalence.*

In its ambivalence, no moral demand system is static or unchangeable; no culture is immortal. It is the fate of all cultures to fall victim to the particular ambivalences by which they are constituted. There appears to be a dialectical tension within the interdictory and remissive contents of every known moral demand system. Permit me to sketch, by way of illustration, one major shift in the moral demand system of seventeenth-century England, and, also the way that social structures have of absorbing those interdictory-remissive shifts and cognate shifts in privileges and deprivations.

When I was a student in high school, I was led to believe that Archbishop Laud was a villain; the Whig tradition of English historiography taught that the anti-Laudians were 'progressive,' fighting for the liberty of the individual. Yet the events can well bear quite another interpretation. Laud and the Star Chambers can be understood as defending, among other things, not only church land but the traditional rights of peasants to use common pasture land, which, of course, the enclosure movements were destroying in the name of the right of private property. In that revolutionary confrontation, as I once learned about it, the 'good guys' were those who fought and argued for the rights of private property and individual liberty, while the 'bad guys' were the judges of the Star Chambers. Perhaps Laud and the church establishment were defending not only their own interests, which were clearly involved, Church lands, but also the common lands of England. Individual rights, civil liberty, and private property indivisibly intermingled in the moral demands of the rising bourgeois, for whom Locke composed 'charters' (in the Malinowskian sense).[4] In that cultural crisis of English history, a complex of demands we now call 'liberalism' and 'democracy' was subversively remissive, asserting a radical break in the way land tenure and personal relations were organized. Who and what was then the revolutionary force? It was the demands of worshippers of private property that became subversively remissive. In due course, a successful reinterpretation changes the structure of social reality. "This demand to change consciousness," Marx and Engels observed, "amounts to a demand to interpret reality in another way, i.e. to accept it by means of another interpretation." By the time the Whig and Liberal historians had finished rationalizing events, the reverse had become the accepted fact: good (what men ought to do) was assigned to the private property advocates, and bad (what men ought not to do) was assigned to those who opposed the enclosures. When a remissive thrust is victorious, it becomes interdictory, while other remissive contents are produced by the transformed complex. In the Marxist idea of history, the bourgeois produced the proletariat, which would grow to subvert the entire capitalist system, which is not only economic and social but primarily a moral system, inducing men to realize themselves in certain possibilities and not in others.

4. It is a charter proposition of liberalism that family and property are prior institutions to the state. Politics develop to protect us, in our private pursuits, from unwarranted interference.

Where and when a significant shift occurs in the moral demand system, there is implicit an incorporation of the contents of that shift into the social structure. Every radically significant shift in the contents of an interdictory-remissive complex transforms what is demanded of us and by us, transforms the distribution of goods, roles and statuses, transforms relations of deference in a given social order. In this sense, the Marxist movement was truly revolutionary; but so were the movements of the bourgeois, as Marx himself proclaimed. Revolutionary orders of moral demand animate social structures.

Every form or school of sociological, psychological or historical analysis implies a symbolic, not least where that symbolic does not assert any such aim to reanimate social structures; no more did the carriers of the early Christian symbolic assert such an aim. Moreover, a symbolic may be incorporated by certain groups having particular powers in the social structure. The comparative position and effect of the incorporating group is vital to any analysis of basic social change; for example, although low in the American social structure, the black lumpenproletariat is probably the single most influential social formation on the inner attitudes of certain sections of white youth. In effect, a shift of moral demand may bypass apparently protection strata of the social structure in its transformative effect upon character structures. Thus, the eroticizing of American life from the bottom up, through the influence of the blacks, as whites, in fear and envy, understand them,[5] represents, at least in its initial phase, no significant shift in the social structure.

Unlike Marx, who is supremely political, Freud appears apolitical—even antipolitical. Here, precisely, Freud made his great contribution to our revolutionary condition. He established again that knowledge the ancients possessed: that revolutions are, at once, a stirring of the depths, out of which new men are created, to act out once suppressed possibilities. Then, and only then, in the acting out of new possibilities, can there be truly new regimes.

The new man Freud tried to avoid imagining, lest he become too committed to his vision, would be capable of analyzing his own symptomatic behavior, in a culture at last free of its bankrupt inheritances of moral demand. As Freud wrote to Pfister, a Protestant pastor who was one of his more distant disciples, there could be no more the happier state of earlier times when religious faith stifled the neuroses. That way of disposing of the matter will no longer work, Freud thought. Thus, in Freud's own mind, it was the historic failure of the Christian (and Jewish) moral demand system that called forth his revolution. Freud confirmed a radical discontinuity; he did not invent one. It is from the *failure* of the repressions, not their success, and from the more general failure of the moral demand system to compen-

---

5. Further discussion of this influence involves the entire ambiguous question of racism in contemporary American society.

sate men satisfactorily for the necessary deprivations imposed upon their impulse lives, that Freud thought to derive his revolutionary explanations of the modern translation of common faith into individual symptom.

Individual symptoms may be collectively creative; they may be the beginning of yet another generalization of faith. But because Freud pays relatively little attention to social structures, it is unclear how one symbolic succeeds another. He sees concentrated in individuals those symptomatic consequences of the systemic failures he has to treat. What can a therapist do in such a situation? Can he return men therapeutically, as Jung proposed, to the very moral orders which are the predicates of their symptoms? Freud cannot believe, as Jung did, that the cure lies hidden still in what has become the disease. What then remains to be done, by the therapist, self-proclaimed successor to the pastoral guide?

The revolutionary component in Freud's thought is precisely that through analytic insight men are to give up all thought of salvation. They will become new men the moment they cease sacrificing themselves, and others, to what has become an impossibility: salvation. Then real possibilities of living will open up, closed down as they have been by cultures that promise salvation. Like a neurotic, this failing culture hangs on desperately to the particular stabilities, created in its neurotic condition, through which faith neither can stifle impulse nor express it. Freud's hostility to 'religion' was due to the 'readiness' with which religions "fit in with our instinctual wishful impulses,"[6] rather than oppose them, as Freud knew they must.

Patently, the therapist is no neutral. The very ground of his discipline is the failure of the social symbolic that produces the too lightly individual patient. Even profound revolutionary movements are caught up in structural failures truly and realistically to oppose the impulse life. Of Marxism Freud wrote, in a famous passage:[7] "Theoretical Marxism, as realized in Russian Bolshevism, has acquired the energy and the self-contained and exclusive character of a *Weltanschauung*, but at the same time, an uncanny likeness to what it is fighting against . . . It has created a prohibition of thought which is just as ruthless as was that of the religion of the past . . . And although practical Marxism has mercilessly cleared away all idealistic systems and illusions, it has itself developed illusions which are no less questionable and unprovable than the earlier ones."

Thus, in Freud's analytic, Marxism has become yet another repressive order of moral demands. Although he admires the power of the Marxist analytic, Freud marks it too, at least in its Russian form, as a symbolic. As yet another ideology of the superego, Marxism has not escaped the past. Offering an analytic that helps men think against all ideologies of the superego,

---

6. *New Introductory Lectures*, Standard Edition, volume 22 (London, 1964), 175.

7. Ibid., 179–80.

Freud is truly revolutionary. He has opened the possibility of suspecting, in a diagnostic way, all symbolics: he has given us a mode of analyzing them. Finally, Freud leaves us with that most revolutionary attitude of all, the analytic attitude, which closes off in the resolution of the transference the ancient possibility of creating, by its success, yet another ideology of the superego—yet another moral demand system. In this sense, Freud promises no politics but an antipolitics, no faith but an attendance to a shifting sense of well-being that marks, I suggest, a new man: the therapeutic. As a therapeutic anticreed, Freudianism denies that it is a symbolic—an ideology of the superego—at all. How can there be clinical evidence for the therapeutic when he is the clinician? As clinician to all ideologies of the superego, Freud may well be the most profound and transformative revolutionary of all.

Implicit in the Freudian analytic is the main lesson of a revolution that runs deeper than politics. That main lesson is not easily or swiftly learned. Yet, in a growing capacity even among the officially devout, Christian and Communist, to ride loosely to all symbolics, there is a hint of Freud's victory, of his permanent revolutionary assault upon precisely what he (departing from many among his disciples) considered tragically necessary: a moralizing culture. Because he considered culture, as a moral demand system, a tragic necessity, Freud did not enjoy even the fantasy of a victory for his analytic. Rather, in his criticism of that tragic necessity, Freud, the revolutionary, also draws the limit within which all revolutions must play themselves out. (72:1)

48

By What Authority? Post-Freudian Reflections on the Repression of the Repressive as Modern Culture

For the last time psychology!
                                        —Kafka, *Diaries*

In face of the metaphysical, even if you should have no other word for it than simply death, all political concerns dwindle into nothingness.
                    —Huizinga, "Conditions for a Recovery of Civilization"

There is a memorable change in the face of authority in an otherwise poor play by Shaw, *The Devil's Disciple*, the first of his three plays for Puritans— showing them up, as he thought. Richard, the disciple who has pledged

Reprinted, abridged, with changes, from *The Problem of Authority in America*, edited by John P. Diggins and Mark E. Kann (Philadelphia, PA: Temple University Press, 1981); 225–55.

himself to the "devil," as he calls himself, must end, as he does, a minister of the living God while the official minister, Anderson, finds himself, at the end, a soldier—a man of power. Early in the play, Richard sounds the great and attractive prophecy of the therapeutic, at his solicitous worst: "No child shall cry." [1]

Imagine a world in which no child cries. Where would be his joy if he were incapable, even so young, of sorrow? As a source of civilizing sorrow, as a refining device of realistic melancholy, some decently irrational *Cannot* must be felt at their fingertips by all ages among wanton boys and girls; if they are to become civilized, then, very early in life, all must feel the offense, even before they think of doing something so harmless as pulling the wings off a fly. If it be true, then guilt is the civilizing emotion. False guilt follows another path, as we shall see. Throughout this essay, I shall deal with this essential and suprarational—if not irrational—dynamic of *Cannot*, inseparable as I think it to be from the dynamics of *distaste/taste* or *sense/sensibility*. I intend to argue that true guilt is the distinguishing thing, as between higher authority and lower.

From authority itself there is no escape. A "crisis" of authority derives not least from some more or less intellectually elaborate failure to understand that authority, higher and lower, is immortal and unalterable in its form. In that form, unchangeably vertical, however ingeniously the big children of modernity may try to level it, every lowering act produces the pain or fear humans experience as true guilt; every raising act produces a saving sense, as of being redeemed from guilt or of a remission from pain or fear.

A certain inversion now characterizes our common and received sense of what is lowering and what is raising in the form of authority. No culture can survive a widespread treatment of this common and received sense as if it were false and unworthy of enlightened minds. This essay proposes, without hope, a counter-enlightenment. Our great enlightenment, the slow work of the centuries since the Renaissance, has ended catastrophically, in our own time, not in the failure of authority, as is widely believed among the late enlightened themselves; rather, the catastrophe of our enlightenment lies in the success of its lowering movements.

Gulag and Dachau, torture and terror, are the dry-eyed children of our enlightenments. Some of our greatest talents are the last officers of our enlightenment and coeval with its dying genius. Nietzsche is the first fully self-conscious theorist of authority in modernity. I reckon Picasso the greatest painter of modernity and Joyce its chief storyteller. Not for the first time, and for more than reasons of familiarity, I shall work through certain facets of Freud, from whom I have taken certain hints toward a portrait of the true and yet always masked face of authority.

1. George Bernard Shaw, *The Complete Plays* (New York: Dodd, Mead, 1971), 80.

Imagine an authority that will not fail and cannot disappear. What, then, of its crises? I imagine that we mortals can only enact, and re-enact the raising or lowering possibilities of action stipulated in the social organization of our received culture. Any reference to a "crisis of authority" in contemporary American culture would refer to those strange pleasures that may be taken in lowering acts, or thoughts, within a vertical order of possibilities in their primacy. From that primacy culture delimits its operative acts.

Works of art, acts of thought, all sensibility and expression, are even more illuminative than they are operative acts. Hands may be washed as an illuminative gesture; they may be washed operatively. Both acts tend to merge; by that mergence, authority is carried in its culture. There can be no culture without authority as the mergence of illuminative and operative acts. From illuminative acts, which ordain the direction of operative acts, life takes its meanings and culture its energies. An act, in culture, can only become operative in the vertical. Try as we may, we cannot live horizontally in the vertical world of culture; so to prostrate oneself would be to live beyond the range of authority; such a life—such a culture without an authority that is either raising or lowering, and both—is impossible.

One way to imagine an impossible culture is to imagine the primacy of possibility, rather than its repression, as precisely that rebus we call "culture." I propose that what Freud named "primal repression" is the unrelievable pressure, in any and all cultures, against the primacy of possibility. That primacy cannot happen even in our wildest imaginings. Chaos is itself an order. Within a vertical of specifically operative acts become illuminative, the most disorderly acts take their positions in an order that is sacred. Those positions, in sacred order, must be, wherever they are, raising or lowering; or that complex of both I shall call "remissive."

Authority is that about sacred order which will not brook its levelings, however brilliantly they may be conceived. The very effort at leveling sacred order must be sensed as guilt. Pain is the objectification of guilt even at the possibility of a move downward in the vertical along which cultures express themselves as closures of possibility. The primacy of possibility is a negational inference of secondary realities in sacred order. A raising act, I shall call *interdictory*. A lowering act, I shall call *transgressive*. Mixed acts, what is not done, yet done, I have already called *remissive*. Much of our lives are spent in a remissive flux. The order of that flux is unchanging—I daresay, sacred.

Cultures give readings of sacred order: these readings are their arts and sciences. In this both natural and supranatural capacity, every man, born as he is into a culture, is both artist and scientist. Man is a reading animal, to the sacred manner born. Every effort to unlearn the sacred manner, even the most ingenious, must fail. Even our highest conceivable illiteracy is itself an achievement of those complex motifs by which, in our thoughts as well as actions, we are no longer able to read our endless rise and fall along that vertical of illuminative acts inseparable from every operative act. In the face of the metaphysical, "to be" is to suffer, more or less gladly, generally less than more, our raisings and lowerings within a vertical of possibilities otherwise not even to be entertained by the secondary imagination in safely distorted and distanced images. As we cannot cease to be fearful, but only resist knowing what we are fearful about, so we cannot lower ourselves permanently into the transgressive depths of authority. Fear prevents this free fall. Fear is the original respect in which we receive the fact that sacred order is evident even in our disorders. That we cannot kill authority is the beginning of wisdom. A fearful recognition of authority, even at its lowest, may also be the end and purpose of wisdom. Without timely readings of timeless order, no authority can put on even its briefest dress, to play hide-and-seek with freedom, conjuring such nervous tics of self-justification as would make an angel weep.[2]

What Freud psychologized as "primal repression" can be seen, less darkly, as that mindfulness that denies entry into consciousness of any and all lowering possibilities. Before such closed mindfulness, the true name of what Freud recognized negationally as the repressive unconscious, every fear in lowering position, persists both active and unaltered.[3] Equally active and unaltered: possibilities high enough to need no negations. Mind is not necessarily a reformed whore. I see no reason to call every risen possibility by its Freudian name, "sublimation." What is sacred does not rise out of what is profane. Interdicts do not derive from their transgressions: that theory is sheer gnosticism and so rings true to the modern mind. But its truth is challenged by the fact that enactable possibilities, including sexual acts, are not spiritualized. What is spiritual is always present, in our shifting obediences to the hierarchy of repressive imperatives from among which we are free to choose both what we are not to be and be, in our irreducibly complex responsibilities as enactors of sacred order.

Artful Self in Sacred Order

In its shifts within the vertical, self is an artful dodger; that would appear to go best without saying. Yet precisely what is self-evident, being sacred, occurs in constant repetitions. Repetition is authority in its form, making clear, in endless variations of such knowledge experienced, that self cannot endure a world imagined entirely profane, possibility undenied to consciousness. Authority is the achievement of rank order out of a primacy of

2. But see *Measure for Measure*, II, ii, 118.
3. Sigmund Freud, "Repression," in *The Complete Psychological Works of Sigmund Freud, Standard Edition* (London: Hogarth Press, 1953–), XIV, 148.

possibilities so slow to change that primary possibility itself can only be inferred from secondary imaginings of it. Those secondary imaginings, generally named "Culture," direct humans in the manner and matter of what to deny to themselves. By these teachings of denial, the more commanding in their characteristic indirections—distortions and distancings—self has contained its own artfulness. Freud's rebus for these distortions and distancings, self in its unalterable artfulness, is negationally named "repression." In the equal and opposite rebus "sublimation," he supplied the negation of the negation. Sublimation is to repression as secular is to sacred order. It is the preferred term of modernity for those indirections by which artful self sounds out its directions, in painfully and slowly achieved addresses to the complexity of sacred order. Sublimations, themselves unconscious, by Freudian definition, will not be divorced from repression. Both occur with whatever cleverities of denial the mind contrives to conceal the worshipful element in the addresses that are self, more or less articulate, in sacred order. "Sublimation" is a concealing word, in face of what is sublime, for the prevalent doctrine of faithlessness, which is different from bad faith.

Theologies are but one form of address to sacred order; and by no stretch of the imagination always the most illuminative. Indeed, as Nietzsche thought, theologies reek of bad faith. Read aright, as a modernist reading instrument of sacred order, in which readings can be given only in negational language, Freudian doctrine reveals itself in the paradox of a faithless address to sacred order. That order is a dream from above. All the other dreams Freud interpreted were dreams from below.

It is widely acknowledged that Freud, like Weber, claimed to be religiously unmusical. But this is only to say that both Freud and Weber took their unconscious vows of faithlessness so early in life that neither could recognize himself for what he was: an intellectualizing rebel in sacred order, substituting for the specific commands of faith in life those terrible abstractions of command that pass for psychology or sociology. Beyond bad faith lies faithlessness. Freud's faithlessness is announced in the matter of his interpretation of dreams as possible only if they come from the bottom up and never from the top down: "If I cannot bend the Higher Powers, I will move the Infernal Regions." Freud never came closer to recognizing the downward direction of his movement in sacred order.

Though elsewhere I shall choose to work through Nietzsche, Kafka, Joyce, Picasso, Wilde, and other inversionists of obedience in sacred order, here Freud's works have been again chosen because none have had greater or more popular authority in the modernist culture to which the others also belong. That greater authority, downward, has come of popular, often caricaturing, imitations of Freud's resistances in sacred order. It is Freud's negationally sacred manner, far more than the apparently sexual matter of his doctrine, that accounts for his appeal to the classes re-educated in lowering versions of that manner. If that appeal is now ending, as I reckon, then the indirections of authority may be again turned around. We may be at the end of modernist inversions of sacred order. We can only have faith and wait; and see. Meanwhile, in the act of waiting, essays such as this are nothing more than wordy versions of proverbial wisdom successfully forgotten by the cultivated classes. All the intellectualizings that follow have been said far better and briefly in Proverbs 27:20: "The nether world and Destruction are never satisfied; so the eyes of men are never satisfied."

The Culture of the Never Satisfied

To be cultivated is to know, at least by indirection, through the artfulness of our recognitions, what it is to be obedient, and what is not, in those stipulations of sacred order that constitute authority in every culture. Authority must be deeply cultivated and long prepared. Every *Not*, if it is operative, needs settling enough in time to be conveyed, mainly through casuistries of excusing or critical reasons, across the generations by teaching classes that are sanctioned more by their propriety than property. Propriety is always subject to a certain nervousness about being breached. Authority is bound to take its toll in nerves. To live within the limiting dynamics of authority is to measure up to the prohibitions and permissions from which the metamorphic range of *illuminative/operative* acts derive. These metamorphoses stipulate, as they moralize, social reality. To live amorally may be possible to the Machiavellian or Nietzschean imagination, but that imagination can never satisfy the requirements of real life. In real life, nothing is neutral and moral indifference a pose.

Everything real is real because it exists within limits, a verticality at once illuminative and operative. Is handwashing obsessive or worshipful, symbolic or functional? A handful of dust takes direction in sacred order from its complex of illuminative and operative relations in the risings and lowerings we call "experience." A place, or we ourselves, can be more or less clean. Polluted or cleansed, brought down or up: there is fright at living in either extremity, interdictory and transgressive, of sacred order. Our fears, expressed in unconsidered rejections, first teach us what is acceptable, what heart's ease there may be in laughter and tears before thought. Every child must cry. Freud first named this fright, at the primacy of possibility, interior "flight."

There is an interior flight that leads self deeper into sacred order. It is this flight, necessary and inescapable, that now goes by its popular nickname, the apparatus of pain Freud named "repression." Daring as he was, Freud dared make little more than negational sense of repression. He admitted it into his theory on condition that it become, and never cease to be, his crucial problem. The illuminative facet of repression was itself repressed by the operative. Before this gatekeeping *Not* Freud sat all the main part of his intellectual life, without being able to know how cleverly he had recognized sacred order. That cleverity had to be negational. It follows that in Freud's unconscious denial of it, sacred order is like a woman who can never say no; her virtue is her complete want of virtue. With her, everything is possible and nothing is true. With Freud, the repressive, unadmitted as predicate of repression proper, imagines itself a little freer at last of its own limits.

To admit the repressive would have confronted Freud with the most frightful theoretical necessity: "of postulating a third *Ucs.*, which is not repressed."[4] That third unconscious, predicate of the second, raised a possibility superior to Freud's lowering second: that of making the "characteristic of being unconscious lose significance."[5] In the repressive repressed we may find the combination that unlocks again the meaning of authority. The repressive thus rendered by Freud, unrecognizable in its imperative as sacred order, becomes that very general rule, about the degree of distortion and remoteness from the primacy of possibility achieved by linked repressions proper, that Freud himself could not see.[6] Distanced from sacred order, tastes and distastes, addictions and abhorrences, become inexplicable or historical in their determining origins. Culture becomes the history of otherwise inexplicable splittings into oppositional modes of that primacy of possibility that aims only at its own expression.

Repression is to psychoanalysis as unknown gods are to pagan theologies. Repressive splittings make of every cultural expression an illuminative act that refers to Freud's own radical dualism more than it refers to the distancing arts of obedience and disobedience in sacred order. "Ambivalence," along with "ambiguity," becomes the code word, favored in modernity, for a faithlessness that forbids knowledge of sacred order. Freud's repression of the repressive allowed this forbidden knowledge to play upon its enactors. "Repression" became Freud's word for what culture must include: deeply forbidden knowledge; that which is, at once, known and unknowable. These intellectualizing and paradoxical resistances to the repressive predicate of repressions show the brilliance of the one kind of knowledge forbidden to us: of sacred order, for which art and/or the science of society are the chief

4. Freud, "The Ego and the Id," in *Standard Edition*, XIX, 18.

5. Ibid.

6. In Freud's negational symbolic, the symbol is what it represents. So instinct and its vicissitudes represent the primacy of possibility. Secondary imaginative processes suffer complete inversion. What is primacy becomes secondary and vice versa. On Freud's inversive inability to lay down, in his theory of repression, a general rule of a little more or less in sacred order, those necessary degrees of distortion and remoteness by which self, in its artfulness, is constituted as our continuous address in sacred order, to it: See Freud, "Repression," 150 *et pass.* The papers of 1915 are specially important in working through Freud's negational recognitions of sacred order. See Freud, "Repression," 117–307.

substitutes. What we modernists fear to know, we admit back into our arts and sciences on condition of Its denial. Where It is, there the sacred once was. Freud's ingenious repressions of the repressive serve continuously, and in an intensely stipulative manner, against admitting sacred order back into a modern consciousness pregnant from the father of these repressions. The repressive father unacknowledged, except as "primal repression," modern sensibility has been achieved at the cost of a critical insensibility. The sacred is denied even as the arts of its address are celebrated as ends in themselves—as art or science, but more as art. Rather than science, art is our repository of faithlessness. How much more easily Freud is accepted nowadays as artist rather than scientist; and rightly so. Our culture feeds on its doubly critical addresses: to a sacred order that is allowed to exist only for purposes of lowering everything high in it. Critical intellect becomes something "criminal," as Freud was not the first or last to remark.

Our endlessly critical culture is ending, I reckon, in its movements of inversion. To lower the interdictory motifs, to raise the transgressive: in sum, this is the function of that criticism for which our humanists and other enlighteners held such high hope. To come nearer understanding modernist movements of inversion, authority celebrated in its lowering modes, we must first recognize its love affair with death as the interdict of interdicts that modernism would abolish as meaningless. In his negational language of the "death instinct," Freud framed his most completely up-to-date resistance to the eternal yesterday that is sacred order. Authority must be eternally past, in every culture, however unstable. The sense of the past may be in it. Compared to others less negational in their traditions of acknowledgment, our culture may be rightly considered more unstable. But all cultures are unstable precisely in their vitality: all are moving balances of abhorrences and idealizations, one the predicate of the other. Repression is best imagined in its mobilities rather than, as popularly conceived, in its immobilities. If the repressive in culture is not constantly renewed and attached to fresh possibilities, then authority will lower, and so destroy, itself. It is in this repressive mode, raising and lowering the threshold of possibility in its denials, that cultures constitute unstable responses in sacred order to it.

What parental authority is not suspect, nowadays? A litany of "nots" may survive, but all in quotation marks, for liberating use only; else, what would be the pleasure of understanding the "harshly restraining, cruelly prohibiting quality," of "even ordinary normal morality"? As for that old-time religion, which none of us can recover, it is from its cruelly prohibiting quality that "the conception arises of a higher being who deals out punishment inexorably."[7] Kafka's treatment of this higher being, as the creator of our inher-

7. Freud, *Standard Edition*, XIX, 54.

ited order, itself an obsolescent punishment colony, both to its last officer
and to its evasive explorer, puts the need for punishment at the center of
authority. That need for punishment is a negational version of understanding
in sacred order. Such understanding must remain uncommunicable to its
critics—if, indeed, not also to its last officer, despite the fact that he acts
out, in his nakedness and death, the ancient mode of that understanding.[8]

In our penal colony, at the end of its existence as sacred order, the very
nature of spiritual discipline is no longer understood, perhaps not even by
its last officer. Reordered abstractly, as in modern sociological thought, all
individuals reduce to whatever they have in common, their class or some
other abstract sameness. Regarded in sacred order, that sameness does not
exist at all. Strictly speaking, each shifting for himself in the vertical of authority, no one has anything in common with anyone else. What seems to be
common, among God's children, becomes in fact uncommon in the individualities of their responsive address to sacred order, from wherever they are,
at any given moment, inside it. As all of us, in our bodies, have our own
special constitution, which a doctor must examine in its uncommon particular, so the mind of each is so distinct from all other minds that each may be
said to live as it must die—alone. How well Newman knew, in his *Grammar
of Assent*, that we are all ourselves alone, in our identity, in incommunica-
bility, in personality. The mystery of authority so communicates to each that
every other must feel the force, if not the understanding, of that communication. My paraphrase of Newman on the range of that "illative sense" without
which authority does not communicate, as from one to another, should
end here and direct quotation begin: "There is something deeper in our
differences than the accident of external circumstances." For "objective
truth . . . we need the interposition of a Power, greater than human teaching
and human argument, to make our beliefs true and our minds one."[9]

The ultimate test of authority is its vitality. It proves itself by exercising
itself, in one direction or another, interdictory or transgressive. Remissive
authority, the characteristic modern kind, wants a vitality of its own; it is
transitional, in one direction or the other, subserving or subverting the interdicts. That vitality wanting, we cannot be surprised that the master mind of
our remissiveness, Freud, imagined the primacy of possibility as sexual energy. Reverse the ordination of energy, see it from the bottom up, as desexualization, rather than from the top down, as obedience, and "sublimation"
follows; for this reason, I have read sublimation as the antisacral equivalent
of obedience to the repressive imperative. As sublimations, cultural achieve-

8. Franz Kafka, "In the Penal Colony," in *The Complete Stories* (New York: Schocken
Books, 1972), 140–67.

9. John Henry Cardinal Newman, *An Essay in Aid of a Grammar of Assent* (New York:
Image Books, 1958), 293 (1st ed.: 1870).

ments reduce sacred order to sexual energy raised somehow to a condition in which it becomes something wholly other than itself. In fact, "sublimation" is the most genteel religion without god, humanism deified, that modernism has yet contrived.

Was Jesus sublimating? Not without his completion and perfection in obedience to a superior will: "Thy will be done." Was Hitler sublimating? Is the art of Picasso desexualized? If we concede the artist as a special case of cultural achievement without desexualization, then what of the modernist aesthetic in its concentration precisely on sexuality? I have said that the cultural value of sublimation can be as much a lowering as a raising act. However we tinker with the mechanism of sublimation, it cannot work, I think. And after sublimation, what?

> After sublimation the erotic component no longer has the power to bind the whole of the destructiveness that was combined with it, and this is released in the form on an inclination to aggression and destruction. This defusion would be the source of the general character of harshness and cruelty exhibited by the ideal—its dictatorial "Thou shalt." [10]

Having made its own historic contribution to the destruction of our mindful obediences in sacred order, the dictatorial No, "thou shalt not," has been sublimated into the democratic Yes, "I will." The reverse of desexualization takes place. Where once, in Freud's obsolete vision of it, aggression "extended beyond the id to the super ego," and "increases its severity towards the innocent ego," [11] now, in modernity, severity itself becomes sexualized. On the basest level, that severity can be seen sexualized in such a film as *The Last Tango in Paris*. On an incomparably higher level, we can literally read the sexualization of modernist culture in the remorseless last forty pages of Joyce's *Ulysses*. There, the true meaning of the sublimating yes practically suffocates us in its embrace. Joyce has the heart of modernist sublimating sexuality going like mad as the climax of his novel: "Yes I said yes I will yes."

Against that yes, so repeatedly urged as sublimation, the received and immemorial shalt-nots proved to be playthings, toys of re-educated morality, here yesterday for discard tomorrow. But the nots have a history that is more than repetitional; they test us in their repetitions. Superior ego has no choice but to draw "upon the experiences of past ages stored in the id." This strength of repetition in the ego may derive from reviving shapes of former egos. "Resurrection" makes its fleeting ghost of an appearance in Freudian theory as these "reviving shapes of former egos." [12] This way only true super-ego comes into being. This true way recalls the fact that there is a piety of

10. Freud, *Standard Edition*, XIX, 54–55.
11. Ibid., 55.
12. Ibid., 38.

mind, however little that piety is recognized nowadays. It is piety of mind, superior to its critical powers, that marches out to the progressive conquest of id.[13] Critical intellect, without its pieties, cannot conquer its own imagined primacy of possibility. Precisely in its abstraction, ego idealism, Freud's supposed "reaction-formation *against* the instinctual process of the id,"[14] we are given a glimpse of impotent gods in their mythic modern dress. These gods are trimmers of a familiar sort. Politic ego

> disguises the id's conflicts with reality and, if possible, its conflicts with the super-ego, too. In its position midway between id and reality, it only too often yields to the temptation to become sycophantic, opportunist and lying, like a politician who sees the truth but wants to keep his place in popular favor.[15]

"Popular favor" is to social order as "primacy of possibility" is to sacred; both may be achieved only by a systemic mendacity of critical intellect in search of its self-justifying abstractions. In that specially *revealing/concealing* passage, where Freud's death instinct is called "an abstract concept with a negative content for which no unconscious correlate can be found,"[16] the negational truth that every fear is ultimately fear of death is stated only to be denied. As a negational theorist, Freud properly says that such a "high-sounding phrase . . . has hardly any meaning, and at any rate cannot be justified." Yet Freud also says that in the fear of death "the ego gives itself up" to what used to be called final "judgment,"[17] or spiritual salvation.

Fears of death are linked by Freud with an anxiety to please the punitive superego. Here, in the great canon of our century, as in Kafka's penal colony, we see a typical failure to grasp the object of an illuminative act. Self surrenders its identity but only to the superior identity from which it derives its own. This is translated into: "the ego relinquish[es] its narcissistic libidinal cathexis in a very large amount." That to which the ego relinquishes itself is unidentified, except negationally as death. All others denied, this aspect of the sacred must appear like a revenant to a self so doubtful about sacred order that it would protect against precisely its own surrender to the sacred. Hamlet is such a figure of anxiety, threatened by the sacred even as he would obey its command to remember that he must live, or die, obedient to it. Hamlet's anxiety signals his primal doubt in sacred order. Were I his therapist, I would reckon that that university man has been rather too long and hard at his studies. Hamlet has come home from university with a bad case of *contemptus mundi*, which can only confirm everything that is rotten in Denmark. From his primal doubt about everything, Hamlet tries escape into bad faith, a pseudodecisive act of putting his world right, as if vengeance would become operative if only it were illuminative. Hamlet has

13. Ibid., 56.
14. Ibid., 56; my italics.
15. Ibid.

16. Ibid., 58.
17. Ibid.

confused, in an impossible and destructive way, the question of his parents with the parent question that he must face alone, though not he alone has faced it. Claudius makes a politic effort to answer the parent question of authority, in his remarks on the death of fathers. Not less a political man than King Claudius, Prince Hamlet does not understand that in matters of authority, as in country matters, winning is one thing, understanding another. This prince has confused winning with understanding, operative acts with illuminative.

There is nothing to be learned from politics except who won and who lost; no more is there anything to be learned from society, except who is in and who is out. The confusion of performance with insight makes professors turbulent and intellectuals specially subject either to the seductions of power or to what is almost as bad—graphomania. This confusion is so widespread that Freud can easily conflate obedience in the illuminative mode with death in the operative. It is the oldest confusion: of faith and power. Kafka's officer in the penal colony, and Shakespeare's prince, in Denmark, in their confusion of faith and power, decisive action and winning, see themselves in what is called, nowadays, a "no-win situation"; they feel "deserted by all protecting forces." Freud reads this desertion from sacred order in purely political terms, as punitive superego demanding ego sacrifice itself to its protecting, and therefore sovereign, forces.

> The ego gives itself up because it feels itself hated and persecuted by the super-ego, instead of being loved. To the ego, therefore, living means the same as being loved—being loved by the super-ego, which here again appears as the representative of the id. The super-ego *fulfills the same function* of protecting and saving that was fulfilled *in earlier days* [my italics] by the father and later by Providence or Destiny. . . . Deserted by all protecting forces, [ego] lets itself die.[18]

This abstraction cannot but be inexact when applied to immortal characters. Hamlet is seeking vengeance. The officer is seeking obedience to his old commandant. If both may be said to let themselves die, it is in desperately illuminative acts, to show themselves that they have not deserted forces that demand the obedience even of those desperate acts.

What a typically modern sadness: to see nothing but ineffectual fathers where almighty gods once were. To reduce "all protecting forces" to representations of parental authority must turn the tragic sense of life into one family quarrel after another. Conflating ultimate authority with the function of parents, Freud himself popularized that lowering which, more than any other, has increased our spiritual confusion. We can see the drama of this decline, from Hamlet to James Dean (or Jim Stark) in *Rebel Without a Cause*.

18. Ibid.

Facing the fact of his spirituality, James Dean can only treat it as radical doubt about the authority of his father. With its knife-fight, chicken-runs, and sexual gropings, in its lowly way, *Rebel* fatally misunderstands the parent question of humanity for the question of parents. The parent question, correctly understood, questions us: 'Am I thy Master, or art thou Mine?' James Dean does not begin to understand the parent question anything like so well as Hamlet, of which he is a therapeutic mockery. Jim Stark thinks he hates his mother and loves his father. At the end of the film, Jimmie's father yields to his need for authority and promises to become one. Unlike *Hamlet*, at the end of *Rebel* it appears that Jimmie is going to be all right; a winner. Here repeated is the model of all spiritual confusion; winning and understanding amount to the same thing. If Jim Stark had died, as Hamlet does, he would have lost and failed to understand. But life in sacred order is not the same as the struggle for power in country matters or more obviously political forms of war. From Jim's uncorrected confusion of winning and understanding, there spreads, like a fatal disease, the untragic anti-hero himself the carrier, more transgression—until the most innocent and vulnerable of those 'involved' with Jim dies. Plato dies. Plato is the youngest son, the most completely deserted by all protecting forces. Jim is unable to protect himself or anyone else among his innocent peers from the miasma of evil spreading from the defaulting authority of parents. He lives in what appears to be an utterly profane world, yet Jim can do nothing right.

All *Rebel* youth in that film suffer desertion. Therefore, they suffer primal doubt about *authority/love*, which appears to them only as the inexplicable stupidity of parents. Authority reappears, in *Rebel Without a Cause*, in two plausibly split roles: first, a strong and sympathetic plainclothes policeman who specializes in trying to protect the young from the danger to themselves of living in a world otherwise void of authority; second, in some unseen but invincibly stupid uniformed policeman, who kills the most deserted child. Jim, the new and utterly confused authority figure, has deserted Plato temporarily to begin in earnest his race toward full sexuality. Though he appears to oppose them, Jim himself belongs in that horde of rutilant sons without fathers, posturing before daughters not yet ready to distribute more than their symbolic favors. Jim's own search for love is a desertion from his assigned role of authority and fatal to its assigner: the smallest boy, who can scarcely entrust his empty gun to so young and untried a father surrogate.

The modernist equivalent of faith is the achievement of self-satisfaction. Jim Stark's dissatisfactions with himself are so great that he would become a knight of faith in search of himself. The authority of his own father is his own ego as he would strengthen it for his own trip through life. Yet, withal his ignorance, James Dean knows what authority is in its simplest and least deniable demands upon him: he is obedient, above all, even in a society that allows it practically no place, to the sense of honor. Honor is the noble trait that ego, on the evidence of its realistic deals with those lowerings that often spell success in life, would declare obsolete; and, yet, cannot.

The modernist mind cannot think of self-surrender in anything except terms of defeat. It has deserted all knowledge that does not advance its own power to break any rule that inhibits power. That "guilt is never to be doubted"[19] announces that grace is always to be doubted. Kafka's officer and Shakespeare's prince wait as long as they can before they give up the struggle against primal doubt in a self-destruction that becomes, as a surrogate of faith, performed in order to produce a concluding performance. On the gravestone of authority, Kafka inscribed, "in very small letters," the full mendacity of a culture that gives birth only to one death of authority after another. The last sentence on the gravestone of the old commandant runs: "Have faith and wait!"[20] Never have I read a sentence so inseparably compounded of despair and irony. The truest expression of the officer's faith is that he waited no longer. The truest expression of the officer's faithlessness is that he waited so long.

Worse: the nakedness and death of the officer suggest nothing to the explorer (not to mention the author and his readers) except the sincerity or authenticity of the officer. Poor, sincere old fool. There is nothing we can see through in his eyes to suggest that his total sacrifice of everything to the command of his *immediate and ultimate* superior, to be just, is anything more than plain self-murder. Indeed, the explorer understands just enough to continue, as before, in his office. That office is to keep anyone, by force if necessary, from "attempting the leap"[21] of faith, which must always appear as a sacrifice of everything self-willed. That sacrifice of everything to god has about it the ancient character of a true holocaust. Modernity knows of holocausts only as meaningless deaths. The most horrible aspect of modern holocausts is that they are sacrifices of everything to nothing.

Shifting Responses to Sacred Order: The Unrepressed Repressive Re-enacted

So far as there is a crisis of authority, it is complicit in the efforts of our explorer classes, those ever on the move, as from life-style to life-style, virtuoso order hoppers, to discourage leaps of faith. Nor would Freud, in the adamancy of his rebellion against sacred order, countenance ideological parodies of leaps, such as Marxism. Yet Freudian theory, like Durkheimian, has served to diffuse parodies of faith, so far as it would see authority lower itself by finding in itself nothing more than residues of primitive *taboo*, or, at

19. Kafka, "In the Penal Colony," 145. 21. Ibid.
20. Ibid., 167.

best, interdicts.[22] It is in this particular that Freud's internal surrogate for what is interdictory, superego, implies the completest leveling of authority. Psychology is to the leveling of authority as publicity is to charisma. Imagine everyone in modernity intimately famous for five minutes and you have experienced the grace of our new god. Yet Freud, for one, had the grace to be unable even to dream of a world deprived of its truthful distancing and obscurities. Mind's eye cannot see clearly. Whether in its upward movements, or down, the obscure truth of authority is never lost; its complex, shifting balances, movements upward and down, never end. A veridical of vital indirections—interdictory, remissive, transgressive—guides us always and everywhere, whether we can follow, in something other than negational ways, those indirections or not.

Repressive commands, the sacred in its stipulations as culture, form normally around interdictory motifs and their remissions—what is not to be done, yet done. By their efforts to rationalize away the interdicts as merely obsolete "taboos," suitable to earlier, less enlightened states of social evolution, the enlightened in American culture have attacked, largely unaware of what they are doing, the fundamental form of culture in any possible content. Huizinga hints at the secret truth of this cultural suicide when he commented on that

> early stage of social organization [when] obligation expands into conventions, rules of conduct and cults, in the form of *taboos*. In wide circles the popularisation of the word *taboo* has led to an undervaluation of the ethical element of the so-called primitive cultures, not to say anything of that body of sociological thought which with truly modern simplicity disposes of everything called morality, law, or piety, as just so many *taboos*.[23]

The suicide of a culture can be seen in its leveling of differently valued facts. The contents of experience come nearer and nearer to their ultimate and original condition of meaninglessness. Critical intellect can teach nothing except one critique of "meaning" after another. Then our obligationss expand no longer into conventions of commands and obediences as into conventions of remissive explanations that put in doubt the very idea of obligation. Authority leveled is authority destroyed. An authority that cann brook its own lowering must be transgressive. The predicate of transgression is remission. Our remissive teaching elites have made a piety of endless criticism. The more obligation expands into convention, limiting the range of

22. See Émile Durkheim, *The Elementary Forms of Religious Life*, translated by J. W. Swain (Glencoe, IL: Free Press, n.d.), 299–307 *et pass*. Freud likens "a general taboo" to "a Papal Interdict." These "prohibitions are mainly directed against liberty of enjoyment" (Freud, *Standard Edition*, XIII, 21).

23. Johan Huizinga, *In the Shadow of Tomorrow*, translated by J. H. Huizinga from the Dutch (New York: W. W. Norton & Co., 1936), 44–45.

action otherwise open to human "impulse"—"impulse" being secondary to "habit," as Dewey rightly argued, not prior to it—the higher a culture. Low culture is the doing, more or less openly and in the wrong time space, of what is not to be done. It is high culture that is under siege in American society. This siege has taken the form of a fusillade of critical lowerings, a critique of all raisings, sacred order acknowledged only in the identification of culture with endless criticism. This endless criticism is of neither the "Left" nor "Right"; rather, it is a nothingness that can be both radical and reactionary at the same time. Nihilism stood at the door of European culture in the late nineteenth century. In America, as the successor to European culture, the door has been opened.

Behind its closed doors, high culture develops in expressive limits upon the primacy of possibility. If, at the commanding heights of every culture are its interdicts, then the more interdictory a symbolic, the more is "not done," if that symbolic is "true"—that is, if it has descended deeply enough into self and society. To do nothing lowering would be the highest cultural achievement of all. Some ancients called this "nothing doing" the "contemplative life." Aristotle came close to this meaning, when he declared leisure the first principle of action.[24] Prepared in contemplative leisure, the interdicts can challenge the primacy of possible acts even in the world of its technological facility.

Modern technology gives the primacy of possibility an immediacy not dreamt of in the magic universe that is its true ancestor. Modern therapy will soon have nothing of the authoritative past left to interiorize except the panic and emptiness of the cult of experience. The doubly strange thing about this cult is that our experiences teach us nothing and therefore none appears worth giving up. Every experience being, in modernity, worth having, an unprecedented cultivation of vulgarity has set in. The culture of panic and emptiness is indistinguishable from one in which idealizations are admitted only as constructs, never as realities beyond our will to construct.

Balancing this endlessly lowering effect of culture as experience, there is the blind spot in every vision that permits what is envisioned. The veto complicit in every vision warrants the manifold hierarchies in which we live. These hierarchies will not be rationalized. To say that it is against God to kill animals, depends upon the acceptance of animals within the manifold hierarchies that are sacred order. Saint Francis pitied fire. Blake thought of a white cloud as sacred. Thomas More thought animals were made for innocence. What, then, is beneath sacred order?

There is always something with which, in its identity, we cannot identify. I may feel regret at throwing away an old tie. But what of Gregor Samsa, who awoke one morning to find himself transformed into a gigantic insect? A man

24. See *Politics*, VIII.

cannot maintain sympathy with himself as such a body ego. Gregor's decision to disappear expressed at once his act of faith that there are sacred orders for insects as for humans and that he was a member of neither. "The Metamorphosis" is Kafka's story of such a lowering in sacred order that only the death of so lowered a body ego can raise its sibling, the sister body ego, into full life.

Kafka's story of a lowering is a terror to read, worse than any horror film; indeed, that genre depends upon our terror at being lowered, or at being attacked by lower creatures, even if they descend from above. But, as modern culture is levelled down, our lowering acts are more and more experienced as the possibility of unlimited pleasure. Plato understood the insolence of that kind of possibility.

> The goddess of limit, my dear Philebus, seeing insolence and all manner of wickedness breaking loose from all limit in point of pleasures and self-indulgence, established the limit of law and order, of limited being; and you say this restraint was the death of pleasure: I say it was the saving of it.[25]

The death of pleasure is no small cultural achievement; it may be the most powerful, though not the highest, of modernist cultural achievements. As Trilling noted, in "The Fate of Pleasure,"[26] modern spirituality has long rejected, as repressive or specious goods, those restraints and refinements established by the Platonic goddess of limit or the Judaic God of commandment. Instead, the heart of everything authoritative was to be sought in the cultivation of lowering violence, in pain. The destruction of what is interdictory, regarded in a variety of specious goods—or as "bourgeois," or "repressive"—is "surely one of the chief literary enterprizes of our age." Modern spirituality proposes a return to the ethos of holy fools; to madness as the expression of faith; to a perverse fundamentalism of "insistence upon the sordid and the disgusting"[27] rather than upon the noble and the pleasing. We can see this perverse fundamentalism, this insistence upon truth as the experience of what is lowering, captivate the liberal imagination. The negational work of the prophets of modernity, in search of the sacred in its transgressive modes, has triumphed in the tremendous variety of demoralizations, of lowerings, marketed as "life-styles," in contemporary culture.

---

25. *Philebus*, 26c. Some praise of the political meaning of "law and order" seems in order here. The monarchical principle is the best political expression of law and order wherever a heterogenous association of people have nothing else necessarily in common except submission to one sovereign power. A king rules according to law: that is his fundamental distinction. Despots, tyrants, modern totalitarian rulers—none of them rule according to law, which is nothing if not a stipulation of the interdictory.

26. Lionel Trilling, *Beyond Culture* (New York: Harcourt, Brace, Jovanovich, 1963), 57–87.

27. Ibid., 76.

Transgressive spirituality for mass consumption makes Freud as much a figure of the past as his immediate predecessor, Nietzsche. As practiced by the remissive parental generations of modern social order, by our leaders in "lifestyles" and lowering conduct, the affects of transgression, identifications down the unalterable order of culture, are constituted by less limited and more self-expressive being. The ethic of honesty is now played out, like a game, against our cunning uses of that ethic. Inversely moralizing revolts against the eternal vertical of existence, its interdicts unalterably in place, once played out as tragedy by King Oedipus, have been transformed into the democratic comedy of the Oedipus complex. The parent question, asked of humanity in every variety of its universal experience of existence in sacred order—"Am I thy Master, or art Thou Mine?"—was persuasively disguised by Freud, as therapist, but not as metapsychologist, in the question of parents. It is always surprising when parental authority is caught out by transgressive spirituality, as if that were something youthful. What is youthful, to the point of being infantile, is the denial of spirituality, not celebrations of its downward motions. The death of Satan, that tragedy of the Western imagination, has been succeeded by an aesthetic that admits no evil. In the culture of the therapeutic, there are neither raisings nor lowerings. Everything is on the level. So honest, we live in a world of "comic ugliness or a lustred nothingness."[28] Sacred order has become nothingness lustred, studied nostalgias, for that "place in which to be is not enough to be."[29]

This modernist tradition, of spirituality like a tongue touching a cavity, will always have its risible aspect. The pleasure of our lowerings can appear comic no less than the pain of our raisings can appear false. Something rotten is always there for those with a nose twitching for it.[30] We can always be joked out of our straightforward obediences, from which the true sense of guilt derives.

As an example of man as joker, pretend with me a moment to Hamlet as

28. Wallace Stevens, "Esthétique du Mal," in *Collected Poems* (New York: Alfred A. Knopf, 1976), 313–26.

29. Ibid.

30. Hamlet knows and does not know, that those who will "nose" the body of Polonius, should it not soon be found, will also nose his own deed. 4.3.34–39. Hamlet's act is itself lowering, however cleverly he talks about it. After Hamlet, there have been veritable armies of young men who have declared, specially in the most warring moments of their lives, specially if they are caught into a war, that: "I don't know what to think. . . . The world's rotten" (Ford, Maddox Ford, "No More Parades," in *Parades End* [New York: Alfred A. Knopf, 1961] 304). In Hamlet, above all other addresses to sacred order, the question is raised, in Tietjen's truest last words, whether "the game is worth more than the player" (Ford, "No More Parades," 305). God intended Prince Hamlet for Intelligence, as He intended animals for Innocence, and "not for the footslogging department," where real wars are always fought (ibid., 307). The intellectualizing, and consequent abstraction, of the Western imagination spells the real tragedy of Western culture.

the case history of a student who studied philosophy too long in a German university. In German, the word *sein* stands not only for *to be*, but also for the possessive pronoun *his*. Hamlet's problem, all but self-understood, but not, that he belongs to nothing and no one, certainly not to the memory of his father, must turn, upon a therapeutic reading, into a question about his questionable attitude toward his parents. The tragedy of a transgressive Hamlet cannot be played, in the Ernest Jones-Laurence Olivier version, as a family problem; that would make it a role fit for Woody Allen, spreading sad cheer rather than deadly evil round him.

Hamlet is a tragic hero because it is he, more deeply than either his transgressive uncle or mother in theirs, who doubts authority in its sacred order. Suffering his case of primal doubt about it, testing sacred order as if against his own will, Hamlet knows his rebellion must fail as surely as none can be "the indifferent children of the earth."[31] The permanent crisis of authority, and the tragic hero caught in that crisis, has now been democratized. Oedipus was neither intellectual nor democrat; nor joker. It is Hamlet who should have got himself to a monastery. His crucial problem is more spiritual than sexual. Because the No seems to him, as it has to every other rebel against it, mortal, Hamlet finds his world-rejections, as they are, no less suspect than the acceptances made by others. Nothing can satisfy his sense of justice. The famous "dream of evil" extinguishes all "noble substance."[32]

Freud might have more accurately named the nuclear complex after Hamlet instead of Oedipus. In his blindness, Oedipus never ceases to blame the gods. Still, he accepts the reality of sacred order. Hamlet accepts nothing of the sort. Though both are asked the parent question under the concealment of questioning their parents, Hamlet seems to me the more fanatical questioner; his is nearer that modern fanaticism that expresses extreme skepticism in the most destructively violent manner. It is from Hamlet that veritable contagion of what is transgressive spreads, to take in even Ophelia.

The rebellion characteristic of modernist fanatics, against the subtleties and indirections of sacred order, can never be doubted. That rebellion is no matter of crude certainties. It is primal doubt, not certainty, that has led to the present monstrous compound of fanaticism and unbelief, as in Nazism and Marxism. This faithless fanaticism in our politicized experience of it, gives the lie to the notion that authority is whatever legitimates power. The most elementary fact of the Nazi regime was that it recognized no authority superior to its own; nor does any Communist regime recognize an authority superior to winning and keeping power, despite the Marxist rhetoric of a

31. Hamlet, II, ii, 231.
32. Ibid., I, iv, 36.

class that, when triumphant in the class war, will abolish all winnings including its own. Somewhere in the Zurich of the next social order, its next officer walks and talks away the time until he succeeds and brings with him his own capital of the spirit, to invest in his own paradise of winning meanings. So Weber imagined, in his ideal typology, the modern capitalist, son of a Calvinist father. But in the Weberian typology, as in the Marxist, the capitalist must be the last officer of a sacred order. After all, Marx celebrated the bourgeoisie as the most revolutionary class, abolitionists of everything sacred. In the capitalist and rationalist "as if," that last officer strips his paradise of winning meanings. Rather, "meaning" itself becomes a critical glass-bead game, the intellectual form of "legitimation." Engaged in such gamesmanship, upon which their offices depend, the officers of our radically desacralized reality, one in which every construct deserves its deconstruction, win their right, as authors, to invent our next winning "meaning," by which even the weakest noodles can make their critical refusals of sacred order. In such a culture, the final solution of the criticism problem can happen: the primacy of possibility will be treated as if it were a reality. In such a "reality," asceticisms would be prescribed as needed: the therapeutic need exclude nothing from his repertoire of roles—including "sainthood" and "martyrdom." Even Kierkegaardian "decision" would become an endless performance, not excluding life-and-death performances. The world as hospital would be transformed into the world as hospital-theater.

How to describe the anticritical critic? I am reminded of his predeceasor, the artful dodger turned artist, as once described by the Abbe Galiani:

> Imagine an artist whom the police have commissioned to paint in large letters on a wall: "It is forbidden to commit any nuisance here under penalty of a fine or corporal punishment." The painter gets to work, but in the midst of his work he feels the call. Down he climbs and, while breaking the law, admires the beauty of his own inscription.

The artistry of a therapeutic culture heroically remissive has been easily imagined since at least the late nineteenth century. Empathy, *feeling*, is in widest supply. Dr. Johnson was well ahead of the modernist game when he was hard-headed enough to make his famous remark:

> If Baretti should be hanged, none of his friends will eat a slice of plum pudding the less. . . . You will find these very feeling people are not very ready to do you good. They *pay* you by *feeling*.

And, if they go beyond the payment of feeling, and would volunteer to be hanged in your stead, or at least go to prison, you will find these very activists are self-consciously making a fine spectacle for themselves—rather like the character played by Woody Allen in *The Front*. That character is seen off to prison on camera, with feeling people paying him off with "Free Howard Klein" placards jerking up and down—all on camera. The secret is now open. It is publicity, not relentlessly critical intellect, that will bend the higher powers. The "aesthetic yes" of the early modern artist, as in Joyce or, earlier, in Nietzsche, in which suffering is experienced as a pleasure,[33] has become no less obsolete than the spirituality of knowing oneself. To the modernist mind, "know thyself" is the greatest public relations slogan ever devised.

The power of publicity as therapy may be inferred from the famous little "just suppose" story Freud once told.

> Suppose . . . a number of ladies and gentlemen in good society have planned to have a picnic one day at an inn in the country. The ladies have arranged among themselves that if one of them wants to relieve a natural need she will announce that she is going to pick flowers. Some malicious person, however, has got wind of this secret and had printed on the programme which is sent round to the whole party: "Ladies who wish to retire are requested to announce that they are going to pick flowers."[34]

As I have implied elsewhere[35] in remarking on Freud's easy target practice, malice is no basis for the ethic of honesty. The artfulness of those ladies was without malice. As a result of his malicious action, Freud's story against himself continued:

> No lady will think of availing herself of this flowery pretext, and, in the same way, other similar formulas, which may be freshly agreed upon, will be seriously compromised. What will be the result? The ladies will admit their natural needs without shame and none of the men will object.[36]

That cant phrase, "natural needs," begs the question of how easily and elaborately all such "needs" must go well beyond anything that can be called the "call" of nature. To be "without shame" is scarcely possible in the sacred order from which every culture derives, for that condition would admit nothing as transgressive, that is, as shameful before the blind eye of whatever god's body may be in that culture.

High culture is a flowering of pretexts; shame follows upon not abiding by them. In the *Laws*, Plato understood these matters differently and perhaps better than Freud. Only through its concealments can the body express itself

---

33. Friedrich Nietzsche, *The Will to Power*, no. 852, "The Tragic Artist," translated by Walter Kaufmann and R. J. Hollingdale (New York: Vintage, 1968), 450. "It is the *heroic* spirits who say yes to themselves in tragic cruelty; they are hard enough to experience suffering as a *pleasure*."

34. Cf. Philip Rieff, *Freud: The Mind of the Moralist*, 3d ed. (Chicago: University of Chicago Press, 1979), 316–17.

35. Ibid.

36. Freud, *Standard Edition*, XI, 49. Cf. Garry Watson, "The Impossible Culture . . . ," *The Compass* (Winter 1979), 52.

beautifully in a profane world. The nude belongs in the world of the sacred.[37] These manners of reticence express that divine fear, commonly experienced in reverence and shame before the primacy of possibility, which less
religious minds than Plato's, including Freud's, ascribe to a fastidiousness
and taste so powerfully ordaining that it acquires the character of religiosity.

Guided, as it must be, by just and noble fear of the sheer movement humans can achieve in the vertical of possibility, a true officer class in that
order will not be too embarrassed to take up arms at the approach of an
insolence of lowerings that publicizes its movement as a "liberation."[38] In
either case, raising or lowering, authority, in its moral range, is always
present and invariably presides over our lives; this remains so, even in the
modernist conceit of identifying downward, as if that downward identification were somehow anti-authoritarian. (81:1)

49
For the Last Time Psychology

The joys of this life are not its own, but our dread of ascending to a higher life;
the torments of this life are not its own, but our self-torment because of that
dread.
                    —Kafka, "Reflections on Sin, Pain, Hope, and The True Way"

The Triumph of the Therapeutic first appeared twenty years ago. Ten years
later, titling the book 'prophetic,' the editor of *The American Scholar* referred to the American "state of unconditional surrender"[1] to the type. The
surrender is now no longer American. As Western culture continues to be
Americanized, the therapeutic, in his triumph, has spread beyond these
borders and even beyond Europe. As I shall suggest below, Soviet man and
the therapeutic may have affinites. I offer these afterthoughts on the therapeutic where others have appeared earlier.[2] Heaping these afterthoughts di-

37. Cf. Titian's "Sacred and Profane Love." "God creates out of nothing, but here, if I
dare say so, He does more by clothing an instinct with the beauty of love, so that the lovers see
only the beauty and are unaware of the instinct. Who would dare to do that? The ideal beauty
is the veiled beauty and . . . the sea by its half-transparency tempts only half so strongly as
the . . . wife through the veil of modesty." Søren Kierkegaard, *Stages on Life's Way* (New
York: Schocken, 1967), 125–26.

38. Cf. *Laws*, 671d.

Reprinted from *Salmagundi* 74–75 (Spring–Summer 1987): 101–17.

1. See 'Aristides,' "Incidental Meditations," *The American Scholar* (Spring 1976):
173–74.

2. "Fellow Teachers," *Salmagundi* (Summer-Fall 1972): 5–85; and commentary on that
article in *Salmagundi* (Fall 1973).

rect upon the original text of *The Triumph of the Therapeutic* would be to disturb the irenic tone essential to it. Those dispassionate respects of recognition respected the tension of possibility that, in his triumph, the therapeutic can create an enduring culture. The disrespects paid the therapeutic most explicitly in the earliest pages of my epistle to the Skidmoreans, and in the preface of the book that followed,[3] respected all the more the increasing authority of the therapeutic in our culture.

Even if he does not succeed in abolishing the last interdict in our culture, the first death, of the body, if the therapeutic succeeds in establishing his own social order, then he will have succeeded in securing a social order never seen before anywhere on earth: a social order entirely divorced from sacred order. In that new order prevalent in the lives of the cultivated classes but not yet established fully among the populace, life would be lived without reference to eternal vertical in authority. That vertical is interdictory in its heights and reciprocally transgressive in its depths. But most of more ordinarily human time is spent shuffling and sidling along the remissive horizontal that always crosses and may easily double-cross the vertical. That is why the cross, and double-cross, strait or crooked, is so potent a symbol still in our culture. In his rationalizations of excusing reasons, in his enlightened rejections of one criterion the better to tolerate all, so to become a more agile order-hopper, the therapeutic organizes that mentality most accurately termed 'modern.'

On the other hand, if the therapeutic should prove to be yet another sick physician, recycled on the couch of world-affirmations and/or world rejections, each suited to differing circumstances, then, unable to go on indefinitely as the physician healing himself, therapeutic social order must yield various partial selves to sacred order. Then, entirely new commentators will arise to confirm our old prophets. 'Entirely new prophets' are part of Weber's Nietzschean despair. As I shall remark at greater length below, sacred history never repeats itself, except when it is being abused for the construction of yet another moralizing mythology—Freud's murderous analytic mythology about the Egyptian Moses, for example, as he has led so many Jews back to a new Egypt, strangely like a California, of the mind. If he can be cured, then therapeutics will learn on their body the way *guilt/knowledge* is acquired in a punishment colony: that therapies, however well they work, cannot transfer to themselves, democratic and mortal as they are, the immortality of revealed and aristocratic, even monarchial, truth. From the magisterial vertical of authority, there is no escape; but only shufflings and sidlings in its remissive and pseudo-democratic horizontal.

Yet it is not certain that a therapeutic culture cannot survive its own democratic genius. The leveling languages of the therapeutic, against the

3. *Fellow Teachers: Of Culture and Its Second Death* (Chicago, 1985), in particular pages ix–4.

ladder languages of faith, may yet succeed in eliminating both the dreadful joys of ascending to a higher life and the dreadful self-torments of failing to make those ascents. Even more tormenting: the dread of descents into immemorial transgressions that may leave even the therapist himself suffering the residual effects of magisterial and eternal truths repressed. For this reason, if no other, therapists need therapy. On the other hand, if the therapeutic cannot be reconverted from his long disciplines of deconversion, then he will have proved that he is not ill. This possibility of proof, never terminable in the case-history of humanity, is the weakness in their own case recognized by the faithful masters of our spiritual history, from the early sayings of R. Simeon b. Lakish to a saying of the late Dietrich Bonhoeffer.

In his comment on Exodus, in Midrash Rabbah, Reb Simeon is quoted in the usual marvelous rabbinical brevity of true sayings:

> If they are ill, they can be cured; but if they are not ailing, then I know not what to do. For this reason does it say, 'This is my weakness.'[4]

The Protestant Bonhoeffer, being more academic in style, was more prolix in his sayings. But this saying, taken from one of his *Letters from Prison*, is the more true when read in its historical conductibility charged with that same weakness reported in my Midrash:

> We should all give up our clerical subterfuges and our regarding of psychotherapy and existentialism as precursors of God. The importunity of these people is far too unaristocratic for the Word or God to ally itself with them. The word of God [from above] is far removed from this revolt of mistrust, this revolt from below. But it reigns.[5]

Not less authoritatively than the Marxist, but in a different style, the therapeutic leads a multicolored ideological revolt from below that, in its brown-shirted uniform, cost Bonhoeffer his life. Led by the psychologically re-educated elites of the West, our revolt from below resolves the authority of faith, the love of divine justice tempered with mercy, into a bargain-basement of one resolved erotic transference relation after another, all sold as the opportune life-style of the moment. Buy it while it's hot. It, or one of its many attributions, is bound to cool off. Mussolini once remarked that Fascism was not a doctrine, but an opportunity. Faith entails doxologies. Therapy entails opportunities of sensual satisfaction, which are like serial doxologies; which, in turn, are like serial monogamies; which are like adulteries—which are *not* to be done, no more than abortions or murders or homosexualities. Therapeutic movements, of whatever ideological color, including black, are modes of negational eroticism against the positive divine law of love, transformed into a politics.

As the symbol of an eroticized social order divorced from its predicative

4. Midrash Rabbah, Exodus XLV.3.
5. Bonhoeffer, *Letters From Prison* (London, 1953).

sacred order, the therapeutic is even more true now to the reality he represents than he was when I first gave him his name and described his way of
life. In his symbolic truth, the therapeutic is what he represents: the most
revolutionary of all modern movements—toward a new world of nothing
sacred.

A new generation of readers have grown up in this new world of the therapeutic. They will know little of the old and therefore risk illiteracy in the
high art of reading themselves out of the new world they never made. As a
teacher in the traditions of the old world, I say that in this old world, the
surest signs of something sacred are and remain ever in its highest powers of
prohibitions: those *shalt not/wilt not* directives from absolute authority that
gave to each a common sense of direction and sacred fear at not taking that
direction. Fear is anticipatory dread of what is coming. From that common
sense of what is coming to them, that judgment from which they cannot get
away, however 'repressive' they may call it in their own condemnatory post-
Freudian way, each knew and knows where he belongs, however insecurely:
in the sacred vertical of authority. Once given, divine law, and the merciful
character of salvation through grace, neither changes nor repeats itself. If
sacred history is real, then it never repeats itself. The authority of the past is
historical and commands doxological memory. The children of Israel cannot
stand more than once at Sinai. There is only one Christ. "Communities of
memory" are a therapeutic and professional abstraction without doxologies
of observance. To use any doxology of observance therapeutically is already
to parody it, as our contemporary evangelicals often do. Even the mythic
hero of my own boyhood, Lincoln, no longer has a birthday to celebrate publicly. As surely as residual faiths recur as present neurosis, the notional religion of the cultivated American classes, 'civility,' becomes a quaint Anglo
myth, circulated by some sociologists and by all travel agents specializing in
'ye olde England.'[6] It is only in the mythic cum neurotic time of the therapeutic that history repeats itself and is reduced to cases of repressed instinctual impulses frustrated by powers too high and punishing for human
endurance.

In the world of my new readers, there is therapy where theology—but
rarely civil—once was. There are hospital theatres where churches once
were. I had remarked these displacements in detail to an earlier generation.
There is now a large literature of further detail and theoretical variations.[7]
To repeat the message risks speaking in the discredited old style of despair
and hope; and, what is worse, that style shorn of its psalmist poetry. I take
that risk in these unpoetic afterthoughts just long enough to remind the new

6. Against such sociologists and travel agents, read the poetry of Philip Larkin: "And that
will be England gone / . . . There'll be books; it will linger on / In galleries; But all that
remains / For us will be concrete and tyres."

7. See, for leading examples, Christopher Lasch, *The Culture of Narcissism* (New York,
1978); and Robert Bellah, et al., *Habits of the Heart* (Berkeley, 1985).

generation of what terrible danger there is in trying to realize or actualize each his own self in the asphalt world, full of glass-houses and showing itself, to its own increasingly sick satisfaction, how free it is at last of sacred authority; free of an historical past that reaches into every present; free of such revelations from above that tell us, if we knew how to read sacred order and ourselves the mess in it, that 'repression' from below can never displace, at least not for those who remember the ancient knowledge, not less Greek than Jewish and Christian, that there is no piety without law. Now, without the law that cannot be changed by Congress or the Supreme Court, divine law, piety has not died but merely shifts crazily from antigod-term to antigod-term. So the culture of criticism has displaced the culture of command. And what a Babel of criticism. Now we learn that criticism itself is the ultimate literature.

Just who and what is it that was commanded and, in his radical unbelief in his own existence as other than a fiction of the historical moment, is engaged in pleasing his critical beliefs? The historical fact is that, in the new and unordained world of the therapeutic, there is neither self nor text to which he can be true; even if he tried. Truth lies in the criticism of it. But that professorial brains truster to the politics of whatever you can get away with, Polonius, was as Hamlet described him when he dragged the corpse of the old professorially political man off stage: a foolish prating knave. The true self derived from the one self, self-disclosed in Exodus III.14: "I am that I am." That 'I' once took no nonsense about being as well the excusing circumstances of every 'I' turned case-history instead of ultimately responsible participant-creature in the otherwise wholly other creator-self. Each self is commanded to be according to this creator-self and not to become a cast of characters no longer in search of their author. The 'self' to which we insistently refer in our therapeutic languages can only be an old sacred world courtesy title. In the new utterly profane world of therapeutic anticulture, every one of our partially realized selves is bound to know the one thing necessary to the anticulture as a device of survival: that the centered self, however held, can be nothing more than another glass bead in the endless European culture game.[8]

---

8. In *Magister Ludi*, by Hermann Hesse (New York, 1969), Father Jacobus, on visiting an order of cultural therapeutics who call themselves 'Castalians,' denounces a faith turned, at its best, learned and aesthetic:

> You measure the weight of the vowels in an old poem and relate the resulting formula to that of a planet's orbit. That is delightful, but it is a game. And indeed your supreme mystery and symbol, the Glass Bead Game, is also a game. I grant that you try to exalt this pretty game into something akin to a sacrament, or at least to a device for edification. But sacraments do not spring from such endeavors. The game remains a game.

On the European culture game, see, further, my "Intimations of Therapeutic Truth: Decoding Appendix G in *Moses and Monotheism*," in this volume.

Specially for whatever readers of *The Triumph* there may be in the next
generation of culture game players, perhaps the next game to go video, I
should draw, in these afterthoughts, silhouettes of two enabling allies of the
therapeutic, both instrumental to his triumph. That profane history, too, is
unlikely to be repeated, except as myth, Freudian or otherwise; all aimed to
end the compulsions and increase the uses of faith.

The therapeutic is in historical fact not the only member of the officer
class by which the new anticulture is ruled. He did not triumph alone or
unassisted. Rather, the therapeutic is the youngest and therefore most influential member of an unholy trinity of character types sovereign over the
modern anticulture, of which therapy is the modal experience.

Of that ruling trinity, Nietzsche's actor in the comedy of his own existence is eldest, each role as true to his character as any other. As I see him
still, the therapeutic enactor of everyday life need have no faith except in
his right to change roles, on demand of his totalitarian society (early Communist), or on demand of his consuming will (later Capitalist). The therapeutic needs no criterion for conduct because he is willing and able to use
all criteria. When will our sociologists of culture learn this lesson? Never, I
suppose, until they see how mythic are both their sociologies and their civil
religions. But, as myth-maker, modern man is a beauty in his brutality. He
knows he can get away with murder if he can treat it mythically enough.

Here is that element in the Western doctrine of human rights by which
the freedom to make the right choice and to remain steadfast in it, is sub-
verted by the therapeutic compulsion to make choice after choice, after
choice: so long as no choice be thought true. Such rights, advanced by radically politicized movements clean outside any of our inherited cultures of
commanding and eternal truth, amount to dedeified parodies of histrionic
fictions. In his hospital theatres, some of them made over from churches and
synagogues, in his schools and in such television dens he calls home, most
of all, during the last twenty years, in politicized movements of "liberation"
from everything sacred, from anything absolutely prohibited, the therapeutic actor in his infinite role-faiths knows he has become the most pious fraud
ever on earth; a pious fraud who celebrates his fraudulencies.

The piety of the therapeutic is historically most peculiar. It is a piety that
shifts endlessly from object to object.

The pious frauds of this therapeutic anticulture welcome all manner of
criteria, the better to hop another order while staying put. These impietists
can handle all sorts of old pieties, such as Eros and/or *Amorfati*; or even
Ananke or Thanatos; or even *Jihad*, if they are post-Muslims mobilizing their
masses for revenge against the West and for their own fuller symbol-system
employment, as in the manner of Shari'ati. Or, in the manner of Franz
Fanon, they can rationalize black terror therapy. Any therapy can be therapeutic. But what works is not the therapy but the anxiety it conceals. Anxi-

ety animates both repression and therapy. The essential anxiety can be seen
most clearly in Bergman's character of the knight, home from the Crusades,
in *The Seventh Seal*. Anxiety is the absence of faith. There are two polar
resolutions of anxiety. One resolution is given in the familiar despairing and
hopeful old style of various knights of faith: 'I believe, O Lord; help Thou
mine unbelief.' The other resolution is therapeutic: in the absence of faith,
anxiety can be resolved by organizing and celebrating the primacy of possibility—Freud called that primacy 'instinct.' I call it 'Hitler.' For the Hitlers,
and many an anti-Hitler impietist, the impossible is precisely what can be
done. Liberation movements come in all ideological colors and anticreeds.
However else opposed, all are agreed in opposing what is interdictory in
sacred order. The intellectual expression of this liberation movement downward in sacred order is itself always historical. Nowadays, that expression
appears often in such questions as: 'Why not homosexuality and Christianity?' 'Why not abortion, even infanticide, and animal rights?' And so on and
on. Anticulture is constituted by an assault upon the eternally given *Nots* of
our historically received faiths. It is the vocation of every teacher in this
culture to take away from the big children of this therapeutic culture all
those psychological rubber nipples on which they suck in order to escape
the authority of their anxieties.

To supply himself with pacifiers, so to ease his anxieties in the absence of
faith, the therapeutic can even use new prophets in the old style of despair
and hope. But, having nothing other than a style of coping with the anxiety
of faith in its absence, new prophets cannot but be therapists in religious
drag, transvestite priests in those fatherless religiosities by which all therapeutics acquire a special freedom to do in bad faith precisely what was not
to be done in the good faith taught, in unbroken traditions, by ordained remembrance of revelation. From the origins of our old cultures of command,
revealed from above, there followed those moralizing demands that doing
what is not to be done may be forgiven but not justified. What is needed by
all who now justify what is not to be done yet done is an impersonal authority
to stage-manage the transgressive freedom to do precisely what is not to be
done in our social order as it derives from our historical sacred order.

This is where the second member of the new officer class comes in. Max
Weber named him 'bureaucrat.' Knowing the work of the church historian,
Rudolf Sohm, Weber knew that in Western culture the first bureaucrats were
those who managed the most helpless members—widows, orphans, the
sick, the dead—of the *ecclesia*, sacred order so far as it could be realized
charitably in social order. The last bureaucrats are the therapists of our regnant, democratic anticulture. They are the regnant managers of our passionate indifferences, of our moralities at a distance and distinctly ideological in
character.

Therapeutics derive their authority from their role faiths: as experts in resolving our transferences to the graven character of original authority. This new guiding character of our therapeutic anticulture makes his presiding presence felt only in order to abolish his presiding presence. This abolitionist movement feeds straight into the world of the bureaucrat.

With his artist and bureaucratic friendly enemies, at the end of the historical road taken by the Western spirit, there, waiting with his endless supply of rubber nipples to transfer the anxieties of faith in its absence to himself, the last charismatic to parody charisma, is the therapist. Where public and family festivals of divine recognition were, there let private, even intimate, resolutions of transference relations be made over into movements of liberation from sacred order in any of its historical realities. So changed is the face of authority that, in fact, therapeutic authority has no face. More precisely, his face is all mask and make-up. As actor-manager of his own indefinitely changeable identities, the therapeutic as therapist pretends to no eternal truth; rather, to passing emotive values.[9]

That the therapeutic would effect a merger of therapy and politics, that this merger requires an ungrantable divorce between morality and religion, will not surprise us in this present age of liberation movements. The new Gletkins not only have no gods but have eroticized both democratic and totalitarian cultures. The cat-house of the Soviet elites is less well-known than the cat-house of the Western elites. But it will come into view, surely as did the cat-house of the Nazi elites.

A plague on both cat-house elites, Eastern and Western. Not that I reckon these most highly miseducated classes, the enemy selves most decisively and publicly active in both East and West, moral equals or comparably transgressive. That would be fantasy, and a subversively remissive kindness to the anticulture peculiar to the Soviet elites. The sin of greed for money and sex cannot be considered quite so abysmal as the sins of pride in, envy of, and lust for power.

For the West, it can be said that the self in sacred order, our freedom of movement in its vertical of authority, is not officially abolished. By contrast, the many selves of which the Soviet I appears constituted may be best understood as the shadow me and mine of our Western elites. In that shadow, sacred order is already abolished. Created out of that abolition, enemy selves endlessly adjust their ideological masks and put on fresh makeup so to conceal even from themselves, when they look in the mirror, that they are all artifice. So they put on passionate expressions of life, indifferently liber-

---

9. On our emotive value civilization and on its ruling unholy trinity, the finest philosophical work yet to appear is Alasdair MacIntyre's *After Virtue: A Study of Moral Theory* (Notre Dame, 1981). That trinity should be a quaternary, I reckon. I consider, in a Baconian manner, scientists as making up in their corporate body the caterpillar girdling our world and producing, from out of their body, metamorphoses of power. But, no more than the artist, bureaucrat or therapist, can the scientist authorize his services to power.

ated and committed only to winning the game of games, the political power game, and therefore serious only in that play, which takes in everything, including sex and the bad faith of an egalitarianism in which some are bound to become ever so much more equal than others.

In the West, the therapeutic leads levelling assaults upon everything necessarily interdictory, against every high sign in sacred order. To level the vertical in authority would be to abolish it. Both psychological and Soviet man lead abolitionist movements in the name of liberating everything human from everything sacred and undeniable. In his fundamentally denying role, the therapeutic plays leader of the modern movement no less well than his completely politicized Soviet counterpart. Both assault what is interdictory in our sacred order and therefore ought to be forbidden absolutely, though forgivable in our social orders.

In sacred order—interdictory and remissive and transgressive—each mode of conduct has its own authority in the everlasting hierarchy. Try to turn that hierarchy upside down: even so, no subversively remissive or transgressive act can remain for long superior to what is interdictory. That is an article of good faith. Prohibition precedes positive law. What is not is the predicate of what is: grace. Man cannot, and therefore ought not, play God. Man is transgressive so far as he makes up his God-play, as he crashes through or sidles around one sacred barrier after another. There is the authority of good faith: in punishment where there is no repentance. But there is also justice and mercy, both of which have nothing to do with therapy.

Theology cannot become therapy. Psychological rubber nipples cannot be made to ride political hobby-horses into movements of liberation toward social orders that will never be more sacred than those they displace. All those red dawns in the East, and now in the South, have turned out to be blood red and more like new and darker nights for humanity. Utopian hope, like the dream life, lives in the desires of the night. Utopian hope is one thing. Observant faith in sacred order is quite another. "Desire not the night," the angel Elihu warns.[10]

Humans have always desired the night. That desire sleeps in what Freud renamed the 'unconscious.' In their nightlives, humans take the royal road to the satisfaction of their transgressive impulses. Nietzsche wrongly prenamed Freud's unconscious, where the *either/or* gives way to the *both/and*, by a Buddhist and Europeanized term: "Nihilism."

Our rubber nipples of transgression therapies, given us to hold against the anxiety of faith in its absence, are nothing so exalted as 'nihilism.' Those rubber nipple therapies, brought to life as a politics of transgression—call those transgressive movements by whatever direction, left or right or middle of the True Way—become monsters of entirely faithless conceit of political

10. Job 36:20.

desire after desire. For the therapeutic, winning or losing is the only game in town. In the politics of sex, in every game, politicized, happiness is being on the winning side. 'Not to be' is to lose, surely as the unremembered dead are complete losers. So the modern true therapeutic can adopt any anxiety of faith useful in the winning game. Victory is truth. Truth belongs to winners. It was our teacher Nietzsche's brilliant and sinister contention that the all-time losers in Western *power/history,* first of all the Jews and following them the few Christians that have lived in our teacher Kierkegaard's Christendom, win by perpetuating the sense of guilt. That sense must die before sacred order can be abolished. The sense of guilt, and of the repentance that should follow, is a wound in the side of a humanity that has had the wrong idea of healing. What is highest in sacred order, not any lowering in it, constitutes the wound modernizing Humanity has suffered. Freud's infamous and unavoidable 'sense of guilt,' which precedes any event that might elicit true guilt, is what he would not have it represent: shame in a sacred order otherwise false. Guilt, whether in thought or deed, is shame in sacred order.

Job truly believed he had done nothing in sacred order, as in social, of which he must be ashamed. Therefore, he rightly rejects all explanatory justifications of his suffering. Resolutions of Job's complaint are made, first by Elihu, and then by God speaking for Himself. The answer is constituted by divine rejection of therapeutic reciprocity. To complain about suffering is to risk the role of God. To forgive, even a cruel or hidden God, is to risk being as near God-like as any man can be.

It follows that not only morality but mercy will go out of the world when faith is perfect: then and only then. That next world will be an entirely different kind of kingdom: if and when it comes. Meanwhile morality with mercy, the vertical in authority, including its shufflings and sidlings in the remissive horizontal, is inseparable from faith. The trouble with the therapeutic triumphant is that he uses faith merely as a weapon to free his various and unrealized enemy selves from both the morality and mercy that must represent, however imperfectly, the invisible world in which our visible world is enclosed: the world of sacred order and of the presence presiding in both worlds. The therapeutic no longer believes he is suffering from sin, but from the disease of too elevated a faith; from some residue of life in sacred order. So it was that Freud contributed his judicious mite to the visible world: by counseling some lowerings of the ambition to live well in the world within which our world lives.

By this present age, the giant patient has risen from his knees, or lain down from his unanswered prayers. Kneeling or standing, the tragic cures were always of one faith pitted against another. Now the patient has gone political instead of prayerful. Political cures are always and entirely faithless. The therapeutic politicized is the latest rough beast slouching toward his own imaginary Bethlehem. He knows that Bethlehem is a fiction.

Not being ill of sin, but only of some residual and unacknowledged fixation upon his true self, self-caught in some sort of dreadfully embarrassing position, the politicized therapeutic cannot be cured by prating parody god-terms in the old style of despair and hope.

The religious appear to be among the last to know that any therapeutic faith is bad. Moreover, all have something horribly comic about them. Though no therapeutic faith dare judge itself truer than any other which works, the conflicts between them are as deadly and irreconcilable as any between the good faiths that were once the doxologies of holy wars. I persist in thinking, until better informed, that even Islamic jihadists are really therapeutic ideologists, who, like the Irish Catholic terrorists of the IRA, mobilize backward masses to gain power any man in good faith may live to regret.

What has succeeded the terrible tragedies and outrageous cruelties of religious existence? Nietzsche knew: the even more terrible tragedies and more outrageously cruel comedies of post-religious existence. The Inquisition is not the moral equivalent of the Holocaust, though Christian Jew-hatred undoubtedly prepared the way for post-Christian, even anti-Christian, Jew-hatred. Anticreedal comedies may be even more horrible than their precedent creedal tragedies. Horrors can be better carried out in rationalized bad faith than in good, I suppose. Bad faith evolves, as in the case of 'unsere Adolph,' into no faith. I shall return to this case below.

It is only in their faithless thrusts against the interdicts and their subversive remissions that psychological and Soviet men are antiauthoritarian. In these wars of liberation from what is highest in sacred order, the Soviet and Western elites *are* uncannily alike. Their identity kits contain all the cosmetics necessary to produce the human face. In all the various and competing lowering movements with a human face, both elites approach the future anticulture as the friendliest of enemies, all equally selves and none truer than any other.

These friendly enemy selves know, in their unconscious, that there is nothing more therapeutic than a transgression: nothing more authoritarian than this transgressively moralizing revolution from below led even against their own interests by our higher culture classes. The revolution against culture in its very form, as an address to sacred order from somewhere inside it, was bound to displace the cultivated elites that started it by ever more barbaric elites that will finish it. Modernist barbarism is anything but primitive; even its 'primitivism' is a sophistry.

From the successes of their prototypal assault upon the sexual interdicts, therapeutics now lead assaults upon others equally high. Their subversively remissive cadres, not least notably in law and medicine, lead movements toward sacred order inverted.

Inversion is nothing like abolition. Where interdicts were, there, equally bored by both, our remissive elites would let transgressions be. That is the law our subversively remissive elites now try to lay down. The therapeutic revolution is being conducted from the top down, not from the bottom up; that is reality, not romance. It must follow, for example, that a judicial voice, like that of a turtle, would be heard to say, in the land of judgment without condemnation: "This is only a murder, Mr. Greenbaum, and I have heard it over, and over, and over again. Only a murder, and we are talking about an eighteen-year-old."[11] Under such endlessly excusing judgments, which I like to call 'remissive' rationality, constrained as it is by sacred fear, murder would become common as the death of sons at the hands of fathers. Here is the Freudian mythic prototype inverted. Anything is possible in mythological order; even probable, if never certain.

By way of another mythic possibility, in the new anticulture of the possible primary and dominantly desirable, let us treat rape as mental illness rather than as transgression in the flesh against what is sacred in social order. If the human body is no longer the temple of God, then rape could be better treated, I suppose, as a 'paraphilic coercive disorder.' Just suppose it happens, later if not sooner, like divine wrath, that 'paraphilic coercive disorder' is listed in *The Diagnostic and Statistical Manual of the American Psychiatric Association*. Many other crimes have been divorced from their origins in sin. Social orders have always liked the idea of deciding for themselves, by way of their elites, just how to live as they are minded. In the mind of our remissive elites, there is always an excusing reason for everything; or, worse, there is always some more or less elaborately rationalized indifference to the horror of a social offense in sacred order.

The first and model offense had been well known for a long time: a lowering disobedience of what is interdictory.[12] For this transgression, man was made mortal as a due punishment for the soul's endless suicide of separations from sacred order. Those separations cannot be granted except as punishments and panaceas.

Sacred order and the self centered in it, both apparently abolished, we can better understand medical science in its new, magic god-role. A medical *cost/benefit* expert has said aloud what is ultimately on the remissive mind: "I think we can beat this thing called death."[13] Here we have stumbled upon a new truth: that death is the last interdict respected and feared in Western anticulture, the one evident in all our lives that still commands something like sacred fear. With that ultimate victory, of mortality recycled as immortality by transplant technology administered by *cost/benefit* com-

11. Judge Altman (of all surnames), quoted in A. R. Kaminsky, *The Victim's Song* (Buffalo, 1985), 63.

12. On man's first disobedience and all that, the 'Old Testament,' if not Milton, will grow more important in our residual church culture even as our anticulture grows more and more dangerously unaware of those old canonical books.

13. Dr. Carl J. Schramm, quoted in the *New York Times*, 18 January 1985, p. B3.

mittees of experts on *life/death* recyclings, what endless balancing acts, what multiple perspectives, what rich shows of life-styles, what a riot of selves, would be put on the world stage. In his display performances of the second death, as the unminded life, the therapeutic as therapist would perform his scientific *role/faith* with a syncretic zest that would say yes to everything sensual and use everything spiritual to keep the show on the road. Can the therapeutic live long enough to live as all his endlessly unrealized selves may please? Can he avoid being bored to death by his own recurrent remythologizings where unique and eternal truths once were? These, indeed, are long-term God-term questions of 'values.' (Whenever I hear that word, I know yet another god has died.)

The therapy of therapies, in post-modernity, as it is already constituted, is one assault upon another upon the enabling human gaiety, and its dignity: upon the high life in sacred order, and the necessary human dread of ascending in it. The histrionic politics of the therapeutic are the same in all his front organizations: to lower the truth of what is interdictory until it splits, repressively and therefore into an unfailing failure to choose rightly; splits, I hate to think, into merely human 'values,' exchangeable at whatever the current rate of each 'value' may be. Where revelation was, there let 'values' and repressions be.

Repressions keep intellectuals fully employed complicating the plain truths of revelation. Intellectuals, and first of all theologians, make the direct communication of truth so indirect that we may consider the intellectualization of the modern world its greatest catastrophe. Nietzsche rightly asked who began this relentless intellectualizing if not the theologian? His ultimate usurper, the therapist, serves the theologian right. Neither is poetic enough to tell the truth once revealed and still commanding, if not obeyed. In his negational genius, the therapeutic as therapist revalues his values whenever he grows displeased with them. These constant revaluations by psychological man may well be called 'therapy neuroses' or 'life-style' as a parody of true culture. Truth endures. Life-style always changes.

Negational genius in earlier periods of this culture was given more to tragedy than to therapy. Hamlet was nothing like a therapeutic. Concealed as it is revealed, behind his manifest question of parents, was Hamlet's latent parent question: whether or not he belonged to sacred order. Concealed as it is revealed behind that parent question is another even more ancient: whether sacred order is or is not. That last is the question of being or not being, which is one and the same as belonging or not belonging to sacred order. Knowledge of that membership constitutes good faith. Stripped of good faith, the many enemy selves of Hamlet were poised and unpoised against his true self even before he saw the questionable ghost of dead authority.

In our present age, 'to be or not to be' seems a merely suicidal question.

And so it is, so long as we do not question the established dogma of the therapeutic: that there is no sacred order, now, if ever there were any, to which anyone can belong. I suspect Hamlet asked that question long before we see him on stage. The rest, for him, was bound to be tragedy and silence.

For us, there is nothing tragic in the sound of psychobabble. Even the most terrible transgressives of our time have something comic about them. That is why, I reckon, nothing occurred to Karl Kraus worth saying, wittily, about Hitler. 'Unsere Adolf,' as one ex-Nazi described that terribly bad actor, Hitler, to me, was a bad joke, rather like Freud's 'instinctual unconscious.' Better call it, as my old rabbi did, the 'evil impulse.' Because the instinctual unconscious contains no either-or, it is worse than immoral: amoral, positively transgressive. Therapeutic neutrality in this matter is more than mistaken: it has been a tragedy for our, or any other, culture and for anyone alive to its deadly condition.

There is said to have been a time when transgressive figures could be nobly tragic. The devil was a fallen angel; Prometheus, the original supreme trickster and high technology thief, was a god. Now the transgressive has lost all dignity. Now, he is merely base, and the more terrifying for being so uncommonly common. Hitler was not a tragic figure, though he may well be, with Stalin, death's greatest historical ambassador of a health entirely profane and without limits. How Freud, in his modern genius, vacillated between criticism of overcivilized limits and fear of instinctual health. Sacred fear remains the cure of all therapeutic and neurotic health.

Not less fundamentalist in their negations of sacred order than the more easily understood fundamentalists appear in their affirmations, our post-Freudian therapeutics will end well, all defeated later if not sooner, I trust. Meanwhile, remissive authority, the therapeutic in the horizontal, commands our anticulture. Its end must come. Remissive conduct, shufflings and sidlings in the horizontal, cannot go on dominant interminably. Dominant, they lead to transgressive falls, deeper and deeper down into an abyss of unprecedented danger from which Science can supply no raisings. Science remains fixed in its Baconian services to power.

What is interdictory and remissive and transgressive, in that vertical unchanging, sacred order even in the tragic conflict of its irreconcilable cultures, commands culture in its very form and each of us individually. No matter how often its god-terms lapse into silence, once spoken, divine law and grace remain. Human beings have ridden their hobby horses many times to do battle against this eternal truth. Much and many more may fall to the perishing point before therapeutics, riding their new mottled mythic-political hobby horses, discover their triumph has taken them farthest toward being nowhere.

Here I am brought back, in an older ladder language of despair and hope, to the uses and abuses of the faith that was and is the question, asked, irenically as I know how, of these present and permanent culture class wars. To that generation born during the triumph of the therapeutic, I would repeat Kafka's great exordium on the first thing he, and not he alone, thought necessary for recognizing faith in our received sacred order:

For the last time psychology!
      —"Reflections on Sin, Pain, Hope and The True Way"

Sentences

I

Psychological man is, of course, a myth—but not more of a myth than other model men around whom we organize our self-interpretations . . . I am merely announcing his presence, fluttering in all of us, a response to the absent God.

II

Conscience, not passion, emerges as the last enemy of reason.

III

A universal culture is a contradiction in terms. We Jews of culture are obliged to resist the very idea.

IV

I suspect that the children of Israel did not spend much time elaborating a doctrine of the Golden Calf; they merely danced around it, until Moses, their first intellectual, put a stop to the plain fun and insisted on civilizing them. Now, although there is some dancing again, the intellectuals mainly sit around and think about their instincts, disguising their self-worship in the religion of art.

V

It is the deadly fault of the modern intelligensia that it refuses to assert even the possibility of innocence.

VI

I, too, aspire to see clearly, like a rifleman, with one eye shut; I, too, aspire to think without assent. This is the ultimate violence to which the modern intellectual is committed. Since things have become as they are, I, too, share the modern desire not to be deceived.

367

VII

Contempt is the readiest emotion of one intellectual confronting another.

VIII

Experience is a swindle; the experienced know that much.

IX

In therapy, interpretation is chiefly a weapon of ideological reconstitution.

X

The therapy of all therapies, the secret of all secrets, the interpretation of all interpretations, in Freud, is not to attach oneself exclusively or too passionately to any one particular meaning or object.

XI

The therapy of all therapies is not to attach oneself exclusively to any particular therapy, so that no illusion may survive of some end beyond an intensely private sense of well-being to be generated in the living of life itself.

XII

Violence is the therapy of therapies. . . . There is less and less to inhibit this final therapy, least where the most progressively re-educated classes seem ready to go beyond their old hope of deliverance, from violence as the last desperate disciplinary means built into the interdicts, as punishment, to violence as a means toward a saving indiscipline, as self-expression.

XIII

The therapy of therapies, in post-modernity, as it is already constituted, is one assault upon another upon the enabling human gaiety, and its dignity: upon the high life in sacred order, and the necessary human dread of ascending in it.

XIV

Every trespass increases the probability of yet another trespass. The "domino theory" of morality is correct, I think.

XV

Survival: that is the meal ticket of all acceptable immoralities.

XVI

We are, I fear, getting to know one another. Reticence, secrecy, concealment of self have been transformed into social problems; once they were aspects of civility, when the great Western formulary summed up in the creedal phrase "Know Thyself" encouraged obedience to communal purposes rather than suspicion of them.

XVII

The combination of a repressive political order with a permissive moral order is not unheard of in human history.

XVIII

No state is a moral entity, none are holier than Thou, whatever is said for them: that is one thing we teachers must know.

XIX

I have said that *there are no aggressions except as transgressions;* that is Rieff's first sociological law, applicable to all public life.

XX

But the essence of repression lies in a necessary turning away from direct and conscious expression of everything that is before praise and blame. A culture without repression, if it could exist, would kill itself in closing the distance between any desire and its object. Everything thought or felt would be done, on the instant. Culture is the achievement of its unconscious distancing devices made conscious, yet indirect, in a variety of visual, acoustical, and plastic registrations. In a word, culture is repressive.

XXI

Rieff's first law of private life reads: *You only live once, if then.*

XXII

What is needed today are more communities, and some that have a sense of their holiness, to save democracy from the pestilence of indifference and impersonality that characterizes modern society. But holy communities are not raised by fiat, or by UNESCOS. They must come of themselves, or at least from unplanned situations. Men are powerless to create them if they will not live in them.

XXIII

Religion can no longer save the individual from forming his private neurosis, for he has become his own religion: taking care of himself is his ritual now, and health is the ultimate dogma. With the end of religious community, the sects become countless, each with a membership of one.

XXIV

No ideal has been more misleading than that of scientific detachment. The cult of neutrality that dogs the rationalist and scientific traditions was no original part of those traditions, but developed much later—when rationalism no longer had to contend seriously with its great enemy, dogmatic theology. For rationalism, and the sciences of which it is composed, arose first as a negative instrument, to penetrate the spurious logics of dogma. When dogma failed, rationalism lost its object and became, in lieu of an object of attack, objective.

XXV

The true world of ideas will not yield to force or ambition. You cannot politic your way to an idea. Both joy and understanding are what they are, ideal existences, delicate, sudden, unannounced just before they occur but never unprepared.

XXVI

There is a danger in laying oneself open to new ideas: as original disciples, the first consumers of new ideas develop inordinate desires to produce their own.

XXVII

As a rule, every creator of authorizing concealments must suffer them to succeed in shallow, more transparent versions. The statics of vulgar piety overcome the dynamics of subtle revelation.

XXVIII

The piety of the therapeutic is historically most peculiar. It is a piety that shifts endlessly from object to object.

XXIX

The faith of the rich has always been in themselves. Rendered democratic, this religion proposes that every man become his own eleemosynary institution. Here is a redefinition of charity from which the inherited faith of Christianity may never recover. Out of this redefinition, Western culture is changing already into a symbol system unprecedented in its plasticity and absorptive capacity. Nothing much can oppose it really, and it welcomes all criticism, for, in a sense, it stands for nothing.

XXX

The whirligig of fashion has suffered its intellectualization at the cost of feeling intellect; with the discipline of modesty, against openmouthedness, intellect confuses itself with ego.

XXXI

Sublimation without soul, as literary achievement, is a polite word for graphomania.

XXXII

As academics, our vocation is to teach the intellect tried resistances . . . in disciplines that refuse the easiest option of all: an imagination full of nothing but options.

XXXIII

When art seeks to become a work of life, the artist fails; his failure, transferred from art to life, produces terror instead of what is sublime. A failed artist, Hitler, became a successful politician. Incite experience to riot and it will assault precisely what art and science, as moral forms, defend.

XXXIV

Be grateful for your sense of true guilt and doubly grateful if it has not been badly damaged. Without that guilt, an elaborately cultivated strength of inhibition preventing or punishing transgressive activity, there can be neither aristocracies of the feeling intellect nor democracies of obedience. Guilt, subserving the interdicts, is inseparable from the working of high culture.

XXXV

By false guilt, I mean to remark again that praise of the perverse, cultivated in the tone of every voice aggrieved enough to ask "By what authority?"

XXXVI

It is part of the oral, teaching tradition from which I descend, without conscious dissent, that whoever is a true master of his guardian dogs of thought, knows which way they are going without holding a manuscript full of directions in his hands. To those of us in the oral tradition, print is alienating; even manuscript shows a trace of magic; knowledge is personal, inward, and best conveyed in conversation—the most civilized art of transaction—between persons and, not least in schools, across generations.

XXXVII

Teaching begins long before a student reaches the classroom. Until there are vast numbers of true parents, we cannot expect vast numbers of true teachers—or true students. How can we teachers expect to achieve disciplines of the feeling intellect so late in the student day, and in a cultureless society—one that divorces us from the interdicts?

XXXVIII

It is the vocation of every teacher in this culture to take away from the big children of his therapeutic culture all those psychological rubber nipples on which they suck in order to escape the authority of their anxieties.

XXXIX

Only under the name of right theory can we preserve our saving sense of what is not to be done.

XL

The repressive imperative cannot be repressed.

Sources for Sentences

Bibliographia Rieffiana

1949

49:1   Reviews of *American Freedom and Catholic Power*, by Paul Blanshard; *Essays on Freedom and Power*, by Lord Acton; *The Vatican in World Politics*, by Avro Manhattan. *The Chicago Jewish Forum* 8, no. 2 (Winter 1949–50): 140–41.

1950

50:1   "A Jesuit Looks at Proudhon: Competition in Damnation." Review of *The Un-Marxian Socialist*, by Henri de Lubac. *Modern Review* 3, no. 2 (January 1950): 166–71.

50:2   Review of *Union Guy*, by Clayton A. Fountain. *The Chicago Jewish Forum* 8, no. 3 (Spring 1950): 220–21.

50:3   "The Future of the Middle Class." Reviews of *The English Middle Classes*, by Roy Lewis and Angus Maude, and *The Decline and Fall of British Capitalism*, by Keith Hutchison. *The New Leader* 33, no. 39 (30 September 1950): 20–21.

50:4   Reviews of *Authority and the Individual*, by Bertrand Russell; *On Power*, by Bertrand de Jouvenel; and *The Twentieth Century* by Hans Kohn. *The Chicago Jewish Forum* 9, no. 1 (Fall 1950): 74–75.

1951

51:1   "The Meaning of History and Religion in Freud's Thought." *Journal of Religion* 31, no. 2 (April 1951): 114–31.

51:2   Review of *Lust for Power*, by Joseph Haroutunian. *Journal of Religion* 31, no. 2 (April 1951): 141–42.

51:3   "Judaism and Democratic Action." *The Chicago Jewish Forum* 9, no. 3 (Spring 1951): 165–70.

51:4   Reviews of *Everyman's Talmud*, by Rev. Dr. A. Cohen; *The Jews in Medieval Germany: A Study of Their Legal and Social Status*, by Guido Kisch. *The Chicago Jewish Forum* 9, no. 3 (Spring 1951): 218–19.

51:5   Review of *Puritanism and Liberty*, edited by A. S. P. Woodhouse. *The Chicago Jewish Forum* 10, no. 2 (Winter 1951–52): 156–57.

1952

52:1   "Disraeli: The Chosen of History." *Commentary* 13, no. 1 (January 1952):
        22–33.

52:2   "Is Democracy Calvinist?" Review of *Democracy and the Churches*, by
        James Hastings Nichols. *The New Leader* 35, no. 1 (7 January 1952):
        17–18.

52:3   "The Theology of Politics: Reflections on Totalitarianism as the Burden of
        Our Time." Review of *The Origins of Totalitarianism*, by Hannah Arendt.
        Journal of Religion 32, no. 2 (April 1952):119–26.

52:4   "Education and the Priestly Lie." Review of *Education and American Civ-
        ilization*, by George S. Counts. *The New Leader* 35, no. 43 (27 October
        1952):26.

52:5   "A Framework for Political Inquiry." Review of *Power and Society*, by
        Harold D. Lasswell and Abraham Kaplan. *The Chicago Jewish Forum* 10,
        no. 4 (Summer 1952):289–90.

52:6   Review of *Systematic Theology*, vol. 1, by Paul Tillich. *The Chicago Jew-
        ish Forum* 10, no. 4 (Summer 1952):294.

1953

53:1   "History, Psychoanalysis, and the Social Sciences." *Ethics* 63, no. 2
        (January 1953):107–20.
        Reprinted in *American History and the Social Sciences*, edited by Edward
        N. Saveth (Glencoe: Free Press, 1964), 110–24.

53:2   Review of *Marsilius of Padua, the Defender of Peace, Vol. 1: Marsilius of
        Padua and Medieval Political Philosophy*, by Alan Gewirth. *Journal of Re-
        ligion* 33, no. 1 (January 1953):67–68.

53:3   "Aesthetic Functions in Modern Politics." *World Politics* 5, no. 4 (July
        1953):478–502.

53:4   "Are Intellectuals Chained to Policy?" Review of *Social Order and the
        Risks of War. The New Leader* 36, no. 34 (24 August 1953): 16–17.

53:5   Review of *A History of the Cure of Souls*, by John T. McNeill. *Church His-
        tory* 22, no. 4 (December 1953): 337–40.

1954

54:1   "Beichman Upbraided for Lack of Humanity on Thompson." Letter to the
        Editor. *The New Leader* 37, no. 13 (29 March 1954): 28.

52:2   "George Orwell and the Post-Liberal Imagination." *Kenyon Review* 16, no.
        1 (Winter 1954): 49–70.
        Reprinted in *Orwell's Nineteen Eighty-Four*, edited by Irving Howe (New
        York: Harcourt-Brace-World, 1963), 227–37.

54:3   "The Case of Dr. Oppenheimer, I." *The Twentieth Century* 156, no. 930
        (August 1954): 113–24.
        "The Case of Dr. Oppenheimer, II." *The Twentieth Century* 156, no. 931
        (September 1954): 218–32. Reprinted, see 69:3.

54:4 "World Revolution from Above." *The New Leader* 37, no. 34 (23 August 1954): 18–20. Reprinted, see 55:4.

54:5 Review of *The Prophet Armed: Trotsky, 1879–1921*, by Isaac Deutscher. *Chicago Jewish Forum* 13, no. 1 (Fall 1954): 66–67.

56:6 "Eros Re-Examined." Review of *Agape and Eros*, by Anders Nygren. *Kenyon Review* 16, no. 4 (Autumn 1954): 645–52.

54:7 "The Authority of the Past: Sickness and Society in Freud's Thought." *Social Research* 21, no. 4 (Winter 1954): 428–50.

Reprinted as chapter 6 in Philip Rieff, *Freud: The Mind of the Moralist*, 1st ed.: 186–219, 2d ed.: 205–40; 3d ed.: 186–219.

Reprinted as "Freud and the Authority of the Past," in *Explorations in Psychohistory: The Wellfleet Papers*, edited by Robert J. Lifton, with Eric Olson (New York: Simon and Schuster, 1974), 78–108.

Reprinted in *Social Research: 50th Anniversary* 51, nos. 1 and 2 (Spring/Summer 1984): 527–78. See 59:1.

1955

55:1 "Psychology and Politics: The Freudian Connection." Review of *The Life and Work of Sigmund Freud, Vol. 1: The Formative Years and the Great Discoveries, 1856–1900*, by Ernest Jones. *World Politics* 7, no. 2 (January 1955): 293–305.

55:2 "Freud's Jewishness." *Chicago Jewish Forum* 13, no. 3 (Spring 1955): 162–70.

55:3 Review of *Understanding the Sick and the Healthy: A View of the World, Man and God*, by Franz Rosenzweig. *Journal of Religion* 35, no. 4 (October 1955): 262–63.

55:4 "Organize a World System of Welfare States." Chapter 7 in *Alternatives to the H-Bomb*, edited by Anatole Shub (Boston: Beacon Press, 1955), 71–82. See 54:4.

1956

56:1 "Freudianism as a Movement." Review of *The Life and Work of Sigmund Freud, Vol. II: Years of Maturity, 1901–1919*, by Ernest Jones. *Midstream* 2, no. 1 (Winter 1956): 101–6.

56:2 "The Origins of Freud's Political Psychology." *Journal of the History of Ideas* 17, no. 2 (April 1956): 235–49.

Reprinted as chapter 5 in *European Intellectual History Since Darwin and Marx*, edited by Warren Wagar (New York: Harper Torchbooks, 1966), 89–109.

56:3 "The Doctor and the Rabbi." Review of *Judaism and Psychiatry: Two Approachs to the Personal Problems and Needs of Modern Man*, edited by Simon Noveck. *Midstream* 2, no. 3 (Summer 1956): 91–94.

56:4 "Socialism and Sociology." Review of *The Power Elite*, by C. Wright Mills. *Partisan Review* 23, no. 3 (Summer 1956): 365–69. Reprinted, see 68:8.

56:5   Review of *Man in Reciprocity: Introductory Lectures on Culture, Society and Personality*, by Howard Becker. *American Sociological Review* 21, no. 5 (October 1956): 636

56:6   "Introduction." *Delusion & Dream and Other Essays*, by Sigmund Freud, edited by Philip Rieff (Boston: Beacon Press, 1956), 1–21.

1957

57:1   "A Character Wrecked by Success." Review of *The Organization Man*, by William H. Whyte, Jr. *Partisan Review* 24, no. 2 (Spring 1957): 304–10.

57:2   Review of *Education and Sociology*, by Emile Durkheim. *American Sociological Review* 22, no. 2 (April 1957): 233–34.

57:3   "Freudian Ethics and the Idea of Reason." *Ethics* 67, no. 3, part 1 (April 1957): 169–83.

57:4   "Introduction." *Outlines of the History of Dogma*, by Adolf Harnack (Boston: Beacon Press, 1957), xiii–xxxv.

1958

58:1   Review of *Marsilius of Padua, The Defender of Peace, Vol. II. Journal of Religion* 37, no. 1 (January 1958): 57–58.

58:2   Review of *The Life and Work of Sigmund Freud, Vol. III: The Last Phase, 1919–1939*, by Ernest Jones. *American Sociological Review* 23, no. 2 (April 1958): 211–12.

58:3   "Max Weber: 'Science as a Vocation'" (Introduced by Philip Rieff). *Daedalus* 87, no. 1 (Winter 1958): 111.

58:4   Review of *Psychology and Religion: West and East*, by C. G. Jung. *American Sociological Review* 23, no. 6 (December 1958): 741–42.

1959

59:1   *Freud: The Mind of the Moralist* (New York: Viking Press; London: V. Gollancz, 1959; rev. ed., New York: Anchor Books, 1961; 2d ed., London: Methuen, 1965; Italian ed., Bologna: Il Mulino, 1968 (trans. by Anna Oppo);

59:1a   3d ed., with Epilogue, "One Step Further" (Chicago: University of Chicago Press, 1979).
        Excerpts reprinted in *An Age of Controversy: Discussion Problems in 20th-Century European History*, edited by Gordon Wright and Arthur Mejia, Jr. (New York: Dodd, Mead & Co., 1963), 416–21.

59:2   "The Evangelist Strategy." Chapter 4 in *Religion and the Face of America*, edited by Jane C. Zahn (Berkeley: University Extension, University of California, 1959), 17–24.

59:3   "The Function of the Social Sciences and Humanities in a Science Curriculum." *Religious Education* 54, no. 2 (March–April 1959): 156–63.

59:4   "Freud Will Fade Only From Faddists' Minds." *San Francisco Sunday Chronicle* (21 June 1959), 23.

59:5   "He Discovered a New Image of Man." Review of *Collected Papers*, by Sigmund Freud. *The New York Times Book Review* (19 July 1959), 1, 16.

59:6   "Fearless at the Feet of Freud." Review of *Free Association: Memoirs of a Psychoanalyst*, by Ernest Jones. *Saturday Review* 42, no. 40 (3 October 1959): 40–41.

59:7   "Social Scientist Attacks 'Cult of Objectivity.'" Review of *Personal Knowledge—Towards a Post-Critical Philosophy*, by Michael Polanyi. *The Unitarian Register* 138, no. 8 (October 1959): 15.

1960

60:1   "Reflections on Psychological Man in America." *What's New* (no. 220, 1960) Abbott Laboratories What's New Anniversary Issue, Contemporary Comment no. 13, pp. 17–23.

60:2   "Priest Reconciles Science and Piety." Review of *The Phenomenon of Man*, by Pierre Teilhard de Chardin. *The Unitarian Register* 139, no. 5 (May 1960): 15.

60:3   "Two Honest Men." *The Listener* 63, no. 1623 (5 May 1960): 794–96; presented as a broadcast talk on the BBC Third Programme.
Reprinted in D. H. Lawrence, *Sons and Lovers, Text, Background, and Criticism*, edited by Julian Moynahan (New York: Viking Press, 1968), 518–26.

60:4   "Cosmic Life Energy Was Just What the Doctor Ordered." Review of *Selected Writings*, by Wilhelm Reich. *The New York Times Book Review* (11 September 1960), 3, 26.

60:5   "A Burden of Knowingness." Review of *Letters of Sigmund Freud*, edited by Ernst L. Freud. *Saturday Review* 43, no. 48 (26 November 1960): 23–24, 37–38.

60:6   Review of *The Masks of God: Primitive Mythology*, by Joseph Campbell. *American Sociological Review* 25, no. 6 (December 1960): 975–76.

60:7   "A Modern Mythmaker." Chapter 14 in *Myth and Mythmaking*, edited by Henry A. Murray (New York: George Braziller, 1960), 240–75.

60:8   "Introduction." *Psychoanalysis and the Unconscious* and *Fantasia of the Unconscious*, by D. H. Lawrence (New York: Viking Press, 1960), vii–xxiii.

1961

61:1   Review of *The Unconscious Before Freud*, by Lancelot Law Whyte. *New York Herald-Tribune* (1 January 1961), 32.

61:2   "The American Transference: From Calvin to Freud." *The Atlantic Monthly*, Special Supplement, 208, no. 1 (July 1961): 105–7.
Reprinted as "The Freudian Ethic—Self-Help Through Self-Knowledge." *Psychiatry in American Life*, edited by Charles Rolo (Boston: Little, Brown, 1963), 168–76.

61:3   "The Mirage of College Politics." *Harper's Magazine* 223, no. 1337 (October 1961): 156–63.

Reprinted in *Reading and Rhetoric From Harper's*, edited by Leo Hamalian, John C. Sherwood, and Edmond L. Volpe (New York: Harper & Row, 1962), 45–65.

1962

62:1   Review of *The Social Theories of Talcott Parsons: A Critical Examination*, edited by Max Black. *The Annals of the American Academy of Political and Social Science* 339 (January 1962): 211–12.

62:2   "The Analytic Attitude." *Encounter* 18, no. 6 (June 1962): 22–28.

62:3   "On the Side of the Enemy." Review of *Black Ship to Hell*, by Brigid Brophy. *The American Scholar* 31, no. 4 (Autumn 1962): 642–46.

62:4   "Introduction." *Social Organization: A Study of the Larger Mind*, by Charles Horton Cooley (New York: Schocken, 1962), v–xx. Reprinted by Transaction Books, 1983.

1963

Collected Papers of Sigmund Freud. 10 Volumes (New York: Collier Books, 1963). Each volume edited and introduced by Philip Rieff:

63:1   *The History of the Psychoanalytic Movement*, 9–35.

63:2   *Early Psychoanalytic Writings*, 7–10.

63:3   *Therapy and Technique*, 7–24.

63:4   *Dora: An Analysis of a Case of Hysteria*, 7–20.

63:5   *The Sexual Enlightenment of Children*, 7–13.

63:6   *General Psychological Theory*, 7–20.

63:7   *Three Case Histories*, 7–11.

63:8   *Sexuality and the Psychology of Love*, 7–10.

63:9   *Character and Culture*, 9–13.

63:10   *Studies in Parapsychology*, 7–13.

63:11   "Black and White in America." Audio Cassette Program #67, The Robert Maynard Hutchins Center for the Study of Democratic Institutions.

1964

64:1   "Introduction." *Human Nature and the Social Order*, by Charles Horton Cooley (New York: Schocken, 1964), ix–xx. Reprinted by Transaction Books, 1983.

64:2   "Jung's Confession." *Encounter* 22, no. 5 (May 1964): 45–50.

64:3   Review of *Communication and Social Order*, by Hugh Dalziel Duncan. *American Sociological Review* 29, no. 4 (August 1964): 602–3.

64:4   "The World of Wilhelm Reich." *Commentary* 38, no. 3 (September 1964): 50–58.

64:5   Review of *Psychiatry and Religion*, by Samuel Z. Klausner. *The Annals of the American Academy of Political and Social Science* 356 (November 1964): 184.

1965

65:1   Review of *Protestants and Pioneers: Individualism and Conformity on the American Frontier*, by T. Scott Miyakawa. *The Annals of the American Academy of Political and Social Science* 360 (July 1965): 199–200.

65:2   Review of *European Positivism in the Nineteenth Century*, by W. M. Simon. *American Sociological Review* 30, no. 5 (October 1965): 790–91.

1966

66:1   *The Triumph of the Therapeutic: Uses of Faith After Freud* (New York: Harper & Row; London: Chatto & Windus, 1966).

66:1a   2d ed., with a new preface (Chicago: University of Chicago Press, 1987). Excerpts reprinted in *The Psychology of Society*, edited by Richard Sennett (New York: Vintage Books, 1977), 357–64.

66:2   Review of *The Fusion of Psychiatry and Social Science*, by Harry Stack Sullivan. *Social Work* 11, no. 1 (January 1966): 121.

66:3   Review of *The Collected Works of C. G. Jung*, vol. 10: *Civilization in Transition;* vol. 14: *Mysterium Coniunctionis: An Inquiry into the Separation and Synthesis of Psychic Opposites in Alchemy;* vol. 16: *The Practice of Psychotherapy: Essays on the Psychology of the Transference and Other Subjects. The Annals of the American Academy of Political and Social Science* 366 (July 1966): 199–201.

1967

67:1   "A Preface for Parents." *Reynard the Fox (The Most Delectable History of)*, edited by Joseph Jacobs (New York: Schocken, 1967), ix–xi.

67:2   Review of *The Paths of Culture: A General Ethnology*, by Kaj Birket-Smith. *The Annals of the American Academy of Political and Social Science* 370 (March 1967): 187–88.

67:3   "14 Points on 'Wilson.'" Review of *Woodrow Wilson*, by W. C. Bullitt and Sigmund Freud. *Encounter* 28, no. 4 (April 1967): 84–89.

67:4   Review of *Madness and Civilization: A History of Insanity in the Age of Reason*, by Michel Foucault. *The Annals of the American Academy of Political and Social Science* 371 (May 1967): 258–59.

67:5   Review of *Evolution and Society: A Study in Victorian Social Theory*, by J. W. Burrow. *The Annals of the American Academy of Political and Social Science* 372 (July 1967): 191.

1968

68:1   "Introduction." *Radicals & Conservatives and Other Essays on the Negro in America*, by Kelly Miller (New York: Schocken, 1968), 7–24.

68:2   "Cooley and Culture." In *Cooley and Sociological Analysis*, edited by

Albert J. Reiss, Jr. (Ann Arbor: University of Michigan Press, 1968), 32–47, 161–162n.

68:3   Review of *The Other Victorians: A Study of Sexuality and Pornography in Mid-Nineteenth Century England*, by Steven Marcus. *The Annals of the American Academy of Political and Social Science* 375 (January 1968): 233–34.

68:4   Review of *The Problem of Slavery in Western Culture*, by David Brion Davis. *The Annals of the American Academy of Political and Social Science* 375 (January 1968): 237.

68:5   Review of *The Radical Reformation*, by George Huntston Williams. *The Annals of the American Academy of Political and Social Science* 376 (March 1968): 164–65.

68:6   Review of *On Quality in Art: Criteria of Excellence, Past and Present*, by Jakob Rosenberg. *The Annals of the American Academy of Political and Social Science* 379 (September 1968): 189–90.

68:7   Review of *Psychoanalysis: The First Ten Years, 1888–1898*, by Walter A. Stewart. *The Annals of the American Academy of Political and Social Science* 379 (September 1968): 191–92.

68:8   "Socialism and Sociology." *C. Wright Mills and the Power Elite*, edited by G. William Domhoff and Hoyt B. Ballard (Boston: Beacon Press, 1968), 167–72. See 56:4.

1969

69:1   Review of *Freud and His Early Circle*, by Vincent Brome. *The New York Times Book Review* (12 January 1969), 30.

69:2   Review of *Freud: Political and Social Thought*, by Paul Roazen. *The Annals of the American Academy of Political and Social Science* 382 (March 1969): 188–89.

69:3   *On Intellectuals, Theoretical Studies/Case Studies*, edited by Philip Rieff. Contains a reprint of "The Case of Dr. Oppenheimer" (New York: Doubleday, 1969), 314–40; paperback ed. (Garden City, NY: Anchor Books, 1970), 341–69. See 54:3.

1970

70:1   "The Impossible Culture: Oscar Wilde and the Charisma of the Artist." *Encounter* 35, no. 3 (September 1970): 33–44.

70:1a   Reprinted in slightly different form as "The Impossible Culture: Wilde as a Modern Prophet." In *The Soul of Man Under Socialism and Other Essays*, by Oscar Wilde (New York: Harper & Row, 1970), vii–xxxiv.

70:1b   Reprinted in slightly expanded form as "A Last Word—The Impossible Culture: Wilde as a Modern Prophet." *Salmagundi*, no. 58–59 (Fall 1982–Winter 1983): 406–26.

1971

71:1   "Per Una Teoria Della Cultura." *Rassegna Italiana di Sociologia* 12, no. 1
        (January–March 1971): 15–28. See 72:1.
71:2   Review of *American Students in Israel*, by Simon N. Herman. *The Jewish
        Journal of Sociology* 13, no. 2 (December 1971): 238–39.
71:3   "The Loss of the Past and the Mystique of Change." (An interview with
        Michael Glenny broadcast over Radio Free Europe.) *Can We Survive Our
        Future?* A symposium, edited and with an introduction by G. R. Urban
        (London: The Bodley Head, 1971), 44–56.

1972

72:1   "Towards a Theory of Culture: With Special Reference to the Psychoana-
        lytic Case." In *Imagination and Precision in the Social Sciences* (Essays in
        memory of Peter Nettl), edited by T. J. Nossiter, A. H. Hanson, and Stein
        Rokkan (London: Faber & Faber, 1972), 97–108. See 71:1.
72:2   Review of *Freud: Living and Dying*, by Max Schur. *New York Times Book
        Review* (18 June 1972), 23–24.
72:3   "Fellow Teachers." *Salmagundi*, no. 20 (Summer/Fall 1972): 5–85.
        Reprinted in part in *The Salmagundi Reader*, edited by Robert Boyers and
        Peggy Boyers (Bloomington: Indiana University Press, 1983), 17–48. See
        73:1.
72:4   Review of *The Culture of Unbelief*, edited by Rocco Caporale and Antonio
        Gumelli. *Contemporary Sociology* 1, no. 6 (November 1972): 505–7.

1973

73:1   *Fellow Teachers* (New York: Harper & Row, 1973).
73:1a   2d ed., *Fellow Teachers/ of Culture and Its Second Death*, with a new pref-
        ace: "A Pretext of Proof Texts" (University of Chicago Press, 1984). See
        72:3.
73:2   "Comments on Dr. Scholem's Paper." Conference on "The Religious
        Dimensions of Judaism." Audio Cassette Program #685, The Robert May-
        nard Hutchins Center for the Study of Democratic Institutions.

1974

74:1   Review of *The Social Question: Philosophical and Sociological Founda-
        tions of Marxism*, by T. G. Masaryk. *Contemporary Sociology* 3, no. 1
        (January 1974): 26–27.

1975

75:1   "The Impoverishment of Western Culture," and "Observations on The
        Therapeutic." *Psychological Man*, edited by Robert Boyers (New York:

Harper & Row, 1975), 3–17, 18–26. ("The Impoverishment of Western Culture" is chapter 2 in *The Triumph of the Therapeutic*, see 66:1; "Observations on The Therapeutic" is excerpted from *Fellow Teachers*, pp. 45–55, see 73:1.)

1976

76:1   "'Herald Nothing': Wrong and Right Ways of Heralding the Future." *Proceedings of the American Conference of Academic Deans, Thirty-Second Annual Meeting*, 8–10 February 1976, Philadelphia, PA. Edited by Frederic D. Ogden (Ann Arbor, Michigan: University Microfilms, 1976), 9–22.

1977

77:1   *Moral Choices in Contemporary Society*, edited by Philip Rieff and Isaac Finkle (Del Mar, CA: Publisher's Inc., 1977).

77:2   "Culture in Crisis: American Society Void of Principles." *Wichita Eagle and Beacon* (23 January 1977), pp. 1B, 9B.

77:3   "What Everybody Has Always Known About Sex." *The Washington Star* (2 October 1977), Section F, pp. F1, F4.

1979

79:1   "Culture in Crisis: American Society Void of Principles." *The Challenge of the Future: Visions and Versions*, edited by William A. Conboy (Lawrence, Kansas: Independent Study, Division of Continuing Education, University of Kansas, 1979), 147–49. See 77:2.

1981

81:1   "By What Authority: Post-Freudian Reflections on the Repression of the Repressive as Modern Culture." Chapter 9 in *The Problem of Authority in America*, edited by John P. Diggins and Mark E. Kann (Philadelphia: Temple University Press, 1981), 225–55.

81:2   "Intimations of Therapeutic Truth: Decoding Appendix G in *Moses and Monotheism*." *Humanities in Society* 4, nos. 2 and 3 (Spring and Summer 1981): 197–201.

1984

84:1   "Psychoanalyse en sociologie: Het debat Rieff-Vandermeersch," edited by Jan Aarts and Marianne Broder. *Sociologisch Tijdschrift* 11, no. 3 (December 1984): 503–29.

1985

85:1   Review of *From Clergyman to Don: The Rise of the Academic Profession in
Nineteenth-Century Oxford*, by A. J. Engel. *Contemporary Sociology* 14,
no. 3 (May 1985): 347–48.

1986

86:1   "The Life and Death of Death." Review of *Images of Man and Death*, by
Philippe Ariès. *Contemporary Sociology* 15, no. 4 (July 1986): 510–11.

1987

87:1   "For the Last Time Psychology: Thoughts on the Therapeutic Twenty Years
After." *Salmagundi*, no. 74–75 (Spring/Summer 1987): 101–17.

1988

88:1   Review of *Idols of Perversity: Fantasies of Feminine Evil in Fin-de-Siecle
Culture*, by Bram Dijkstra. *Contemporary Sociology* 17, no. 6 (November
1988): 818–20.

Acknowledgments

I am grateful to many people who have helped me to find various of the writings that are reprinted in this volume or listed in the bibliography. Martha Pamplin Rosso provided me with the first draft of the bibliography when I was still a graduate student at the University of Pennsylvania. We exchanged new discoveries for many years.

Of all those who have shared in the admiration of Philip Rieff's teachings and writings, Alan N. Woolfolk of Oglethorpe University has remained my closest ally. We began our studies with Philip Rieff together and have steadfastly pursued the devoted students' search to uncover every last piece of published writing extant. What began as delightful one-upmanship has culminated in this volume. Professor Woolfolk has been a silent partner in this enterprise, and I wish to acknowledge his friendship and colleagueship over the same number of years that I have known Philip Rieff.

Finally I write in thanks to my wife, Amy, and our daughter, Elizabeth, who have both patiently waited for husband and father on enough occasions that I ask for a blanket pardon. I hope this book will demonstrate to them that conformative and constructive theory begins at home and that no higher purpose would be truthfully felt without their presiding presences. In the pantheon of remissive gods, goddesses, and other doorkeepers there is, I hope, always some room for laughter. The departmental gods (see p. 35) and the household goddesses occupy considerable time in the modern pursuit of vocation. To know which of these gods or goddesses are worth living and dying for, which are the distractions and which sustain us, the remissive presiding presences and myself in my acknowledgment of them must acknowledge the Presiding Presence in a sacred order and eternal time where all "higher purposes" are first and last illuminated. The cultural reconquest of the therapeutic thought-world begins first in showing what is at stake in our acknowledgments (see p. 336).

No one else could ever be admitted here, since this gate was made only for you. I am now going to shut it.

—Kafka, "Before the Law"

Index